REGION, CULTURE, AND POLITICS IN INDIA

Region, Culture, and Politics in India

Edited by
RAJENDRA VORA and ANNE FELDHAUS

MANOHAR
2006

First published 2006

ISBN 81-7304-664-6

Published by

Ajay Kumar Jain for
Manohar Publishers & Distributors
4753/23 Ansari Road, Daryaganj
New Delhi 110 002

Typeset at

Digigrafics
New Delhi 110 049

Printed at

Lordson Publishers Pvt Ltd
Delhi 110 007

Distributed in South Asia by

FOUNDATION BOOKS
4381/4, Ansari Road
Daryaganj, New Delhi 110 002
and its branches at Mumbai, Hyderabad,
Bangalore, Chennai, Kolkata

Contents

Introduction

Rajendra Vora and *Anne Feldhaus*

A region is a mental construct. It is always a human product, whether the product of scholarship, political ideology, or daily life. Geographers, sociologists, economists, and political scientists divide land into regions according to 'objective' criteria such as elevation, rainfall, flora and fauna, crops, styles of clothing or domestic architecture, means of livelihood, transportation networks, language, script, family structure, or voting patterns. Parallel to but distinct from these kinds of understandings, people living in worlds of various sizes inherit and develop 'subjective' but shared conceptions of the areas they live in and move through. They understand those areas as regions, attach meanings to them, and develop loyalty to a region as well as to those with whom they share a sense of its meaning. Politicians attempt to harness such loyalties and meanings to create movements of regional unification and separatism. But, in all cases, whether identified 'objectively' by a social scientist, recognized 'subjectively' by a poet or pilgrim, or cultivated 'cynically' by a politician, regions are created and nourished by human minds and emotions.

Because a region is a geographical unit, the academic field most basically concerned with regions is geography. Geographers distinguish between 'area' and 'region' and define 'region'—as 'an area of specific location which is in some way distinctive in relation to other areas and which extends as far as that distinction extends' (Hartshorne 1959: 130). Stressing the importance of perception, Schwartzberg (1967: 93) defines 'region' as 'a perceived segment of the time-space continuum differentiated from others on the basis of one or more defining characteristics'. Hartshorne (1959: 130-1) emphasizes the abstraction involved in the concept, pointing out that in order to apply the term 'region' it is essential 'to abstract particular areal characteristics from the total reality'.

The study of economic and social regions also comes under the purview of geography and brings that discipline nearer to the social sciences, which have come to study regions in their respective fields and contexts. It is the non-physical—historical, linguistic, economic, cultural, or social-structural—characteristics of region that are of special interest to social scientists. Sociologists and anthropologists have found the study of regional cultures significant, while economics differentiates between developed and underdeveloped regions, and the rise of regionalist politics has made political scientists look into the question of region and regionalism. In addition, the development of 'humanistic geography' in the 1980s and 1990s (see Agnew and Duncan 1989; Feld and Basso 1996) has brought the work of some geographers close to literary criticism, ethnomusicology, art history, religious studies, and other fields in the humanities.

For such scholars, regions are not always physically given entities; many regions, for example, cross natural boundaries. Being historically and politically determined, regions change their boundaries over time. Finally, a region must always be defined with reference to a context. If the context changes, the boundaries or definition of the region can change radically. When a region that is part of a national domain is sufficiently unified to have a consciousness of its customs and ideals and thus to possess a sense of identity distinct from the rest of the country, it is often not easily demarcated on the basis of any fixed or objective indicator. Because a region is fundamentally a mental construct, in many instances it remains an amorphous idea and thus poses a challenge to scholars.

Regionalism, by contrast, is a more systematic expression of regional consciousness. Regionalism is an ideology founded on the linguistic, ethnic, and cultural identity of the people of a particular area. Not all regions necessarily enter into the phase of regionalism, even though the rise of regional consciousness gives a region a distinctive identity and an implicit political dimension. Regionalist ideology is initially based on some vague ideas, but later on, as regional movements develop, regional elites create a more-or-less defined set of arguments or justifications. A regionalist political movement makes demands for greater autonomy and a larger share in power for the region, or for a separate political existence within the boundaries of the nation-state, or even for secession from the nation-state. In some cases, regionalism gives vent to feelings of economic deprivation and backwardness, and demands a larger share of available resources; it can also take the form of nativism or a sons-of-the-soil argument.

This volume examines the processes through which regions and regional consciousness are formed and maintained in India. South Asia, home to five other nation-states besides India, is a part of the world that is particularly rich in regions. Not only does it have numerous old (named) cultural regions and former little kingdoms, but in recent decades South Asia has seen an often-contentious nationalistic and regionalistic splintering with sometimes horrifying, bloody consequences. The process of transforming conceptual, cultural regions into administrative and political units continues in India to this day, with ever-more-refined regional identities becoming the basis for carving up larger states into smaller ones.

In modern India, the idea of region emerged during the course of the nationalist movement. The colonial power challenged the very notion of an Indian nation, and argued that India was a conglomeration of diverse regional cultures, lacking unity in any substantive sense. Nationalists, on the other hand, stressed the essential unity of India and claimed that it had been one from time immemorial. Jawaharlal Nehru's *Discovery of India* (1951), the best-known text of the nationalist interpretation of the Indian past, emphasized that the diversity of Indian people was only outward. What had held India together for ages, Nehru claimed, was a 'tremendous impress of oneness'. A 'dream of unity', he thought, had 'occupied the mind of India since the dawn of civilization' (Nehru 1951: 53-6).

In Indian history there have certainly been long periods when regions have been more significant than overall unity. Schwartzberg's historical atlas of India shows how regionalism and overall political disunity were clearly manifest from the eighth to the twelfth century. During that half millennium, the absence of a single predominant power provided regional polities the scope to promote their regional cultures (Schwartzberg 1978: 186). There have also been periods in Indian history when one or another imperial power brought most of the subcontinent under its control and established political unity. However, the consciousness of belonging to India developed only during the colonial period, especially in the late nineteenth century. The nationalist movement fostered this feeling, but the oneness could grow because there existed a basic commonality and coherence among various parts of the country. India, therefore, need not be seen only as an invention of colonialism or of the nationalists (Khilnani 1998: 155). The modern Indian nation-state was constructed on the foundations of a civilizational bond.

The notion of regions with distinctive identities based on language or ethnicity was also articulated during the nationalist movement. The Sikhs of the Punjab and 'Dravidians' of the Madras Presidency developed separatist tendencies, and language loyalty nurtured regional identity in places like Maharashtra and Bengal. The Indian National Congress, representing the mainstream of nationalism, appealed to the colonial government in 1920 to reorganize provinces on the basis of language; the Congress also restructured its own organization on that basis (Schwartzberg 1985: 155). Clearly, by the early 1920s, regional identities had taken shape within the nationalist movement.

Writing in 1942, D. P. Mukerji, one of the founders of the discipline of sociology in India, maintained that Indian culture is more a union of the distinctive cultures of different regions than it is a unity (Mukerji 1978: 60). By contrast, Louis Dumont (1957) and McKim Marriott (1976) held views more like Nehru's, considering India a 'single culture area'. Leavitt (1992) labels this position 'cultural holism' and argues that, in spite of providing insights into Indian society and culture, it underestimates the reality and importance of regional and historical specificities.

In our view, both positions (unity-in-diversity and the importance of regional cultures) are historically tenable. Although there were elements of regional consciousness in pre-modern India, colonialism and the anti-colonial struggle did much to sharpen the focus of regional as well as national consciousness. Region and nation are both realities in the contemporary period, the tension produced between them being sometimes manageable, sometimes not.

It is possible to distinguish three phases through which regionalism has passed since Independence. The first phase (from 1947 through the early 1970s) was influenced by Partition, which cautioned the first government of independent India against any kind of regionalist demand. In this phase, all regional expressions were seen as threats to Indian unity. The central government resisted regionalist demands based on religion or ethnicity, but did recognize and accommodate linguistic regions. Nehru's charisma, combined with the Congress party system, helped the project of maintaining unity. Where regional parties were elected to power, regionalism did not grow into separatism.

In the second phase, during the regimes of Indira Gandhi and Rajiv Gandhi (early 1970s to early 1990s), when the Congress party imposed unity from above and the centre tried to displace regional powers, regionalist movements became extremist and challenged the tendencies of centralization. In this phase, regionalism also became an expression of a sense of economic deprivation: development planning, which was not in a position to generate sufficient surplus, failed to distribute resources equitably among various regions. By this time, linguistic regions had become a fact of political life. Regional identities came to be organized around ethnicity (as in the North-east), and (in the Punjab) religion-based regionalism became more and more separatist and violent. Indira Gandhi's regime used four methods to deal with the question of regionalism: (1) giving some regions the status of constituent states, (2) refraining from competing with regional parties in their respective states, (3) giving regions a larger share in the resources of the centre, and (4) using force—the police and the military—to quell separatism.

In the third phase, which began in the mid-1990s and continues into the present, on the one hand, the militancy of regionalism has died down, while, on the other, regional parties have come to play a significant role in national politics and are being accommodated within the coalitional system at the centre. In this phase, the state units of national parties are functioning like regional parties, and regional parties are working as extensions of national parties. In addition, as with the Rashtriya Janata Dal in Bihar or the Biju Janata Dal in Orissa, single-state parties have arisen which at times take a regionalist stance.

Region thus figures prominently in the society, culture, and politics of India, and many scholars have studied the question of region and its place in comprehending the complexity of India in the past and at present. Secessionist movements, along with less radical regional movements demanding autonomy and a larger share in power and resources, have received the most scholarly attention, especially from political scientists (for example, Hardgrave 1965,

Barnett 1976, Ram and Sharma 1979, Nag 1990, Devalle 1992, Hussain 1993, Lam 1993, Puri 1993, Basu 1994, Jeffrey 1994, S. K. Das 1997, Baruah 1998, Baruah 1999, and Nag 1999) analysing regionalist politics in Tamil Nadu, Punjab, the North-east, and Jammu and Kashmir. A very large number of studies have concentrated on what we have identified as the second phase of regionalism, because the question flared up during that period and acquired violent dimensions (e.g. T. D. S. S. 1987, Akhtar 1984, Bharati 1992, Palanithurai and Thandavan 1992, Datta 1993, Bhavani Singh 1993, and Majumdar and Bhanwar Singh 1997).

Some scholars (e.g. Pathy 1988, Brass 1991, S. L. Sharma 1996, Chadda 1997, S. L. Sharma and T. K. Oomen 2000, and Jodhka 2001) have studied the second phase from the angle of ethnicity—that is, of identity based on religion, tribe, race, language, or geographical area. Regional parties function as vehicles of regionalism and play an important role in electoral politics in India; a number of political scientists (see Bhatnagar and Kumar 1988; Palshikar 2003) have analysed such parties' behaviour and their place in the political process. Studies on federalism as well, while discussing centre-state relations as they appear in the Constitution and in practice, take note of demands made by regionalist movements (see Copland and Rickard 1999). General works on Indian politics cover the problems raised by regionalism and its resolution within the system, while studies of state politics deal with the question of regionalism as it surfaces in states like Assam, Punjab, or Tamil Nadu (e.g. Brass 1994, Chatterjee 1998, Corbridge and Harris 2000, Frankel and Rao 1989, Kohli 2001, Rudolph and Rudolph 1987, Sathyamurthy 1996, Vanaik 1991, Weiner 1989).

Studies on Indian culture also refer to regional variations, and there have been several anthologies and monographs dealing with the culture of particular regions (Attwood et al. 1988, Deshpande 1983, Eck and Mallison 1991, Eschmann et al. 1978, Flueckiger 1996, Israel and Wagle 1987, McDonald 1968, Mohapatra 1996, Ramaswamy 1997, Ryerson 1988, Schomer et al. 1994, Talbot 2002, Wagle 1980, etc.). The discipline of sociology in India, however, has primarily been preoccupied with the idea of the cultural unity of the land, and with those factors and features that promote this unity (Chaudhari 2000: 5-11). There have been very few major sociological studies that pay serious attention to regional cultures.

This brief survey suggests that, for social scientists, region becomes a 'relevant' category principally when it enters the political arena, and that such scholars pay attention to it only when regionalist politics take an extremist turn. While students of Indian politics and society take an interest in the question of region primarily in relation to regional movements or ethnic agitations, folklorists, ethnographers, and scholars of literature and religious studies generally take regional cultures as givens. The idea of the region—its latent and manifest forms or the stages of its development from origin to full-fledged manifestation—does not seem to attract many scholars. In this context, we must take note of four important exceptions: four collections of papers in the social sciences and humanities on region in India.

The first of these books is *Regions and Regionalism in South Asian Studies* (Crane 1967), a collection of papers presented at a symposium held at Duke University in 1966. This symposium was the first major attempt to define region in South Asia from historical, sociological, and political perspectives. It brought together historians, geographers, sociologists, and political scientists in order to understand and analyse ways in which regions have formed and developed in Indian history and society. The second book, edited by Richard Fox (Fox 1977), also the result of a symposium at Duke University, is *Realm and Region in Traditional India*. Fox's volume throws light on the evolution of regional power configurations in the pre-modern period, on ways that the boundaries of states were determined in ancient and modern times, and on the sociological definition of regions. The third book, edited by David Sopher (1980), the product of research carried out primarily at Syracuse University, investigates the 'geographical patterning of culture' in India, studying cultural, social, and linguistic regions and arguing for the significance of regional variation. Unlike the other three, which are multidisciplinary, Sopher's volume consists exclusively of contributions from geographers. Finally, *Region and Nation in India*, edited by Paul Wallace (1985), is a collection of papers from a symposium held at the University of Wisconsin, Madison, in 1982 in memory of Richard L. Park. This volume contains studies on regional cultures, kingdoms, history, linguistic states, and politics, as well as papers that try to relate region and nation as these categories are understood and perceived in India.

The present volume may be considered a fifth of this kind. It continues the discussion started by the previous four collections, and touches on several new themes relevant to understanding the phenomenon of region in India. The essays in this volume examine various modes through which people in different parts of India express, create, and foster a sense of their area as a distinct, coherent, significant unit to which they belong in some important way. The modes we examine include language, oral and written literature, festivals, pilgrimages, everyday rituals, domestic wall-calendars, caste and religious identity, and political movements. The contributors to the volume belong to a wide variety of academic disciplines: linguistics, folklore, history, religious studies, sociology, and political science. The regions the essays discuss range from Kerala to the Punjab, including Tamil Nadu, Karnataka, Maharashtra, Gujarat, Orissa, and the Hindi-language areas of north India. The areas considered range in size from the few square kilometres of the Sringeri area to the whole Hindi-speaking region of north India—or, for that matter, all of India—with two of the essays focusing on a single city each: Mumbai and Ahmedabad.

We have organized the essays into three groups based not so much on the academic disciplines of the authors or the parts of India they cover as on the types of material they deal with. Part I comprises studies based on historical documents and literary sources. Part II, while also containing one article that uses such sources, has as its common theme the treatment of spatial conceptions in ritual and cosmology. Part III examines the politics of regions: in particular, the ways in which the region interacts with such other important ascribed identities as caste and religion in configuring political choices and loyalties.

Rich Freeman's essay deals with the earliest period discussed, and considers the question of regional consciousness in a most fundamental way. Freeman discusses linguistic and literary practices in medieval Kerala, practices of a sort that are basic to the formation of those regions that eventually achieved statehood in the modern Indian republic. Given the assumption of a linguistic basis for the states of contemporary India, Freeman points out that, paradoxically, Malayalam emerged during a period when Kerala was not politically united. Most importantly, in setting the stage for our discussion of regional consciousness, Freeman argues that expressions of regional culture differ in the degree to which they explicitly articulate the kinds of connections between land, people, and language that modern-style regionalism brings to the fore.

Whereas Freeman's emphasis is on 'literary practices', including the development of a literary language, Glushkova deals with language in another sense, illustrating the emotive and ideological power of words. Glushkova carries out a semantic analysis of two terms around which regional consciousness has crystallized in Maharashtra. One dates back to at least the fifteenth century, while the other is a more recent coinage. Whereas she finds that the meaning of the older term, 'Maharashtra *dharma*', has shifted over time, Glushkova cannot pin down any particular content for the other term, *asmitā*—a fact that she illustrates in rich detail. Such words, she concludes, fulfil a function that transcends their precise, literal meaning.

Prachi Deshpande focuses, like Glushkova, on Maharashtra, but moves away from the emphasis on language in the papers of both Freeman and Glushkova. Deshpande argues that, besides the 'emotive power' of language, there are other aspects of a region's culture that serve to unify its people. She examines the academic and popular practice of history in nineteenth- and twentieth-century Maharashtra. She shows that, besides being 'the prime cultural resource for forging a modern Maharashtrian regional identity', the history of the Marathas also provided a way to relate Maharashtra to the Indian nation.

Bishnu Mohapatra writes on the emergence of a particular kind of regional identity among the middle class in Orissa in the late nineteenth century, an identity based on a pervasive sense of inferiority to the Bengalis and other neighbours. This sense of inferiority, which Mohapatra traces ultimately to political, social, and especially economic conditions brought on by colonial rule, prompted Oriyas to articulate their common identity in terms of language, literature, and religion, and led to a strident insistence on Oriya's status as a language independent of Bengali, one that ought to be used in schools, the courts, and administrative offices.

In stark contrast with the self-deprecation that brought Oriyas together in the late nineteenth century, Sumathi Ramaswamy discusses a self-aggrandizing geographical theory that has formed a recurring theme in the regional identity of Tamil speakers since the same period. Ramaswamy argues that nostalgia for a place that is distant in time and space provides a powerful means of uniting the people who imagine themselves to have come from there. No matter that the continent of Lemuria no longer exists: as an ancient paradise that was the birthplace of humanity, this lost homeland of the Tamils allows them to understand themselves as the earliest of peoples, the ancestors of the human race. Beyond this, the 'collective yearning' for Lemuria 'holds together a people otherwise riven apart by caste, class, and religious differences'.

Jim Masselos turns our attention to yet another kind of powerful, imaginary place: the city of Mumbai. Maintaining the focus on the nineteenth and early twentieth centuries, Masselos examines the varying contexts in which Mumbai, as it was created and rose to prominence under the British and continued as a major centre of power in independent India, was separate from and linked to the region and nation around it, and the ways in which it served as a 'threshold' to the region and the nation. That Mumbai seemed distinct from the countryside around it becomes clear from the accounts of Indian travellers. To travellers arriving from Europe, by contrast, Mumbai at first represented India in all its foreignness, before becoming for them the safe, secure base from which to venture into the 'quintessential India' that lay beyond.

Part II takes us out of the nineteenth and early twentieth centuries and away from historical documents and literary texts. The four papers of this section are based primarily on ethnographic research. Anne Feldhaus, working from a number of particular cases of pilgrimage circulation and religious images and stories current in Maharashtra, shows how such religious phenomena serve to support and define a sense of place in numerous small, overlapping regions. But she also points out that these little regions are not universally known or recognized; they become relevant in particular ritual contexts, and even the residents of the regions have varying degrees of awareness of their existence. In Feldhaus's view, the multiplicity and variety of culturally defined regions of South Asia present a convincing argument that there is no particular political teleology to the cultural valorization of regions.

Leela Prasad provides the stunning example of a micro-region and the kinds of everyday and annual customs that form its people's cosmology and provide them with a sense of community and identity.

Prasad analyses three 'moments of collectivity' in the small region of Sringeri that illustrate three different kinds of regional consciousness and three different aspects of the relationship between the region and the Śaṅkarācārya *maṭha* that is its most prominent institution. She shows that even a region as small as Sringeri is an 'elastic construct', and that the relationship of the locality to the region fluctuates. The notion of community is formed by a process in which spatial conceptions interact with social distinctions between insider and outsider and with a cultural sense of the links between the past and the present.

Daniel Jasper's paper takes on a particular case of the celebration of the past in the present. Describing an urban festival that contrasts sharply with the rural and small-town setting of Prasad's work, Jasper shows how the name or image of the heroic seventeenth-century king Shivaji Maharaj can support and even sanctify a relatively wide range of political positions. In all cases, though, for all who claim him, Shivaji is seen as a Hindu king and as a king who was and is tied to the people, the language, and the land of Maharashtra.

If there is one modern object more ubiquitous in Maharashtrian homes than the picture of Shivaji it is the *Kālnirṇay* calendar on the wall. Sanjay Palshikar presents a study of this calendar, along with a discussion of its history and an analysis of its editorial policies. By including all manner of festivals and holidays—even secular holidays, and festivals of even the numerically smallest minority religions—from a motley set of places at all ends of Maharashtra, the calendar 'produces something internally continuous' that it identifies as Maharashtrian, or even Indian, culture. Time, not only as nostalgia and history but also as the at-once-linear-and-cyclical phenomenon represented by the squares on the calendar, becomes as important as space in forging regional identity.

In the vast majority of cases, regional identity remains politically dormant, but when it does have political consequences these can be powerful and dramatic. The political significance of the phenomena discussed in Parts I and II of the book becomes explicit in Part III. This section contains four papers that discuss the interaction of regional consciousness and other forms of identity that are politically significant in contemporary India.

Unlike the other papers in this volume, which each focus on one region, large or small, Suhas Palshikar's paper provides an overview of many regions in different parts of India. Palshikar highlights the regional character of caste-based politics at the end of the twentieth century. Rather than studying caste-based regional parties, he analyses the caste-based regional politics of the all-India parties. Since, as Palshikar argues, caste is basically local and regional in its scope, it is primarily at the regional level that the hegemony of a particular caste can take effect or be contested in the political arena.

The remaining three papers in the last part of the volume investigate not caste but religious identity as a factor or a focus in regional politics and social unrest. Surinder Jodhka provides a historical survey of the demography and political geography of the Punjab, showing how the territory of the Indian Punjab shrank and the proportion of Sikhs living there rose in the twentieth century. Jodhka presents the case of a relatively small religious community making its religious-ethnic identity more important than language in defining a territorial region. Here religion plays the part that history plays in Prachi Deshpande's chapter: Jodhka, like Deshpande, points out that language is not always the sole or the primary factor in forming and bolstering regional consciousness in India.

Rajendra Vora analyses the political behaviour of Muslims in the Hindi heartland. He shows that the vast 'cow-belt' of north India is a 'sacred' region for Muslims as well as for Hindus—despite the fact that residents of the region do not even think of it as a region, let alone a Muslim region. The diametrical opposite of the Sikhs in this respect, north-Indian Muslims are a religious community without territory. As a result, they form an identity group whose strategies must circumvent the fact that they are not identified with any one region. Vora argues that forming alliances with other large but relatively powerless groups ('majoritarianism') would be more effective than 'minorityism'—that is, focusing on such minority-rights issues as the protection of mosques, personal law, Urdu, and the Muslim character (and name) of Aligarh Muslim University.

Sujata Patel, working on a much smaller area (Ahmedabad and its surrounding region) and a much more dramatic type of activity than electoral politics (riots), comes to conclusions very similar to Vora's with respect to the most effective means for Muslims to pursue their own social and political advantage. Patel studies the communal riots in Ahmedabad in 1985-6 in terms of the intersection of caste, religious, economic, and political factors in the city and its region. Her primary focus is the city-region nexus as it expresses itself in the prism of politics and riots. Thus, in a very different historical and cultural context, Patel is carrying on a study of the relationship between city and region that is similar to Masselos's analysis for Mumbai.

While our work represents a significant development beyond the earlier interdisciplinary volumes on regions in South Asia, there are many aspects of this topic that remain to be addressed, or that need to be explored in greater depth. It is our hope that this book will inspire more and more scholars to turn their attention to the genesis and dynamics of regions, regional consciousness, and regionalism.

REFERENCES

Agnew, John and James S. Duncan, eds. 1989. *The Power of Place: Bringing together Geographical and Sociological Imaginations*. Boston: Unwin Hyman.

Alam, Javeed. 1999. 'Behind the Verdict: Another Look at the Nation and the Regions'. In Copland and Rickard 1999, pp. 184-96.

Attwood, D. W., M. Israel and N. K. Wagle. 1988. *City, Countryside and Society in Maharashtra*. Toronto: University of Toronto, Centre for South Asian Studies.

Barnett, Marguerite R. 1976. *The Politics of Cultural Nationalism in South India*. Princeton: Princeton University Press.

Baruah, Sanjib. 1998. 'Politics of Subnationalism: Society versus State in Assam'. In Chatterjee 1998, pp. 496-520.

———. 1999. *India Against Itself: Assam and the Politics of Nationality*. Philadelphia: University of Pennsylvania Press.

Basu, S. 1994. *Jharkhand Movement*. Shimla: Indian Institute of Advanced Study.

Bhatnagar, S. and Pradeep Kumar, eds. 1988. *Regional Political Parties in India*. New Delhi: ESS Publications.

Bhatt, Bharat L. 1980. 'India and Indian Regions: A Critical Overview'. In Sopher 1980, pp. 35-61.

Brass, Paul R. 1991. *Ethnicity and Nationalism: Theory and Comparison*. New Delhi: Sage.

———. 1994. *The Politics of India Since Independence*. Cambridge: Cambridge University Press.

———. 1999. 'Regionalism, Hindu Nationalism and Party Politics in India's Federal System'. In Copland and Rickard 1999, pp. 137-65.

Chadda, Maya. 1997. *Ethnicity, Security and Separatism in India*. New Delhi: Oxford University Press.

Chatterjee, Partha, ed. 1998. *State and Politics in India*. New Delhi: Oxford University Press.

Chaudhari, Maitrayee. 2000. 'Cultural Policy in Indian Sociology'. Paper presented at the National Workshop on Knowledge, Institutions, and Practices: The Formation of Indian Anthropology and Sociology, Institute of Economic Growth, Delhi, 19-21 April.

Copland, Ian and John Rickard, eds. 1999. *Federalism: Comparative Perspectives from India and Australia*. New Delhi: Manohar.

Corbridge, Stuart and John Harris. 2000. *Reinventing India: Liberalisation, Hindu Nationalism and Popular Democracy*. New Delhi: Oxford University Press.

Crane, Robert, ed. 1967. *Region and Regionalism in South Asian Studies: An Exploratory Study*. Durham, NC: Duke University.

Das, Samir K. 1997. *Regionalism in Power: A Case of Gana Parshad*. New Delhi: Omsons Publication.

Dasgupta, Jyotindra. 2001. 'India's Federal Design and Multicultural National Construction'. In Kohli 2001, pp. 49-77. Cambridge: Cambridge University Press.

Datta, Prabhat. 1993. *Regionalisation of Indian Politics*. New Delhi: Sterling Publishers.

Deshpande, Madhav M. 1983. 'Nation and Region: A Socio-Linguistic Perspective on Maharashtra'. In Israel 1983, pp. 111-34.

Devalle, Susana B. C. 1992. *Discourses of Ethnicity: Culture and Protest in Jharkhand*. New Delhi: Sage.

Dumont, Louis. 1957. 'For a Sociology of India'. *Contributions to Indian Sociology* 1: 7-22.

Eck, Diana L. and Françoise Mallison, eds. 1991. *Devotion Divine: Bhakti Traditions from the Regions of India*. Groningen: Egbert Forsten/Paris: École Française d'Extrême-Orient.

Eschmann, Anncharlotte, Herman Kulke, and Gaya Charan Tripathi, eds. 1978. *The Cult of Jagannath and the Regional Tradition of Orissa*. New Delhi: Manohar.

Feld, Steven and Keith H. Basso, eds. 1996. *Senses of Place*. Santa Fe: School of American Research Press.

Feldhaus, Anne. 2003. *Connected Places: Region, Pilgrimage, and Geographical Imagination in India*. New York: Palgrave Macmillan.

Flueckiger, Joyce Burkhalter. 1996. *Gender and Genre in the Folklore of Middle India*. Ithaca: Cornell University Press.

Fox, Richard G., ed. 1977. *Realm and Region in Traditional India*. New Delhi: Vikas.

Frankel, Francine and M. S. A. Rao, eds. 1989. *Dominance and State Power in Modern India* (2 vols). New Delhi: Oxford University Press.

Hardgrave, Robert L. 1965. *The Dravidian Movement*. Mumbai: Popular Prakashan.

Hartshorne, Richard. 1959. *Perspectives on the Nature of Geography*. Chicago: Rand McNally.

Hasan, Zoya. 1999. 'Region and Nation in India's Political Transition'. In Copland and Rickard 1999, pp. 166-83.

Hussain, Monirul. 1993. *The Assam Movement: Class, Ideology and Identity*. Delhi: Manak.

Israel, Milton, ed. 1983. *National Unity: The South Asian Experience*. New Delhi: Promilla.

Israel M. and N. K. Wagle, eds. 1987. *Religion and Society in Maharashtra*. Toronto: University of Toronto, Centre for South Asian Studies.

Jeffrey, Robin. 1994. *What is Happening to India? Punjab Ethnic Conflict and the Test for Federalism*. London: Macmillan.

Jodhka, Surinder, ed. 2001. *Community and Identities: Contemporary Discourse on Culture and Politics in India*. New Delhi: Sage.

Kaviraj, Sudipta. 1992b. 'Writing, Speaking, Being: Language and the Historical Formation of Identities in India'. In *Nationalstaat und Sprachkonflikte in Süd- und Südostasien*, edited by Dagmar Hellmann-Rajanayagam and Dietmar Rothermund. Stuttgart: Franz Steiner Verlag, pp. 25-65.

Khilnani, Sunil. 1998. *The Idea of India*. London: Penguin.

Kohli, Atul, ed. 2001. *The Success of India's Democracy*. Cambridge: Cambridge University Press.

Lam, Alastair. 1993. *Kashmir: A Disputed Legacy 1846-1990*. Karachi: Oxford University Press.

Leavitt, John. 1992. 'Cultural Holism in the Anthropology of South Asia: The Challenge of Regional Tradition'. *Contributions to Indian Sociology* 26, 1: 3-49.

Majeed, Akhtar, editor. 1984. *Regionalism: Developmental Tension in India*. New Delhi: Cosmo Publications.

Majumdar, A. K. and Bhanwar Singh, eds. 1997. *Regionalism in Indian Politics*. New Delhi: Radha Publications.

Marriott, McKim. 1976. 'Interpreting Indian Society: A Monistic Alternative to Dumont's Dualism'. *Journal of Asian Studies* 36: 189-95.

McDonald, Ellen E. 1968. 'The Growth of Regional Consciousness in Maharashtra'. *Indian Economic and Social History Review* 5: 223-43.

Mohapatra, Bishnu N. 1996. 'Ways of "Belonging": The *Kanchi Kaveri* Legend and the Construction of Oriya Identity'. *Studies in History* (n.s.) 12: 203-21.

Mukerji, D. P. 1979. *Sociology of Indian Culture*. Jaipur: Rawat.

Mukherjee, Bharati. 1992. *Regionalism in Indian Perspective*. Calcutta: K. P. Bagchi and Co.

Nag, Sajal. 1990. *Roots of Ethnic Conflict: Nationality Question in North-East India*. New Delhi: Manohar.

———. 1999. *Nationalism, Secularism, Secessionism*. Jaipur: Rawat.

Nehru, Jawaharlal. 1951. *The Discovery of India*. Calcutta: The Signet Press.

Palanithurai, G. and R. Thandavan, eds. 1992. *Perspectives on Indian Regionalism*. New Delhi: Kanishka Publishing House.

Palshikar, Suhas. 2003. 'The Regional Parties and Democracy: Romantic Rendezvous or Localised Legitimisation?' In *Politics, Parties and Party Systems*, edited by Ajay Mehra, B. D. Khanna and Gert W. Kueck. New Delhi: Sage.

Pathy, Jagannath. 1988. *Ethnic Minorities in the Process of Development*. Jaipur: Rawat.

Puri, Balraj. 1993. *Kashmir: Toward Insurgency*. New Delhi: Orient Longman.

Ramaswamy, Sumathi. 1993. 'En/gendering Language: The Poetics of Tamil Identity'. *Comparative Studies in Society and History* 35: 683-725.

———. 1994. 'The Nation, the Region, and the Adventures of a Tamil "Hero" '. *Contributions to Indian Sociology*, n.s. 28: 295-322.

———. 1997. *Passions of the Tongue: Language Devotion in Tamil India, 1891-1970*. Berkeley: University of California Press.

———. 1998. 'Language of the People in the World of Gods: Ideologies of Tamil before the Nation'. *Journal of Asian Studies* 57: 66-92.

Reddy, G. Ram and B. A. V. Sharma. 1979. *Regionalism in India: A Study of Telangana*. New Delhi: Concept.

Rudolph, Lloyd and Susanne Hoeber Rudolph. 1987. *In Pursuit of Lakshmi: The Political Economy of the Indian State*. Chicago: University of Chicago Press.

Ryerson, Charles A. 1988. *Regionalism and Religion: The Tamil Renaissance and Popular Hinduism*. Madras: Christian Literature Society.

Satyamurthy, T. V., ed. 1996. *Region, Religion, Caste, Gender and Culture in Contemporary India*. New Delhi: Oxford University Press.

Schomer, Karine, Joan L. Erdman, Deryck O. Lodrick, and Lloyd I. Rudolph, eds. 1994. *Rajasthan: Explorations in Regional Identity*. Vol. I: *Constructions*. New Delhi: Manohar/American Institute of Indian Studies.

Schwartzberg, Joseph E. 1967. 'Prolegomena to the Study of South Asian Regions and Regionalism'. In Crane 1967: 89-111.

———. 1985. 'Factors in the Linguistic Reorganisation of Indian States'. In Wallace 1985.

———, ed. 1978. *A Historical Atlas of India*. Chicago: University of Chicago Press. Second impression, with additional material: New York: Oxford University Press, 1992.

Sharma, S. L. 1996. 'Ethnic Challenge to Indian Identity: Rethinking Culture-Politics Interface'. In *Theory and Ideology in Indian Sociology*, edited by Narendra K. Singh. Jaipur: Rawat.

Sharma, S. L. and T. K. Oomen, eds. 2000. *Nation and National Identity in South Asia*. New Delhi: Orient Longman.

Singh, Bhavani, ed. 1993. *Regionalism and Politics of Separatism in India*. Jaipur: Printwell.

Singh, Yogendra. 1988. *Modernisation of Indian Tradition: A Systematic Study of Social Change*. Jaipur: Rawat.

———. 2000. 'Is Globalisation a Threat to Regional and Local Identities?' In *Pluralism and Equality: Values in Indian Society and Politics*, edited by Imtiaz Ahmad, Partha S. Ghosh, and Helmut Reifeld. New Delhi: Sage.

Sontheimer, Guenther-Dietz. 1989. *Pastoral Deities in Western India*. New York: Oxford University Press.

Sopher, David E. 1980. 'The Geographical Patterning of Culture in India'. In Sopher, editor 1980.

———, ed. 1980. *An Exploration of India: Geographical Perspectives on Society and Culture*. Ithaca, New York: Cornell University Press.

Stein, Burton. 1977. 'Circulation and the Historical Geography of Tamil Country'. *Journal of Asian Studies* 37: 7-26.

Suri, Ratnapala. 1999. 'Federalism as a Response to Ethnic Regionalism'. In Copland and Rickard 1999.

T. D. S. S. 1987. *Nationality Question in India*. Pune: T. D. S. S.

Talbot, Cynthia. 2002. *Precolonial India in Practice: Society, Region, and Identity in Medieval Andhra*. New York: Oxford University Press.

Unnithan, T. K. N., Indra Deva and Yogendra Singh, eds. 1965. *Towards a Sociology of Culture in India*. New Delhi: Prentice-Hall of India.

Vanaik, Achin. 1991. *Painful Transition: Bourgeois Democracy in India*. London: Verso.

Vance, Rupert B. 1968. 'Region'. In *International Encyclopaedia of the Social Sciences*, edited by David L. Sills, Vol. 13. London: Macmillan.

Wagle, N. K., ed. 1980. *Images of Maharashtra: A Regional Profile of India*. London: Curzon Press.

Wallace, Paul, ed. 1985. *Region and Nation in India*. New Delhi: Oxford and IBH Publishing Company and American Institute of Indian Studies.

Weiner, Myron. 1989. *The Indian Paradox: Essays in Indian Politics*. New Delhi: Sage.

PART I

Regions in History and Literature

1

Literature and the Development of Regional Consciousness in Medieval Kerala

Rich Freeman

This essay offers some reflections on the nature and development of regional consciousness in the context of pre-modern literary identity in medieval Kerala. While a number of pieces in our volume touch in various ways on the importance of language for the formation and maintenance of regional identities in South Asia, I wish to draw attention to the specific importance of literary language within the domain of linguistic consciousness. I find this kind of research fruitful both on theoretical grounds, because of certain properties that literature as a kind of discursive practice tends to exhibit, and on substantively historical grounds, because of the important role that literary claims to regional identity have played as we track these discursive practices through time.

Theoretically, I find an interesting convergence between the operations that literature works on language, and the role that language itself plays in articulating identity. Whatever grander claims recent literary theories have advanced, most still recognize the special function of literary language in both (1) formalizing everyday speech according to explicit or implicit meta-rules of structure and usage and (2) calling attention to that formalization as the sign of its literariness, its 'art'.[1] In simpler terms, literature is reflexive, in that it calls attention to itself as literature. In relation to identity formation, linguistic practices more generally are one of the key means by which communities recognize and demarcate group membership, and this includes the reflexive use of language itself to label that membership. Literature, as a special kind of language practice that complexly figures such reflexivity, can obviously play a vital role in creating and indexing various sorts of cultural capital and cultural identity, both regional and trans-regional.

Historically, some version of this process has been indigenously claimed as tantamount to *the civilizing process* on the Indian subcontinent for over two millennia—ever since the invention of that linguistic and cultural formation called 'Sanskrit'.[2] More than a mere language, Sanskrit projected a world-view of culture-building predicated on the disciplinary regimes it laid down for grammar and poetry. Whatever the political and religious forces accompanying this projection (and they seem to have been historically varied), this disciplining of language into literature was implicit, if not explicit, in legitimating the promotion of most other pre-modern South Asian regional languages into literary media.[3] In modernity, these particular regional legacies additionally became an important resource for demonstrating the historical depth, and hence the authenticity, of claims to culturally legitimated regional identities within the framework of the nation. These issues have been furthermore entangled with writing the modern histories of regions as well, since they have helped adjudicate whose history is to be written, and who gets an identity with the cultural clout and capital worthy of chronicling.

I do not develop these specifically modern entailments in any depth here, though they implicitly frame and lend the weight of their greater political relevance to the material that follows. Instead, I wish to take up the issue of regional consciousness as it partly converges with the reflexive properties of literary language, and to consider this convergence in pre-modern Kerala, before the advent of the complexities that colonialism and modern cultural politics introduced into the equation.

Specifically, I wish to relate the issue of reflexivity in literature to a named, spatially figured awareness of identity, to the extent that these converge in the sense of a developing regional consciousness. I prefer the term regional 'consciousness' here rather than 'imagination' because of a particular contrast I wish to keep in view. Since I suggested above that literary reflexivity can operate either through a formal discipline of explicitly worked-out rules, or implicitly, through an intuitively developed sense of practice, I think we can and should recognize a similar distinction in regional identity. That distinction, which really charts out a continuum, concerns the relation between largely unreflective practices that cluster spatially because people interact over a region, and those that become thematized as indices of a self-consciously articulated regional identity. In a way that most invocations of the 'imaginary' do not, I pose the problematic as to when the people of Kerala became aware of belonging to any such region in literary-linguistic terms, at what level of conscious awareness this might or might not have operated, and what difference this makes.[4]

After a brief overview of the development of language and literature in Kerala, highlighting some key historical and theoretical problems of regional identity this raises, I present three cases of literary textual practices that illustrate different points along a continuum of the explicitness of identity consciousness implicated in literary production. Finally, I venture a provisional correlation between this explicitness and the power relations of the respective authors.

The Regional Literary Language in Historical Overview

One of the greatest problems in the linguistic-literary demarcation of a specifically Kerala identity has to do with the long imbrication of this identity with that of the Tamils. While there seems to have been an established usage of the geographic term 'Kerala' in the Sanskrit sources, the earliest literature associated with that land was in classical Tamil. As the earliest regional-language literature on the subcontinent, dating from roughly the early first to about the sixth century, this Tamil bardic corpus celebrated the martial and romantic exploits of peoples living in territories under three principal kingly lines: the Cēras, the Pāṇḍyas, and the Cōḻas (Marr 1985; Zvelebil 1974). The Pāṇḍya and Cōḻa territories were centred in what is today Tamil Nadu and reasserted their named identities, as such, in political and cultural form throughout subsequent Tamil history. While some of the poetry associated with the Cēras pertained to places in what is today the Kerala coast, some of it did not, and there have been long scholarly disputes as to whether various Cēra capitals were located on the coast, or on the eastern side of the Ghats in Tamil Nadu.

Modern Kerala scholars have been caught between wishing to claim membership in this Tamil literature, thereby lending modern

Malayalam a literary affiliation as deep as that of Tamil, on the one hand, and recognizing that this historical identification implies that Kerala was merely part of the greater Tamil cultural-political sphere, on the other.[5] Indeed, if this Cēra branch of the classical Tamil literature did pertain prominently to the Kerala territory, then it disappeared from that land with no significant cultural memory, except for some scraps of reconstructed folklore and the close genetic relationship between the later languages of Malayalam and Tamil. These Cēra-affiliated works were preserved only indifferently as part of the larger Tamil corpus in the Tamil country. Although the Tamil language and literature continued to develop into their medieval forms, and this early literature was largely forgotten until its rediscovery by modern scholars, Tamils did maintain the continuity of an explicitly distinctive Tamil linguistic and cultural identity across the centuries that could later avidly reappropriate this literature for the authenticating projects of the modern regional state and Dravidian language politics. Kerala's position in this project was, at best, ambiguous and marginal.

In Kerala itself, we have a complete literary gap, down to the ninth century, when fragmentary inscriptions begin appearing there in what looks linguistically like a slightly variant dialect of medieval Tamil (Ayyar 1983 [1936]; Sekhar 1953). This inscriptional language only gradually diverges over the following centuries towards grammatical forms that anticipate those appearing in the later literature of the region. For the ninth to the twelfth centuries, the only non-Sanskrit literature we have treating persons and places in the region is again in literary Tamil, this time the medieval Tamil of the bhakti literary corpus. This literature celebrates numerous temples and associated saints of the Tamil Śaiva and Vaiṣṇava bhakti movements, only fourteen of whose temples were in the Kerala country. Two kings of Kerala lineage were also included among these saints in terms of poetic attribution and later hagiography, though most of the poetry attributed to them celebrates temples not in Kerala itself, but in Tamil Nadu (Narayanan 1994; Peterson 1991). As with the earlier classical poetry, all these bhakti poems were saved only as part of the compendia preserved in Tamil Nadu, and if they were ever produced or circulated in Kerala, they again disappeared from that land *in toto*.

From the aforementioned inscriptional record, supplemented with the attribution of a number of Sanskrit works and later legends in Malayalam, modern local scholars reconstructed for this period a 'Second Cēra' dynasty which supposedly ruled all of Kerala from the ninth to the twelfth centuries. By comparison with neighbouring regions, these inscriptions are meager and fragmentary, and all very suspiciously lack the dedicatory formulaic introductions of praise (*praśasti*) which allow the identification and correlation of royal reigns everywhere else in India. Many do give dates reckoned in the regnal years of named individuals, however, and by equating a number of these with each other and correlating them, scholars have reconstructed a partial list of the kings who made up this supposed dynasty (Narayanan 1996). Claims for this polity, variously styled the Second Cēra Empire, the Perumāḷs, or the Kulaśēkharas, have ranged from a celebration of its imperial status across the length of Kerala, checking and rivalling the imperial Cōḻas, to reckoning it as a mere province of the Cōḻas, confined to central Kerala, to doubts as to whether it ever existed at all as a unified polity.[6]

The consensus among professionally vested historians seems still to be that these kings constituted a dynasty that reigned in some fashion throughout Kerala, and that their rule marked 'the key period in Kerala history since it was the formative period of all that is distinctive in Kerala society and culture' (Narayanan 1996: vi). The peculiar problem for the way this history meshes with the literary record is this: why would there be no indigenous-language literary efforts to either chronicle or celebrate the accomplishments of this major cultural-political formation which supposedly reigned for more than three centuries?

On the subsequent political trajectory of Kerala history all are basically agreed. Following the break-up of the posited Second Cēra polity, the territory was fragmented for the next six centuries into some dozen or more chronically feuding chiefdoms that alternately split and fused with shifting boundaries and fortunes until their eventual subjugation and amalgamation into the three administrative territories of British imperial rule. Significantly, it is only in the state of political disorder that set in after the twelfth century that literary efforts based in the local language made their appearance. Linguistically, the shift out of a dialect of middle Tamil can be gradually charted in different genres and registers of the local language over the following centuries of literature and inscriptions, to eventuate in something close to grammatically modern Malayalam only around the end of the sixteenth century. If we are thus troubled by the absence of any Kerala-specific claims to literary identity and production during the so-called Cēra period, then we confront the opposite problem with later medieval Kerala: why is it only during the period of the socio-political disunity of Kerala that the regionally distinctive Malayalam language emerges?

Naming Practices of the Language and Region

Having posed the substantive historical problem this way, I wish to broach the theoretical problem of consciousness of this process of literary language formation itself in relation to the region. While linguists can chart a number of structural shifts in the language that mark off the practices of literary production in Kerala as giving it an objectively distinctive, regional identity, how aware were literati themselves of this identity, and at what level of self-conscious activity was the project of literary linguistic identity operative? The answers to these questions turn out to be complex and rather ambiguous, but we can make a start on the issue of reflexive practices by looking at the issue of naming.

It does not seem that the occupants of Kerala had a distinctive name for their language until perhaps the sixteenth century or so, when the modern name *Malayāḷam* emerges. Even then, this was mixed up with other cognates (*Malayāṇma*, *Malayāḻma* and *Malayāyma*), and there is uncertainty as to what the word's original etymology or signification was, other than having something to do with the mountains (*mala*). The semantic scope is similarly vague, since whatever its linguistic pertinence, the word also referred both to a kind of script and to the territory itself. The latter meaning has continued virtually into modern usage, where, though *Malayāḷam* usually refers to the language, it can still be used in certain contexts to refer to the country of Kerala. *Malayāḷi*, as the word for an inhabitant of the territory (never for the language), seems rather older, has a different semantic coverage, and does not imply the existence of the corresponding names for either the language or the territory.[7]

The name *Kērala* was itself a Sanskrit designation that was extended to the territory, but more centrally pertained to royal lineages of the Cēras and their associated subjects, as I discuss below. The longest standing and most pervasive indigenous word for the land, from the earliest literature until modernity, was simply *Malanāṭu*, the Mountain Country. While there was a widespread mythical charter for the divine founding of thirty-two brahman settlements in *Malanāṭu* (along with another thirty-two to the north, in *Tuḷunāṭu*), this network of villages did not coincide with any single political or territorial entity that we know of, aside from its partial relevance to the brahmans themselves. In sum, what we learn from the internal designations in the literature is that while there was a vaguely defined territorial sphere called *Malanāṭu* (and later, *Kēraḷam*), this was not congruent in any clear fashion with a singularly named language or literature or people or polity. To get a better sense of the various disjunctures that any developing sense of regional consciousness had to overcome, both in the horizontal relations of political territory and in the vertical complexities of social relations, we must turn to a closer consideration of the literature itself, its cultural uses, and its social structuring.

The Performance of Literature in Social Hierarchies

While one line of analysis that I have partly drawn on monitors the development of language, as a discretely 'linguistic' entity, through the literature, this is a distinction of analytic levels, and not of linguistic substance and practice. Indeed I would argue that the linguistic development of Kerala cannot be historically abstracted from the production and circulation of literature, and that rather than literature passively reflecting the patterns of some underlying everyday language form, active and continuous literary interventions played a key role in the very creation of what we today call Malayalam. It is important to understand in this context, however, that the 'literature' to which I refer cannot be comprehended under the modern form in which we tend to produce and interpret it.[8]

Print capitalism, with its historically Western patterns of producing and consuming the book form of literature, has thoroughly conditioned the way modern subjects, and most modern scholarly modes of analysis, view the form and use of 'literature'. The default assumption is that the units of literature are books, designed to be silently read in privately individual acts of consumption. I am convinced by both internal and ethnohistorical evidence that this was not at all the character of literature in medieval Kerala (Freeman 2003). If Kerala is culturally famous for anything it is the legacy of its medieval temple arts, and this is directly related to the performative intent of most genres of its literature—devotional chanting, recitation or sung lyrics in formal settings, and background song, narration, or scripts for staging. What modern scholars in Kerala, following Western exemplars, have turned into a corpus of prosaic and exegetical book-literature, 'Malayalam literature', was poetically constructed to be sung, drummed, danced, and enacted.

This further suggests that we should approach the various configured units that this literature takes, its 'genres', not merely as graphically patterned forms of literary structure, but as enacted forms of social practice (Hanks 1987). In keeping with this perspective, we know that most genres were directly related to the social identities of who could perform them for certain audiences in particular forums. These social identities were themselves structured by the hierarchies of caste, especially as mapped into the performative spaces of the Kerala temple, where most important literature had its venue.

The temple, in its architectural layout, formed virtually a spatial representation of the peculiar caste system of Kerala. Centred on the image of the deity, whom only the highest brahmans could directly worship, features of the temple grounds charted out concentric zones of allowable approach dependent on the perceived purity of the different caste blocs. This served as a key for strictures on social interaction and communication in the society at large, where the various degrees of caste were reckoned not just by physical contact and interaction, but even by measured distances of permitted approach on the social landscape. Temple theatres and other venues of performance within temple compounds were thus areas ritually cordoned off for particular caste blocs of audience, with further internal differentiation as to traditional seating and patterns of ritual interaction governing particular performance genres. For the performing castes as well, there was an internal hierarchy of knowledge practices and linguistic resources of performance that was largely congruent with ritual status. Most genres known to Kerala's premodern literature thus had stereotypical associations with the castes or caste-blocs who produced and consumed them, meaning that the overall field of literary production, and the cultural-regional identity this projected, were both inherently stratified by the hierarchies of the social system itself.

The most discriminating meta-discourse that this culture produced on the relation of its literature to linguistic and regional identity provides our first example for analysis. Exhibiting the most self-conscious articulation of these matters, this work also belongs to the least 'performative' and most 'textual' of the genres I discuss here. I would argue, however, that even such a text-about-texts, in both its production and its intended use in regulating other performances of literature, discloses its social position through a kind of meta-performative exposition.

EXPLICIT REFLECTIONS ON A REGIONAL LITERATURE: *MAṆIPRAVĀḶAM* AND THE *LĪLĀTILAKAM*

Within the region of what is today Kerala, we have seen that the first real literature to appear in the local language (excepting the inscriptions in dialectal Tamil) dates from the twelfth or thirteenth century. This is followed rapidly by a number of works during the fourteenth century that culminate at the end of that century with the only premodern treatment and discussion of this Kerala language or literature that is extant, a remarkable work called the *Līlātilakam*.[9] In keeping with my earlier observation on the mutual imbrication of literature with language, this text provides at once a kind of rudimentary grammatical sketch and a poetic manual for producing literature in a medium based on the local language. Remarkably, however, this treatise itself is written principally in Sanskrit. Though it does cite passages in the local language to exemplify the poetic practices it wishes to extol or disparage, the text itself takes the form of a disciplinary *śāstra* in aphoristic *sūtras* with an auto-commentary, both entirely in Sanskrit.

Sanskrit was of course the transregional language of India's literary and intellectual elite, and in Kerala, as much as or more so than elsewhere, this knowledge was largely confined to a brahmanical formation (brahmans, temple servants, and some select others). Since the *Līlātilakam* was clearly intended as a treatment of the language of Kerala for a Kerala audience, transregional communication could not have been the principal intent of writing it in Sanskrit (no one outside the region would have cared), and its audience within Kerala could only have been a restricted elite. The purpose of using this Sanskritically learned form therefore seems to have been, as is stated once in the text, to put the local language it teaches on a shastric footing, to discipline it into an elite artistic medium and authorize it with the weight of the poetic and cultural capital of Sanskrit.

But what is the language thereby authorized? It is not the ordinary language, *Kēraḷa-bhāṣa*, but rather an amalgam of this with Sanskrit into a special medium termed Maṇipravāḷam. This name refers to the stringing together of the rubies (*maṇi*) of the local language with the coral (*pravāḷam*) of Sanskrit, for it is only in the lexical, grammatical, and poetic union with Sanskrit that the *Kēraḷa-bhāṣa* can in fact be legitimated for the production of high literature (*kāvya*). It is this fusion at the phonological and lexical levels that fundamentally reshapes the 'Tamil' of the Kerala country into Malayalam over the subsequent centuries. The *Līlātilakam*, however, is not happy with just any such amalgamation, but requires instead a particular collocation of forms and usages from both languages that it stipulates as fit for literary production. As the necessary counterpart of the positive union it enjoins between the languages, and in keeping with preserving its elite cultural base, it must thus also exclude other varieties of language from its purview. It this way it had to inventory the competing, and perhaps more popular, language forms over which it wished to assert its superiority.

A rival form of poetic language that it prominently singles out for contrast is one it calls *Pāṭṭu*, meaning literally just 'song'. According to the *Līlātilakam*, Pāṭṭu uses only the Dravidian phonology (i.e. that of Tamil), particular metrical patterns of phonetic euphony, special non-Sanskrit metres, and heavily Pāṇḍyan (Tamil) usages. All of these features, perfunctorily stated as they are in this text, are in fact characteristic of classical Tamil poetry, and this clearly attests (as do two surviving works written in this style) to the retention of Tamil literary conventions in the Kerala country, in fairly direct opposition to the trend that Maṇipravāḷam poets sought to establish for their own poetry. In the subsequent history of development of the language we can say somewhat crudely that the Sanskritic, Maṇipravāḷam poets won out phonetically and lexically, while the

Tamilian, Pāṭṭu poets prevailed grammatically and in terms of poetic metre and euphonic line structure.

But how did the *Līlātilakam* perceive the base language, the terrain of *Kēraḷa-bhāṣa* over which it sought to assert its Sanskritic authority in vying with Tamil influence? First, following Sanskrit usage, the word *Kēraḷa* never stands uncompounded in that text as the name of a land, but rather with plural, personal terminations as the proper name of a people, or a line of kings, the Kēraḷas. So by implication *Kēraḷa-bhāṣa* was the language of a people associated with a royal line. This exactly parallels the usage of the names Pāṇḍya and Cōḻa for the rival Tamil kings, and Kēraḷa is, in fact, just a Sanskrit cognate of Cēra. Within the corpus of Maṇipravāḷam poetry, we do find the invocation of a Cēra's polity (Cēramān Nāṭu), confined only to central Kerala, but this provides merely a notional, ceremonial centre for the mythically founded Malanāṭu, and the Cēra line was by this period shorn of any substantial power or political centrality.[10] The association of the Kēraḷa lineage with a land and language thus need not suggest any tight region-wide congruence between various units of polity, the boundaries of geo-political territories, and the networks of cultural-religious centres; nor need it indicate the existence of an ethnically integrated populace; nor need it imply that all of these spheres were united under the unitary practices of a single language community. My reading of this literature suggests a far looser and more historically fluid set of associations around the related names Cēra and Kēraḷa.

The principal issue of nomenclature with which the *Līlātilakam* had to contend, however, was that the common name for what it prefers to term *Kēraḷa-bhāṣa* was in fact simply Tamil! The inhabitants of Kerala indeed continued to call their language by this name for centuries after the *Līlātilakam*. It is therefore in the context of defining Maṇipravāḷam as the union of 'Tamil' and Sanskrit that this text must provide a description of distinctive grammatical and lexical usages (that we would recognize as Malayalam), in order to prove that 'Tamil' here refers to a distinctive *Kēraḷa-bhāṣa*, and not to the Tamil that is the *Pāṇḍya-bhāṣa* or *Cōḻa-bhāṣa*. Although a number of the grammatical and phonetic peculiarities that had begun to mark off Malayalam as a distinctively diverging west-coast dialect of Tamil were captured with some astuteness, the overall concern of the Maṇipravāḷam project with establishing an elite register of literary language also characterizes the treatment of the *Kēraḷa-bhāṣa* that forms its local language component. We are thus informed that *Kēraḷa-bhāṣa* comes in noble (*utkṛṣṭa*) and debased (*apakṛṣṭa*) varieties, and that only the former is fit for Maṇipravāḷam. While the former is the speech of the educated, who are of the upper three *varṇas* (brahmans, temple-servant castes, and royalty, excluding shudras), the latter is of the low castes and is incidentally described as phonologically deviant from the upper-caste dialect (in ways that look, by the way, a lot like Tamil). So even within the field of its 'own' language component of the Maṇipravāḷam-mix, the text must posit a language-identity against others, both inter-regionally, in terms of Pāṇḍya and Cōḻa varieties of Tamil, and intra-regionally, in terms of lower-caste strata closer to home.

While the *Līlātilakam* deploys its forms against 'Tamil', both at the level of linguistic identity in grammatical terms, and in terms of Tamil's classical poetic legacy constellated around the Kerala form of Pāṭṭu, the meaning of Tamil, as a broader cultural construct, and the Kēraḷas' relation with it are quite complex. Rather oddly, having argued against an identity with other Tamils at these levels, the *Līlātilakam* also argues for the Kēraḷas' common Tamilness with the Cōḻas and Pāṇḍyas under the construct of their shared 'Dravidianness' (*Dramiḍa-tva*, where *Dramiḍa* is just a Sanskritized form of Tamil!). The first argument for their common Dravidianness links language with religious scripture: the Kēraḷas and the other Tamils are both Dravidian, because their languages, though different, are neither very far from the earlier medieval Tamil Vaiṣṇava *bhakti* literature, which our text calls the 'Dravidian Veda'. The second argument links these groups together around what I would call a notion of literary polity. In this sense, the Kēraḷas are Dravidian because the classical Tamil literature (of which the elite in Kerala must have still retained some knowledge) was written in praise of the Three Kings (*Mūvēntar*), who were the Cēras, Pāṇḍyas, and Cōḻas. While the 'polity' of this triumvirate had clearly had no real political purchase in south India for some seven or eight centuries, the literary corpus built around it still must have had sufficient cultural capital among the 'Tamils' that our author wanted to stake Kerala's continued claim to it. Thus, even as the *Līlātilakam's* author wanted to establish a regional-language literary identity for the Kēraḷas that was distinctive from the construct of Tamil in linguistic and poetic terms—partly through claims of local language differences and partly through the embrace of Sanskrit—it wanted to maintain ties to a larger Tamil cultural sphere in terms of certain religious and literary-political legacies.

The *Līlātilakam* provides as explicit and sophisticated a set of reflections on the self-identity of a language with a literature and a region as we can find in premodern South Asia. From one perspective, micro-distinctions of phonology, grammar, and poetic form are used to index a literary language and its correlated everyday speech with a people and some loosely notional territory. From another perspective, however, we can see that there are a set of fairly incoherent inclusions and exclusions that lie at the very basis of the project. On the one hand, the Maṇipravāḷam proponents wish to differentiate the Kēraḷas from the Tamil traditions of literature and polity with which they are historically imbricated, partly by resort to trans-regional status gains through Sanskrit, while on the other hand, they seek the continued embrace of their shared Tamil identity in terms of the greater cultural capital its grammatical, literary, political, and religious traditions offer compared with the fledgling Kēraḷa productions. Similarly, in its local sphere of operation, Maṇipravāḷam must position itself in a field of competing literary forms which it must disprivilege, just as it must distance itself from the everyday speech of the region's lower caste communities. The sense of regional consciousness this produces is thus internally divided and externally spread over its inter-regional relations with Tamil, and its trans-regional relations with Sanskrit, with little concern for demarcating the cultural or political sphere of the Kēraḷas or the territorial boundaries of Malanāṭu.

Implicit Practices of Literary Mobility: The Messenger Poems

The second case I take up, more briefly, addresses the issue of territory and polity in literary regional consciousness a bit more directly, through reviewing a genre-theme of Maṇipravāḷam. While the *Līlātilakam* was meta-literary in the sense of being a treatise about literature, I turn here to the actual practice of figuring cultural space within these literary texts themselves. The genre that is most useful in this regard is called the messenger poem (*sandēśa kāvyam*) by Malayalam scholars. It is modelled explicitly on the first and most famous prototype in Sanskrit, Kālidāsa's *Meghasandeśa*, and involves the theme of lovers separated over long distances who send a messenger to carry their intimations of love over the intervening natural and cultural territories that divide them. Despite the trans-regional impact of Kālidāsa's Sanskrit work, arguments have been made for this theme's original locus in classical Tamil literature, which might also account for the explosion of *tūtu* (messenger) poems in medieval Tamil Nadu and south India more generally.

In any case, the interest for our purposes has to do with the major focus these texts have in describing the territory over which their messengers move. I have argued elsewhere that one of the principal functions this theme seems to serve, at least at this period in south India, is to figure (or prefigure) the territorial circulation of these works and their performance for the concerned authors and patrons.[11] As with the whole project of Maṇipravāḷam in relation to Sanskrit *kāvya* generally, we find here that a Sanskrit model of pan-Indian scope gets spatially transposed to a more restricted, but more intensively regional, set of usages.

At the broadest level of this adaptation we have a number of Kerala-focused messenger poems in Sanskrit itself. The most prominent of these, however, are inter-regional with respect to Kerala and Tamil Nadu, and seem to clearly trace the migration of their brahman authors from patronage bases in the courts of Tamil kingdoms to those in Kerala (often via Andhra and Karnataka). These works are thus trans-regionally trans-political in scope and are composed, fittingly, in the cosmopolitan language of Sanskrit. Their descriptive content, however, is focused on the praise of regionally prominent temples and palaces found along the rather meandering routes their works trace across a scale and variety of cultural and political patronage bases in south India.

When we shift to the Maṇipravāḷam messenger poems, we encounter an expected restriction of territorial sphere to that based on Kerala-language speech communities. Their range of description, however, is not over the greater region of 'Kerala'. Their compass is rather a particular network of localities over which the messengers' itineraries take them. In keeping with the temple-based and courtly provenance of this literature, the points of travel are mapped by stopping for descriptions of temples, brahman estates, and various royal capitals and residences. As the messenger-vehicles move over this circuit they encounter political territory only in micro-regional terms: the *nāṭus*, the various chiefdoms of shifting alliance and enmity into which the greater region was parcelled up. Notionally, there were eighteen of these, but this was a poetic figurement (found also in contemporary Tamil Nadu) and the actual number, names and boundaries fluctuated through conquest and fission across time.

The same travel and description that are explicit in the emplotment of the messenger poems (of which only two are extant in premodern Maṇipravāḷam) are implicit in earlier and later genres of the language as well, showing the same compulsion to travel and describe the same kinds of centres of cultural and political eminence. What is interesting is that most of these itineraries are transpolitical in terms of encompassing a chain of adjoining *nāṭu*, but all of them map only partial segments of the territory of what we today call Kerala. It is not clear whether this reflected existing political alliances within which the poets composed, or an intended sphere of influence which they projected poetically on behalf of their patrons or themselves. In addition, there are cases of leap-frogging comparisons that figure places in *nāṭus* off the poet's circuit in an unfavourable light, reflecting inter-*nāṭu* rivalries. In only some of the works do we encounter the dim framing invocation of a greater geographical sphere of Malanāṭu, centered on a king of the 'Kēraḷas' who was supposed to be resident at Mahodayapuram (near Cochin). If such a personage was not mythical by this time, he must merely have had some residually ritual entitlement, for he is promptly forgotten in these works to celebrate local chiefs as more prominently powerful.

The larger point I wish to make here in terms of regional consciousness is this. While there is none of the explicitness of the kind of attention to regional identity in terms of language and literary form that we encountered with the *Līlātilakam*, the practice of literature itself articulated a certain practical sense of territory that only partly and incidentally engaged segments of the region of the 'Kēraḷas', the mythically established and fuzzily bounded 'Malanāṭu'. The issue of linguistic-regional identity did not arise explicitly for these poets as it did for the *Līlātilakam*, and typologically discrepant literary forms and linguistic media co-existed in their works. Nevertheless, through the practice of literature itself (which, we must recall, was performatively grounded), the various micro-territorial mappings confronted and overlapped each other in competitive interaction, to create a larger sphere of territorial circulation. This overall pattern roughly coincided with that of neighbouring chiefly *nāṭus* intermittently warring and allying with each other, and with the inter-*nāṭu* mobility of certain brahmans and poets. But it is important to realize that literature was not just a passive reflection of a sense of a territorial sphere, but was helping to articulate and hence create it. This activity seems not to have been consciously harnessed to any larger project of shaping a regional Kerala identity. It was rather embedded in the habitus of being a poet and moving in these circuits of shifting patronage.

The Implicit Practice of Poetry: The Metric Aesthetic

The literary ventures treated so far doubtless circulated in the elite sectors of society, those centred on temples and courtly residences. For my final case I want to take up an aspect of literary genres that reflects the performative nature of this literature, and, at least inferentially, its caste stratification, to suggest how practices from excluded sections of society might come to invade and even inform upper-caste literature, without making their intervention in discursively explicit form. Indeed as James Scott (Scott 1990) has persuasively argued, such 'arts of resistance' cannot mark their interventions except indirectly and in disguise.

As I noted earlier, in the context of performance most Kerala literature was sung and drummed. This was and is as true of high-caste temple arts as of low-caste folk-genres. Paralleling their membership in completely different language families with completely different phonological and grammatical structures, the basic principles of metre in *Kēraḷa-bhāṣa* and Sanskrit were equally contrastive. Going back to the classical Tamil, Dravidian metres are based on rhythmic beat (*tāḷam*), while the canonically classical Sanskrit metres required a determinate sequence of long and short syllables.[12] In the former case I would argue that these *tāḷam* metres, as the word suggests, were derived from percussion instrumentation, to which they remained largely adapted. In the Sanskrit case, it is in fact difficult to find singers maintaining vowel quantity (and often even quality) in the context of Kerala's performance arts. The result is a kind of internal contradiction between Sanskritically metred text in the literary mode of Maṇipravāḷam, and its sense of appropriate performative realization. The popular performative sense of metre was in this way ideologically suppressed, even while it struggled for practical realization. Let us now look at two genre fields of Kerala literary production to document this return, and ultimate triumph, of the repressed popular sense of 'literature'.

A prominent genre of Maṇipravāḷam literature was called *campu*. This being, in theory, a direct adaptation of the Sanskrit genre of nearly the same name (*campū*), it was similarly defined as a poetic form that mixed poetry with prose. In the Sanskrit genre, what did not conform to metre was definitionally prose (*gadyam*), though in *kāvya* this usually took special literary forms of long and elaborate compounds with ornamental patterns of alliteration. In the Maṇipravāḷam *campu*, one finds that this 'prose' slot is frequently occupied instead by text in Dravidian metre.

It will be recalled that in this matter of metre, the *Līlātilakam* stipulates only Sanskrit metres for Maṇipravāḷam and excludes the peculiar non-Sanskrit metres as belonging to the Tamil-like genre of Pāṭṭu. But in the case of *campu*, since prose is allowed, and since Dravidian metrics, through not meeting the criteria of Sanskrit poetry, are stipulatively 'prose', they could be smuggled into the heart of this Sanskrit form. The innovators initially prominent in this process were most likely of the Nambyār-caste, drummers for the sacred theatre who had a special performative association with prose recitations. This convention, however, was taken up in the later *campu* form even by brahman authors.

Finally, the development of the Pāṭṭu genres reveals even more clearly a popular association that is initially and most prominently linked to shudra authors. As the soldiers and political and economic managers of Kerala's *nāṭus*, these shudras (under caste names like Nāyar, Paṇikkar, etc.) were at once the lowest caste-bloc allowed in the temple and those who mediated between the brahmanical formation and the rest of the labouring and productive castes of society outside the temple. In their hands, Kerala literary form was synthetically transfigured. For while, on the one hand, the typically Tamil phonological and lexical stipulations of the *Līlātilakam's* Pāṭṭu came to be completely dropped in favour of Sanskrit patterns, on the other hand the metrical principles of Dravidian prosody became the dominant feature for the whole stream of literature that indeed comes to define the emergence of the Malayalam language, as such.

From at least the late fourteenth century, poets who are explicitly shudra began adapting (with apologies to brahmans) Sanskrit works, evidently for their own communities' liturgical use. Such works, which are clearly composed for recitation and singing, develop different kinds of metres which are not classical Tamil, but Malayalam divergences that are built on similar principles. These compositions indeed swell to a stream that finally eclipses the force of Maṇipravāḷam. Eventually even some brahman and temple-servant authors took up these metrical forms for the popular compositions that are still a part of living Malayalam literature performed in religious contexts.

What is interesting in historical perspective, and my major point as regards the literary consciousness of these authors, is that all of these complex metrical patterns were developed and deployed in the absence of any meta-treatment of the language such as the *Līlātilakam* constitutes for Maṇipravāḷam. *Campu* authors, to my knowledge, never aver to the fact that their 'prose' is conforming to local metric patterns. No treatises of shudras or others ever treat, discuss, or acknowledge their distinctive poetic practices. We do not even have the names for any of the metres until a modern Sanskrit pandit-grammarian invented names for them as part of an effort to formalize them for teaching in schools. Though still a standard textbook for teaching Malayalam composition, this descriptive effort fails, since nearly all these '*bhāṣa*' metres are adjudged from the pundit's Sanskrit perspective to be deviant and defective, in principle.

Yet not only have these metres flourished as the very basis of a Malayali sense of what is rhythmically appropriate for poetry, but they were clearly differentiated in the premodern poetical compositions themselves for their distinctive performative virtues. The unmistakable evidence for this is the number of poetic works which bear elements in their titles like the 'Ten Metres', the 'Twenty-four Metres', and so on. This refers to their composition in pastiches of these distinctive metres, in which the stipulated number of metres are played off against each other, section-by-section, in a fixed sequence.[13] What this shows is that highly 'literary' composers were wielding these metres in the absence of any recorded poetics that would describe or stipulate or even name their poetic structures, and crafting their language out of the aesthetic sense that they had embodied through performance. It is this matrix of metrics, perhaps more than any other quality, which would have characterized their 'regional' sense of their own literature, without anyone apparently needing to think in these terms. Rather like the physical circulation of the literature itself through territory, the phonic circulation of an aesthetic through these authors was thus a matter of practice.

CONCLUSIONS: PRACTICE AND CONSCIOUSNESS IN THE LITERARY REGION

We have seen that literary practices in medieval Kerala, entailing both the identification of languages and literary media, and the relating of these to social and territorial identities, seem to run along a continuum of conscious articulation. At the most explicit level of discursive treatment, we find a concerted attempt to discipline linguistic and literary form in the *Līlātilakam*. This work also makes the clearest attempt to 'regionalize' the literary language by positioning it in relation to the trans-regional sphere of Sanskrit, the inter-regional sphere of the Tamil kingdoms, and the intra-regional sphere of locally competing literary media and caste dialects. I would argue, however, that in the absence of any overarching politically integrated or territorially bounded sphere of operation, and in the presence of its own internally riven social positioning, it did not yet articulate that identity of language with a people or a territory (except, perhaps, as an intermittently royal aspiration) that modern regionalists attempt to read back into the record. This is reflected, I believe, in the absence of a common name for the language itself until the brink of modernity.

We came up against these limitations most clearly in the second case, where we took up the thematic of territorial figurement through travel, within the literature itself, and saw that there were only partial circuits of territorial integration, confined to movements within and between a limited number of *nāṭus*. To the extent that these were either projective of poets' and patrons' expanding aspirations for territory, or competitive between patronage circuits, they seem to have worked towards a greater sphere of literary language circulation, even in the absence of integrating polities. These efforts were only partially consciousness, however, and did not rise to the level of region-wide projects, but emerged from the practices of poets working in the existing political configuration of patronage.

The final case of Dravidian metre showed how the results of such language practices, circulating through a region through time as performative enactments, could embody an aesthetic that would put its regional stamp on the overall literature, in the absence of any explicitly articulated literary discipline. The smuggling of this metric into the elite literature of Maṇipravāḷam, as well as the seeming insurgency of these metres in shudra literature as against their Sanskrit counterparts, suggests something of the power dynamic that was also in play. Paralleling the gradient from conscious literary discourse to embodied practices, we can see the contours of a struggle to control the forms and functions of literature in Kerala.

This effort at conscious control was most refined in the *Līlā-tilakam*, which was most concerned with developing and implementing discriminating hierarchies of language forms and pinning them to particular groups in society. Above these Sanskritizing vernacular intellectuals was the trans-regional model of Sanskrit itself; below their own ideal of Maṇipravāḷam came a welter of relatively disprivileged but evidently thriving media, and, embodying the spectre of Tamil's continuing cultural clout, there was Pāṭṭu. Though most powerful in terms of controlling the intellectual capital of Sanskrit, the Maṇipravāḷam model of literary-regional articulation was also the most explicitly hierarchical and exclusionary. Its literary forms failed to hold ultimate sway in Kerala, but they seem to have been undermined not by countermoves of rival expository subtlety, but by actual practices of literature that had different social bases and agendas.

To practise literature rather than expound it was the work of the poets who travelled the *nāṭus*, reiterating the political linkages and rivalries that held Kerala into a patchwork of contending, yet interacting polities. They were concerned with the substance of description that would please their local constituencies, and it was in these contexts that we have the earliest instances of that 'prose' (*gadyam*) that reflects the local metres. It was the advance edge of this popular sense, which was at once socially 'lower' and less formally articulated, that was seized on by the shudra poets for their later devotional and recitational literature. What was first smuggled into literature in a Sanskritic frame came to escape it altogether and without declaring itself—without daring to or needing to—became a new literature which aimed at, and achieved, a greater inclusivity.

In its overall contours, however, the profile of Malayalam is not that of a popular victory. Though the most widely circulated works in Malayalam were in the local metres, the Sanskritizing influence of Maṇipravāḷam's centuries-long reign had been considerable. The very sound-structure of the phonology had been irrevocably changed (though not exactly as intended),[14] and the native vocabulary of Tamil had been swamped by the Sanskrit lexicon, a trend that continues to the present.

While we can thus glean the workings of power along the continuum of consciousness—from those with the cultural resources to expound and refine, to those armed only with their practical engagements and their inarticulate 'tastes'—it turns out that the outcome of these struggles in terms of winners and losers is far from clear. The region of literary language practices that became 'Malayalam' can be claimed only by an amalgam of social forces that contended in ways seen and unseen through the historical record. For me, then, neither end of what I have characterized as a gradient of literary-regional consciousness can be privileged, since there was a complementarity between the actual practices of literature and the articulatory projects that attempted to give them their form. In this case, the simultaneous presence of various practices, expository and practical, contended and played off each other in creating the form that the regional identity of Kerala projected through its literature.

NOTES

1. This understanding of how literature is constituted probably entered English-language scholarship most prominently with Jacobson 1960, and one could argue that even more recent deconstructive theory still presupposes this basic meta-structural insight as fundamental to the latter's conceptualization of language and literary analysis.
2. Sanskrit means literally 'perfected' or 'polished'. This was self-descriptive of its own dominant linguistic ideology, wherein the disciplining of language through grammar and literature was itself the principal sign of culture. Compare its close cognate *saṃskāra*, for its various senses of 'refining' human beings ritually and educationally into

social, moral, and civilized beings, and the modern coining of *saṃskṛti* for 'culture'.

3. This modelling on Sanskrit prototypes of grammatical, literary and religio-cultural disciplines was true even of the Pāli-Prākrit language cultures of the Buddhist and Jaina world, as well as of Tamil, the most refractory of the language cultures in its interaction with Sanskrit. See the essays in Pollock 2003.
4. This is in partial response to comments by Sumathi Ramaswamy, who suggested that 'regional imagination' implies 'consciousness', and by Jim Masselos, who suggested that regional consciousness sounds too 'Jungian'. I hope this clarifies what is at stake in my use of the term, and I thank them for prodding me. On the necessity of reference to consciousness in the context of even the most stringently empirical analysis of mundane, everyday conversation, see Chafe 1994.
5. A discussion of some of these vexed issues can be found in Freeman 2003.
6. Since most of these debates are in Malayalam, I will refer the general reader to Sreedhara Menon 1980, Narayanan 1996, and Gurukkal 1992 for rather different interpretations. A fuller set of references can be found in Freeman 2003, though I there missed the new, relatively 'official' perspectives on these matters in English (Cherian 1999).
7. The personal suffix *–āḷi* is productive through all phases of Kerala language, down to the present (as with *toḷil-āḷi*, 'labour-er'). This is not the case with the other suffixes, which occur more sporadically, mostly as parts of received, frozen forms. I thus see no warrant in stating, as some scholars do, that the earlier use of the term *Malayāḷi* (which really just means 'mountaineer') presupposes the existence of a language community speaking *Malayāḷam*.
8. A body of anthropologically linguistic thinking regarding the constructively creative powers of textualization, as well as the continuum between text and performative modes, is reviewed in Baumann and Briggs 1990.
9. For a fuller analysis of this fascinating and unique text see Freeman 1998. Some historical placement and textual references are given there.
10. A Sanskrit work that deals with the west coast, the *Prapañcahṛdayam*, though of uncertain medieval date, confirms that the lineage name 'Kerala' pertained only to the central part of the modern region, areas to the north and south being named after different kingly lines (Sankunni Nair 1995: 48, n. 19).
11. The treatment of the messenger poems presented here is partly adapted from Freeman 2003.
12. I am not forgetting the Sanskrit *mātrā*-based metres, but these are different, in principle, from the rhythmic framing by *tāḷam*. This basis of Malayalam metres on *tāḷam* has generally been noted by scholars more

sensitive to Dravidian linguistics than the earlier Sanskrit-trained pundits (Subrahmanyan 1977, from a comparative perspective, and Krishna Warrior 1977, more centrally focused on Malayalam). A performatively-based analysis of *tāḷam*, however, differs from these essentially textual linguistic treatments, with some interesting consequences, as I hope to demonstrate empirically in a future publication.

13. The inclusion of some Sanskrit-derived metres into this compositional matrix of local metres should be noted, but this only strengthens the point that the local metres had been promoted to the point where they could appropriate and formally subordinate Sanskrit metres in the absence of any higher authority for their own metres or compositional forms.
14. The Malayalam script adopted the Sanskrit alphabet and can thereby render the ubiquitous loans graphically correct, but in practice their actual pronunciation collapses critical Indo-Aryan distinctions, conforms more to an underlying Dravidian set of functional contrasts, and introduces a hybrid system of co-articulation.

REFERENCES

Ayyar, L. V. Ramaswami. 1983 [1936]. *The Evolution of Malayalam Morphology*. Thrissur: Kerala Sahitya Akademi.

Bauman, Richard and Charles Briggs. 1990. 'Poetics and Performance as Critical Perspectives on Language and Social Life', *Annual Reviews in Anthropology* 19: 59-88.

Chafe, Wallace. 1994. *Discourse, Consciousness, and Time: The Flow and Displacement of Conscious Experience in Speaking and Writing*. Chicago and London: University of Chicago Press.

Cherian, P. J., ed. 1999. *Perspectives on Kerala History: The Second Millennium*. Kerala State Gazetteer, Vol. II, Part II. Thiruvananthapuram: Government of Kerala.

Freeman, Rich. 1998. 'Rubies and Coral: The Lapidary Crafting of Language in Kerala', *Journal of Asian Studies* 57 (1): 38-65.

———. 2003. 'Genre and Society: The Literary Culture of Pre-Modern Kerala'. In *Literary Cultures in History: Reconstructions from South Asia*, edited by S. Pollock. Berkeley: University of California Press.

Gurukkal, Rajan. 1992. *The Kerala Temple and the Early Medieval Agrarian System*. Sukapuram, Kerala: Vallathol Vidyapeetham.

Hanks, W. 1987. 'Discourse Genres in a Theory of Practice', *American Ethnologist* 14 (4): 688-92.

Jakobson, Roman. 1960. 'Closing Statement: Linguistics and Poetics'. In *Style in Language*, edited by T. Sebeok. Cambridge, MA: M.I.T. Press.

Krishna Warrior, N. V. 1977. *A History of Malayalam Meter*. Trivandrum: Dravidian Linguistics Association.

Marr, J. R. 1985. *The Eight Anthologies: A Study in Early Tamil Literature*. Tiruvanmiyur, Madras: Institute of Asian Studies.

Narayanan, M. G. S. 1996. *Perumals of Kerala: Political and Social Conditions of Kerala Under the Cēra Perumals of Makotai (c. 800-1124 A.D.)*. Calicut: Author.

Narayanan, Vasudha. 1994. *The Vernacular Veda: Revelation, Recitation, and Ritual*. Columbia, SC: University of South Carolina Press.

Peterson, Indira. 1991. *Poems to Śiva: The Hymns of the Tamil Saints*. Delhi: Motilal Banarsidass.

Pollock, Sheldon, ed. 2003. *Literary Cultures in History: Reconstructions from South Asia*. Berkeley: University of California Press.

Sankunni Nair, M. P. 1995. *Points of Contact between Prakrit and Malayalam*. Trivandrum: Dravidian Linguistics Association.

Scott, James. 1990. *Domination and the Arts of Resistance: Hidden Transcripts*. New Haven: Yale University Press.

Sekhar, A. Chandra. 1953. *Evolution of Malayalam*. Poona: Deccan College Postgraduate and Research Institute.

Sreedhara Menon, A. 1980 [1967]. *A Survey of Kerala History*. Kottayam, Kerala: National Book Stall.

Subrahmanyan, S. 1977. *The Commonness in the Metre of the Dravidian Languages*. Trivandrum: Dravidian Linguistics Association.

Zvelebil, Kamil. 1974. *Tamil Literature*. Vol. X, Fasc. 1, *A History of Indian Literature*, edited by J. Gonda. Wiesbaden: Otto Harrassowitz.

2

A Philological Approach to Regional Ideologies[1]

Irina Glushkova

'Maharashtra dharma' is a concept bound to the name of Shivaji (1630-80), the founder of the Maratha Empire. (There do not exist toponymic dharmas of other socio-cultural or administrative units of India.) Stewart Gordon (1993: 65-6) writes in this respect:

> The Brahmin historians of the twentieth century, starting with Rajwade, especially wanted to prove that Shivaji was guided by Brahmin advisors from early in his life, and that he had a vision of a state based on something called Maharashtra Dharma. Much of this, if not all, has been shown by later research to be an artifact of the researchers, not a fact of the period. The only articulation of a 'Maharashtra Dharma' is in a text that predates Shivaji by four hundred years. Further, it details only relations between castes, not any sort of a Hindu political program. Finally, there is no evidence of any connection between the text and Shivaji.

The text mentioned (but not named) by Stewart Gordon is the *Mahikāvatīcī bakhar* (*Māhīmcī bakhar / Bimbasthāncī bakhar*), edited by Vishvanath Kashinath Rajvade in 1923 and since recognized as the oldest example of the *bakhar* literature, chronicles of political events. *Mahikāvatīcī bakhar* consists of six chapters composed by different authors in different times and brought together in the seventeenth century. It starts with the enthronement of Pratap Bimba in 1138 and ends with the arrival of the Portuguese in Konkan in 1500. Every chapter bears a chronological marker; the second, composed in verse by the brahman Keshavacharya in 1448, is the oldest. Keshavacharya narrates some events from the beginning of the fourteenth century, and, inspired by a dream of the kshatriya Nayak-rav, recommends for inhabitants of Maharashtra rules for behaviour based on a strict social hierarchy and the accurate execution of rituals of the life-cycle and the calendric cycle. While enumerating the rules he constantly refers to Shankaracharya (eighth or ninth century), who, besides other things, won fame by a rigid regulation of caste prescriptions. 'Dharma' appears about twenty times in the sermon of Keshavacharya, and five of those times it is found in proximity to the toponym 'Maharashtra' (*Mahārāṣṭra*) or 'Marashtra' (*Mārāṣṭra*) (Rajvade 1923: 53-61).

At the first occurrence it is said that on learning about general moral decay, the Devi sent a dream for protection of *dharma māhārāṣṭra* to Nayak-rav (*jāṇon devine dharma māhārāṣṭra rakṣāyā kāraṇe rājśrī nāyakorāyās svapna dilhē*). Here *dharma* precedes *mahārāṣṭra*, which makes doubtful the attributive function of the latter. Taking into consideration the possibility of grammatical ellipsis and/or the dubious character of a link between parts of a compound, this passage can be interpreted as 'Devi gave a dream [about correct actions] for protection of dharmic Maharashtra' or 'for the protection of dharma and Maharashtra'. Two lines later Devi is called a defender of *mahārāṣṭradharma* (*mahārāṣṭradharma-rakṣikā*). This can be interpreted as 'a defender of dharma in/and Maharashtra'. An additional argument in favour of these options can be found in the next line, which tells about a dream sent by Devi 'for the protection of one's own dharma (*svadharma*)', i.e. the dharma of a varna, caste, family, or clan. After two and a half pages, Shankaracharya is called an incarnation of Mahadev (Shiva), and his birth is explained by the necessity to re-establish hierarchical social links. Here Shankaracharya is called *śrījagadguru dharma mārāṣṭrāce ṣoḍaśakarmādhikarī*. In this case of spatial proximity of 'dharma' and 'Maharashtra', the first word, of masculine gender and singular number, precedes again the genitive form of the second, which functions as an attribute of masculine gender and plural number to a compound 'an authority [supervising the execution] of sixteen rituals'. This title with regional ('Maharashtrian') connotation is applied to Shankaracharya, a brahman from Kerala. The fourth usage demonstrates an attributive function of the compound *mahārāṣṭradharma* which defines the word 'a place' (*sthān*), and the sentence as a whole describes an area of dissemination of *mahārāṣṭradharma* which lies within Shvetambaradharameshvar in the south, Kashi in the north, Dwarka in the west, and Tuljapur in the east. This statement by no means reflects the real territory occupied by Marathi speakers in the fourteenth century, and thus the *mahārāṣṭradharma* is left without actual localization. In the fifth case 'dharma' precedes 'Maharashtra' again; in addition, 'dharma' is defined by its own attribute—'main' (*muḷ*)–*muḷdharma mārāṣṭra snān guru-upadeś mantrajap pratyahi karāvā*. The whole phrase can be translated as '[one] should take ablutions, [listen] to the precepts of the guru, [and] repeat a mantra every day—this [is/should be] the main dharma for/in Maharashtra'.

The discord in the illustrations testifies to the lack of a fixed composite *mahārāṣṭradharma* at the time of the composition (fifteenth century) of the text, which is projected to an earlier time (fourteenth century) and filled with references to Shankaracharya, who lived sometime in the eighth or ninth century. Furthermore, the grammatical classification of types of compounds gives grounds to treat this composite as a *dvandva* (Maharashtra and dharma), a *tatpuruṣa* (dharma in/for Maharashtra), or a *karmadhāraya* (Maharashtrian dharma). No other occurrence of 'dharma' has a toponymic attribute, the rest are attached either to Shankaracharya or to Devi, and once to 'Mahadev, a defender of dharma, who appeared incarnated as a woman from Kolhapur' (*aise asāṃ śrīmahādev dharmarakṣaṇik raṇḍākolhāpurī avatar ghetlā*).[2] Shankara, whose propagandistic and reformistic activity (aimed at the reinforcement of Hinduism) took place mostly outside Maharashtra, is in the Marathi speaking region too a 'teacher of dharma' (*dharmagurū*) (Mulansathi 1964: 45) and 'founder of the empire of dharma' (*dharmasāmrājyācā saṃsthāpak*) (Joshi 1976: 178). This illustrates the attempt to elevate the process of the restoration of dharma by invoking an authoritative name. (The projection of historical Shankara as the propagator of this instead of a legendary Manu was the handiwork of the author of the chronicle.) This neither makes dharma specifically Maharashtrian nor makes Shankara a defender of dharma in the face of Muslims who invaded Maharashtra a couple of centuries after his death. Yet the second chapter of the chronicle treats the question of dharma within the context of a confrontation between Hindus and Muslims.

Notwithstanding the fact that the *Mahikāvatīcī bakhar* does not confirm the existence of 'Maharashtra dharma' as a well-formed concept, Rajvade treats it as such in his commentary on the chronicle, and describes the essence of the concept in his own words.

According to him the first feature of *mahārāṣṭradharma* should be understood as the superiority of the brahman who acts as guru. The second feature is that *mahārāṣṭradharma* is the soul (*jīv*) of all other dharmas. The third feature is daily ablutions (Rajvade 1923: 108). These features could hardly lay claim to be regionally unique. Rajvade explains that Keshavacharya and Nayak-rav admonished brahmans and kshatriyas who had came for a meal about the need to create a 'unified society and a unified state which will be followed by the creation of their own dharma, their own polity, their own language etc., which will lead to obtaining prosperity'. Rajvade glosses *mahārāṣṭradharma* by the term *pravṛttidharma*, which means 'dharma of action' (Rajvade 1923: 106). Eventually he draws the conclusion that *mahārāṣṭradharma* is not the religious norms of the region but the 'dharma of the country + caste dharma + family dharma + clan dharma + religion' (ibid.: 109): in other words, it is everything which is available in Maharashtra. Thus, stimulated by his own active life position, Rajvade, even before the discovery of *Mahikāvatīcī bakhar*, interpreted *mahārāṣṭradharma* as a dharma 'aimed at victory' (*jayiṣṇu dharma*) (Rajvade 1967: 169), and chose to neglect the fact that the text deals mostly with the dharma to be established *in* the region to preserve its originality. There is an even earlier text which expresses a preference for Maharashtra and speaks about dharma *in* Maharashtra: 'Maharashtra is *sattvic* . . . Maharashtra does no wrong itself, and allows no one else to do wrong. Maharashtra is [where] *dharma* gets accomplished' (Feldhaus 1986: 541). This statement affirming the well-being of dharma *in* Maharashtra is found in a commentary on *Sūtrapāṭh*, compiled by the Mahanubhavas around AD 1300.

'Maharashtra dharma' as a compound appears in another text, the *Gurucaritra*, compiled by Gangadhar Sarasvati around 1538.[3] This is a hagiography of Narasimha Sarasvati (1378-1458), the founder of the Datta cult in Maharashtra, and is still treated as a kind of Bible by the devotees of the god Dattatreya. Narasimha Sarasvati, appalled by the life conditions of Maharashtrians under Muslim rulers, turned to the brahman caste to remind them about their leading role in the society. He urged them to pay respect to the Vedas, to follow the four-*āśrama* way of life and to carry out rituals. Describing the moral decay in society, the author links prosperity to the pious behaviour of a king who should act as a servant to brahmans (*viprasevak*). Only by fulfilling this condition (*aisā hā rāv astāṃ*) and living according to the Maharashtra dharma (*mahārāṣṭradharmi vartatāṃ*) will such a king 'not bring evil—know this!' (*āplā dveś tatvatāṃ / na karīl kīṃ jāṇpāṃ*).

Thus, two sources treat the polysemic notion of dharma in its brahmanical usage as the ethical and religious core of human life responsible for spiritual and social stability which can be achieved by recognition of brahman leadership and the execution of all rituals guided by them. Both authors aim their prescriptions at a particular cultural and geographical locus, and by imposing all-pervading rules prepare the ground for the formation of such a cultural-geographic composite as Maharashtra dharma. So Stewart Gordon was more or less right when he denied the existence of a Hindu political programme inherent in this formula in pre-Shivaji times. Like old Russian literature, which contains occasional spontaneous references to 'fabulously rich India' (Bongard-Levin and Vigasin 1984; Shokhin 1988), *mahārāṣṭradharma* emerges twice in the writings of Keshavacharya and is used once by Gangadhar Sarasvati, both brahmans. Their appeal for adherence to the general pattern as perceived by brahmans testifies to the fact that there were some common elements in their mental programmes which had the potential to turn into a regional symbol.

After a gap of almost one hundred years, in the second half of the seventeenth century, the term Maharashtra dharma was revived by the energetic brahman Ramdas (1608-81). He explains in his letter to Shivaji, 'There is no protector of dharma on this earth but you. The Maharashtra dharma has survived due to you' (*yā bhūmaṇḍalāce ṭhāyīṃ/ dharma rakṣī aisā nāhīṃ/mahārāṣṭradharma rāhilā kāṃhī / tumhāṃkaritā//10//*) (Pawar 1971: 99). Ramdas glorifies Shivaji as a defender of 'gods, dharma, cows and brahmans', and refers a number of times to dharma. Examples include: *dharmakṛtyeṃ* (activity corresponding to dharma), *dharmamūrti* (an embodiment of dharma), and *dharmasthāpnā* (establishment of dharma). The composite *mahārāṣṭradharma* appears only once, and, in the context of the epistle, nothing prevents us from treating it as a *tatpuruṣa* (and not a *karmadhāraya*), thus translating it as an adverbial phrase, 'dharma in Maharashtra'. After the death of Shivaji, Ramdas appealed to his son and successor Sambhaji, and having described the pains of the country, which was suffering under the 'dogs who despise god', he advanced his famous slogan, 'Bring together all marathas and spread our Maharashtra dharma!' (*marāṭhā tetukā meḷvāvā / āpulā mahārāṣṭradharma vāḍhvāvā*). An unflattering epithet is aimed at the non-Hindu invaders, and Hindu marathas are called to unite.

Henceforth 'Maharashtra dharma' or 'dharma in Maharashtra' emerges from time to time in different sources: letters, *bakhar*s and *sanad*s. Thus, Shivaji's grandson Shahu, in a letter dated 1735-6, remarks that the imprisonment of a brahman family is not Maharashtra dharma (or is not [the right execution] of dharma in Maharashtra).[4] The *Śrīśivdigvijay* chronicle of 1818[5] contains a story about a skillful woman warrior who belonged to a kshatriya family and fought for Aurangzeb against Shivaji. Commenting on this, the author makes Shivaji proclaim that to fight an armed woman is Maharashtra dharma (or [the right execution] of dharma in Maharashtra) (Bhat 1925: 273).

Mahadev Govind Ranade (1842-1901), a prominent political figure of the nineteenth-century *prabodhan* (awakening), is acknowledged as a founder of the nationalist approach to the history of the Marathi-speaking region. Like Shivaji, who has been elevated to the position of 'the father of Maharashtra dharma', Ranade is known as a person who rediscovered and interpreted this slogan at the right time and attracted broad attention to it. Actually it was Rajaram Shastri Bhagwat who exposed the hidden potential of Maharashtra dharma in a lecture on this subject in 1895 (Bhat 1925: 27). Digging into the political past of Maharashtra, he found the source of 'Maharashtra dharma' in the *Bhagavad-gītā* and named Dnyaneshvar of the thirteenth century, who wrote a Marathi commentary on the *Bhagavad-gītā*, along with other saint poets of the bhakti period, the genuine initiators of the concept in question. Bhagwat, finally, ascribed a religious status to Maharashtra dharma, and was eager to make it acceptable to the whole region. Thus he chose to trespass on confessional barriers: 'Marathi is [a person] who speaks Marathi. And Maharashtra dharma, which can easily embrace Muslims too, is the dharma of the Bhagavad-gita [or, as was explained by its God, *bhāgavatīdharma*]. There is no progress without understanding it' (Bhat 1925: 35).

Ranade became curious about Maharashtra dharma in 1894 (Ranade 1961: ii-iii), and wrote a famous essay, 'The Saints and Prophets of Maharashtra'. Due to the high standing of the author, the position he expressed there became standard. According to Ranade, Maharashtra dharma is nothing but the patriotic religion of Maharashtra bound tightly to the political upheaval of the end of the seventeenth century that resulted in the formation of the Maratha empire, so that it would be impossible to treat religion and politics separately (Ranade 1961: 78). Presuming that the national ideal of spiritual perfection was molded by charismatic saint-poets from the thirteenth to the seventeenth century irrespective of their creed, Ranade does not differentiate among their worldly positions and teachings, but relies a great deal upon miracles described in the hagiographies as testifying to their impact on the Maharashtrian mind. Notwithstanding the absence of a reference to Maharashtra dharma in the writings of the poets of the Varkari tradition, he unites them together with Ramdas as initiators of an all-Maharashtrian religious movement, and concludes, 'It [the religious movement] tended in all these ways to raise the nation generally to a higher level of capacity both of thought and action and prepared it, in a way no other nation in India was prepared to take the lead in re-establishing a united native power in the place of foreign domination' (Ranade 1961: 92). These appeared to Ranade to be the principal features of the religion of Maharashtra, and that is how he read Ramdas's words.

Rajvade, who had started to expound his understanding of Maharashtra dharma in dependence upon the same Ramdas even before coming across the *Mahikāvatīcī bakhar*, differed from Ranade on almost every point. He clung to the Marathi language as the only medium of expression, and while trying to draw out the meaning of the compound that Ramdas had used only twice, he dug into the totality of the works of the militant prophet and took advantage of a broad span of the political history of Maharashtra. In one of his introductions to a volume of historical sources, he states, 'Marathis had been constructing this notion from 1646 to 1796 and throughout 150 years were guided by it' (Rajvade 1967: 168). In another introduction he specifies that the notion in question had been in the main shaped by 1720 and that 'the distinguishing streak of the marathas' activity in Hindustan was their spread of the Maharashtra dharma' (Rajvade 1967: 187). Only Ramdas, who appealed to Shivaji to regulate the ethnic structure of his troops, is acknowledged by Rajvade as the creator of a Maharashtrian polity (*rāṣṭrīytva*) and a national feeling (*rāṣṭrabhāvnā*); he assigns Shivaji the role of an executor (Rajvade 1967: 208). And, finally, Rajvade names the god Vithoba 'an embodiment of a meek Hindu dharma' (*sahiṣṇu hindudharmācī mūrti*) and the god Maruti 'a banner of victorious Hindu dharma' (*jayiṣṇu hindudharmācā patākā*) (Rajvade 1967: 169). The historian thus succeeded in driving a wedge between the Varkaris, followers of the Varkari saints and devotees of merciful Vithoba, and Ramdasis, adherents of Ramdas, who beautified the land of Maharashtra with images of bellicose Maruti. Against this background, it seems odd that in Satara in 1917 a book series entitled *Mahārāṣṭradharma* was launched with the publication of Dnyaneshvar's commentary on the *Bhagavad-gītā*, edited by Rajvade.

P. N. Joshi summed up Rajvade's views on Maharashtra dharma as follows: 'Achievement of [marathas'] own polity, punishment of foreigners (*yavan*), unification of marathas, punishment of those who create obstacles, and other similar traits form roughly the substance of Maharashtra dharma' (Joshi 1965: 50). Thus the mobilizing and even aggressive character of Maharashtra dharma was reiterated in the second half of the twentieth century.

However, forty years before this summing up, in 1925, Bhaskar Vaman Bhat, a fervent adherent to the ideas of Ramdas, used the term Maharashtra dharma to fight off what seemed to him an ill-meaning conclusion drawn by an anonymous Bengali author about Maharashtrian brahmans. This author had stated that the fact that 'they [maratha brahmans] were not actuated by the same feelings in the days of the Peshwas is due to the fact that the virtue of patriotism as understood in these days was unknown to India' (Bhat 1925: 2, 100). Explaining the reasons which stimulated him to write a 508-page volume, Bhat says,'There is no unanimity with regard to what meaning should be extracted from this word [*mahārāṣṭradharma*] and what should be included in it, but there does exist an uncertainty which has become constant' (Bhat 1925: 38, 385). After a detailed analysis of the positions of Bhagwat, Ranade and Rajvade, of maratha history from the Yadavs to Shivaji and onward, of the concept of dharma in Hindu law and Marathi documents, as well as of the caste system in general, Bhat holds with Rajvade that the bhakti period was time lost for Maharashtra, and that none of the Varkari poets had had anything in common with Maharashtra dharma. He reminds his readers that initially Maharashtra dharma had two meanings—the dharma of kshatriyas and the common dharma of all Maharashtrian Aryans (Bhat 1925: 40), and he speaks ironically, without naming names, of somebody who compared Maharashtra dharma with 'pride in one's own country'. Maharashtra dharma is 'patriotism turned into real deeds' (Bhat 1925: 44). Finally, Bhat states that one should not search for a 'second or third meaning of Maharashtra dharma as it is clear [from the whole analysis] that this compound is characteristic of the same essence that is found in dharma as propagated in the Vedas or other shrutis and in the books of Manu, Yajnyavalkya or other smritis' (Bhat 1925: 355). So, accepting Maharashtra dharma as an all-embracing entity and ascribing a sacred status to it, Bhat marks out nine additional dharmas that form 'Maharashtra dharma': life rituals and vows, ruler's and subject's dharmas, etc. (Bhat 1925: 357-9). Irrespective of this, he never writes about dharma *in* Maharashtra. On the contrary, Bhat again recollects the Bengali author who vexed him so brutally, and exclaims that any kind of patriotism is exceeded by feelings intrinsic to Maharashtra dharma. A few pages further he concludes that 'love for Motherland is a kind of soul's motion, while Maharashtra dharma is bound to no display of feelings but just a dharma found in shruti and smriti' (Bhat 1925: 367, 389).

In 1923 Vinoba Bhave, a prominent follower of Mahatma Gandhi, authored and published a monthly entitled *Mahārāṣṭradharma* in which he explained the title by resorting to both popular etymology and his own universalistic views:

> In spite of the fact that Maharashtra is limited by the general understanding of this word, judging by its origin it has a broad sense. In the capacity of 'a great state' it is representative of the whole of India. . . . That is why this compound (*mahārāṣṭradharma*) contains a triple meaning: the special regional dharma of Maharashtra, the all-Indian dharma of the 'Great state', and the all-embracing dharma of the 'Whole great world'. It might seem a dwarf at first sight, but in reality it is similar to Trivikramu, who covered the earth in two steps' (Maitri 1990: 351).

Thus the regional symbol as interpreted by Vinoba Bhave transcends that in Bhat's interpretation and reaches the level of outer space.

Almost at the same time, *Rāmdās āṇi rāmdāsī*, a periodical published from Dhulia, launched a series of articles under the encompassing title of 'Maharashtra dharma', which treated in co-ordination the religious and political motives of Shivaji and the role of Ramdas as his counsellor (*Rāmdās āṇi rāmdāsī* 1925-6). There also appeared *Hindupadpadshahi,* by the militant nationalist V. D. Savarkar, who turned the 'Maharashtra dharma of Ramdas' into the 'hindupadpadshahi of Savarkar' (Fasana 1999: 57). Against this background the observation made by R. Vora seems almost inevitable: 'Each school of nationalism had tried to relate to Maharashtra dharma or appropriate and interpret this pre-colonial form of national consciousness' (Vora 1999: 24). Vora concludes: 'Maharashtra dharma was thus another name for Maharashtrian nationalism and was rooted in the historical experience and cultural traditions of the people of Maharashtra' (Vora 1999: 29). In that way, being restored to life from temporary oblivion, Maharashtra dharma, notwithstanding what it comprised, was in universal demand. All subsequent users of this compound either clung to the position of Rajvade or Ranade, or tried to synthesize the two, despite the incompatibility of the 'attacking activity' of Ramdas and the 'defensive passivity' of the Varkari saints.

There is nothing surprising in the fact that the Marathi-speaking region of the end of the nineteenth and the beginning of the twentieth century manifested such a special, even oversensitive attention to Maharashtra dharma. In the *prabodhan* period Marathi people compiled their own pool of symbols, which included, along with the 'nectar of the Marathi language', the god Vithoba and the poets who praised him, a heroic past and brilliant Shivaji, the god Ganesh,[6] and, eventually, a verbal formula possessing no definite meaning but consisting of two parts, both of which carressed the Marathi ear. Precisely the lack of semantic clarity and the constant metaphorical usage of this compound with its capacity to be filled with anything, caused the fossilization of Maharashtra dharma as an 'above-any-party' ideologem with the function of mobilization. This is vividly illustrated by one of many examples. During the *satyāgrah* in Mulshi (1921-4), the fight of the people of the Maval against the construction of the Mulshi dam and the consequent submersion of surrounding lands was inspired by references to Shivaji, who had started his quest for *svarāj* from the precise place and who was backed by followers from this subregion of Maharashtra. Vora comments on this instance as follows: 'That volunteers from every remote corner of Maharashtra came to join the Mavalas in their struggle indicates that this appeal to Maharashtra dharma on the part of Congress leaders had the desired mobilizing effect' (Vora 1999: 27).

The Indian National Congress used this almighty regional mantra aptly in the colonial period. Yet, after Independence, at the time of the administrative reorganization on a linguistic basis, the Congress made a mistake by ignoring the rhetorical formulae sacred to Maharashtrians. Acharya Atre, a famous playwright and satirist and one of the leaders of the *Saṃyukta mahārāṣṭra āndolan* (Movement for a United Maharashtra), did not fail to notice this.[7] Knowing the right chords to touch to awaken sentiments hidden in stern Marathi hearts, he appealed to Maharashtra dharma in his speeches and writings. Once, reminding his audience that the movement for a United Maharashtra had been started by Shivaji and had been decorated with the famous slogan of Ramdas, he skillfully incorporated other symbols to make an impact on the Marathi psyche: 'In order to make our Marathi language purer, richer and more beautiful, and Maharashtra dharma more powerful, we should bring together [to cast a vote in elections] all forty million Maharashtrians' (Atre 1967: 40). When he started the publication of *Dainik Marāṭhā*, subordinating it to the course of the Movement for a United Maharashtra, Acharya Atre used Ramdas's motto (*brīdvākya*) along with pictures of Shivaji, Lokamanya Tilak, and Mahatma Phule as the paper's logo. Later, in an editorial dedicated to the official inauguration of the new Maharashtra state incorporating the city of Bombay, he wrote: 'Ramdas's project behind the "Spread the Maharashtra dharma" [motto] might have implied turning the whole of India into "Ma-ha-ra-shtra" [a "Great State"]' (Atre 1997: 11). It is interesting that Acharya Atre himself became curious much later with regard to the meaning of this 'great mantra' (*mahāmantra*). In 1968, completing his memoirs, he raises this question in the last chapter, entitled 'A song of Maharashtra's glory'(*Mahārāṣṭrācī gauravgāthā*): 'What is the genuine essence of this Maharashtra dharma, the one that was articulated by Ramdas as a great mantra?' He answers by referring to various passages of Ramdas's poetry, including, for example, the following:

> [One] should die while fighting (*māritā māritā marāve*)
> [such death] leads to salvation
> [If] another birth [occurs,] enjoy
> [such] a great fate.

Hold the god on your forehead,
shout with all [your] strength,
destroy the country
to establish dharma.
A brave [man] needs a brave [man],
a tough [one] needs a tough [one],
an impudent [one] needs an impudent [one]
to advance.[8]

According to Atre, this admonition (or rather manual) explains the technique of bringing the Maharashtra dharma into effect (ibid.: 669). He also supplies some new information regarding the worldview of Ramdas and the contents of the great mantra: 'Maharashtra dharma was strongly opposed to discrimination on the basis of affiliation to a country or a region, to a varna, to a particular set of behavioural norms, or to a religious group' (ibid.: 669). Further, the renowned satirist proclaims: 'Pandharpur is a spiritual centre of Maharashtra dharma, and Raygad [one of Shivaji's fortresses] is its political centre.' Just a few lines later, Atre names all Maharashtrian saint poets—from brahman to untouchable—as founders of Maharashtra dharma! And he states that Indian independence would not have been achieved without drawing on Maharashtra dharma.

The semantics of the phrase 'Maharashtra dharma' has been under scrutiny by Maharashtrian historians, politicians, publicists, and satirists for more than a hundred years. D. B. Chauhan, the representative of the Kolhapur historical school,[9] derives 'Maharashtra dharma' from 'kshatriya dharma', and even brings to light a historical figure—a certain Satyanaga, a bodyguard and general of the Scythian king Shridharavarmana—as a 'winner in [establishing] dharma' (*dharmavijayin*). According to Chauhan, this Satyanaga was a native of Maharashtra who channelled kshatriya dharma to his homeland in the fourth century. With the passage of time, those ideas were remoulded into Maharashtra dharma and remained as 'a faint image' in the memory of such leaders as Nayak-rav and Keshavacharya of the *Mahikāvatīcī bakhar,* then in that of Ramdas and his followers, until it was required on a full-scale basis again (Chauhan 1971: 8, 9).

Purusottam Ganesh Sahasrabuddhe devoted a whole chapter to Maharashtra dharma in his 835-page volume entitled the *Culture of Maharashtra* (Sahasrabuddhe 1979: 344-61). Contrary to Chauhan, who considered 'Maharashtra dharma' invariable in its meaning throughout time, Sahasrabuddhe looks upon this concept dialectically. He reminds his readers that Ramdas, the creator of this notion, used the phrase only twice and never bothered to explain it. This is why Sahasrabuddhe took on the burden and examined all the explicit and implicit postulates found in the works of Ramdas with respect to the formula. According to Sahasrabuddhe, Maharashtra dharma is defined by six features which can be lined up in a logical sequence: (1) a desire for pecuniary prosperity in this world, which is not achievable without (2) carrying out the responsibilities and affairs of everyday life; (3) realization of this idea requires mass awakening strengthened by (4) force and (5) persistence to (6) build up one's own polity. For all this, Sahasrabuddhe affirms that the polity is not attainable without experiencing a 'proud feeling of a double nature' (*dvividh ahaṃkār,* the last word usually means 'haughtiness', 'arrogance', or 'conceit'). This proud feeling is nurtured by an understanding of one's own and collective peculiarities, and this feeling was unknown to any other Indian ethnic group but Marathi folk. Who else, asks the author, has managed to exclaim, 'Bring together all Rajputs, or Kannadigas, or Bengalis?' (Sahasrabuddhe 1979: 351-2). By the same token, none of the saints of the Varkari tradition has anything to do with Maharashtra dharma, because they were occupied with extinguishing the very essence of *ahaṃkār*. As for Shankaracharya, who is constantly invoked in the *Mahikāvatīcī bakhar,* he bears no relation to dharma at all, to say nothing of Maharashtra dharma, because he propagated a 'quietism' (*nivṛttivād*), which paved the way to an era of decay in India (Sahasrabuddhe 1979: 358).

V. P. Bokil, who compiled the biography of Ramdas, sees Maharashtra dharma as a way of life. '. . . Dharma is that which holds men together in a society and in a political unit; as it can also bind man to God. In this sense then Maharashtra Dharma connoted the social peculiarities of the Maharashtrian people as formed by the geographical conditions in which they lived and by the ancestral traditions in which they were brought up' (Bokil 1979: 142-3). And J. Gokhale-Turner, reflecting on regionalism through the example of Maharashtra, raises Maharashtra dharma to the rank of an ideology. She thinks that, pronounced by Ramdas as a part of a slogan, it meant an aggressive Hinduism directed outward, against the Muslim rulers, with the goal of establishing a Hindu polity (Gokhale-Turner 1980: 95). At the same time, Gokhale-Turner suggests that each social group extracted something of its own from this slogan. Thus, among brahmans, who were the most consistent followers of Ramdas, Maharashtra dharma could have meant the restoration of the leading role of brahmans as interpreters and propagators of dharma in general. Warrior marathas could have perceived it as the quintessence of the values they protected, and consequently they could have thought of themselves as the very embodiment of this dharma. The lower strata, and especially untouchables, could have apprehended the idea of Maharashtra dharma in the spirit of the ideals of humanity and equality. Gokhale-Turner comes to the conclusion that the relevance of this regional ideology was related to 'specific socio-economic and political factors' and that 'it cannot be assumed that a regional ideology and a regional consciousness impose a vertical unity on the region . . . ' (Gokhale-Turner 1980: 96). So it appears as if Maharashtra dharma aimed at mobilization but somehow failed.

Eventually, J. V. Naik compromises to the highest level on all disputable questions of Maharashtrian history and makes an attempt to cover Maharashtra dharma with the garb of inter-regional harmony, preserving loyalty to all-Indian unity. He says that Maharashtra dharma was not directed against Islam, 'nor was it intended for the propagation of Hindu religion. It was certainly not meant to establish a communal empire. Its basic aim was to preserve and carry forward the ancient religion and culture of all the people who reside in Maharashtra and who are all known by the comprehensive term Maratha' (Naik 1974: 81).[10] Being a mere philologist I can only guess what could be hidden behind 'the ancient religion' and what methods were used in medieval times 'to preserve and carry forward' the culture.

Here I stop my queries, not because the list of quotations has been exhausted—it is limitless—but because despite a century of debates, there is a very limited number of ideas which are used to fill the elastic capacity of the term 'Maharashtra dharma'. Untiringly repeated in one of its few interpretations in various mass publications, including school textbooks, and constantly evoked, Maharashtra dharma has frequently been reinforced as a national symbol. It has long framed the collective mind of Marathi speakers, and it is hard to imagine an event on a regional scale without a fresh appeal to this ritual formula. The *Indian Express*, dated 06.02.1994, stated that (then) 'President Shankar Dayal Sharma, who declared open the [World Marathi] conference, called upon people to fully understand and popularize the concept of Maharashtra Dharma. He said the ideology of brotherhood and understanding was part of the Maharashtra Dharma, an outlook which even inspired Maratha ruler Chhatrapati Shivaji.' As not only Marathi people themselves but representatives of other Indian regions and even the highest central authority imagine that Maharashtra dharma does exist, it should be reckoned with. Be that as it may, nobody will ever doubt that there exists a long and amusing history of what it implies.

I became curious about Maharashtra dharma while writing a chapter on Maharashtrian culture for a volume on 'India and its regions' (Glushkova 2000a).[11] At that time my colleague Boris Ivanovich Kluev, who was preparing a chapter on Maharashtrian politics, approached me with a question, 'What is Maharashtrian *asmitā*? Why does this word appear untranslated in Indian papers in English?' By that time I myself had already become bewildered by innumerable occurrences of this word in Sahasrabuddhe's *Culture of Maharashtra* and its absence from Marathi-English dictionaries.[12] In Pune in early 2000 I exasperated everybody by asking repeatedly about the meaning of *asmitā,* but nobody could explain. Three of my victims reverted to the question on their own. A teacher from a school in Deccan Gymkhana conjectured that *asmitā* originated from Sanskrit *smita* (smile) by adding a negative prefix *a.* However the Sanskrit-English dictionary did not support this guess, preferring instead to treat the word as 'egotism'. A professor of Sanskrit pointed out that *asmitā* is found in Patañjali's *Yoga-sūtras* (2.3, 2.6) and is interpreted in the English translation of J. H. Woods as 'feeling of personality' (Woods 1972: 106). A librarian was generous with his time, and after a long discussion summarized, 'Asmita is a feeling of personal pride and anxiety for Maharashtra (*svābhimān, mahārāṣṭrācī kāḷjī*).' And precisely at that time I was surprised to find that the house of my old acquaintance Madhu-kaka (Damodar Dinkar) Kulkarni, a well-known publisher from Pune, is named 'Asmita'. I had visited this house for fifteen years but discovered its name only on 22 February 2000, the day of the sudden death of Madhu-kaka, when I came to pay last respects and could ask him nothing. His son later told me that the house was built in 1961.

The earliest resort to *asmitā* that I have found in the context of 'anxiety for Maharashtra' occurred in a speech by the writer G. T. Madkholkar in 1946 at the opening session of the 30th annual meeting of the *Marāṭhī sāhitya pariṣad.* It was cited from a written copy in the above-mentioned memoirs of Acharya Atre, who states that it was at this session that a detailed substantiation of the urge of unification within a United Maharashtra of all territories inhabited by Marathi-speaking people was exposed for the first time in Marathi. Madkholkar said, '. . . Marathi literature should fill in all corners of Maharashtrian life. As soon as Maharashtrian *asmitā* spread from the Narmada to the Tungabhadra starts flowing in tangible streams from fates of Maharashtrian folk we will be able to experience pride . . . ' (Atre 1975: 388). The vague rhetoric of this utterance implies that there is some *asmitā* related somehow to Marathi literature which dwells somewhere implicitly, and its exposure will lead to the emergence of a feeling of pride in Maharashtrians.

As the first usage of *asmitā* turned out to be bound up with a political demand, I resorted to those passages of the five-volume memoirs of Acharya Atre which are related to the *Saṃyukta mahārāṣṭra āndolan* and to the stages of the struggle for the creation of a monolingual state. Addressing a meeting before the Bombay municipal elections in 1957 and calling for support of the candidates of the Committee for a United Maharashtra, Acharya Atre proclaimed, 'The precept given by Ramdas 400 years ago—Bring together all marathas!—today is being carried out in real life. This miracle is taking place because Maharashtra's feeling of self-pride is hurt, and Maharashtrian *asmitā*, along with the very existence [of Maharashtra], has been dealt a severe blow' (Atre 1968: 357). This statement is of special interest for two reasons. First, it sticks to the first part of Ramdas's popular slogan, while the 'Maharashtra dharma' of the second part is replaced by *asmitā*. Secondly, there is a notable proximity of 'pride' (*svābhimān*) and *asmitā*.

Narrating the course of events during the fight for the formation of a united Marathi-language-based administrative entity, Acharya Atre refers to a number of politicians of various positions, and cites an utterance made by one of them (Shankarrav Dev, a Gandhian) in relation to disturbances in Bombay: 'I feel an *asmitā* with regard to

Maharashtra. But if Maharashtra disregards human values I will have to burn out this *asmitā*!' (*Mahārāṣṭrabaddal malā asmitā āhe. Paṇ mānvī mūlyāce jar mahārāṣṭrakaḍūn pālan hot nasel tar malā hī asmitā jaḷūn ṭākāvī lāgel!*) (Atre 1968: 200-1). The politician treats *asmitā* as a feeling: this is expressed by the syntactic construction used for such cases. Most probably, he speaks about his pride for Maharashtra—but what is wrong with the words *abhimān* or *garv*, which have the same meaning?

Asmitā, mysterious as the smile of Mona Lisa, emerges again in Acharya Atre's memoirs in the chapter 'What is Marathiness?' related to the question of self-identity. The writer states that at the time of the struggle for United Maharashtra the Congress was in power and promoted the idea of a bilingual (Gujarati and Marathi) composite state along with an independent status for Bombay. This politics of the Congress is described by Acharya Atre as 'conscious actions to destroy Maharashtrian asmita' (Atre 1968: 634). He proceeds further to define the Marathi national character as 'tightly stuffed with self-pride (*svābhimān*) and unyieldingness (*bāṇedārpaṇā*)'. The Maharashtrian 'is ready to pay whatever cost for his principles and ideals. He behaves as if he has forever accepted a challenge to sacrifice himself for his country and freedom. . . . He is absolutely unaware of fear before an enemy or death. Precisely these [qualities] are what we call Maharashtrian *asmitā* or Marathiness' (ibid.: 639). In this way Acharya Atre tries for the first time to present the verbal expression of a vague notion, juxtaposing it again with pride, inserting an indomitable craving for risk for the sake of achieving a goal, and eventually equating it with the concept of Marathiness. Thus, *asmitā* is allotted the status of an identifying substance.

After my preliminary study of the semantics of *asmitā* in its Marathi usage I shared the information with Boris Ivanovich Klyuev and requested him to let me know the precise examples that had provoked his question on Maharashtrian *asmitā*. Sadly, Boris Ivanovich died on 8 July 2000, his promise unfulfilled, and I launched a search for Maharashtrian *asmitā* in the files of press-cuttings which he had collected over forty years. It came to light that *asmitā* appears in press entries related chiefly to election campaigns or any *force majeure* developments in Maharashtra, and to a great extent shapes the rhetoric of the Shiv Sena. My assumption was substantiated by facts found in the press in general and by statements of Marathi people in particular. The *Times of India* dated 16.02.94 writes: 'When Shiv Sena raised the question of Maharashtrian *asmitā* in the 1960s, it was the fear of the middle class about competition from the South Indian migrant for salaried jobs that enabled it to mobilize support.' Commenting on the Shiv Sena and the BJP (Bharatiya Janata Party) entering into an alliance, the *Times of India* dated 11.10.89 notes: 'The championship of Hinduism has been paying the Sena far greater dividends than its fight for jobs for "sons of the soil" or its assertion of the Marathi *asmita* did.' Nikhil Wagle, the *Mahānagar* editor, said in the *Times of India*, 19.03.95: 'The issue of regional identity was brought up long before the Sena by the Samayukta Maharashtra movement. Thackeray [the leader of the Shiv Sena] hasn't done much except exploit it.' The implication of *asmitā* in this passage is proven by the immediate proximity of the statement made by Amol Palekar, an actor and director, in the same article: 'I sincerely hope that Thackeray now [after the party victory at the legislature elections and formation of its own government] goes beyond mere talk of Marathi Sasmita [*sic*]. If his government can help revive Marathi cinema which has gone to the dogs, if it can support Marathi literature and take it all over the country, it will be truly representative of what he has been talking about.' This illustrates a change in the attribute used to qualify *asmitā:* 'Marathi' instead of 'Maharashtrian'. Besides, there is a spelling error: the word in question is preceded by the Sanskrit prefix *sa* meaning 'with'. Whoever made this mistake, it testifies to the kind of uncertain treatment of a word which has already turned into a cliché but has not yet become habitual and intelligible.[13] The last usage is also indicative of a connection between the perception of *asmitā* and the politics of protectionism. In the Marathi-language *Mahārāṣṭra Times* dated 6.2.2000, Sanjay Ketkar directly acknowledges a link between *asmitā* and the practice of the Shiv Sena and its leader: 'I will hardly be wrong if I affirm that nobody in Maharashtra but Bal Thackeray has been protecting Marathi *asmitā* and Marathi glory.' In the 1980s, at the time of the heated debates which followed the declaration by the Marathi scholar Ramchandra Chintaman Dhere that the image of the god Vithoba kept in the temple in Pandharpur was not genuine, the Shiv Sena headed a powerful campaign of protest. Among its publications, there was an article in

Mārmik which contained a section entitled, 'The hands [touching] the pleats of Marathi *asmitā*' (*Marāṭhī asmitecyā nirīlā hāt*). It is hard to overlook an allusion to the insult of Draupadi by Duhshasana in the *Mahābhārata* in this metaphorical expression. Nobody can assert that women in ancient India wore saris, but the Indian mass consciousness under the impact of mythological films and Ravi Varma's oleographs conceives of Draupadi clad in a sari, and consequently of Duhshasana as pulling out her sari's pleats. By resorting to this metaphor the Shiv Sena reminds its readers of the course of events which were stimulated by this epic episode. On the occasion of the silver jubilee of the Shiv Sena, Datta Salvi, one of its functionaries, made the following statement quoted by the *Times of India* dated 23.06.91: 'Yes. We were close to the Congress. But our main aim was, and still is, to restore the *asmita* (pride) of Maharashtrians.' Here again an English gloss is attached.

In the foreword to a small pamphlet, *Mumbaī*, dealing with the renaming of Bombay, Bal Thackeray writes, 'Name and *asmitā* are closely associated and nobody will manage to tear these associations apart' (Samant 1988). With regard to the renaming of Marathvada University in Aurangabad after Dr. Ambedkar, and the Shiv Sena protests against it, the *Times of India* dated 17.01.94 writes: 'If the Shiv Sena continues to indulge in violence, it will only expose its hollow commitment to the cause of social justice and Maharashtrian *asmita* (self-respect).' At the same time, the forces who lobbied for the perpetuation of the memory of the fighter for lower-caste rights described their goal as no less than 'Marathvada *asmitā*-[containing] renaming' (*marāṭhvāḍyācī asmitā nāmāntaraṇ*),[14] while an influential Dalit magazine is named *Asmitādarśa*. This can be translated either as 'Philosophy of *asmitā*' or 'A display of *asmitā*.'

Arun Tikekar, former editor-in-chief of *Loksattā*, has recourse to *asmitā* six times in an article on the problems of caste differentiation (20.2.2000), and each time he defines it as 'related to caste' (*jātīy*) and uses it as a direct object of the verb 'to awaken' (*jāgṛt karṇe/ ṭhevṇe*). The latter usage, which is quite frequent, implies the predisposition of *asmitā* to stay mired in drowsiness.

Reporting about the First World Marathi Conference, which took place in 1989, the *Times of India*, dated 25.9.89, observes: 'They [the Marathi elite] spoke in terms of *asmita* (self-identity), pride, and cultural and literary glory, and not in terms of jobs and a livelihood.' It is notable that here *asmitā* is not understood as 'pride', which occupies its own place, but as something else that needs to be explained with the help of English 'self-identity'. The Committee for Erection of a Memorial to Immortal Soldiers (*Amar javān smārak nirmāṇ samitī*) suggested the reconstruction of the Gateway of India in Bombay. This news was published in the *Loksattā* on 21.02.2000 under the title, 'Wipe Off the Stain of Disgrace and Turn the Gateway of India into a Monument to a National *Asmitā*' (*Gulāmīcā kalaṅk pusūn 'Geṭve of Indiyā' rāṣṭrīy asmitece smārak karā*). This example, along with the others given above, demonstrates the elasticity intrinsic to *asmitā* (similar to the same quality of Maharashtra dharma): it can shrink to the size of Marathvada and a caste or it can grow to the size of the whole nation.

A small article in the same paper dated 17.02.2000 reports a law suit brought by an organization from Baroda against ambiguities and obscenities in songs and dances in Hindi cinema. The grounds for bringing an action is set forth by the Marathi language paper as 'an assault upon Indian culture and women's *asmitā*' (*bhāratīy saṃskṛti āṇi nārī asmitece ullaṅghan*).[15] If harm done to *asmitā* becomes a reason for taking someone to court it should be recognized that this notion is in urgent need of semantic qualification. The writer Tara Bhavalkar also invokes *asmitā* when, meditating on emancipation, she names saint poets responsible for 'awakening of human *asmitā* in a human being [i.e. a woman]' (*māṇsācī māṇūs mhaṇūn asmitā jāgī kelī*) (Bhavalkar 1994: 166). I would have easily accepted the substitution of the permanently sleepy *asmitā* for the more appropriate 'consciousness' here, for example. R. C. Dhere, who was severely attacked by the Shiv Sena, states that 'Dnyaneshvar is in all respects the originator of Marathi *asmitā*' and then adds, 'The age of Dnyaneshvar is the genuine time of the conception of Marathi *asmitā* in the true sense, and among those who contributed to its creation Dnyaneshvar was in the lead' (Dhere 1991: 9, 13). Who doubts that 'originality', going hand in hand with the formation of the Marathi language, is implied here? It will not be out of place to recall that Dnyaneshvar is acknowledged in Maharashtra as the initiator of the worship of Vithoba within the bhakti fold. The same Vithoba, or rather his image in Pandharpur, scrutinized by Dhere for its authenticity, turned out to be a reason to incriminate a scholar for encroachment upon Marathi *asmitā*! In the introduction to the book *Mahārāṣṭradharma-smaraṇ* recently published by the Society [for the propagation] of the dharma of Gita (*Gītādharmamaṇḍaḷ*), G. V. Karandikar, the publisher, reminds the readers about the important contribution of Dnyaneshvar, Namdev, Eknath, Tukaram, and Ramdas—all saint poets—in consolidating and augmenting the dharma of India and Maharashtra. He elucidates that 'through their discourses Marathis became aware of bhakti and Maharashtra dharma. These saints filled with the taste of nectar the Marhati [an earlier term for Marathi now used affectionately] language which nourished Marathi *asmitā*' (Limaye 1999: 1). Thus, in the mental programme of Marathi speakers, the saint poets, notwithstanding their ideological divergences, are conceived of as creators of both Maharashtra dharma and Maharashtrian *asmitā*.

The emergence of a reinterpreted Sanskrit term in the Marathi lexical armoury (I insist on this military metaphor) etymologically related to a Sanskrit verb *asmi* (I am) did not go unnoticed by scholars of the humanities in Maharashtra, who made an attempt to implant this notion deeper in the regional context and to associate it with predictable (or manipulated) emotions as its stable semantics eludes the grasp. With this in view, a 696-page volume with an inverted title—*Asmitā Mahārāṣṭrācī*—was published in 1971 (Kulkarni 1971). The volume starts with an introduction which explains that the main goal of this publication is to introduce to readers the idea of *asmitā* along with its exploration. The goal is expected to be achieved by answering the following questions: 'What is our [Marathi people's] constant feeling evoked by our collective life?' 'What are the forces that bring us together?' etc. Most questions are formulated in such an elusive way and impregnated with such polysemic words (*āplyā astitvāce svatantra adhiṣṭhān, āple sattva ghaḍaviṇāryā śakti*, etc.) that they give broad scope for varying interpretations. As a result it is felt that all questions are in one way or another related to what is habitually called a 'national character'. This impression intensifies as none other than Shivaji, normally associated with Maharashtra dharma, is chosen to illustrate 'the best personification of *asmitā*' (*asmitecī ek udatt pratimā*), and the description of *asmitā* is reminiscent of a divine incarnation which 'manifests itself in different times in various ways' and which 'has shone by all possible colours and shadows during the last three or four decades', demonstrating its 'play' (*asmitecā vilās*).[16]

The subsequent 53 articles deal with all imaginable and unimaginable spheres of Maharashtrian life—from theatre and the standing army to district management and rural education. The majority proceed easily without a single reference to *asmitā* while others make the most of it. For example, Yadunath Thatte, in his article 'Marathi *asmitā* in the age of sciences' (Kulkarni 1971: 102-9), deviates from all assumptions made in the introduction and virtually accuses *asmitā* of being incongruous with the times. Thatte affirms that 'nowhere—from literature to mechanical engineering—is there felt an independent manifestation of Marathi *asmitā*.' Besides this attack, he marks out various types of *asmitā* corresponding to different social groups—for instance, rich farmers or urban bureaucrats, and describes all-Maharashtrian *asmitā* as laying obstacles for the collective labour of the Marathi-speaking community and being responsible for its inner alienation. Whether explicated or hidden, the *asmitā* is charged by the author with an inferiority complex, neglect of social justice and technical progress, and other sins. In short, *asmitā* is labelled as mobilizing for separation instead of unification. In the article 'Political aspects of Marathi *asmitā*' (Kulkarni 1971: 146-59), P. S. Ghare first corroborates that 'Maharashtrian political *asmitā* was truly born at the time of the movement for a united Maharashtra'. On second thought, he reaffirms that 'it was well known at the time of Shivaji and Ramdas' (could it have manifested itself in the disguise of Maharashtra dharma?), and thirdly he finds it 'in the form of different movements that emerged after establishment of British power'.

The *Culture of Maharashtra* by Sahasrabuddhe that was mentioned earlier falls back upon *asmitā* incessantly. The very first section of the opening chapter ('Maharashtrian individuality') is entitled 'Culture [emerges] from *asmitā*' (*Asmitetūn saṃskṛtī*) (Sahasrabuddhe 1979: 1-2). The author proposes that each man and each country enjoys his/its own personality (*vyaktitva*). Awareness of being different from others, of one's own superiority, is a 'source of creative activity for a human community', and this is nothing but *asmitā.* The second chapter, 'The origin of *asmitā*', contains 'Regional *asmitā*' as a section. Here Sahasrabuddhe declares that '. . . the genuine trait of a state's individuality is comprehension of it' and this is nothing else but 'regional *asmitā*, or haughtiness (*ahaṃtā*)' (Sahasrabuddhe 1979: 43-4). Although he appeals to the understanding, Sahasrabuddhe also juggles with Sanskrit words which are difficult to understand, such as *pṛthagātmatā* (individuality), *abhimān/ahaṃtā*, *pṛthagahaṃkār* (a feeling of conceit [due to one's own] exclusiveness), *asmitece tādātmya* (oneness/identity with *asmitā*), etc. He uses all of them as synonyms for *asmitā* or explains the latter with their help. As a whole the book teems with such subtitles as 'Enrooted *asmitā*' or 'The urge for pecuniary prosperity and *asmitā*' or 'New *asmitā*', marking stages in the awakening of Maharashtrian *asmitā*. The first stage, dated third century BC (ibid.: 43), is followed by the stage, from 235 BC to AD 55, when *asmitā* got stronger (ibid.: 78). In the period from the thirteenth to the seventeenth century, Dnyaneshvar, Namdev, Eknath, and Tukaram provided Maharashtra with 'independent *asmitā*' (*svatantra asmitā*) (ibid.: 333), which leads one to think that before that period the *asmitā* was dependent. Whatever it was, Shivaji 'built a new *asmitā*' for Maharashtra, one that contained the message, 'We are marathas and our country is Maharashtra' (*Amhī marāṭhe va āmcā deś mahārāṣṭra*) (ibid.: 421). It is not difficult, then, to substitute *asmitā* for Maharashtra dharma, especially if one recollects the way Sahasrabuddhe twisted the latter notion in the same book. In any case, there is much more that he tries to make clear: he speaks of an indissoluble connection between *asmitā* and the Marathi language (ibid.: 344-5), and, without going into details, divides *asmitā* into national (*rāṣṭrīy*) and personal (*vaiyaktik*) (ibid.: 425), making it analogous to *vyaktitva,* which has the same two types. Either as 'personality' or as 'individuality' *vyaktitva* goes hand in hand with *asmitā,* occasionally giving way to *pṛthagātmatā.* Eventually *svatva*—one more synonym for 'individuality'—is added (ibid.: 333) for the reader's better understanding or deeper confusion.[17]

Chronologically, the last attempt to deal with *asmitā*, not on a philological level but the level of globalization, was undertaken by Pramod Talgeri. On the occasion of the eleventh anniversary of a popular Marathi weekly, *Sāptāhik sakāḷ,* he delivered a lecture in English. The lecture was translated into Marathi and published under the title, 'How to Test for Indianness' (*Bhāratīytva koṇtyā nikaṣāvar tapāsāve?*) (Talgeri 1999). Talgeri dwells on three notions crucial for a contemporary Western mind—modernity (*ādhuniktā*), identity (*asmitā*), and nationalism (*rāṣṭravād*)—which he considers to be linguistic and ideological translation loan words introduced to India. According to Talgeri, personal identity has not yet become an imperative category in a traditional society, and it still can be shaped in India as *asmitā* if and when there appears a reality corresponding to this notion, comprising the idea of individualism as well. Sticking to philological criteria, I ought to remark that the neologism *asmitā* (unlike *ādhuniktā* and *rāṣṭravād*) has been created not by borrowing as a translation loan word but by a semantic shift. Although it derives from *asmi,* as a part of a syntagma in its Marathi usage this word is always preceded by a genitive attribute which refers to a collective referent and not an individual one, for example Maharashtra (*mahārāṣṭrācī asmitā*), and consequently *asmitā* of the Marathi language—irrespective of its actual meaning—is perceived as a function or quality of a community. As such it is not in a position to become *vaiyaktik* (as per Sahasrabuddhe's suggestion), or to replace English 'identity' (as per Talgeri's speculations), which might be described as both collective and individual. As if backing Sahasrabuddhe, Talgeri too speaks of a collective *asmitā* (*sāmuhik asmitā*) as different from an individual one, and converts it straight away to a national one (*rāṣṭrīy asmitā*), interpreting it as something 'favouring bringing people together under a common banner' (Talgeri 1999: 8). Being described by its main function—mobilization—*asmitā* cannot but remind us of 'Maharashtra dharma', especially as Talgeri speaks of the end of the nineteenth century as the time of the 'awakening' of the concept of *asmitā.* A few steps further on, Talgeri's *asmitā* starts to mushroom—there are sociocultural and politico-economic, artificial, Muslim Pakistani, and secular Indian *asmitās*. In addition there appear expressions which are almost impossible to comprehend—such as *ājcyā bhāratīy nāgarikācī, ek ādhunik vyaktī mhaṇūn rāṣṭrīy asmitā* (Talgeri 1999: 8). As Talgeri built his theory originally within the English language and based it on speculative application of English 'identity' to Indian soil, and not on Marathi *asmitā* , some obscurity could be allotted to the mechanics of translation, with the interchangeable use of 'identity' and *asmitā.* To speak philologically, English 'identity' too is able to nonplus anybody, as it possesses two opposite meanings—'the extreme case of resemblance; absolute likeness of two or more things in the respect in which they are considered' and 'the state or fact of remaining the same one or ones, as under varying aspects or conditions.' I am not in a position to recommend, being a Russian speaker, but the latter definition can go smoothly with either 'individuality' or 'originality'. Yet I am well aware that the whole world rushes about in search of identity.

As in the case of 'Maharashtra dharma' the list of examples can easily be lengthened, but those already given testify to at least six facts. First, Marathi (and not Sanskrit) *asmitā* does not have a conventional English equivalent. Those being used for clarification are 'pride', 'self-respect', and 'identity'; A. R. Kulkarni suggested in personal communication that 'self-consciousness' too can be used.[18] Second, this notion is evoked by those who are fighting for a certain goal, and that may explain its frequent but not exclusive usage by the permanently fighting Shiv Sena. Third, *asmitā*, along with Maharashtra dharma, is resorted to as an invocation at the time of jubilee celebrations and in connection with other regional Marathi symbols (Vithoba, Dnyaneshvar, etc.); it is recurrently linked to the activity (or passivity) of saint poets seen to have played the role of integrators of Maharashtra. *Asmitā* is treated as both Maharashtrian and Marathi; it is always found in proximity to 'pride' and/or 'arrogance'; it should be 'fought for', 'protected', 'maintained', and 'awakened'. Fourth, on the one hand it exhibits a tendency to expansion, turning all-Indian, and on the other hand, it tends to contraction, appearing within a caste or a collective image of women. Fifth, *asmitā* frequently goes by the name 'Maharashtra dharma' and even supplants it, taking its place. Regular appeals are made to accept a 'new Maharashtra dharma' or to realize/awaken 'a new *asmitā*'. A periodical published by a literary society in Baroda is entitled *Navāsmitā*. Finally, in accordance with the urge of the moment, Maharashtrian *asmitā,* notwithstanding its being a neologism, is traced to any historical or prehistoric level of Maharashtrian existence. All these facts are bound up with situations when the person appealing expects to receive mass support and approval. It follows that whatever *asmitā* affects—be it self-respect, pride, conceit, or self-identity of Marathi people, a particular caste, or women—and whatever it means, it functions as an invocatory formula for mobilization.

It is no secret that a human community, especially one framed within a state or an administrative unit, needs a unifying idea. This need strongly intensifies at the time of change of political or economic regimes, alterations in social life, and social and natural calamities. In post-communist Russia, for example, the imperative need for detection and verbalization of such a unifying idea has been constantly articulated and the search for it is on the march (though making no progress). Maharashtrian *asmitā* was indeed very much in demand during the struggle for the unification of the Marathi people in post-colonial India, and, possessing the same potential as 'Maharashtra dharma' or 'new Maharashtra dharma' (and differing in no way from 'new *asmitā*' as well), has been adopted in a newly shaped Maharashtra state. Similar to a war horse who cannot but rouse itself at the first sound of a regimental trumpet, the heart of a Marathi person should thrill on hearing 'Maharashtra dharma' or its modern substitute 'Maharashtrian asmita'. The actual meaning of both is of no importance. After all, a Russian may resort to the 'mysterious Russian soul' without giving much thought to what its real meaning could be.[19]

P. L. Deshpande, a renowned satirist, a man whose words carried authority with the Marathi-speaking community, was also among the contributors to the volume of *Asmitā mahārāṣṭrācī*. Perhaps he was the only person who asked whether Maharashtra could boast of a special *asmitā*, different from other regions. In answer, he quoted N. C. Kelkar: 'If it is said that it does exist then it exists, and if it is said that it does not then it does not' (*mhaṭle tar āhe ani mhaṭle tar nāhī*) (Kulkarni 1971: 16).[20] Reflecting on urgent tasks to be taken care of by Maharashtrian society, Deshpande summed up, 'Today, accepting the challenge of the new era as the first step, Maharashtra should accept a new Maharashtra dharma corresponding to modern knowledge' (Kulkarni 1971: 28). So, while easily interchanged for different purposes in various contexts, Maharashtra dharma and *asmitā* can come together too, multiplying their grandeur by propping each other up.

Afterword: While in Pune for the symposium on regions, and a short stay after that (December 2001-January 2002), I went on stumbling upon *asmitā* almost every day in the morning papers. I also found it technically easy to predict the occurrence of this word in a publication at the first sight of its title or the first line. Many of the references I came across unintentionally were related to the *asmitā* of the Marathi language,[21] which needs to be maintained; this is hoped to be achieved by 'launching a movement of all those concerned' (who are not, I wonder!). There also appeared appeals for 'conscious treatment' (*jāgṛktā*) of Marathi that should accompany 'love, pride, and *asmitā*' for the language. The feminist approach revealed a recourse to 'prideful *asmitā*' (*gauravpūrṇ asmitā*), while the late N. G. Nandapurkar, a student of Marathi literature, was named in the jubilee article on the occasion of his centenary 'a personality saturated with the *asmitā* of Marathi and Marathvada'. The above-mentioned librarian from Pune kept an earlier cutting for me in which the RSS chief K. S. Sudarshan makes a demand to introduce changes in the Constitution of India 'to adjust it to our country, our *asmitā* and our needs'. At the same time somewhere else *asmitā* was brought into a sequence with 'anger' (*rāg*), 'hostility' (*dveṣ*), and 'impetuosity' (*abhiniveś*), and all these were qualified as negative qualities which should be extinguished by special training. Back we go to 'egotism'.

NOTES

1. I am grateful to the Open Society Institute, Soros Foundation, which sponsored my two-month stay in Pune in January-February 2000. Most of the research for this paper was conducted during that period.
2. It is not clear why D. B. Chauhan claims that *Mahikāvatīcī bakhar* names Tulja-Bhavani of Tuljapur 'the presiding deity of the Maharashtra dharma' (Chauhan 1971: 10). There is no specification concerning the origin of Devi except for this reference to Kolhapur.
3. The information about *Gurucaritra* is drawn from Tulpule (1979: 352-3, 395, 430). Part of the text containing the reference to *mahārāṣṭradharma* is cited from Bhat (1925: 149-50).
4. This example was suggested by A. R. Kulkarni in his letter dated 24.10.2000. I express my gratitude to him for his help and guidance in regard to various references.
5. This date of composition is mentioned in *Literature of Maharashtra* (Bhave 1963: 974) and *The Concise Dictionary of the Marathi Literature* (Dadkar et al. 1998: 581), while the latter adduces 1668-1726 (136) as the period of Khando Ballal Chitnis, who is named as the author of this chronicle.
6. I have treated this subject in detail in Glushkova 2000a.
7. Congress held a different opinion regarding the future of the Marathi-speaking territory, and, speaking at the meeting on the occasion of a separate Maharashtra state with its capital in Bombay, Jawaharlal Nehru

omitted any reference to Shivaji or his part in preparing the ground for building a Hindu polity. Acharya Atre spared no words to express his indignation, and exclaimed: 'This Pandit Nehru deliberately insulted Maharashtra. Does anybody doubt it?. . . No historical event in our Maharashtra commences without addressing Shivaji—could Pandit Nehru be unaware of this?' (Atre 1968: V, 663).

8. The cited lines are extracted from *Dāsbodh* (19.9), the gospel of Ramdas's teachings, which does not contain a single mention of Maharashtra dharma, though many authors erroneously refer to this work.
9. It is not a secret that Maharashtrian scholars in the field of humanities form informal groups, frequently shaped within this or that sub-region of Maharashtra and/or this or that caste, as regards certain questions, mainly related to the pool of Maharashtrian symbols. I have dwelt upon this phenomenon elsewhere, analysing modern theories on Tukaram and the unsolved mysteries of his biography (Glushkova 2000b).
10. The then Prime Minister, Indira Gandhi, correcting the neglect of Shivaji by her father, contributed a few lines as a preface to the edition. She wrote,'Chhatrapati Shivaji is one of the most colourful heroes of our nation. His dazzling adventures have inspired generations of young people. The strategy of mobile warfare which he adopted brought him brilliant victories and changed the course of our history. The greatest legacy he has left us is his courage, his magnanimity, his sense of justice and the spirit of sturdy independence and self-reliance.'
11. I had even sent a questioning message to two Western scholars who were engaged in studies of medieval Maharashtra. One ignored my curiosity while the other answered, 'I have never been very satisfied with any explanation of Maharashtra dharma that I have heard. What the hell does it mean really?'
12. Rajendra Vora drew my attention to the *Modern Marathi-Marathi English Thesaurus* published by Mehta Publishing House, Pune, in 2000. It seems to be the first lexicographic edition suggesting that *asmitā* means 'individuality, personality, genius, character, ego, identity, essence' (p. 76).
13. Attacking enemies of India and Hinduism, K. S. Sudarshan, a chief of the RSS, proclaimed:'They are making attempts to crush the Hindu *smita* (pride). But the country is waking up' (Prasannarajam 2000: 48). Here again though an English equivalent was added for clarification, the mistake changed the postulated meaning of *asmitā* into a Hindu 'smile'.
14. It is worth noting that a subregion of Maharashtra is also in a position to possess its own *asmitā*.
15. During the last two or three years, *asmitā* started to come in sight in the Hindi language press, too, especially in the context of women's problems. This word is found in the *Hindi-Russian Dictionary* and is

treated by Russian lexicographers as 'egoism', 'vanity', 'arrogance', or 'haughtiness'. It is also present in the *Bṛhat Hindī-Marāṭhī Śābdkoś* and is interpreted as *ahaṃkār* and *mīpaṇ* ('egotism' or 'egoism', 'conceit', 'self-importance', 'arrogance', 'pride', etc.) I doubt though that these meanings would be helpful while interpreting the following episodes from Seth's essay entitled 'Woman: Creation and Realization of *asmitā*'. The essay reflects upon the 'sufferings of realization of inevitability of struggle and *asmitā*' (*saṅgharṣ aur asmitā kī anivāryatā ke ehsas kī yātnā*) or upon the 'very sad sociology of struggle of fighting community for [its] *asmitā*' (*asmitā ke lie laḍtī jāti ke saṅgharṣ kā baḍā karun samāj-śāstra*) or upon 'confidence regarding *asmitā*' (*asmitā ke prati viśvās*) or upon 'recognition of requirements for freedom and *asmitā* as priority' (*svatantratā aur asmitā kī jarurat ko yadi mukhya mānā jāegā*) (Seth 2000: 31-2). All those meanings found in the dictionaries won't be helpful while translating such sequences as 'unsafety of *asmitā*' (*asmitā kī asurakṣā*) (Kavita 2000: 35) or 'questions related to women's *asmitā*' (*nārī asmitā se juḍe savāl*) (Kaur 2000: 94). The frequency of usage of *asmitā* considerably increased at the time of the scandals inspired by *Fire* and *Water*, movies directed by Deepa Mehta. During debates on this subject, besides women's *asmitā* there started to gleam here and there pieces of *asmitā* of regional/interregional scope (as happened in the case of Marathvada). K. K. Mishra, a voluntary secretary of the Committee for the Protection of Kashi Culture (*Kāśī saṃskṛti rakṣā samiti*), declared, 'It is beyond our patience to cope with insults aimed at Mother-Ganga and Kashi, because if there is no *asmitā*, life is worthless' (Mishra 2000: 45). An analysis of the Hindi usage of this word is beyond the scope of my paper, but one cannot fail to notice a trend to juxtapose it with notions of 'struggle' and 'protection'.

16. Pagination is absent in the publisher's introduction. The new sequence *asmitecā vilās* offers a new difficulty for interpretation. This time it is the usage of the word *vilās*, meaning 'sport', 'play', 'pastime', 'dalliance', 'diversion esp. with women and dancers and singers', etc.
17. I wonder about my not coming across *sāmuhik piṇḍ* within the same contexts, as this is another phrase requiring special resourcefulness and one that will look in place here. Anyhow, continuing to play with Sanskrit words (what I am tempted to call *saṃskṛt śabdāncā vilās*) Sahasrabuddhe (1971: 425) explains that extension of *ahaṃkār* leads to unification with Brahma (*ahaṃkār vyāpak karṇe hec paramārthāt uddiṣṭa aste. 'ahaṃ' mhaṇje mī ek vyaktī hī bhāvnā ṭākūn 'ahaṃ brahmāsmi' asā bhāv manāt banvāvā, ase tattvavete sāṅgtāt*).
18. A. R. Kulkarni informed me about this alternative in a letter dated 24.10.2000. He also mentioned that this variant resulted from his discussions with Sanskrit pandits and is based on analysis of the semantics of *asmi*. This means that the meaning was reconstructed

etymologically but irrespective of its modern Marathi usage. The Marathi analogue suggested by Prof. Kulkarni is *mī āhe hī bhāvnā.*

19. I have my own idea of what traits of the Russian character could have been ciphered in this cliché (which is not important here), but there is a general understanding that it is something making Russians look more attractive. A foreigner who had stayed three years in Russia sent me the following message on her departure: 'It has been a special experience to have "be-friended" you. You and your family contributed much to my enjoyment of your extraordinary country and especially of "Russian soul"!!'
20. I am thankful to Ashok Kelkar for his encouraging remarks on this paper. He thinks that a more accurate translation of the phrase of N. C. Kelkar, who succeeded B. G. Tilak as the editor of the *Kesrī,* would be 'There is something to be said for both points of view.'
21. The collection of speeches by the renowned scholar V. B. Kolte, though entitled *Quest of Asmitā of the Marathi Language* (is it something difficult to locate without searching?) does not exploit the word *asmitā* at all but deals seriously with various aspects of Marathi spelling and grammar, its practical (and not decorative) usage as a medium of education and administrative communication within Maharashtra, and its interaction with English and Hindi. The meaningful absence of *asmitā* in writings based on an academic approach testifies again to the rhetorical character of this term.

REFERENCES

Atre, Acharya (P. K.). 1975 (Vol. III), 1967 (Vol. IV), 1968 (Vol. V). *Karhece pāṇī. Ātmavṛtt.* Mumbai: Parchure Prakashan Mandir.

Atre, Prahlad Keshav. 1997. *Jay hind! jay mahārāṣtra!* Mumbai: Manorama Prakashan.

Bhat, B. V. 1925 (śake 1847). *Mahārāṣṭradharmagranthmālā, granth cavathā. Mahārāṣṭradharma.* Dhule: Atmaram Printing ani Publishing Kampani Li.

Bhavalkar, Tara. 1994. *Strīmuktīcā ātmasvar.* Pune: Shrividya Prakashan.

Bhave, V. L. 1963. *Mahārāṣṭra-sārasvat puravṇīsah.* Mumbai: Popular Prakashan.

Bokil, V. P. 1979. *Rajguru Ramdas.* Poona: Master Kamalesh P. Bokil.

Bongard-Levin, G. and Vigasin A. 1984. *The Image of India: The Study of Ancient Indian Civilisation in the USSR.* Moscow: Progress Publishers.

Chauhan, D. B. 1971. 'Maharashtra Dharma—Its Origin'. In *Maratha History Seminar (May 28-31, 1970).* Kolhapur: Shivaji University.

Dadkar, Jaya et al. 1998. *Saṅkṣipt marāṭhī vāṅmaykoś*. Mumbai: G. R. Bhatkal Phaundeshan.

Dhere, R. C. 1991. 'Dñyāndev āṇi dñyāndevī: abhyāsācī sthitī-gatī'. In *Dñyāndev āṇi dñyāndevi*, edited by R. C. Dhere. Pune: Shrividya Prakashan.

Fasana, E. 1999. '*Deshbhakta:* The Leaders of the Italian Independence Movement in the Eyes of Marathi Nationalists'. In *Writers, Editors and Reformers: Social & Political Transformation of Maharashtra. 1830-1930,* edited by N. K.Wagle. New Delhi: Manohar.

Feldhaus, Anne. 1986. 'Maharashtra as a Holy Land: A Sectarian Tradition', *Bulletin of the School of Oriental and African Studies, University of London.* Vol. XLIX, No. 3.

Glushkova, Irina. 2000 (a). ' "Mental'naya programma" marathov' (The 'mental program' of Marathis). In *India: strana i eyo regioni* (*India and Its Regions*), edited by Ye.Yu.Vanina. Moskva: Editorial URSS.

Glushkova, Irina. 2000 (b). 'Sovremenniye strasti vokrug srednevekovogo mistika' (Heated discussions of today regarding a mystic of medieval times), *Vostok-Oriens,* No. 4.

Gokhale-Turner, J. 1980. 'Region and Regionalism in the Study of Indian Politics: The Case of Maharashtra'. In *Images of Maharashtra: A Regional Profile of India*, edited by N. K. Wagle. Toronto: University of Toronto, Center for South Asian Studies.

Gordon, Stewart. 1993. *The New Cambridge History of India. The Marathas 1600-1818.* Cambridge: Cambridge University Press.

Joshi, M. S., ed. 1976. *Bhāratīy saṃsṛtikoś. Khaṇḍ navvā.* Pune: Bharatiya Samskrutikosh Mandal.

Joshi, P. N. 1965. *Rājvāḍe vicārdarśan.* Pune: Vhinas Prakashan.

Kaur, Balvant. 2000. 'Strī vimarś: kṛtiyõ mẽ akṛtiyā̃', *Hans. Jancetnā kā pragatiśīl kathā-māsik.* March.

Kavita. 2000. 'Strī-chavi barakṣ sārthak sinemā', *Hans. Jancetnā kā pragatiśīl kathā-māsik.* March.

Kolte, V. B. 1992. *Marāṭhīcyā asmitecā śodh.* Pune: Shrividya Prakashan.

Kulkarni, Bhimrav, ed. 1971. *Asmitā mahārāṣṭrācī. Marāṭhā-mandīr raupyamahotsavī granth.* Mumbai: Maratha Mandir.

Limaye, R. 1999. *Mahārāṣṭradharma-smaraṇ.* Pune: Gitadharmamandal.

Maitri. 1990. *Maitrī*, 12 September.

Mishra, K. K. 2000. 'Kisī kimat par kāśī mẽ "vāṭar" nahī̃ banne dẽge'. *Demokretik varld*, February-15 March.

Mulānsāṭhī bhāratācā itihās. 1964. Dilli: Publikeshans Divhijan, Mahiti va Nabhovani Mantralay.

Naik, J. V. 1974. *Śivrāj-mudrā.* Raygad/Mumbai: Mahiti va Jansampark Mahasanchalanalay, Maharashtra Shasan.

Pawar, A. R. 1971. 'Shivaji and Ramdas'. In *Maratha History Seminar* (28-31 May 1970). Kolhapur: Shivaji University.

Prasannarajam, S. 2000. 'Vision Hindutva'. *India Today,* 30 October.

Rajvade, V. K. 1923 (śake 1847). *Keśavācāryādikṛt mahikāvatīcī urf māhīmcī bakhar*. Pune: Chitrashala Press.

Rajvade, V. K. 1967. *Rājvāḍe-lekhsaṅgrah,* edited by L. Joshi. Mumbai: Sahitya Akademi/Popular Prakashan.

Ranade, M. G. 1961. *Rise of the Maratha Power and Other Essays.* Bombay: University of Bombay.

Rāmdās āṇi Rāmdāsī. 1925-26. Nos. 85, 86, 87, etc.

Sahasrabuddhe, P. G. 1979. *Mahārāṣṭra saṃskṛti.* Pune: Kantinental Prakashan.

Samant, M. L. 1988. *Navhe 'bāmbe', navhe 'bambaī' yā śahrāce nāv mumbai!* Mumbai: Prabodhan Prakashan.

Seth, Raji. 2000. 'Strī: sṛjan aur asmitābodh', *Hans. Jancetnā kā pragatiśīl kathā-māsik.* March.

Shokhin, V. K. 1988. *Drevnyaya Indiya v kulture Rusi (XI—seredina XV v.).* (Ancient India in the culture of Russia [eleventh to mid-fifteenth century]). Moskva: Nauka.

Talgeri, Pramod. 1999.'Bhāratīytva koṇtyā nikaṣāvar tapāsāve? *Sāptāhik sakāḷ,* 2 January.

Tulpule, S. G. 1979. *Classical Marathi Literature: from the Beginning to A.D. 1818.* Wiesbaden: Otto Harrassowitz.

Vora, Rajendra. 1999. '*Maharashtra Dharma* and the Nationalist Movement in Maharashtra'. In *Writers, Editors & Reformers. Social and Political Transformations of Maharashtra 1830-1930*, edited by N. K. Wagle. New Delhi: Manohar, pp. 23-30.

Woods, J. H. 1972. *The Yoga-System of Patañjali.* Reprint. Delhi: Motilal Banarsidass.

3

Writing Regional Consciousness: Maratha History and Regional Identity in Modern Maharashtra

Prachi Deshpande

After being mired in an excessively statist focus on centre-state relations in post-colonial India, research on regions and regional identities has recently seen some welcome growth.[1] Much of this recent work has focused on regions such as Assam, Tamil Nadu and Kashmir that have demonstrated resistance to the homogenizing and centralizing Indian nation-state. In this sense, the dominant approach to the idea of the region is still as one conceived in opposition to the nation. However, the attention to discursive or imaginative articulations of regional communities and their relationship, albeit antagonistic, to nationalist discourse is long overdue. It has usefully reminded us that regional identities in the subcontinent are not only modern formations rooted in specific historical moments, but also expressions of a 'dialogical relationship with pan-Indian politics'.[2]

Theoretical work on Indian nationalism, for its part, has implicitly assumed that regional identities, especially those that weren't overtly antagonistic to the overarching national narrative, were mere local, usually linguistic, flavours of nationalist discourse.[3] In this context, the emphasis in recent research on the modernity of regional constructions and the *relationship* between regional and national imaginations is a significant departure. It enables us to look at regional identities as products of the transformations that colonial rule and the emergence of modernity brought to the subcontinent. More importantly, it opens up a space to explore regional cultural expressions as sites where new ways of belonging to the new Indian nation were negotiated, at the levels of both discourse and politics.

Several conceptual questions, however, remain. An important one, for instance, highlighted by Sanjib Baruah's use of 'subnational' as opposed to 'regional' identity, is that of the variety of factors that produced some collective identities in the subcontinent as national and others as 'merely' regional within a broader nationalist discourse. My specific concern here, however, is with the conception of the region itself. Baruah and Ramaswamy have both rightly highlighted the 'emotive power' that sustains regional narratives, but explicitly assign this emotive power only to language. Thus, despite his valuable insight that 'the fit between the formally federal structure of the Indian polity and the emotive power of . . . subnational narratives is hardly perfect', Baruah replaces this formal structure with another given, namely language.[4] In this paper, I wish to take issue with the idea that language was the 'cultural foundation of India's regionally based subnationalisms' and argue that this foundation or emotive power can be seen as coming from a variety of cultural resources. The specific resource I will focus on is a sense of history and its relationship to Maharashtrian regional consciousness.

Impressionistic appraisals of the importance of history in Maharashtra abound. Some, such as P. K. Atre's famous declaration during the Samyukta (United) Maharashtra movement of the 1950s, are celebratory: 'There is only one *rashtra* with history in India. That is Maharashtra. Maharashtra can only mean history. To put Maharashtra down is to put history down.'[5] Others, such as T. S. Shejwalkar's remark in the 1950s, are more pessimistic: 'History', he despaired, 'has possessed Maharashtra like a devil.'[6] Other recent commentators have been more specific about the particular importance that attaches to Maratha history in Maharashtra; these observations have only been bolstered by the stark presence of Maratha historical symbols and figures in the Maharashtrian public sphere and the Shiv Sena's rather raucous invocation of Shivaji for Hindu majoritarian politics and mobilization in recent decades.[7]

Historical invocations of a range of figures and themes relating to Maratha rule, however, are not only a feature of post-colonial Maharashtra: they have deeply informed cultural practice and political rhetoric in the region for over a hundred years. The presentist focus on the Sena's activities does not fully explain their presence and power in Maharashtra's public culture. How do we account for this century-long popularity of specific historical narratives and the depth and extent of their deployment? The question becomes even more interesting when we consider the novelty of modern historical practice itself in the late nineteenth century and the colonial conditions under which it was forged. It is important to remember that 'Maratha history' itself was constituted as a discursive field in the late nineteenth century in the context of, and in response to, an emerging colonial modernity. This not only included the inculcation of history as a new, rationalist discipline and its deployment as an attractive vehicle for new identities and aspirations but also the wider and thorough re-examination of the conceptual universes of religious philosophy and practice, social hierarchy and conceptions of belonging. In this paper, I propose to examine some responses of Marathi middle-class intellectuals to this new discipline of history and some practices through which the field of Maratha history was constituted as the prime cultural resource for forging a modern, Maharashtrian regional identity.

The practice of engaging with the past, especially in the context of present exigencies, was not unknown to the Marathas themselves. I have argued elsewhere that the practice of history, in the form of biography, genealogy and heroic commemoration, was an important instrument of expressing power and allegiance in the seventeenth- and eighteenth-century Maratha firmament. Prose chronicles (*bakhars*) and oral ballad traditions (*powadas* and *lavanis*) extolled a complex of qualities, ideals, and values that contributed contested visions of warrior-peasant Maratha identities.[8] The snuffing out of the Peshwai in 1818, however, brought a radical change in the practice and philosophy of this engagement with the past. British officials came to look on Marathi chronicles as entertaining at best and farcical at worst; political subjugation was accompanied by full-scale English narratives that sought to understand and 'know' western India through the lens of 'histories of the Mahrattas'.

Of these narratives, the work that was to become the most important and controversial for more than a century after its publication, was James Grant Duff's *The History of the Mahrattas* (1826). Duff's history not only symbolized the British triumph over the Marathas through its pronouncements on Maratha politics and society, but also became the final word on the subject. In the dominant Whig historical tradition, Duff's was the first complete text that crystallized the political and social upheaval in the Deccan of the preceding centuries into an academic narrative with a coherent beginning, rise and denouement. He made his central focus the category 'Mahrattas', who had a vague and uncertain beginning in the remote ancient period, were conquered by the Muslims from the north by AD 1000, and rose in sudden revolt under Shivaji in the seventeenth century, only to be eventually subdued by British power. His narrative drew generalizations on this category and wove all his characters as being either within it or without, and all the events of western Indian politics and society that he described, dovetailed into a history of this overarching category. Also, despite its extensive use of Persian and Marathi chronicles and documents, Duff's work laid claim to being the first modern history of the Marathas. His ordering and tidying up of the pre-colonial Marathi historical materials exemplified the argument in colonial discourse on the apparent lack of a reliable historical method and consciousness in the Indian intellectual past.[9]

The introduction of Western liberal education also caused a deep-seated change in the perception and production of history in Maharashtrian society. Conventional nationalist thinking traces a happy causal linkage between Western education, a rationalist historical method, and nationalist histories on the Marathas that began to critique Grant Duff's work from the late nineteenth century. As I hope to show below, however, this link between Western education, modernity and nationalist history was rather more complicated. The critiques of Grant Duff were not a natural outcome of an awakening to a 'proper' historical awareness. Instead, the eventual popularity of the period of Maratha history as a prime resource to fight colonialism was produced through a variety of factors, and over other alternative engagements with the past. Within Western education, the positivistic understanding of history as a science dependent on facts, sources and evidence was to be an important factor. Equally important, however, were changes such as the modernization of the Marathi language and the emergence of new classes and political communities and their aspirations, of which history was to become a self-conscious representation.

NEW ENGAGEMENTS WITH THE PAST

As has been pointed out elsewhere, the colonial education system drastically altered the importance and reach of history. History became a powerful instrument of emphasizing Western superiority and triumph over the Orient and an integral part of colonial discourse on Indian society, but also became a means of refuting this discourse and expressing collective identities of different kinds.[10] At the same time, its practice was no longer restricted to scribes with a graceful hand but part of a pedagogical process that every aspirant to a job in the colonial administration and a middle-class existence had to undergo. The history taught in government schools and colleges was almost entirely European in material and method, with an emphasis on chronology and political history. The history of India was taught every year in schools and every other year or so at the college level, but it was not until the 1870s that Maratha history was introduced into college curricula, as an optional subject for the BA level.[11] The first generation of English-educated Marathi intellectuals, accordingly, comprehended history as a subject essential to the advancement of mankind, along with other sciences such as logic, mathematics, grammar and ethics, and part of a wider genre of 'useful subjects'.[12] Some early writings such as those by Lokahitawadi or M. G. Ranade soon took on some patriotic stirrings, but these were still a far cry from the later identification of history as a useful plank against colonial rule and for generating nationalist pride.[13]

The first concerted engagement of the new Marathi middle class with the Indian past was in the field of Indology, an interest greatly encouraged not only by the increased interest in Sanskrit literature and comparative philology among European scholars, but also by the government's continued patronage to Sanskrit learning and the search for Sanskrit manuscripts. The Indian scholars in this field, by the later nineteenth century, not surprisingly, were all brahmans, but these were not traditional shastris; they were Western-educated men, well versed in the rationalist-scientific tradition. The best known among them was the liberal reformer, author of several Sanskrit textbooks, and Professor of Sanskrit at the Elphinstone and Deccan Colleges, Sir Ramkrishna Gopal Bhandarkar.

The principal thrust of Indological research was on Sanskrit sacred texts and poetry. Scholars debated the antiquity and 'classicism' of Sanskrit literature in general and the authenticity and reliability of specific texts. Indian scholars spent much energy painstakingly denouncing European suspicions, such as K. T. Telang's refutation of Albrecht Weber's theory that the *Ramayana* had been copied from Homer.[14] In attempting to establish a civilizational parity between the ancient West and India, Indian Sanskritists such as Bhandarkar firmly placed themselves within the new discourses of scientific research and comparative philology and emphasized the linguistic connections between Greek and Sanskrit.[15]

Bhandarkar's attempts to apply new 'scientific' parameters to judge this ancient material to avoid adversarial debates and arrive at its 'truth', however, led him towards a consensus with his European counterparts about the lack of a genuine historical consciousness in ancient India. Bhandarkar discounted most of the ancient Indian texts as sources of history because their objective had been 'to please . . . the reader and excite the feeling of wonder' rather than 'to record events as they occurred'. He therefore dismissed the epics, *charita*s of kings, and any text with a hint of hyperbole, as a usable historical source. He added, however, that they were the main source for understanding 'the thoughts and feelings, the aims and aspirations, and the manners and customs of the people . . . and present to us a picture of the life and civilization of the period'.[16] While a political history, therefore, could not be gleaned from these ancient texts, cultural matters could certainly be ascertained. Indological research, thus, came to explore the Sanskrit corpus through the framework of literature and religion rather than history.

If brahmans dominated this pool of Maharashtrian intellectuals, why did this particular period of ancient history with its 'classical' bent not become the primary focus for patriotic and historical imaginings? With exclusive linguistic access to these texts, this elite could construct a glorious classical past that also emphasized brahman social and political leadership throughout Indian history. The answer lies in this very 'culturalist' classification of the ancient texts as sources for not political history but civilizational information. As Partha Chatterjee has persuasively argued, one of the most important aspects of colonial Indian society's response to colonialism was centred on the issue of power, and historical writing was deeply imbricated by this question of power, its loss, and its regeneration under the nationalist project.[17] While cultural power could definitely be located in a vibrant civilization that expressed itself through a classical language, religion and ritual, it was ultimately the issue of political power that was most crucial to the creation of a viable and substantive modern, national identity. From the very beginning Indological scholarship, including that of Indians such as Bhandarkar, not only highlighted the 'literary' and 'cultural' approach to ancient India, but also ended up reiterating the argument in colonial discourses about the lack of a genuine historical consciousness in pre-colonial Indian society. Moreover, the increasingly positivistic historical method that interpreted political history in narrow terms of battles and kings underscored the foggy political picture of ancient India that the Sanskrit material presented. Unable to fire the nationalist imagination of the middle classes, Indology remained, in the end, the preserve of a few scholars who did not really lead or influence historical debates and questions in the Marathi public sphere.

The non-brahman thinker and activist Jotirao Phule, who also wrote at length on Indian history, presented a radical alternative to the Indologists. Phule was not only well versed in the ongoing debates between Christian missionaries and brahmans over Hindu philosophy and ritual, but was also aware of the ongoing philological and ethnological debates over 'the Aryan race' in the nineteenth century. To many brahman intellectuals of the time, this 'Aryan' classification of ancient Indian history was an affirmation of brahman leadership over Hindu society, the brahmans being seen as the creators and inheritors of this Aryan heritage. Skillfully turning these debates on their head, Phule applied these insights as well as the emerging research on the closeness of Indo-European languages to depict brahmans as only the earliest of many invaders who had exploited the aboriginal peoples of India. In his 1873 book *Gulamgiri* (Slavery), he wrote:

> Recent researches have demonstrated beyond a shadow of doubt that the brahmans were not the aborigines of India. At some remote period in antiquity, probably more than 3000 years ago, the Aryan progenitors of the present Brahmin Race descended upon the plain of Hindoostan from regions lying beyond the Indus. . . . The affinity existing between the Zend, the

Persian and The Sanskrit languages, unmistakably points to a common source or origin . . . the proverbial wealth of [India] . . . which has more recently tempted the cupidity of the Western nations, no doubt attracted the Aryans who came . . . as conquerors. . . . The aborigines whom the Aryans subjugated . . . appear to have been a hardy and brave people from the determined front which they offered to these interlopers.[18]

Phule elaborated on this argument through detailed and polemical analyses of ancient myths and terms used to describe aboriginal people in Sanskrit texts and legends, especially the legend of Parashurama.[19] Phule was also the earliest to recognize the emotive power of the legend of Shivaji and its potential, with all the ingredients of heroism and determination, for a politics of resistance. Accordingly, his 1869 ballad on Shivaji depicted him as *Kulavadi Bhushan*, the leader and pride of the toiling peasants, the aboriginal masses. In Phule's interpretation, Shivaji protected the Maratha lands from the *Yavanas* (foreigners) who had managed to conquer them due to brahman misrule and mismanagement.[20]

Phule's approach to the past had greater potential than did Indological research, as a rich resource upon which a viable and substantive patriotic identity could be built. The legend of Shivaji had shades of political assertion as opposed to a mere cultural efflorescence. At the same time, it was rooted in the popular culture and language of the peasant masses of Maharashtra, who could relate to it and draw sustenance from it. His explicit mention of these masses in the preface to his ballad and his attempts to cast it in a popular idiom to make it more widely accessible suggest Phule's sensitivity to the possibilities of moulding historical symbols for a popular politics.

Despite his keen awareness of the importance of historical and cultural symbolism to political activity, Phule's ingenious invocation of Maratha history too did not inspire the nationalist imagination in Maharashtra. This was because it had questioned the legitimacy of brahmans, the very social group that was increasingly dominating public activity, in discursive and overtly political ways, in late nineteenth-century Maharashtra. Moreover, given the positivistic intellectual environment of the time, he was also writing against the grain. At a time when history was being increasingly perceived as being fact-based truth in prose backed up by proof, his broad arguments struck a discordant note and the predominantly brahman intelligentsia could dismiss his polemic as being without any historical basis or proof. The popular literary journal *Vividh Dnyan Vistaar* dismissed the ballad as a disgrace. Another review (in *Dnyanodaya*) doubted Phule's ability as a historian. Ironically, even Phule's friend and fellow radical Baba Padmanji, whom Phule had thanked for help with the piece in the introduction, wrote to the *Dnyanodaya* and disclaimed responsibility for the ballad, commenting that it went against the *evidence* of history.[21]

Two different engagements with the past in the later nineteenth century, therefore, failed to strike a chord within the emerging nationalist public in Maharashtra. One causal factor was language. This is reflected most sharply in the divergent idioms employed by these perspectives on history, their audiences and readership communities, and their social contexts. Most Indological writing was in English with a narrow readership of mainly European and American Orientalists and Indologists from other Indian provinces, and the debates were carried out mainly through English journals of a pronounced academic bent.[22] The outlook of writers like Bhandarkar and K. T. Telang was oriented outwards, therefore, to a community of English speakers and readers rather than towards a Marathi readership.[23] The discourse of Indology had, despite these writers' otherwise active political life as social and religious reformers, very little scope for popularization. This was reflected not just in the Sanskrit material that only a few could access, but also in the choice of the research language, English.

What of Marathi? Far from taking place in a social vacuum, the modernization of Marathi by the new colonial elite, as with most other Indian languages, meant structuring it in lexical, syntactic, and textual terms to enable it to express the new concepts Western education brought.[24] Despite English's authoritative position, it was the vernacular Marathi, suitably modernized, that had greater potential for generating public opinion or political debate by reaching out to wider sections of people who were schooled in the new concepts but were more comfortable in their native language. Access to, and control of, the new languages and technologies of modernity such as print and the avenues they provided, most importantly in terms of the ability to legitimize claims of social—and national—representation, was to be crucial not only in shaping forms of cultural production, but also in determining the new social leadership. As

Veena Naregal has shown, this large and growing Marathi public sphere came to be effectively dominated by the late nineteenth century by a brahman intelligentsia that was politically radical, but brooked no protest against the social/caste hierarchies that prevailed.[25]

Despite the entry of different social groups into the business of print, brahmans in Maharashtra largely remained in control of the new media and their dissemination. It is in this broader language context detailed by Naregal that we can understand how the radical visions of history and community put forward by Phule as well as the pre-occupations of the Indologists with ancient Sanskrit culture failed to become popular cultural resources for a national imagination. The predominantly brahman and nationalist middle class, writing in, and reaching out to a modern Marathi language community, came instead to conceive of an agenda for self-representation that tackled the question of political power head on, but not the question of social hierarchy. This agenda was shaped in the main through the writings and efforts of two men, Vishnushastri Chiplunkar and Vishwanath Kashinath Rajwade.

VISHNUSHASTRI CHIPLUNKAR

Vishnushastri Chiplunkar represents the classic 'sign of the nationalist consciousness that [did] not find its own voice in histories written by foreign rulers and . . . set out to write for itself the account of its past'.[26] Born in Poona in 1850 and the son of a highly placed and respected writer and translator, Krishnashastri Chiplunkar, Vishnushastri inspired an entire generation of Marathi nationalists, primarily through essays in a literary journal, *Nibandhamala*, which he started in 1873.[27] His strident, often shrill, denials of any necessity of reform and declarations of brahmanical superiority were certainly instrumental in diluting the social reform agenda of liberals such as Ranade and Bhandarkar. However, in the face of insistent Christian missionary criticism, the widening distance between Indians and Europeans by the late nineteenth century, and growing economic distress that was souring the 'divine dispensation' perspective on colonial rule, his defiance and defence of Hinduism and Indian culture as he understood them were also instrumental in generating a new confidence amongst a younger generation of

Marathi intellectuals. His programmatic essays on history and history writing proved to be especially inspirational.

Like many others in Maharashtra and across the subcontinent, Chiplunkar pondered the uses of history. He believed an interest in history was, first and foremost, a hallmark of enlightenment and modernity. He also wrote extensively about its didactic importance, as a mode of imparting *neetibodh*: the teaching of morality and the importance of certain kinds of behaviour and actions in life. History enabled people to learn from the past the experiences of thousands of people, and to make choices about their own future, especially in the face of adversity. This was, however, not just any kind of history, but necessarily in the form of biographies of great men:

> Would Alexander have existed but for Homer's description of Achilles' glory? Would Shivaji have been able to wrest back his kingdom from the Yavanas but for Vyasa's description of the Pandavas? Why would Caesar have risen but for Alexander? If Shivaji hadn't existed, how would the Marathas, despite the murder of his son and the devastation of their lands have harassed Aurangzeb and forced him to come down to Ahmednagar?[28]

History, by recording deeds of glory, therefore, not only acted as a moral guide, but also as proof of a people's worth. Chiplunkar also wrote extensively about the usefulness of history as biography as a worthy substitute for other forms of entertainment, especially new fictional forms such as the novel that could corrupt and degrade the morals of young men.[29] This concern over morality was part of broader anxieties under colonial modernity over drastically altered gender and caste relations.[30]

The most important use of history Chiplunkar highlighted, however, was in generating pride. The core of his critique of colonialist histories was that the British not only lacked the moral and intellectual authority to write about India, but they also engendered powerlessness among the colonized. The only way this powerlessness could be combated was by developing one's own history, which brought together the ingredients of political power, self-representation, and language. In a long essay on the concept of pride, he argued powerfully that it was to be seen not as arrogance, but as self-esteem and a necessary tool in building this history.[31] Just as a constant self-denial of one's achievements could be extremely annoying, especially to one's listeners, he argued, a constant denigration of a people by another required this self-esteem to withstand the onslaught. Without this buffer, 'all our capabilities [were] bound to be eventually destroyed.' The criticism of 'the likes of Macaulay', he added, 'should not bother real patriots', or, more importantly, 'those who stand by truth'.[32] Interestingly, he argued that such histories instilling pride were not only useful in generating patriotism, but also because they had the backing of 'truth'. This belief in the truth of a history that necessarily generates pride and patriotism in a people is another primary sign of a nationalist consciousness, a belief that was to strongly characterize historical discourse in Maharashtra.

Chiplunkar's treatment of history had a deeply contradictory and complex relationship with colonial discourse. This was of course characteristic of all nationalist writing in colonial India. He used his biting wit and felicity with words to borrow skillfully and selectively from colonial representations of Indian culture and society. He also reiterated the narrow definition of history popular in nineteenth-century Europe as a political domain of military conflict and diplomacy: great wars and revolutions were the 'stuff of history' for him, and he argued that this was the very reason why a spiritually inclined ancient India, far removed from bloodshed and political conflict, witnessed very little by way of history writing. Despite his venomous railing against British commentators on Indian history, especially Mill and Macaulay, he concluded that overall, in the field of history writing as a method, contact with the West had been beneficial, and he reiterated the idea that pre-colonial India had had no reliable historical tradition.

What, then, was the kind of history to be written? History had to be a heady mix of simple prose and exciting passages of bravery and valour, with an emphasis on biographies of great men that would train and discipline a young (man's) mind, and mould his character. At the same time, it had to reflect the identity and culture of a people and enable them to draw sustenance from a past glory. Elsewhere, Chiplunkar specified this programme for a new history in detail:

> The following have to be included in a history of Maharashtra. First of all, the condition of the Maratha people before Shivaji Maharaj, the special qualities he possessed that enabled them to reach such glorious heights later on . . . the specific policies that he enacted for their progress, . . . the condition of the Hindu religion at the time and how . . . it contribute[d] to the decline of yavana power. Then should follow a description of the Mavala

people, information on Shivaji's friends Tanaji, Baji, Yesaji, Shivaji's education, military system and administration, the training of his armed forces, Aurangzeb's darbar, the Mughal army, the saffron banner, Ramdas' political and religious message, Tukarambuwa's kirtan, Vaman's scholarship and literary abilities, the bravery of the Prabhu people. . . . All this should be included in a history of Shivaji.[33]

He outlined this pattern of history for the entire period of Maratha rule in the seventeenth and eighteenth centuries, including political policy, caste rivalries, poetic and literary achievements, and legal treatises, down to marital and filial relations. 'A complete history should thus include festivals, customs, dress, etc., as well. As long as even one piece of information about the Maratha people is missing, "A history of Maharashtra desh" will remain incomplete.'

Through such examples and outlines, Chiplunkar identified the events and figures of Maratha rule as being most suitable for his agenda of self-representation. He also started a journal *Kavyetihas Sangraha*, with three friends, Kashinath Sane, Janardan Modak and Shankar Shaligram, in Poona in January 1878 to publish old Marathi and Sanskrit poems and Marathi *bakhar*s, with the specific purpose of bringing about a 'renaissance and rejuvenation' in these three fields and preserving for posterity the precious material contained in decaying manuscripts. It was these materials that would form the basis on which the new history would be written.

Chiplunkar's call for a history of 'Maharashtra desh' in a nationalist idiom and his repeated use of examples from his specific regional history for a nationalist project raise the important question of how we interpret the use of words such as *desh*, *bhoomi*, *rashtra*, among others, in nationalist writings. Let us look at just one example:

It is not even a hundred years since our country witnessed great warriors. We can still remember how even at the very end we dazzled all of Hindustan with our royal brilliance, even as the whole world watched, bewitched by our glory![34]

Key in this quotation is not only the defiant declaration of a glorious past, but the ambiguity in the usage of 'we' and 'our country'. The latter could conceivably include the broader Indian nation as such, but it is clear that the great warriors who 'dazzled all of Hindustan with [their] royal brilliance' were the Marathas, in power less than 'a hundred years' ago.

How do we understand this ambiguity? Most work on nationalist discourse in South Asia has seen nothing complex in the way nationalist intellectuals in the nineteenth century used religious, regional and broader national affiliations interchangeably. Partha Chatterjee has also argued that the difference between Hindu, Bengali, and Indian in Bengali nationalist writing did not really matter in nationalist visions of the political community.[35] I would argue, however, that Chiplunkar's ambiguous usage of such language is indicative of the concurrent emergence of the modern communities of nation, region, and religion in the later nineteenth century. As we shall see below, ambiguity, at least in the Maharashtrian case, disappeared by the turn of the twentieth century to give way to a clear demarcation between the characterizations of region and nation and a process of continuous negotiation between the two imagined communities.

At the same time, ambiguous usage is also indicative of how a wider, national imagination across the subcontinent was deeply influenced by regional cultures and pasts. Thus, Chiplunkar's vision of a modern pan-Indian Hindu community and its brahman leadership were also refracted through a regional prism of cultural practice, the political context of the loss of 'brahman' Peshwa power in Maharashtra, and low-caste critiques of brahman domination in the region from the 1870s.

Chiplunkar stirred up quite a hornet's nest in his short but brilliant life span of thirty-two years. His sarcastic and frequently offensive critiques of radical thinkers, particularly Lokahitawadi and Phule, generated heat and controversy in Marathi intellectual circles.[36] His appeal for the regeneration of Marathi society through history, however, proved to be inspirational to an entire generation of scholars. He had taken the first step himself, as it were, by publishing old *bakhars* in the *Kavyetihas Sangraha*, and historical research now took an enthusiastic step in this direction. Through the *Nibandhamala*, Chiplunkar consciously attempted, with considerable success, to develop new aesthetic and modern standards for Marathi literary production and consumption. Through a privileged position in the sphere of Marathi print and access to a growing middle-class readership, Chiplunkar was able to put forward his call for an autonomous history that emphasized pride and political glory. In accordance with the uses and frameworks that he had specified for the subject, history now increasingly came to coincide with the 'glorious' period of Maratha rule, and one did not have to go very far to look for great men whose biographies to write as moral guides for young men. There were the exploits of Maratha heroes like Shivaji, Sambhaji, and Bajirao, eagerly taken up by writers of school textbooks and discussed by school teachers.[37]

It is not surprising, then, that most of the participants in this historiographical endeavour were educated brahmans from the burgeoning middle class; most, however, occupied its lower rungs, working in lowly positions in the colonial administration in Pune or the native states of Kolhapur, Baroda and Sangli. Others were school teachers and head masters; still others were steeped in respectable poverty. The *Nibandhamala* was aimed at precisely this lower-middle-class, Western-educated section that worked in the colonial administration, which was socially respectable as brahman, but was not particularly well off.[38] Chiplunkar's biting criticism of colonial attitudes and the emphasis on *swabhimaan* spoke precisely to this social group that experienced the daily humiliations of *chakri.*[39] A great deal of the *Kavyetihas Sangraha's* financial support came from schoolmasters in the hinterlands of Poona and other district towns. The project of publishing *bakhars* and other material itself had links with such people in smaller towns, who often hunted out interesting material and sent it up to Poona for perusal and publication. It is also important to note that such historiography was not restricted to the political boundaries of the present-day Maharashtra state; it spilled over into areas covered by the erstwhile Maratha power such as Baroda, Indore, and Gwalior as well as Belgaum. The imaginary space of Maharashtra produced by this discourse throughout the colonial period, thus, was marked as much by the shared commemoration of Maratha history as by the Marathi language.

V. K. RAJWADE AND 'THE MARATHA ARCHIVE'

The efforts of Vishwanath Kashinath Rajwade, deeply inspired by Chiplunkar's call, were crucial in consolidating the autonomous construction of the 'Maratha past'. Rajwade was responsible not only for giving Chiplunkar's call a definite direction, but also for building an archive for this historiographic practice. In his eagerness to apply the tools and standards of Western historiography to combat colonial discourse on Indian society in a disciplinary, impartial and academic manner, Rajwade sought documents and 'facts' that would help him locate the 'truth' about Maratha history. He was, in effect, displaying the same nationalist confidence that there existed a historical truth out there that was worthy of pride and patriotism. He dismissed the pre-colonial *bakhars* altogether as fantastic, biased, and useless for a true history, but looked high and low for other kinds of historical documents: letters, lists, private diaries, and administrative material. He called out to those interested in history to make such papers their primary focus, and identified one hundred and thirteen locations across Maharashtra and Central India where private *daftars* of chieftains and princely rulers could yield a wealth of historical information.[40]

Firmly believing in the mantra that the 'facts would speak for themselves', Rajwade's historical programme, therefore, was to go out and collect these papers, and collect them he did, with a single-mindedness that has captured the attention of many a biographer. He travelled the length and breadth of India between 1893 till his death in 1926, often on foot, visiting places and *daftars* that he thought would prove useful. Stories of Rajwade's indefatigable search for documents have now become legendary, and tales abound of how he snatched papers from a reluctant chieftain here and lost his temper at a recalcitrant and suspicious chief there.[41] There is no doubt that this was an arduous task. Rajwade eventually published all this material in twenty-two volumes entitled *Sources of Maratha History*, with critical introductions to nine of them. What is significant about this tremendous enterprise is that it was done almost entirely on Rajwade's own steam and at great personal sacrifice. Having published all the volumes himself at great cost, he lived frugally on the proceeds of fifty copies of each volume forwarded to him by the printer, and piled up a huge debt through his travels. As Jadunath Sarkar put it, he was 'a penniless collector' but his 'actual performance, in spite of the severe handicaps of his poverty, temper and environment, was wonderful. He was our pioneer par excellence.'[42] Rajwade's identification of this practice as one of primary focus for nationalist historians received a tremendous response from young Maharashtrian nationalists and further emphasized the importance of the Maratha period for nationalist expression.

Another factor that contributed to this crystallization of 'Maratha history' as a nationalist resource was the colonial government's policy of keeping the principal record office, the Peshwa *Daftar*, closed to Indian researchers well into the 1920s to limit seditious writing. In fact, the Bombay government ironically enhanced the importance of these documents and their publication as a patriotic duty. Following Chiplunkar, several intellectuals and fledgling political associations began taking an interest in the *Daftar*, seeking entry and publication of the materials that were now identified as crucial to an autonomous history. In 1886, after petitions from organizations like the Deccan Vernacular Society, the Government sanctioned a project for printing the more 'valuable' parts of the Peshwa diaries. Accordingly, Ganesh Chimnaji Vad, a government official, was assigned the task of transcribing them, but an extremely tedious approval process laid down by the government ensured that not much headway was made. Any introduction to this material was to be 'approved by Government as an accurate and authoritative exposition', and M. G. Ranade's perceptive introduction to the first of Vad's volumes caused quite a flutter in official circles. Ranade summarized the importance the Peshwa Daftar had come to symbolize in the minds of Indian historians by the 1890s and spoke for a lot of them when he wrote:

> These [records] . . . are simply invaluable and though they have their own defects, in the absence of better materials, they shed a flood of light upon the real movements and the hopes and fears, the strength and weakness of the people for over a century, and for purposes of instruction and guidance. . . .[43]

The Peshwa Daftar, therefore, became a site of conflict between the government and Marathi nationalist intellectuals and somewhat of a political powder keg. Although this was to increase sharply after Tilak's inauguration of the Shivaji festival in 1895, British officials were already becoming aware of the potential Maratha history had for generating public sentiment. Despite the urging of liberal-minded officials that 'every civilized government' was obliged to admit students of history to its archives, caution was advised with the view that there was really no historical public in India, but only 'political pamphleteers'.[44] The government's intransigence, therefore, only served to enhance the importance of the *Daftar*, and, indeed, records of all kinds, in the self-representation project. Rajwade's call to the Deccan chieftains to throw open their record collections and encourage historians to study them has to be seen in this context. With the main *Daftar* out of bounds it was only by scouring the region for material housed in other political and influential establishments that the 'truth' could be discovered.

The creation of a Maratha archive itself, then, became the principal historical as well as patriotic activity.[45] The initial response of many princely rulers to the young nationalists who began scouring the countryside and seeking permission to use their private collections and papers was not enthusiastic. Private papers and state records were important in the negotiation of power with the British, and most chiefs were loath to give up any control over them. Some, like the Patwardhans of Sangli, were open to researchers publishing their records but did not offer financial support, earning Rajwade's wrath and scorn. By the turn of the twentieth century, however, the increased interest in Maratha history led some houses to commission family genealogies and histories of their principalities.[46] Many princely rulers also began dabbling in politics in the early twentieth century, providing financial and symbolic patronage in particular to the non-brahman movement, and supported the aggressive use of Maratha historical symbols witnessed in this movement. Liberal princes like Sayajirao Gaekwad of Baroda, in addition to the focus on the Marathas, also patronized works on the history of other countries of the world, but this trend was clearly an exception.[47] Most chiefs encouraged the publication of their records and financed a history of their own domains, thus ensuring through their patronage an increased production of Maratha history.

MAHARASHTRA DHARMA: REGION AND NATION

Marathi writers inspired by Chiplunkar and Rajwade proceeded, from the late nineteenth century, to critique colonialist interpretations of Maratha history, especially the work of James Grant Duff. This critique produced an enormous body of nationalist monographs, biographies, articles in newspapers and journals, speeches in conferences, and historical plays and novels, emphasizing in the main the idea that the Marathas were not a bunch of marauders inspired by the love of booty but represented a popular movement rooted in a religious and cultural tradition. Many of these were biographies of individual figures of the Maratha period such as Shivaji, Bajirao I,

Nana Phadnavis and Ahilyabai Holkar; others were studies of Maratha military campaigns and diplomatic tactics; still others were explorations of the socio-religious life of the Maratha period.

This emergence of an autonomous history and the popularity of Maratha history were not de-linked from the broader debates over religious practice and reform taking place across the subcontinent in the later nineteenth century. One important strand of debate that emerged from this re-evaluation of history was centred on the popular regional religious tradition of bhakti. Widely referred to in Marathi parlance as *Bhagavata Dharma*, this popular religious tradition was rooted in regional cultural practice not only through a sacred geography of pilgrimage, but also in a vast corpus of devotional verse produced in Marathi from the thirteenth to the seventeenth centuries, disseminated through performative traditions such as the *kirtan*. The Marathi intelligentsia, like their counterparts across the subcontinent, sought to frame these popular religious discourses in the modern vocabulary of a Hindu community and Indian nation.[48] There was considerable debate regarding several aspects of this tradition of bhakti. To reformist critiques exemplified by institutions such as the Prarthana Samaj, the bhakti tenets of individual devotional spirituality represented the ideal middle ground between excessive ritual and a rejection of religious practice altogether. To many brahman nationalist critics of the reformist position, otherworldly spirituality as represented by poets like Tukaram was not as important as the more militant interpretation of religion put forward by Ramdas. However, to Maharashtrian historians in general, despite their differential emphases on this regional religious tradition, bhakti came to be understood specifically in politicized terms, as the moral basis for Maratha nationalism.

This connection between bhakti and Maratha nationalism drew upon one important category: Maharashtra Dharma. During the period of Maratha rule itself, Maharashtra Dharma was used as the 'Maratha way' of living and doing things. In their attempts to root the Maratha struggle in the religious and cultural traditions of the region, however, Maharashtrian historians came to focus on the following usage of the term:

Maratha tituka melavava,
Maharashtra Dharma vadhavava
(Bring all the Marathas together and spread the Maharashtra Dharma).

This couplet is ascribed to the seventeenth-century poet Ramdas, and in popular belief it illustrates the imperatives behind the Maratha upsurge. From the late nineteenth century Maharashtra Dharma, with its attractive religious as well as political-geographic inflections, not only came to represent what bound all the Marathas together, but also became the prime site upon which to debate the heritage of Maharashtra and its relationship to the Indian nation. Recent research on the Marathas practically dismisses the importance of Ramdas or Maharashtra Dharma to Shivaji's policy imperatives; by contrast, the centrality of both in popular perceptions of the Maratha past is another indicator of the many levels of historical awareness and the limits of academic historiography in shaping popular visions of the past.

M. G. Ranade was the first to quote Ramdas on the matter in 1895 in an essay called 'The Saints and Poets of Maharashtra' in the *Sarvajanik Sabha Quarterly*, later included in his famous work *The Rise of the Maratha Power*:

> Saint Ramdas, the spiritual adviser of the great Shivaji, is reported to have exhorted Shivaji's son, Sambhaji, to follow the footsteps of his father and the advice he gave on this occasion was tersely summed up in two sentences—'Unite all who are Marathas together,' and 'Propagate the *dharma* (religion) of Maharashtra.'[49]

Ranade collapsed together sentences from two separate letters in verse written by Ramdas to Sambhaji shortly after Shivaji's death in 1680, urging him to rule well and follow in his illustrious father's footsteps.[50] Rajaramshastri Bhagvat built on this initial interpretation of Ranade through his 1895 essay, *Maharashtra Dharma*. Bhagvat's earlier, 1887 work *A Few Words about the Marathas* had already set the tone for a reformist or moderate interpretation of Maratha history. Both men were prominent intellectuals active in the reform circles of Bombay Presidency and wrote widely about Hindu religious thought and society; their approaches to the history of Maharashtra were not only similar, but also strongly reflected their politics.

Bhagvat and Ranade interpreted bhakti as a vibrant and peculiar set of religious values and practice that had developed in the medieval period in Maharashtra through a blending of traditional Hinduism with the monotheism of Islam. This was a regional culture that began with Dnyaneshwar's Marathi commentary on the

Bhagavad Gita in the thirteenth century and flourished for five hundred years, culminating in the poetry of Tukaram and Ramdas. What made this tradition distinctive was its rejection of Brahmanical values and tenets and the contribution of poets, men and women, from different caste groups, including Muslims, and the establishment of devotional spirituality as superior to the ritual-driven traditions of Hinduism. It produced a popular literature in Marathi that enabled the entire population to participate in this cultural tradition, denied the importance of caste difference, and 'made the nation more humane, at the same time more prone to hold together by mutual toleration'.[51]

According to the reformist view, it was this regional culture that Ramdas termed Maharashtra Dharma; combined with the political unity and upsurge, it successfully established the Maratha power as not the accidental accomplishment of a lone charismatic leader such as Shivaji, but one created through 'a foundation that was laid broad and deep in the hearts of the whole people . . . a national movement or upheaval in which all classes cooperated.'[52] Ranade likened it to patriotism, as part of his broader attempt to cast Maratha history in the framework and historical categories of Western civilization. The bhakti movement too, in his view, was similar in many ways to the European Reformation of the sixteenth century; in both places, he argued, a heterodox spirit of religious devotion had protested against the excesses of a corrupt, ritualistic priesthood, breathing new life into the religion and the nation.

Both Ranade and Bhagvat insisted on the social or caste inclusiveness of the bhakti movement, but Bhagvat was emphatic that it was the disruption of caste hierarchy that enabled the establishment of a community of Maharashtrians, or a *Maharashtra-mandal*. The very idea of being a Maratha, he argued, was to rebel against the idea of social divisions and a religiously sanctioned hierarchy, and it was this special character of the *Maharashtra-mandal* that underlay Maharashtra Dharma. In his words, 'The climate of the Marathi lands simply did not suit the health of conservatives.'[53] Bhagvat was an early proponent of the idea that Ramdas and Shivaji represented the two sides, spiritual and political, of the regional traditions of Maharashtra and that it was impossible to understand one without the other.

Later historians of Maratha history too drew considerably upon the work and personality of Ramdas in their attempt to recover the morality of Maratha rule, and they strengthened the idea that it was underpinned by a Hindu religious identity. In his introduction to the first volume of *Sources of Maratha History*, his multi-volume magnum opus, V. K. Rajwade drew on the lines quoted by Ranade, but added a few others:

> Bring together the Marathas, Spread the Maharashtra Dharma
> Survive even in war, Accept death only after you have killed
> They desecrated places of pilgrimage and polluted Brahman spaces
> The entire earth was in doldrums and Dharma was lost . . .
> Bring all the people together, infuse them with one thought
> Descend upon the foreigners with all your might and effort . . .
> Protect what is already yours and seek to acquire more
> Establish the rule of Maharashtra everywhere.[54]

Recent scholars of Ramdas have taken Rajwade to task for putting together stray phrases from the poet's works in his eagerness to prove Ramdas's nationalist slant, and liberally misquoting the poet regarding the use of words such as 'Hindu dharma'.[55] Aphorisms ascribed to Ramdas, however, were regularly quoted in nationalist texts on the Marathas from the late nineteenth century without exact references to his works. They also form part of the popular and oft-quoted oral repertoire of moral sayings in the Marathi language. Tracking the 'authenticity' of these utterances, given the numerous interpolations and changes that the manuscripts and early printed editions of Ramdas' writings have undergone, is a difficult task. In ascribing patriotic poetry to Ramdas, Rajwade was certainly not alone, but perhaps the most culpable, given his vigorous championing of fact-based, scientific history. His use of these aphorisms certainly influenced their repeated invocation in following decades.

These repeated invocations of couplets attributed to Ramdas—some possibly apocryphal—also reinforce the ways in which religious-moral aphorisms from Maharashtra's regional culture were recast in shaping a modern historical view of the Maratha past. They suggest the fragility of the dominance of a 'scientific' methodology in approaching the past; clearly, not even Rajwade was immune to them. Remarkably, in his critique of Ranade's interpretation of Maharashtra Dharma, he cited as proof the same *bakhars* he had famously dismissed as fantasy.[56] Putting together stray maxims from Ramdas' poetry with some of his own, Rajwade constructed a political programme that placed the ousting of Muslim invaders and the spread of Maharashtra Dharma *across India* at the heart of the Maratha struggle.[57] It was only when this programme and motive for military action was taken into account, he argued, that 'the picture of Maratha warriors scampering aimlessly across [the country] painted by foreign historians [became] clearer.'

Maharashtra Dharma, therefore, was a regional variant of Hinduism, but one that differed significantly from Hinduism in other parts of the country and was enhanced by some definite qualities and purposes. Lest there remain any doubt, Rajwade even provided a formula:

> Maharashtra Dharma (Hinduism in Maharashtra) = Hinduism in other parts of India + establishment of righteous rule + protection of cows and Brahmans + freedom + unity + leadership.[58]

Muslims, he argued, had long oppressed Hinduism in other regions of the country, but these regions had meekly continued to follow their religion throughout the medieval period. Maharashtra was special because Muslim oppression here had been matched by significant political concessions to its elite; the Marathas therefore developed both the urge as well as the ability to oust the Muslims, an urge that had smouldered and reached a peak by the time Shivaji came on the scene. Unlike Ranade, who had described this groundwork as the work of all the bhakti poets, Rajwade focused on Shivaji's father Shahaji and his activities, arguing that the son had accomplished what the father had set out to do.[59] Hinduism itself, in his view, had come to mean the twin sentiments of anti-Muslim fervour and the urge to establish righteous rule that protected cows and brahmans in Maharashtra; freedom was the very essence of Hinduism in Maharashtra, and it was an active, militant Hinduism compared to the rather passive traditions in other parts of the country. The Maratha project, therefore, was to spread this idea of Hinduism embodied in Maharashtra Dharma all over the country and unite the nation.

Rajwade's interpretation of Maharashtra Dharma, clearly, also drew from a regional cultural tradition, but differed significantly from the reformist position. He cast it more overtly in relationship with conventional Hinduism in other parts of the country, and focused exclusively on Ramdas as a brahman, delinking him from the popular bhakti tradition. The passivity of bhakti ideology propagated by poets from different castes, he argued, was responsible for Maharashtra's defeat by the Muslims in the first place; Ramdas's Maharashtra Dharma inaugurated a militant brahman-led revival from this passive tradition. The uniqueness of this Maharashtrian culture for Rajwade, therefore, lay not in the religious practice itself, but in the political project that it inspired and the prospects for Indian unity that it raised.

Other writers such as Bhaskar Vaman Bhat and S. S. Deo, following Rajwade, emphasized further this militant Hindu interpretation of Ramdas, focusing almost exclusively on the protection of cows and brahmans and the expulsion of Muslims as the core of Maharashtra Dharma. Bhat, in particular, argued that Ramdas was not part of the bhakti tradition at all, but represented the revival of Sanatan Hindu values in Maharashtrian Hinduism, adding for good measure that a culture's vibrancy depended on a healthy balance between bhakti and Sanatan values.[60] Deo grafted Ramdas's message advocating the cultivation of 'God's story, politics and awareness, all the time' on to a political programme for Maharashtra in the current colonial situation: spiritual regeneration, political struggle, and a nationalist awareness of the past through historical research.[61]

One result of the identification of bhakti as Maharashtra Dharma and therefore a source for Maratha political inspiration was the over-determination of a complex and diverse philosophy into a generalized and politicized ideology of religious community. Poets like Tukaram and Ramdas, especially the latter, were too often reduced to overt political stances—as advocating either the rejection or the maintenance of caste identity—obfuscating their complex contributions to the tradition as a whole.[62] Religion, in this connection between bhakti poetry and the Maratha struggle, became less a matter of faith and everyday practice and more an expression of the political philosophy of the Marathas; bhakti now became a variant of a modern 'Hindu' religion, one that was less a spiritual world-view, but more the enumerated political Hindu community. This community could be plural, inclusive and tolerant, as put forward in the writings of Ranade and Bhagvat, but it was still conceived of in political, 'patriotic' terms. In the 1920s, the famous Gandhian Vinoba Bhave cast this integrative approach to

Maharashtra Dharma in an overtly Gandhian programme of Hindu-Muslim unity, interpreting Ramdas's teachings as prescriptions for a modern universalism of brotherhood and social service.[63] A couple of decades later, the socialist leader Lalji Pendse, as part of a broader argument about Shivaji's essentially anti-feudal and pro-peasantry policies, interpreted Ramdas's lament, 'The brahmans have lost their senses, devoid of their morality; they have lost their leadership of society and become disciples instead', as a critique of the decadence of upper-caste Hindus in Maratha society.[64] Despite these dissenting visions, the understanding of Maharashtra Dharma that was to become dominant and popular in the twentieth century was Rajwade's, as an overtly political ideology nurtured in Maharashtra to protect Hinduism across India from Muslim invasions.

Crucial in all these interpretations, however, is the identification of the relationship between region and nation. These arguments over Maharashtra Dharma constructed the Marathas as the pioneers of Indian nationalism, but in doing so they also put them forward as emblems of Maharashtra's own regional identity and significance in the contemporary nation. Indeed, all their differences notwithstanding, Maharashtrian historians were unanimous in invoking the 'uniqueness' of the Maratha experience and citing its importance as a lesson for the colonial situation. To writers like Rajwade and Bhat, hitching the Maratha wagon to a larger Indian cart was a means of expressing Maharashtra's role as the militant leader and protector of the Hindu/Indian nation. As Rajwade argued, the Marathas were not the only leaders who realized the responsibility of protecting the nation from Muslim rulers in the eighteenth century, but the only ones who had the daring, resolve, and qualities of leadership needed to succeed in such an enterprise.[65] Vinoba Bhave, for his part, argued that far from representing regionalism, Maharashtra Dharma incorporated universal bhakti values of devotion, respect and tolerance that were relevant not only to Maharashtra, but to India and the whole world. Lalji Pendse, too, was eager to place the left-led farmers' movement within the broad framework of Maratha history and to claim its legacy of protest for his own political programme. Even Ranade's catholic and integrative approach, however, could not escape this idea of regional leadership and control:

> This feeling of [Maratha] patriotism illustrates most forcibly the characteristic result of the formation of a Nation in the best sense of the

word, and constitutes another reason why the History of the Marathas deserves special study. It is the history of the formation of a true Indian Nationality, raising its head high above the troubled waters of Mohamedan confusion. It was this force . . . which . . . enabled them to dream as a possibility the establishment of a central Hindu padshahi or Empire at Delhi, uniting and controlling all other Native Powers.[66]

This centrality of interpretations of the Maratha past to the characterization of the modern region, religion, and nation makes these historical debates crucial to an understanding of how the Marathi middle classes articulated their regional identity in colonial Maharashtra. The reformist plural approach struck an increasingly discordant note as the nationalist movement progressed under the leadership of Tilak into the twentieth century, and lost out to more muscular and triumphalist visions of the past. It was this vision of religion, region and nation that was overwhelmingly invoked in a range of popular fictional forms and the public arena, contributing to its consolidation as the popular consciousness of the Maratha past.

To highlight the regional imagination it is instructive to contrast the approach of Marathi intellectuals with that of the prominent nationalist historian of the Marathas from Bengal, Jadunath Sarkar. In addition to several articles on Maratha history in English journals such as the Calcutta-based *Modern Review*, Sarkar wrote a biography of Shivaji in 1919, which remained, along with Ranade's work, the principal English-language work by Indians on the Marathas during the colonial period. An erudite, painstaking scholar completely wedded to the Rankean tradition of going straight to the sources, Sarkar was also able to access a wide variety of sources through his mastery of Persian, Marathi, and Arabic. His pompous prose, however, earned him considerable hostility from Maharashtrian historians, some of whom saw in him an Indian version of Duff.[67] He concurred with Duff's statements regarding the Marathas' 'cunning and lack of chivalry', roundly criticised their raiding tactics, and displayed little patience for what he saw as 'chauvinism' in the Maharashtrian appraisals of the Marathas.[68] Sarkar's appraisal of Shivaji was also nationalist, but the differences with that of the writers discussed above is obvious:

[Shivaji] has proved by his example that the Hindu race can build a nation, found a state, defeat enemies; they can conduct their own defence; they can protect and promote literature and art, commerce and industry . . . maintain navies and ocean-trading fleets of their own and conduct naval battles on equal terms with foreigners. He taught the modern Hindus to rise to the full stature of their growth . . . [and] . . . proved that the Hindu race can still produce not only jamaitdars (non-commissioned officers) and chitnises (clerks) but also rulers of men and even a king of kings (Chhatrapati).[69]

Sarkar, therefore, looked for evidence of a broader Hindu modernity in Shivaji; in this celebration of the proof of political and civilizational power of 'the Hindu race' it is not surprising that Maharashtra Dharma found no place. To Marathi writers and activists of different ideological persuasions, however, it became impossible to ignore: if Maharashtra Dharma and the history it embodied was the key to the cultural heritage of the region, it was imperative to stake a claim to this history in their own ideological frameworks. It is worth emphasizing that it was this construction of the importance of Maharashtra Dharma—its wide applicability and perceived relevance across ideological boundaries—that makes narratives of Maratha history central to an understanding of Maharashtrian regional identity.

CONCLUSIONS

As a state created in 1960 through a movement to unite the Marathi-speaking areas of western India, Maharashtra appears at first sight to be the perfect example of a linguistic regional identity. As I have tried to show in this paper through a few, but enormously influential middle-class articulations, however, the imagination of a modern Maharashtrian regional identity has, instead, drawn heavily on narratives of Maratha history, which not only gave it a meaningful space within the new Indian nation but also provided the necessary emotive resources for such a regional imagination. It is necessary to emphasize that the centrality of Maratha narratives does not imply that the Marathi language did not play an important role in shaping Marathi identity. The creation of a more cohesive and modern Marathi language community through the processes of 'print capitalism' provided the social and intellectual space within which this discourse on Maharashtrian identity was articulated. This process itself was crucial in shaping the nature, extent and direction of historical imagination; the role of language in shaping how Marathi speakers understood their identity and their space within the Indian nation, therefore, also has to be seen in the context of the changes Indian languages underwent under colonial modernity, instead of as a given, primordial source of identity.

More broadly, this focus on discursively constructed regional communities reminds us that the eventual establishment of a centralized post-colonial Indian state with its constituent linguistic units should not automatically lead to the assumption that throughout the colonial period, regions were mere linguistic sub-sets of the nation. This is especially so with regions that have not always corresponded to their present political incarnations. Viewing the formation of modern imagined communities at the national and regional levels as a constantly evolving process opens up a theoretical space to explore the many attachments to culture, history and ethnicity across the subcontinent that did not achieve a political 'success' in the current federal arrangement (colonial Hyderabad is a good example), but either found expression—or were subsumed—in a linguistically determined federation. Demands for linguistic states in the 1940s and 1950s also have to be considered in the wider arena of centre-region dynamics, the Congress's privileging of the linguistic principle at the expense of other factors for reorganizing states, and the available possibilities for negotiating regional autonomy.[70] Viewing the region-nation relationship from the Maharashtrian perspective, where no opposition to national discourse arose throughout the colonial period, also alerts us to regional imaginations as being more complex than a mere opposition to the nation. Such a perspective and attention to the relationship between region and nation can provide a more historically nuanced approach to problems of dissidence and demands for autonomy facing the fragile but over-centralized monoliths that are South Asian states today, by replacing the old and tired framework of national integration vs. regionalism with an approach that allows for a greater dialogue and parity between the region and the nation. It is also crucial to a better understanding of the complexity of Indian nationalism and its contested history.

NOTES

1. Baruah 1999; Ramaswamy 1997; Zutshi 2004.
2. Baruah 1999, p. 14.
3. Chatterjee 1986.

4. Baruah 1999, p. 21.
5. Atre, 1998, p. 96.
6. Quoted in Phadke, 1989, p. v.
7. Y. D. Phadke, historian of the colonial period in Maharashtra, shared Shejwalkar's gloom, but was more specific. Maharashtrians were crazy about history, he wrote, but only the period from the birth of Shivaji to the fall of the Peshwai, and he concluded that the ordinary Marathi-speaker, although physically resident in the twentieth century, mentally inhabited this 'medieval' period with considerable enjoyment. More recently, Thomas Blom Hansen has also remarked that 'The Shivaji mythology is a nodal point, the historical fiction at the heart of state practices, political rhetoric and historical imagination in this part of India.' Hansen 2002, p. 21. The mob attack and vandalizing of the Bhandarkar Oriental Research Institute in response to Professor James Laine's recent volume on Shivaji has only reinforced this importance of Maratha narratives to contemporary politics.
8. Deshpande 2002, pp. 15-55.
9. Duff 1863.
10. Sarkar 1997, p. 13.
11. 'Syllabus of Studies for the School Department', in Parulekar and Bakshi 1953, pp. 176-7.
12. This was how Bal Gangadhar Shastri Jambhekar, one of the most talented and prolific of this early generation of intellectuals, described it. Jambhekar 1950, p. 192.
13. Lokahitawadi, also known as Gopal Hari Deshmukh, frequently wrote on historical topics in his famous 'hundred letters' to the Marathi newspaper *Prabhakar* in the 1840s. See S. R. Tikekar 1940. Also see M. G. Ranade 1858.
14. See Telang 1972 [1873].
15. Bhandarkar 1933, p. 363.
16. Ibid., pp. 335-66.
17. Chatterjee 1986.
18. English preface to *Gulamgiri* (Slavery) [1873] in Phadke 1991, pp. 117-18.
19. O'Hanlon 1985, pp. 143-6. The Parashuram myth is a particularly contentious myth and has been the subject of much caste-related controversy throughout the nineteenth and twentieth centuries in Maharashtra. An origin myth about the Chitpavan brahman community, it describes Parashuram, a brahman, as destroying all the kshatriyas in the world, leaving it with only brahmans and shudras. He is also described as bringing to life from a pile of ashes a group of people who became Chitpavan brahmans, literally 'purified from the ashes'. Brahman polemicists in the colonial period used this myth to argue that all non-brahmans were shudras.

20. Jotirao Phule, 'Chhatrapati Shivaji Raja Bhosale Yancha Povada' (The Ballad of Chhatrapati Shivaji Raja Bhosale) [1869], in Phadke 1991, p. 42.
21. Quoted in O'Hanlon 1985, p. 175.
22. Some of these were, for instance, *Journal of the Royal Asiatic Society, Journal of the Bombay Branch of the Royal Asiatic Society, Indian Philosophical Review, Indian Antiquary,* and from the early twentieth century, the *Annals of the Bhandarkar Institute.*
23. Bhandarkar, for instance, sent papers to the International Congress of Orientalists at London in 1876, and attended its Vienna session in 1886. He was an honorary member of the Royal Asiatic Society, the German Oriental Society, the American Oriental Society and the French Institute. Significantly, when the Bhandarkar Oriental Research Institute was inaugurated on Bhandarkar's turning eighty, the festschrift volume published on the occasion included contributions from scholars all across India and Europe, with very few Maharashtrians.
24. Pandit 1995, p. 117.
25. Naregal 2001.
26. Chatterjee 1993, p. 77.
27. For a good biography of Chiplunkar, see Phadke 1982.
28. Chiplunkar 1993, p. 65.
29. Chiplunkar's father, Krishnashastri Chiplunkar, was a senior government official, sometime Oriental Translator to the Government of Bombay, a noted Marathi scholar, and famous for his translation into Marathi of the Arabian Nights. He was also given to an active interest in women, and had several extra-marital affairs, his lifestyle getting him into trouble with the government on more than one occasion. It is possible that this had something to do with the rather severe views of Vishnushastri on this matter.
30. The thought-provoking recent work by Uma Chakravarti on this issue of gender in nineteenth-century Marathi debates on nationalism and social reform also highlights the role that colonial law, with its tremendous departure from Peshwa rules regarding caste and gender, played in creating visions of chaos and disorder in the minds of brahman leaders. Chakravarti 1998. Sumit Sarkar's work on the imagery of 'Kaliyuga', with its insubordinate women and lower castes, also relates to this uneasiness of the upper castes about a general chaos and degeneration. Sarkar 1997, particularly the essay 'Kaliyuga, Chakri and Bhakti'. For a detailed discussion of the relationship between such anxieties and the didactic themes within Maratha historical narratives, especially in fictional renderings, see Deshpande 2002, pp. 100-58.
31. Chiplunkar 1993, pp. 223-42.
32. Ibid., p. 239.
33. Ibid., p. 467.
34. Ibid., pp. 90-1.

35. Chatterjee 1986, pp. 55-8.
36. For the critique of Phule see Chiplunkar 1993, Vol. 1, pp. 441-57. For the essay on Lokahitawadi, see Vol. 2, pp. 1046-1204.
37. For examples, see G. G. Joshi, 'The teaching of History I', *Marathi Shikshak*, July 1912, and 'The teaching of History II', *Marathi Shikshak*, March 1913. He elaborated on the method of telling these stories, one that was echoed in the guidelines given by G. B. Borwankar, the author of one of the most popular Marathi textbooks on Maratha history in the early twentieth century. The stories, which included earlier periods of Deccan history, nevertheless had an emphasis on familiar themes and tales of Shivaji's ancestry, his exploits and so on. Borwankar stressed the importance of narrating these tales without a break with gestures and actions to capture the students' attention. G. B. Borwankar 1921.
38. The journal was priced at 4 annas per issue, and an annual subscription was only Rs. 2, if paid in advance.
39. Cf. Sarkar 1997, 'Kaliyuga, Chakri and Bhakti'.
40. Rajwade is generally viewed in Maharashtra as the Father of Modern History and there is a wealth of biographical work on him. For two recent examples, see Joshi 1965; and S. S. Puranik 1989.
41. Jadunath Sarkar's biographical piece on Rajwade has some of these interesting anecdotes. On one occasion, Sarkar writes, 'when about to leave a village in disappointment, [Rajwade] turned fiercely upon the rustic owner of a bundle of historical letters who had refused to let him copy them, and cried out, "These papers are of no use to you, but important for my purpose. Give them to me. . . . You refuse! Well, I shall get them from your widow when she offers them for sale to some dry grocer as waste paper!" ' On another occasion, it appears, Rajwade rescued a bundle of waste paper from a grocer's shop in Paithan, which yielded twenty-three precious letters in the original, eventually published in the first edition of his *Sources of Maratha History*. See Sarkar 1940 [1925], pp. 262-78.
42. Ibid., p. 273.
43. Kulkarni 1993, p. 133.
44. The academically inclined Collector of Nasik district, A. M. Jackson, commented, 'Government is aware that a school of thought has grown up in the Presidency which looks back to the rule of the Peshwas as a sort of golden age and seeks evidence in support of this belief . . . a selection made by the adherents of this school of thought is likely to give too bright a picture of the period and therefore to encourage political dreams which can do no good either to the dreamers or to the Government.' Ibid., p. 135.
45. The *Kavyetihas Sangraha*, started by Sane, Modak, and Chiplunkar, ran, despite intermittent hiccups, for nearly twelve years and by the end of its pioneering run had published 22 *bakhars* and 501 historical letters,

petitions, and other material. Following it there appeared several such journals, which did not have much financial backing and barely survived. Notable among these were two journals edited by Dattatraya Balavant Parasnis, *Bharatvarsha* (1898-9) and the longer running *Itihas Sangraha* (1908-15). Another project that was financially ruinous but extremely valuable was the Miraj-based Vasudeoshastri Khare's journal and later edited volumes, *Aitihasik Lekhasangraha* (1897-1924). The bulk of the material that was published in these journals and volumes was culled from private collections of smaller chiefs and landlords. Besides these specialized periodicals, documents were also published in popular literary journals such as the *Vividh Dnyan Vistaar* and, later, the nationalist newspaper *Kesari*.

46. Notable among these was the Durbar of Dhar, which patronized and financed a history of their domains by K. K. Lele, an official in the Dhar administration. The chief of Aundh too took a keen interest. Anant Narayan Bhagvat, an enthusiastic researcher, deeply disappointed after being refused permission to use the Peshwa *daftar*, went to the princely durbars of Bhor and Phaltan (south of Pune) and requested permission to use their collections and write their histories. Later, as an official of the Indore court, Bhagvat also published some material relating to the Holkars. See Potdar 1935, p. 28, for details.
47. Sayajirao commissioned a Marathi series called *Rashtrakathamala* along the lines of the English 'Story of the Nations' in 1892, and accordingly, histories of Iran, Carthage, Turkestan, ancient France, Spain and the Moors, Germany, Assyria, and Rome were written by different Marathi writers, some translated from English works, others original works. Ibid., p. 80.
48. Cf. Dalmia 1999.
49. This essay was later included in Ranade 1951, p. 78.
50. These poems are included in Karandikar 1982, p. 158.
51. Ranade 1951, p. 92
52. Ibid., pp. 3-4.
53. Bhagvat 1979, pp. 220-1.
54. Joshi 1991, p. 31.
55. For a particularly ferocious critique, see Phatak 1953, pp. 289-303.
56. Joshi 1992, pp. 283-8.
57. Ibid., p. 336.
58. Ibid., p. 32.
59. See 'Shahaji the Foundation Builder of Maratha Power' in Ibid., pp. 205-30.
60. Bhat 1925, pp. 34, 39.
61. Deo 1906.
62. N. R. Phatak's learned study of Ramdas's philosophy strongly argues against his interpretation for political purposes. Phatak places Ramdas

firmly within the bhakti tradition, despite his differences with other poets like Tukaram in the specific method he advocated for devotion and spirituality. The main difference lay in Ramdas's emphasis on cultivating this world and body through discipline and morality in seeking absolution, in contrast to Tukaram's emphasis on renunciation and otherworldly spirituality. See Phatak 1952, pp. 35-40.

63. Bhave 1928.
64. Pendse 1976 [1946].
65. Joshi 1992, p. 92.
66. Ranade 1951, p. 4.
67. Sarkar, who received a vitriolic response from the Marathi press when he reiterated Duff's argument about Shivaji's illiteracy, retained a haughty disregard for his Marathi critics; in his letters to his friend and fellow historian G. S. Sardesai, he referred to the comments of one as 'inspired by ignorance and spite' and to another as an 'infernal liar'. He routinely dismissed the publication of new documents in Marathi journals as 'worthless' and despaired of what he called the 'Poona circle' of 'chauvinist' historians, some of whom distributed handbills protesting his interpretations during his tour to Maharashtra in 1930. See Tikekar 1964. Bhaskar Vaman Bhat's response to Sarkar's work, in turn, was representative of this very circle:

    We do feel a sense of respect [for Jadunath Sarkar and other Bengali historians] for writing [on Maratha history] using newly unearthed materials, but no Maharashtrian can avoid a sense of dismay at their generally prejudicial approach. Instead of trying to explain the ideals that inspired Maharashtrian political leaders in the seventeenth century, they have merely subscribed to the notion of Marathas as robbers. The Bengalis are closer to us than the British. Our culture and religion is one. We are therefore disappointed that they have participated in the spread of this untruth. . . . Maharashtrians have been writing about their history well before Sarkar and other Bengali historians . . . their discussions have established Maharashtra Dharma as the basis for the Maratha struggle.

    Bhat 1925, p. 6.
68. Sarkar 1940, p. 436.
69. Ibid., pp. 442-3.
70. See, in this context, Ayesha Jalal's discussion of the Akali Dal's demand for a Punjabi *suba* in this period. Jalal 1995, pp. 166-7.

REFERENCES

Atre, Prahlad Keshav. 1998. *Karhecha Pani, Atmacharitra* (*Waters of the Karha: Autobiography*). 5th edn. 5 vols. Vol. 5. Mumbai: G. P. Parchure Prakashan.

Baruah, Sanjib. 1999. *India against Itself: Assam and the Politics of Nationality*. Philadelphia: University of Pennsylvania Press.

Bhagvat, Durga, ed. 1979. *Rajaramshastri Bhagvat Yanche Nivadak Sahitya* (*Selected Writings of Rajaramshastri Bhagvat*). 5 vols. Vol. 5. Pune: Varada Books.

Bhandarkar, Ramkrishna Gopal. 1933 [1888]. 'The Critical, Comparative and Historical Method of Inquiry'. In *Collected Works of Sir R. G. Bhandarkar*, edited by Narayan Bapuji Utgikar and Vasudev Gopal Paranjpe. 4 vols. Poona: Bhandarkar Oriental Research Institute.

Bhat, Bhaskar Vaman. 1925. *Maharashtra Dharma Arthat Marathyañcya Itihasace Atmika Svarupa* (*Maharashtra Dharma or the Essence of Maratha History*). Dhule: Satkaryottejak Sabha.

Bhave, Vinoba. 1928. *Maharashtra Dharma* 1, No. 1.

Borwankar, G. B. 1921. *Maharashtracha Goshtiroop Itihaas* (*Maharashtra's History in Story Form*). 12th edn. Pune: n.p.

Chakravarti, Uma. 1998. *Rewriting History: The Life and Times of Pandita Ramabai*. New Delhi: Kali for Women, Book Review Literary Trust.

Chatterjee, Partha. 1992. *The Nation and Its Fragments: Colonial and Postcolonial Histories*. New Delhi: Oxford University Press.

———. 1986. *Nationalist Thought and the Colonial World: A Derivative Discourse?* New Delhi: Oxford University Press.

Chiplunkar, Vishnu Krishna. 1993. *Nibandhamala* (*A Garland of Essays*). 5th edn. 2 vols. Pune: Varada Books.

Dalmia, Vasudha. 1999. *The Nationalization of Hindu Traditions: Bharatendu Harischandra and Nineteenth-Century Banaras*. New Delhi: Oxford University Press.

Deo, Shankar Srikrishna, ed. 1906. *Shri Samarthanchi Don Juni Charitre* (*Two Old Biographies of Samarth Ramdas*). Dhule: Satkaryottejak Sabha.

Deshpande, Prachi. 2002. 'Narratives of Pride: History and Regional Identity in Maharashtra, *c*. 1870-1960'. Ph.D. dissertation, Tufts University.

Duff, James Grant. 1863. *History of the Mahrattas*. Indian reprint edn. Bombay: Exchange Press.

Hansen, Thomas Blom. 2002. *Wages of Violence: Naming and Identity in Postcolonial Bombay*. Princeton: Princeton University Press.

Jambhekar, Ganesh Gangadhar, ed. 1950. *Memoirs and Writings of Acharya Bal Gangadhar Shastri Jambhekar, 1812-1846: Pioneer of the Renaissance in Western India and Father of Modern Maharashtra*. 4 vols. Poona: G. G. Jambhekar.

Joshi, Lakshmanshastri, ed. 1992. *Rajwade-Lekhasangraha* (*Selected Writings of Rajwade*). 4th edn. New Delhi: Sahitya Akademi.

Joshi, Pralhad Narahar. 1965. *Rajwade Vichardarshan* (*The Thought of V. K. Rajwade*). Pune: Venus Prakashan.

Joshi, Shankar Narayan, ed. 1991. *Rajwade Lekhasangraha* (*Collected Writings of Rajwade*). 2 vols. Pune: Varada Books.

Karandikar, V. R., ed. 1982. *Samartha Ramdas: Vivekadarshan* (*Samarth Ramdas: Glimpses of Wisdom*). New Delhi: Sahitya Akademi.

Kulkarni, A. R., ed. 1993. *History in Practice: Historians and Sources of Medieval Deccan-Marathas*. New Delhi: Books & Books.

Naregal, Veena. 2001. *Language Politics, Elites, and the Public Sphere*. New Delhi: Permanent Black.

O'Hanlon, Rosalind. 1985. *Caste, Conflict, and Ideology: Mahatma Jotirao Phule and Low Caste Protest in Nineteenth-Century Western India*. Cambridge: Cambridge University Press.

Pandit, Maya. 1995. 'Translation Culture and the Colonial Discourse in Nineteenth Century Maharashtra'. In *Explorations in Applied Linguistics: M. V. Nadkarni Felicitation Volume*, edited by P. N. Paranjpe and M. V. Nadkarni. Pune: Shubhada Saraswat Prakashan.

Parulekar, Ramchandra Vithhal, and C. L. Bakshi, eds. 1953. *Selections from the Records of the Government of Bombay*. 2 vols. Bombay: Asia Publishing House.

Pendse, Lalji Moreshvar. 1976. *Dharma Ki Kranti? Shivakaryache Vastava Svarupa* (*Religion or Revolution? The True Picture of Shivaji's Legacy*). 2nd edn. Mumbai: Abhinava Prakashan.

Phadke, Y. D. 1982. *V. K. Chiploonkar*. New Delhi: National Book Trust.

———. 1989. *Visavya Shatakatila Maharashtra* (*Maharashtra in the Twentieth Century*). 1st edn. 5 vols. Sasvad, Pune: Srividya Prakashan/Sasavada Ashrama Vishvasta Mandala.

———, ed. 1991. *Mahatma Phule Samagra Vanmaya* (*Collected Works of Mahatma Phule*). Revised 5th edn. Mumbai: Maharashtra Rajya Sahitya ani Sãskrti Mandal.

Phatak, Narhar Raghunath. 1953. *Ramdas Vangmayá Ani Karya* (*Ramdas: Life and Work*). Mumbai: Mauj Prakashan.

Potdar, Datto Vaman. 1935. *Marathi Itihasa Va Itihasasansodhana Vihangama Nirikshana* (*A Critical Survey of Marathi Historical Research*). Pune: Vishnu Panduranga Nene.

Puranik, S. S. 1989. *Vishwanath Kashinath Rajwade, Vyaktitva, Kartrtva, va Vichara* (*Personality, Contribution and Thought of V. K. Rajwade*). Pune: Raviraj Prakashan.

Ramaswamy, Sumathi. 1997. *Passions of the Tongue: Language Devotion in Tamil India, 1891-1970*. Berkeley: University of California Press.

Ranade, Mahadev Govind. 1858. 'English Essay Beta'. *Elphinstone School Paper*.

———. 1951. *Rise of the Maratha Power*. 2nd edn. Bombay: University of Bombay.

Sarkar, Sir Jadunath. 1940 [1925]. *House of Shivaji* (*Studies and Documents of Maratha History: Royal Period*). Calcutta: S. N. Sarkar.

———. 1919. *Shivaji and His Times*. Calcutta: S. C. Sarkar and Sons.

Sarkar, Sumit. 1997. *Writing Social History*. New Delhi: Oxford University Press.

Tikekar, Shripad Ramachandra. 1964. *On Historiography: A Study of Methods of Historical Research and Narration of J. N. Sarkar, G. S. Sardesai and P. K. Gode*. Bombay: Popular Prakashan.

———, ed. 1940. *Lokahitavadinchi Shatapatre (The Hundred Letters of Lokahitavadi)*. Aundh: Usha Prakashana.

Zutshi, Chitralekha. 2004. *Languages of Belonging: Islam, Regional Identity, and the Making of Kashmir*. New York: Oxford University Press.

4

Self-Definitions and Otherness: Contexts and Sources of Early Imaginings in Late-Nineteenth-Century Orissa

Bishnu N. Mohapatra

> We think that due to lack of cooperation from the Oriyas themselves, the government plans are not yielding the desired result. The government, therefore, does not feel inclined to undertake any better projects for Orissa. To the question as to why Oriyas are so apathetic towards the Government plans, our answer will be: their laziness is responsible for such a sorry state of affairs. They are only willing to work for the barest necessities of life—a little food and a piece of clothing—and once these are procured, they while away the rest of the day sleeping, gossiping and playing rather frivolous games. If these people are not lazy then who else answers to this description?[1]

So wrote an anonymous contributor in 1876 in an article entitled 'Why is Orissa in such a lamentable state?' The above passage reflects a preoccupation with 'identity' by generalizing about the collective predicament of Oriyas. Towards the end of the nineteenth century, a genre of writing reflecting these concerns had come into being. An overriding concern with the questions of Oriya identity, character, and above all the dismal condition of the Oriyas was its recurring theme. The question that emerges is, how did such an image of the Oriya come into being? In 1828, Hamilton wrote in the *East India Gazetteer* very much in these terms about the Oriya character:

> The Oorea nation [is] justly described by Abul Fazel as effeminate. They are likewise so dull and stupid that in all ages, and under all governments, since the downfal[l] of the Orissan monarchy, the principal official employments have been always engrossed by foreigners: Bengalese from the north, and Telingas from the South.[2]

Such a portrayal of the Oriyas was a far from isolated phenomenon; most of the colonial literature[3] and documents abounded in descriptions of the Oriyas as timid, stupid, or backward.[4] The Oriyas, to most of the colonial administrators of that time, occupied the lowest rung of civilization. According to Stirling, an official of the colonial government, Oriyas 'rank the lowest in the scale of moral and intellectual excellence, of any people on this side of India'.[5] When Hunter was writing the history of Orissa, he was certainly conscious of giving something new to the British public. It was a history of a historyless people; a people without historical characters and events. In the introduction to his book, Hunter wrote:

> This book endeavours to delineate the inner life of an Indian Province. It tries to bring home to the imagination and understanding of English men, a state of society and forms of human existence far removed from their own. The narrative is embellished by no splendid historical characters, nor does it possess the interest which belongs to striking crimes. To the World's roll-call of heroes it will add not one name. The people with whom it treats have fought no great battle for human liberty, nor have they succeeded even in the more primary task of subduing the forces of nature to the control of man. To them the world stands indebted for not a single discovery which augments the comforts or mitigates the calamities of life. Even in literature—the peculiar glory of the Indian race—they have won no conspicuous triumph. They have written no famous epic; they have struck out no separate school of philosophy; they have elaborated no new system of law.[6]

The above statements are not just ethnocentric observations made by Hunter; underlying them lies the justification for British rule in Orissa. 'If we won the great Province of Orissa with little loss to ourselves', wrote Hunter, 'it is because we deserved to do so.'[7] By the end of the century, pejorative descriptions of Oriyas had become an official orthodoxy. According to Stanley P. Rice, an official in the Madras Presidency, there were two reasons for the persistence of these views about Oriyas. In the first place, he wrote:

> there is a tradition that the Uriya is an inferior animal, and hence arises a desire to prove that tradition correct—by a posteriori arguments, if by nothing better. . . . But there is another cause. It is in just those avocations of life in which the Uriya is thrown into contact with the European, that he fails. . . . Here, then, we have a key to the Englishman's opinion of the Uriya. The two gods that sit in the highest places in his national temple are energy and cleanliness.[8]

These opinions held by the colonial officers were to a great measure internalized by some of the Oriyas themselves, although undoubtedly a product of the colonial encounter. Whether such characterizations of Oriyas are true or false or whether they ever correspond to historical facts is not the question here.[9] The crucial point at issue, as rightly pointed out by Edward Said elsewhere,[10] is how to analyse the 'exteriority' or representation of this body of ideas and above all the colonial politics that institutionalize and reproduce such thoughts in the minds of the 'native' people themselves. The encounter of the British with the Oriyas or for that matter with other ethnic groups in India was bound to be an uneven one. It was the interaction between the ruler and the ruled, where the ruler had to rule not only by sheer coercive power but by an ideological system in which the colonial subjects would lose their subjectivity. Hence it is in this context of power that such encounters can best be grasped and explained.

It may be argued that the vigorous assertion of identity on the part of the Oriyas was a significant consequence of colonial rule. During the colonial period the ethnic consciousness of the Oriyas took a more concrete shape. This was also the phase when Oriyas attempted to enter politics as a distinct ethnic group. However, it would be incorrect to assume that Oriyas did not possess any sense of collective identity in the pre-colonial period. We do not have sufficient historical materials pertaining to this period to reconstruct a detailed account of the self-consciousness of the Oriyas, but historians have found that, beginning in the twelfth century, kings of the Ganga Vamsa and then the Surya Vamsa made the god Jagannath the supreme deity of Orissa. By proclaiming themselves the 'divine agents' of Jagannath, the kings gained legitimacy not only from their subjects but also from the smaller Hindu feudatory kings.[11] For the Oriyas, during this period, Jagannath represented not merely an important religious deity but also a part of their cultural identity. As the Orissan empire fell into the hands of the Afghans in 1568, it disintegrated into various small political units. As the new rulers were Muslims, Jagannath became even more important for Hindu kings as a powerful symbol motivating them and their subjects to fight against the Muslim rulers.

An insightful essay on this theme has drawn attention to the elements of ethnic consciousness, an 'awareness of unity' among the Oriyas, in the pre-colonial period.[12] Drawing upon a number of literary and religious sources of the period, Dash has suggested that Oriyas, in spite of living in separate kingdoms, had an awareness of belonging to a broad cultural region.[13] In the Rajabhoga section of the *Madala Panji* (the Drum Chronicle) written around AD 1600, the expression 'Odissa' referred not to any particular administrative unit but to such a cultural region.[14] The Oriya language was an important component of this cultural unity. The language also became a marker which informed the Oriyas' sense of difference with others. For instance, in 'Jagannath Charitamrta', written probably in the seventeenth century, the poet Dibakar Das mentioned two Vaisnava sects (dividing them in terms of the language they spoke), Utkali (speaking Oriya) and Bengali Vaisnavas.[15] In the author's view, Jagannath became an important symbol which united the Oriyas and also played a major role in Oriya nationalism.

Pilgrimage to Puri—the place of Jagannath—seems in the pre-colonial days to have played a vital role in making Oriyas from different regions aware of their common linguistic and cultural identity. At a time when the mobility of the common people was limited and travelling was difficult, pilgrimage to Puri must have provided the Oriyas with opportunities to reflect on their broader identity. There is also evidence that the Oriyas (in all Oriya-speaking tracts) in the eighteenth century were using a time calendar (known as Anka) that was distinct from those of other areas.

Can it then be concluded that the Oriyas had a notion of collective identity in the pre-colonial period? At best the evidence suggests a rudimentary awareness among the literati of their language and culture. It would, therefore, be incorrect to argue that Oriyas in the pre-colonial period possessed an ethnic consciousness and reflected seriously on their identity. But during the colonial period a rudimentary awareness of language and culture was transformed into an articulate ethnic consciousness. This consciousness in turn acquired a political salience in the colonial period which was unknown in previous centuries. It is only in this sense that the Oriyas' articulation of their identity, and reflections on their collective situations, were products of the colonial context.

One important element that underlined the colonial context was that of domination; and this domination posed various kinds of threat to the Oriyas and created a sense of helplessness among them. The uprising of 1817 in Khurda—popularly known as the Paik rebellion—and a few unsuccessful insurrections of the tribals and feudatory kings against British rule indicate how the interests of the old kings and zamindars were affected by the colonial policies. The Oriyas, like several other communities elsewhere in India, perceived a threat to their age-old customs, religious and social practices. An example of the new dispensation brought into being by the British rule may be seen through the eyes of a poet:

> People would use their pockets for carrying Pan (betel leaves) and would think nothing of touching the infidels. They would not take off their shoes while drinking water. However, these changes were inevitable in Kali Yuga. They would even eat Palau (rice with meat) and would not care to take off their shirts. They had taken a fancy to alien vegetables such as cauliflower, carrots, and beetroots and ate off glass plates. They would not feel ashamed of putting on English clothes. While they are ready to give alms to the blind and crippled, they despise and attack Brahmins. They would even take their meals in ferries and while travelling on trains. They have taken a liking to smoking tobacco. All these deviations are to be expected in 'Kali Yuga'.[16]

This passage, ostensibly written in the apocalyptic vein, represents an extreme form of reaction to British rule. The writings reflecting such anxieties, however, were not representative of Oriya perception of British rule at that time. Such reactions manifested the helplessness of the Oriyas (mostly from the upper caste) in the face of what was seen as the British assault on Hindu customs and religious practices.

The Oriya Hindus certainly did not like their most revered deity, Jagannath, being attacked by British officials and missionaries. To Stirling, Jagannath, 'the most hideous of all the figures', was nothing more than 'wooden busts, about six feet in height, fashioned into a rude resemblance of the human head resting on a sort of pedestal'.[17] To the missionaries (who arrived in Orissa in 1822 and established the Baptist mission at Cuttack) and to some officials, an attack against Jagannath and the annual chariot festival was an assault on the social and religious practices of the Oriya Hindus. In their view, Oriyas were backward, 'steeped in idolatry, and were enslaved by priestcraft'.[18] By about the middle of the nineteenth century, the campaign of the missionaries against Jagannath had reached its peak. Several pamphlets ridiculing Jagannath (in Oriya) were distributed.[19]

The perceived threat and the sense of helplessness formed the context in which the Oriyas were engaged in acts of self-reflection.[20] However, the perceived fear of the intrusion of alien values and religion had little effect on Oriya elites' overall assessment of colonial rule. An attitude of diffidence existed alongside an unconcealed enthusiasm for British rule. The Oriyas conveyed their gratitude to the British for having rescued them from the oppressive and anarchic rule of the Marathas. For their part, most of the colonial administrators justified and legitimized British rule by constantly harking back to the misrule of the Marathas.[21] Between the assertion of Oriya identity and the veneration for British rule, many Oriyas saw no contradiction. However, such a feeling of ambivalence, if not contradiction, continued to characterize this new consciousness. An anonymous writer in a letter to *Utkal Dipika* wrote:

> . . . O my dear sons! Awake. There is no more time to be wasted. . . . If you have warmth in your blood and if you have real devotion towards me, rise to the occasion. Take the vow to serve your nation (swadesha) today. . . . Hail the British Crown! Glory to your rule, to your teachings! It is thanks to your rule since 1803, I am alive. For you my prestige has been enhanced. The darkness of ignorance has disappeared to some extent. Upon your rule depends the future of my children. Uphold the honour of the British flag by helping my children. Yours affectionately, (Mother Utkal).[22]

A positive attitude towards colonial rule was not only typical of Orissa but prevailed elsewhere in India too. Underlying the positive evaluation of colonial rule was the desire of the Oriyas to forge a collective consciousness on which depended the improvement of their conditions. To many historians, the overt presence of such consciousness was a post-1866 phenomenon. 1866—popularly known as Na-Anka, the ninth regnal year of the King of Puri—was the year of a catastrophic famine in Orissa that constituted a turning point in the history of Orissa.[23] On a rough estimate, nearly a third of the population of the coastal districts perished in this famine. Such was the magnitude of the loss that Na-anka has become the synonym for famine. This historic disaster[24] exposed the callousness of the colonial state and the vulnerability of the people. The decades that followed witnessed the beginnings of developmental activities in the state; educational activities also got a boost for the first time in Orissa. The changing situation led to the gradual articulation of interests among the Oriya middle class.[25]

The assertion of identity depended as much upon the internal realities of Oriya society as it did upon external factors. In other words, the concerns that manifested themselves in the perceptions of the Oriyas and the nature and the contents of their self-reflections were inextricably linked to their position within the empire. In the initial phase, Oriyas were defining their identity not only against alien rule but against other communities. In Cuttack, Puri, and Balasore, the Oriyas were asserting their identity *vis-à-vis* the Bengalis and in the Madras presidency against the Telugus; in the Central Provinces they had to struggle against the Hindustanis. It is, therefore, pertinent to ask under what conditions Oriyas conceived themselves as members of a nationality. In other words, what were the circumstances that facilitated the assertion of their identity? The emergence of Oriya consciousness can best be understood by looking into the complex interaction of various factors, economic, social, and cultural. Thus it is essential to outline briefly the political economy of Orissa during the period under study.

The first vital contact between the rural society of Orissa and British rule occurred mainly through the Company's drive to maximize the traditional share of the state in the produce of the country in the form of land revenue. The land revenue administration of the British ushered in a new era of exploitation in the history of Orissa. The revenue assessment, made in ignorance of the real assets on the basis of the reports of interested subordinates, was excessive.[26] Compared with the last twelve years of Maratha rule (1791-1803), the land revenue of the new government in 1804-5 increased by about 12 per cent. The period between 1805-97 witnessed a further increase of 93 per cent.[27] As the landlords in Orissa often failed to pay the exorbitant land revenue in time, this led to massive land sales. In the first few decades alone, more than half the Oriya landlords were dispossessed of their estates. This phenomenon was not merely confined to Orissa; indeed it was a repetition of what had happened in Bengal a few decades earlier. For the Oriya zamindars, however, there was an additional problem: as the lands were auctioned in distant Calcutta and transport was never adequate,[28] the Oriya landlords became easy prey to the machinations of the Bengali speculators. Thus most of the big estates in the districts of Cuttack and Balasore came to be owned by absentee Bengali landlords. During the settlement of 1897-8, 15 out of 29 principal estates (each yielding revenue of 6,000 rupees or more), were owned by Bengalis.[29] It is easy to imagine the threat this must have posed to the Oriya zamindars.

The proletarianization of the peasantry on a massive scale was one of the catastrophic effects of the penetration of colonialism into the agrarian society of Orissa. Rural indebtedness among the Oriya peasants reached phenomenal proportions by the end of the nineteenth century. According to Maddox

> If we expect well-to-do raiyats holding themselves 8 or 10 acres or more land, there are very few cultivators not in debt to the mahajan (money lender). Enquiries made by the Assistant Settlement officers have not resulted in much definite information, but it appears to be well established that the petty cultivator pays away as rent and interest the whole of this crop, except what is left for subsistence allowance, and has almost always to borrow again before the next harvest is ripe.[30]

Perpetual indebtedness forced the peasants to migrate to Calcutta and Assam, where they took up menial jobs in order to survive. Since agriculture in Orissa was less productive and largely based on 'mono-crop', it was not only small peasants who suffered during the British rule; the fate of artisans and people involved in the manufacturing of salt was hardly any better.

In precolonial times and at the beginning of the colonial period, salt was a thriving manufacturing industry in Orissa. By monopolizing the salt trade, the British made an enormous profit exporting salt to neighbouring provinces. By the end of the nineteenth century, however, salt manufacturing had reached a stage of gradual decay. First Liverpool salt and then Madras salt edged the Orissa salt out of the market. Fakirmohan Senapati, the noted Oriya novelist, who had himself worked in the salt manufacturing industry, wrote in his autobiography: 'the Laxmi (Goddess of wealth) left Orissa and came to reside now in Liverpool'.[31] Similarly, the weaving industry, predictably, could not compete with mechanical looms and in consequence fell into disuse.

We do not have enough data to sustain a comparison of Orissa's economy with that of Bengal. Yet there is no question that Orissa did constitute one of the most backward parts of the Bengal Presidency. Perhaps one might explain this by using the 'centre-periphery' model. It is quite tempting to analyse the assertion of Oriya identity as a reaction against the developed metropolis, in this instance

Calcutta. Such an argument forms the core of the 'internal colonialism' thesis.[32] It treats the phenomenon of internal colonialism as an inevitable product of capitalist industrialization. According to this approach, the uneven wave of modernization creates relatively advanced and less advanced groups. As a consequence, the unequal distribution of resources and power between the two groups becomes crystallized. Since the dominant group seeks to maintain the system, the subordinated groups are denied access to the benefits generated by the system. This form of stratification or, as Hechter terms it, the 'cultural division of labour'[33] finally leads to the ethnic identification of two distinct groups. Nationalism, or the assertion of a collective identity, on this view, is an inescapable reaction to such a structure of uneven economic development. This approach certainly throws light on an important aspect of Oriya nationalism and goes some way towards explaining the assertion of Oriya identity against the dominant communities such as the Bengalis in the coastal districts of Orissa. In the newspapers of this period, one can often read of the Oriyas comparing their situation with that of people in Bengal.[34]

However, there are certain limitations of this thesis. Oriya nationalism, of course, emerged when very little industrialization had taken place in India. Second, this approach considers the assertion of identity as a symptom of the relative economic backwardness of one community *vis-à-vis* a prosperous one. This explanation, therefore, does not sufficiently account for the cultural dimension of Oriya nationalism and underplays the role of education and the bureaucracy in the emergence and articulation of regional consciousness in Orissa.

The limitations of the 'internal colonialism thesis' are not merely due to its restricted definition of nationalism. It is the colonial context which also makes the thesis, at least in its European variant, less useful for our purpose. The tension between the Oriya middle class and their counterparts, therefore, should not be seen as a conflict between the exploited and exploiters. The uneven development of the colonial period was a major factor which led to the tensions and ultimately mediated the growth of regional consciousness in Orissa.

By the late nineteenth century the consciousness of one's own backwardness was one of the dominant features of the emerging Oriya consciousness. Throughout the nineteenth century, attempts were made to analyse the causes of Oriya backwardness. Besides analysing the causes of economic backwardness, the middle class focused its attention specifically on the problems of education and employment in Orissa. Once again, it was the colonial context which made the questions significant.

The rise of a vast network of bureaucracy during the colonial period meant, among other things, employment opportunities for Indians. In order to keep the cost of bureaucracy low, the British recruited a sizeable number of Indians to various low-ranking jobs. The introduction of English education in the nineteenth century was designed not merely to impart knowledge to the Indians, or to 'promote the advance of modern civilization'[35] in India; in fact English education was the key to government employment and a passport to literate professions. In the Bengal presidency, the earliest beneficiaries of English education were mostly Bengalis. By the mid-nineteenth century, English education had taken firm root in Bengal and the Bengalis had emerged as a powerful professional class in India.

The Oriyas lagged far behind. In comparison to Bengal, the spread of education in Orissa was slow and consequently the growth of an Oriya professional class was retarded. Hence the anxieties of the Oriyas and their efforts to promote education in Orissa. This situation led to tension and rivalry between the Oriya middle class and their counterparts. For instance, Bengalis had settled in Orissa long before the advent of the British. There is evidence to suggest that during the rule of the Mughals and Marathas, Bengalis came to Orissa as administrators and revenue officials.[36] But it was during colonial rule that tension surfaced between the Oriyas and Bengalis. The size of the Bengali population in Orissa was not the cause of the tension.[37] The root cause was the preponderance of the Bengalis in government offices and in educational institutions in Orissa. In the Oriya-speaking areas of the Madras presidency, the dominant position of the Telugu middle class was responsible for the rivalry between them and the Oriyas.

The spread of education, which could have led to the rise of a middle class in Orissa, was extremely slow. In the 1820s, the missionaries had established a few schools in Orissa. By the mid-nineteenth century, there was only one English school with 85 students and eight vernacular schools with 194 students in Orissa.[38] Wood's Despatch in 1854 was a crucial turning point in the spread of primary education in Orissa. The government's effort to popularize elementary education came in the shape of financial aid to a large number of schools.[39] Within a few years the impact of the new educational policy was evident. In 1870-1, in the three districts of Orissa, Cuttack, Puri, and Balasore, for example, 5,799 pupils were studying in 131 schools.[40] In 1875, the number of students and schools increased to 10,196 and 539 respectively.[41] By the end of the nineteenth century there were 111,795 pupils in 6,480 schools. In the last decade of the nineteenth century the actual number of literate males in Orissa increased by 15 per cent.[42]

These statistics hide the Oriyas' abnormally low share at the higher levels of education. Even as late as 1868, only ten out of fifty-eight students who passed the entrance examination in Orissa were Oriyas, and the rest were immigrant Bengalis.[43] In Ganjam, Oriyas were the most backward even in secondary education. For example, in 1882-3, only thirteen Oriya students of the Madras presidency qualified for the entrance examination.[44] In 1870,[45] an Oriya graduated for the first time from Calcutta. Even by the end of the century, the number of Oriya graduates was very small.[46] The small number of Oriyas literate in English was another indication of their relative backwardness at higher levels of education.[47]

British officials made much of the conservative attitudes of the Oriyas as a factor in the slow progress of education in Orissa. Commenting on the destruction of the Puri Government School by fire, the collector blamed it on the 'religious bigots' of Puri hostile to English education.[48] But there is evidence to suggest that this was only partially true. The crucial reason was the negligence of the government and the lack of adequate funding. In 1845-6, the demand for an English school in Balasore was rejected on financial grounds. The Inspector of schools mentioned this fact in his letter to the Director of Public Instruction:

> For the whole of Orissa, with an area of 52,995 square miles, and population of 4,534,813 souls, less is expended than for the small district of Howrah with an area of 800 square miles and a population of 750,000 souls; the expending in the former for grants-in-aid, and Government schools, inclusive of the school in the estates of Khoorda and Ungool being rupees 552, and in the latter 657 a month.[49]

The lack of progress at the higher levels of education was also partly due to poverty. Oriyas who attained the middle-school level education soon found it impossible to pursue higher education. Naturally, the need for employment was more important than that for higher education. Others, who foresaw the difficulties in obtaining government employment, saw no point in joining educational institutions.

The position of the Oriyas with regard to jobs reflected their relative backwardness in education.[50] As L. S. S. O'Malley wrote in the *District Gazetteer*:

> When we first acquired the province in 1803, there was scarcely a single native of Orissa in Government Employ[ment]. . . . All the best ministerial appointments were consequently in the hands of the Bengali clerks, who, attracted by high pay that had to be offered to procure the requisite standard of efficiency, left their homes in Bengal, and bringing their families with them, settled in the province and became naturalized Oriyas.[51]

In the beginning, the dominant position of the Bengalis with regard to government jobs in Orissa was not due to their English education, as Persian was the language of court and revenue offices until 1837. The late annexation of Orissa, nearly fifty years after that of Bengal, seemed to have contributed to the early recruitment of Bengalis in Orissa.[52] Later, the relative backwardness of the Oriyas at the higher level of education reinforced the dominance of Bengalis. One explanation often put forward for this state of affairs was that Oriyas were not sufficiently qualified for the jobs. There is, however, evidence to suggest that there was also large-scale discrimination against Oriyas. Fakirmohan Senapati wrote in his autobiography:

> During that period, intense rivalry existed between Oriyas and Bengalis. In all government Offices, senior officials were Bengalis and they wanted to replace the Oriya language by Bengali. In order to achieve this objective, they spared no efforts to recruit Bengalis whenever vacancies arose. Even in departments as big as the Public Works and Telegraph, there was not a single Oriya. . . . Since I made efforts to expose this through my writings and speeches, I was treated as an enemy by Bengalis; out of spite, they used to refer to me not by my name but as 'Sala[53] ring leader'.[54]

Fakirmohan fought against the Bengali dominance in Balasore. In the 1860s, while working as a teacher in Barabati School, he had to suffer humiliation at the hands of his Bengali colleagues and the Bengali zamindar who was also an influential member of the school committee. In his autobiography, Fakirmohan recalled how out of seven members of the school committee, he was the only Oriya while the rest were Bengalis; and how the zamindar unsuccessfully tried to throw him out of the committee. In the Education Department, which was one of the largest employers of educated Indians, Oriyas were only to be found in the village schools, 'pathsalas' and as pandits in vernacular schools. For example in 1872-3, Bengalis occupied 'all the highly paid appointments in the Government schools'.[55]

If in the Orissa division the position of the Oriyas with regard to government employment was bad, the situation of the Oriyas in Ganjam (in the Madras presidency) was definitely worse. As late as 1906, of the 214 government jobs (within a salary range of 15 to 250 rupees per month) in Ganjam only 21 were held by Oriyas.[56] All the higher posts in the district were monopolized by the Telugus. In Ganjam, the Collector wrote that 'there [were] no Uriya Deputy collectors, district munsifs or Tahsildars and only two deputy Tahsildars. There [were] no Inspectors of police, Inspector of salt and *abkari* and forest Rangers. There [were] no Uriya engineers or overseers.'[57]

The relative backwardness in education and jobs thus became the root cause of the anxieties which ultimately shaped Oriyas' collective consciousness in the nineteenth century. This situation also explains Oriya resentment against the Bengalis and Telugus. The attitudes of 'superiority' of the Bengalis further aggravated this feeling. Even in educational institutions Oriya students had to endure the contempt of their Bengali counterparts. Madusudan Das, an avowed Oriya nationalist, was a student at Cuttack School during 1859-64. In his unfinished autobiography, he writes vividly about his school days:

> Unlike the Bengalis, who had adopted the life style of the West, Oriyas were not ready to accept this. Between the Bengalis and the Oriyas, the differences regarding the modes of dress and food-habits were considerable. Obviously, therefore, I was an object of ridicule. . . . There were times, when smarting under such ridicule, I would remember my happy childhood in the village and break down and cry. Under those conditions, it was hard to believe that, before coming here, I was treated with the respect and affection due to a scion of an ancient family. It made me wonder if I would ever find such happiness again. However, I chose such a way of life that contempt, ridicule and hatred would be my eternal companions.[58]

During the period under discussion, it was not the economic backwardness of the province alone but also the unequal competition between Oriyas and Bengalis in the job market that created tension and ill-feeling between the two communities. The question of dignity and self-respect haunted the Oriya mind during this period. Since Oriyas had to go to Calcutta for higher education, they were vulnerable to the stereotypes Bengalis had formed about the Oriyas. Thus reflected Godavaris in his autobiography:

> Around 1910 or thereabouts, there were in Calcutta more than hundred thousand labourers from Orissa. They enjoyed little respect. Oriyas were scared of admitting their identities. On several occasions, I had had the opportunity to talk to Oriyas in Calcutta; they would always speak to me in a strange language: broken Oriya interspersed with words of corrupted Bengali. Oriyas were sarcastically referred to as 'Udes'. This became a by word for stupidity. Any stupid man, irrespective of the fact that he was from Madras or Bombay, was referred to as 'Ude'. On the stage, portrayal of the stupid Oriya servant was commonplace. This explains why Oriyas, although they comprised 10% of the population of Calcutta, had to remain unobtrusive.[59]

The growing awareness of Oriya backwardness and the general feeling that the neighbouring ethnic groups threatened their interests gave the regional consciousness an exclusivist edge. In this context, the controversy regarding the Oriya language brought the regional consciousness into a sharper relief.

The issue of language remained throughout an important dimension of Oriya nationalism. But the origin of the issue has to be traced back to the nineteenth century. As the number of vernacular schools in Orissa started to increase after Wood's Despatch came into effect in 1854, the crucial question surfaced: which language should be the means of instruction in those vernacular schools?[60] As late as 1868, teaching in the schools was mostly in Bengali. For example in the Normal School (meant for training teachers for primary schools) in Cuttack, with certain exceptions such as prose and geography, all subjects were taught in Bengali. It was only in 1869 that students were first allowed to take the examinations in Oriya.[61] In the Oriya-speaking areas of Ganjam also, Telugu was the medium of instruction in schools.

Before 1868, the absence of a clear policy on the medium of instruction in schools meant that the dominance of Bengali and

Telugu was secure in Oriya-speaking areas. In a letter to the Secretary of the Government of Bengal, Mr. Molony, officiating commissioner of Orissa, wrote that education in his province was affected by the 'introduction of too much of Bengali element into the schools'.[62] This should not be taken to mean that all officials in the Education Department in Bengal were sympathetic to the Oriya cause. For example, the Director of Public Instruction, W. S. Atkinson, advised the government not to interfere in the 'language controversy' and also hoped that Bengali would become the medium of instruction in Orissa.[63] In spite of the opposition in the Education Department, the government's intention was to alter the status quo. Government policy was clearly in favour of 'establishing Uriya as the recognised language of all schools in Orissa, and leaving Bengali as an extra language if preferred, to be taken up in addition to Uriya, but not in the suppression of it'.[64]

Many Bengalis resented the decision in favour of Oriya language, for it meant the reduction of jobs for them in the Education Department. In a letter to the editor in a magazine entitled *Cuttack Star* (July 1869), Umacharana Haldar advocated the use of the Bengali alphabet for writing Oriya. Writing Oriya in the Bengali script, Haldar argued, would help the British and the outsiders to learn and understand the language far more easily than writing Oriya in its own script. Haldar also questioned why print and ink brought from Bengal should be used in printing Oriya script. To Haldar, Bengali letters are as beautiful as diamonds and appear as attractive as pearls, and in contrast, Oriya letters are round-shaped and ugly![65]

Utkal Dipika, the first newspaper in Oriya, was in the forefront of advocating the cause of the Oriya language. In a letter to the editor, an anonymous writer included a poem glorifying the Oriya script.[66] In another letter to the editor, published in *Utkal Dipika* (24 July 1869), the author satirized the view of Rajkrishna Mukherji (then lecturer in law in Cuttack) that Oriya was a 'bastard' language and a corrupt form of Bengali. Rajkrishna Mukherji, in turn, took exception to such criticisms and filed a defamation case against the editor of the newspaper. Although the case was dismissed and did no harm to the editor, it underlined the bitterness that surfaced, during the language controversy, between the two competing middle classes.

The issue regarding the medium of instruction in schools was thus quickly transformed into a tussle between the two languages. The final blow came from Kantichandra Bhattacharya, a Sanskrit teacher in Balasore, in the shape of a pamphlet entitled *Udiya ek Swatantra Bhasa Nahe* (Oriya is not a separate language).[67] Kantichandra argued that Oriya was not a separate language but a mere dialect of Bengali. For the Bengalis advocating the replacment of Oriya language in schools of Orissa, Kantichandra's pamphlet was obviously a great support.

Rajendralal Mitra, defending Kantichandra's book, reiterated the views that he had already expressed some time earlier at Cuttack: Oriya should be replaced by Bengali in the educational institutions in Orissa. In his view, the relationship between Bengali and Oriya is that between mother and daughter and not between two sisters.[68] Part of his argument was grounded on sheer expediency: a people with a small population and a backward economy could not afford to have a separate language and literature; if Oriyas adopted Bengali as their language, they could share the benefits from a developed printing industry and an easy supply of books for the educational institutions. The other part of Rajendralal's argument rested on his ill-concealed Bengali chauvinism. About the prospect of replacing Oriya by Bengali, he wrote:

> Nor is the fusion of their language into ours at all impracticable. The experiment has already been tried and found to be completely successful. Some twenty years ago when the district of Midnapur was transfered from the Commissionership of Cuttack to that of Burdwan, the language of the Courts there and of the people was Uriya. The new Commissioner, for the sake of uniformity in all his districts or some other cause, suppressed Uriya, and introduced the Bengali language, and nearly the whole of Midnapur is now become a Bengali speaking district, and men there often feel offended if they are called Uriyas. That similar measures in Balasore, Cuttack and Puri would effect a similar change, I have no reason to doubt.[69]

The essence of this argument lies in its firm belief in the cultural assimilation of the small and weak community into the bigger and more powerful one.[70] Philologically, Kantichandra's pamphlet and Rajendralal's statements had little significance;[71] but politically, they had tremendous implications for the Oriyas. In *Utkal Dipika*, the book got an angry review and the arguments therein were rejected with vehemence.[72] It is true that the views of people such as Rajendralal against the Oriya language could not bring about its replacement. They tended to make the Oriya middle class more aware of its interests.

If the condition of the Oriyas in the areas where they were in a majority was precarious, the situation for the Oriyas living in the Madras Presidency and in the Central Provinces was even worse. In 1895, the government notified that as from January 1896 Oriya would be completely replaced by Hindi in the courts of Sambalpur (an Oriya-speaking district in the Central Provinces). After persistent appeals Oriya was restored as the court and official language of Sambalpur in 1903. Similarly, in Ganjam (an Oriya-speaking district in the Madras Presidency) Oriya was restored as the court language in 1890.[73] Even as late as 1912, in some areas of Ganjam district the government's decision to make Oriya the court language remained unimplemented.[74] Oriyas living in these areas persistently complained that they were being excluded from all higher-ranking jobs in the colonial administration and that they had been relegated to lower positions compared to the Hindustanis and Telugus.

It is not difficult to see why the issue of language occupied a paramount place in Oriya consciousness for a considerable period of time. The question therefore arises: why was the issue of language so crucial for the Oriyas? Is this to be seen as a fight between the Oriyas and Bengalis?

In the pre-colonial days, Sanskrit had received support from the Oriya kings. Sanskrit was exclusively the language of the priests and the learned. As a language of ritual, it was instrumental in safeguarding the caste system and played a mediatory role in preserving royal power. The emergence of Oriya literature in the sixteenth and seventeenth centuries was the product not of royal patronage but of plebeian initiative.[75] Evidence suggests that brahmans were contemptuous of Oriya literature on grounds that it was written by plebeians and in a language of the masses. Brahman apathy towards the Oriya language persisted even until the nineteenth century.

However, during the colonial era, the spread of vernacular education meant that knowledge of Oriya was a passport to the lower-ranking jobs in the Department of Education. The Oriya middle class's struggle for its language was also an effort to protect economic interests. The introduction of Oriya meant more employment opportunities for Oriya teachers, more opportunities for the publishers to print Oriya textbooks; similarly the retention of Oriya as the language of offices meant more jobs for Oriyas. The fate of the Oriya printing industry too was inextricably linked to the survival of the language itself. The issue of language thus became a weapon of the Oriya middle class in their struggle against the middle class competitors of other communities. It would, therefore, be wrong to suggest that the fight as such was between the Oriyas and Bengalis.[76] It would also be incorrect to suggest that the tension between the Oriyas and the Bengalis was always at the same pitch as it was during the 'language controversy'.[77] The support of several domiciled Bengalis including Gaurisankar Ray, Radhanath Ray, Ramashankar Ray and Baikunthnath De was indicative of this fact. Support for the Oriya language was also linked to the economic interests of some domiciled Bengalis. For instance the fate of Gaurishankar's printing industry was dependent on the survival of the Oriya language.

The Oriyas were becoming increasingly aware that the protection of their language and the promotion of vernacular education could only be ensured by Oriya officials in the Education Department. The demand for the withdrawal of Bengali school inspectors from Orissa was a manifestation of this growing awareness.

However, to reduce the Oriya middle-class consciousness to a bundle of economic motives would amount to undermining the subjective dimension of this phenomenon. It is true that the defence of Oriya language was intimately connected with the material interests of the Oriya middle class. But the implications of the 'language controversy' went beyond the material dimensions. The defence of the language on the part of the Oriyas clearly was more than a mere instrumental identification of their community with the language; it was an assigning of authenticity to their language, as being experientially unique and, therefore, functional in a way that no other language, however close it may be to theirs, could match.[78]

The growth of literary associations and similar organizations in Orissa was a significant product of the language controversy of the nineteenth century.[79] The major objective of the associations was to enrich Oriya language and literature and to make the Oriyas aware of their rich literary heritage. The literary associations also contributed to a subjective definition of Oriya identity.

The contribution of the printing industry was to sharpen this awareness and bring about its quick dissemination. The Cuttack Printing Company was the first to be established, at Cuttack in 1866.[80] After another two years, Fakirmohan Senapati introduced a printing press to Balasore. In the wake of the language controversy, the number of printing presses rose dramatically: by the turn of the century, the number in the three districts of Orissa was thirteen. With the arrival of the printing press, newspapers in Oriya appeared. They provided an important platform for the Oriya middle class to articulate their views and voice their grievances. Newspapers also provided the arena for the fight between various interests and ideas. Most of the newspapers gave wide coverage to local issues by highlighting the problems of Orissa. The perceived threat to the Oriya language encouraged the printing companies to publish more Oriya textbooks and literary texts.[81] The printing press, above all, 'arrested the drift' of the Oriya language. It enriched and standardized the vernacular and made way for the codification of the language. As well as disseminating the myths and symbols on which depended the making of Oriya identity, printing reinforced the mother-tongue 'Oriya', learned naturally at home, with a homogenized print-language.[82] Benedict Anderson has emphasized the role of the printing press in the emergence of imagined national communities.[83] In his view, it is through print-language that communities are imagined. The print-language for the Oriyas was no doubt essential for the survival of their language and, by extension, their identity as an ethnic group.

It is also true that it is through the medium of print that the gradual emergence of an Oriya collective consciousness can best be detected. For instance, in a large number of letters published in the Oriya newspapers during this time, authors signed themselves as 'an Oriya', or 'a real Oriya', or 'Mother Utkal' rather than revealing their names and personal identity. This provides an interesting insight and suggests the gradual articulation of interest in terms of the community rather than individuals in Orissa during the period under study. It also points towards the fact that Oriyas perceived themselves not as mere individuals but as part of a larger 'Oriya identity'.

While discussing the reactive aspect of Oriya consciousness in the nineteenth century we must not lose sight of its positive side. The educated Oriya middle class voiced their protest against child marriage and drinking liquor, and championed the cause of education in Orissa. The attempts to improve Oriya language and literature were also a positive feature of this collective endeavour.

The gradual emergence of an 'Oriya consciousness', to repeat, was a crucial feature of the nineteenth-century socio-political development in Orissa. This form of consciousness emerged primarily as the product of the middle-class's continuing acts of self-reflection. The 'reflections' in the nineteenth century were essentially a record of the Oriya middle class's reactions, in thought and feeling (more feeling than thought) to the changing historical contexts. The reactions of the Oriya middle class were to a great extent shaped by interaction with other forces. The first area of interaction was with the British, the second with other ethnic groups such as the Bengalis, Telugus, and Hindustanis, and the third interaction was among themselves. These interactions within the overarching context of colonialism came to determine the shape of the emerging Oriya consciousness.

It has been argued earlier that with the impact of colonialism in Orissa, the old manufacturing industries such as salt and weaving were completely ruined. Orissa became a source of cheap labour for the industries in Calcutta and plantations in Assam. Oriyas felt that the colonial state was not taking enough economic and welfare measures in the Oriya-speaking tracts.

In this context of backwardness, the relationship among the various ethnic groups underwent a profound change and it was in the context of this change that one has to understand the assertion of Oriya identity *vis-à-vis* other ethnic groups. One could argue that the assertion of an Oriya identity was a reaction to the Oriyas' disadvantageous position among the ethnic groups. In other words, it was a result of the competition between the Oriya middle class and its counterparts for scarce resources. The economic factor, as argued earlier, was a necessary but not sufficient condition for the growth of Oriya consciousness. In Oriya consciousness the demarcation line between the economic and cultural was very thin. Economic backwardness did, of course, present 'various layers of meaning' to the Oriya middle class. For instance, the lack of adequate textbooks in the Oriya language could very well be a result of lack of Oriya printing presses, or might be due to some economic reasons; it could also represent a cultural malaise. Similarly, the language controversy not only had cultural implications for Oriyas, it also presented for them a great deal of economic and political meaning. In the emerging Oriya consciousness, economic and cultural issues were often an integral whole; issues became simultaneously economic as well as cultural. The articulation of identity thus represented a fight for economic benefits as well as for dignity and self-respect.

However, the awareness of their backwardness did not automatically lead to the politics of identity. It was easy to generate a collective awareness among Oriyas; but to translate it into political action was a different matter. In spite of the concerns common to the Oriya middle class living in Bengal and the Madras presidency, there was no organization in which they could come together. As a result political activity in the late-nineteenth century was largely confined to the local level. It was through local-level associations that the Oriya middle class was trying to emerge as a distinct pressure group. But their power as an interest group was compromised by several factors. First, in spite of the government's policy to recruit more Oriyas in the Oriya-speaking areas, the number of Oriya employees remained small. The progress of higher education was also slow. Second, perhaps no less important, was the economic condition of the Oriya middle class. In the absence of adequate financial support, the position of Oriya associations was precarious.

In the absence of an all-Oriya organization the regional consciousness of the Oriyas had yet to achieve political potency. The issue of employment and education was powerful enough to mobilize and unify the Oriya middle class. But in mobilizing those Oriyas who were not affected by the issue of education and employment, issues such as the threat to the Oriya language and culture had tremendous propaganda and emotive value.

What the Oriya middle class needed then was an organization for mobilizing the Oriyas and for concerted action to pursue their interests. By the end of the nineteenth century, the Oriyas were thus well on their way towards forging a link with their brothers in other administrative areas. There were also attempts to transform a 'general feeling' of backwardness into an articulate political voice. But the progress towards those goals was not unilinear or smooth. The historical events from 1869 onward brought about significant changes in the perceptions of the Oriya middle class. From this emerged a distinct and exclusive identity and aspirations that came to impinge upon the future political development in Orissa.

NOTES

1. *Utkal Dipika*, 19 February 1876.
2. Walter Hamilton, *The East India Gazetteer* (2 vols.), Vol. 2, London, 1828, p. 346.
3. H. E. Beal, *Indian Ink*, London, 1954. The setting of the novel is colonial Orissa. Krupasindhu, a clerk in the colonial bureaucracy, is the central character of Beal's novel. Beal makes his protagonist say: 'Sir, we Oriyas are lazy men, and we are not enterprising' (p. 66). When it comes to the perception of the natives about their masters, Beal's narrative falls back on stereotypes. 'These men', he (Khursid, a colleague of Krupasindhu) said, 'are English Sahibs. Why do they tell lies like black men' (p. 55).
4. 'The people of Orissa, though mild and submissive to the very verge of timidity, are a backward and conservative race, impatient of novelty and suspicious of anything which affects to depart from long-established custom.' *Report on the Census of Bengal*, 1871, p. 36.
5. Andrew Stirling, *Orissa: Its Geography, Statistics, History, Religion, and Antiquities*, London, 1846, p. 14.
6. W. W. Hunter, *Orissa*, Vol. 1, London, 1872. See Introduction, p. 3.
7. Ibid., p. 59.
8. Stanley P. Rice, *Occasional Essays on Native South Indian Life*, London, 1901, pp. 20-1.
9. This is perhaps a direction along which research might be conducted, as was done by S. H. Alatas in his study of the image of the Malayas, Filipinos and Javanese from the sixteenth to the twentieth century. See his book *The Myth of the Lazy Native: A Study of the Image of the Malays, Filipinos and Javanese from the 16th to the 20th Century and its Function in the Ideology of Colonial Capitalism*, London, 1977.
10. Edward W. Said, *Orientalism*, London, 1978. See the Introduction.
11. Hermann Kulke, 'Jagannath as the state Deity under the Gajapatis of Orissa', in A. Eschmann, H. Kulke and G. C. Tripathi (eds.), *The Cult of Jagannath and the Regional Tradition of Orissa*, New Delhi, 1978.
12. G. N. Dash, 'Jagannath and Oriya Nationalism', ibid.
13. These are some of the works G. N. Dash has referred to in his essay: Sarala Dasa's *Mahabharata* (sixteenth century); Biswanatha Khuntia's *Bichitra Ramayana* (seventeenth century) and Brajanatha Badajena's *Samara Taranga* (eighteenth century).

14. Ibid., p. 360.
15. Ibid., p. 361.
16. *Sambalpur Hitaisini* (Oriya), 14 August 1889. This is a short extract from a long poem titled *Kali Bhagabata* published in this newspaper. For the sake of convenience, I have rendered the translation in prose form. It should be pointed out that the author of this text has adopted the style of *Bhagabata*, a popular religious Oriya text written in the fifteenth or sixteenth century. This poem belongs to the category of 'apocalyptic literature' predicting inevitable cosmic doom which would follow a severe crisis of social and moral order.
17. Quoted from J. Peggs, *India Cries to British Humanity*, London, 1830, p. 250.
18. J. Peggs, op. cit.; Andrew Stirling, op. cit.; W. F. B. Laurie, *The Idol-Shrine; or The Origin, History, and Worship of the Great Temple of Jagannath*, London, 1851; David B. Smith, *Report on Pilgrimage to Juggernauth, in 1868*, Calcutta, 1868; Nancy G. Cassels, *Religion and Pilgrim Tax Under the Company Raj*, Delhi, 1988.
19. *Jagganath Parikhya* (Oriya), Cuttack, 1867. *Debapuja Birudhare Dharmapustakare Pramana* (Oriya), Cuttack, 1874. Hence the common English metaphorical usage of Juggernaut: 'An institution, practice, or notion to which persons blindly devote themselves, or are ruthlessly sacrificed.'
20. For a view of the Colonial encounter in Bengal in the nineteenth century, see Tapan Raychaudhuri, *Europe Reconsidered: Perceptions of the West in Nineteenth Century Bengal*, Delhi, 1988.
21. See, W. W. Hunter, op. cit., and A. Sterling, op. cit.
22. *Utkal Dipika*, 16 June 1883.
23. Nivedita Mohanty, *Oriya Nationalism: Quest for a United Orissa, 1866-1936*, Delhi, 1982. S. C. Patra, *Formation of the Province of Orissa: The Success of First Linguistic Movement in India*, Calcutta, 1979. J. K. Samal, *Orissa Under the British Crown (1858-1905)*, Delhi, 1979. P. K. Mishra, *The Political History of Orissa, 1900-1936*, Delhi, 1979.
24. See *Report of the Commissioners Appointed to Enquire into The Famine in Bengal and Orissa in 1866*, 2 vols., Calcutta, 1867.
25. 'Middle class' is not a precise term. I have used the term to refer to the educated class which emerged during the colonial rule.
26. L. S. S. O'Malley, *History of Bengal, Bihar and Orissa under the British Rule*, Calcutta, 1925, Ch. IX.
27. Dharma Kumar and Meghnad Desai (eds.), *The Cambridge Economic History of India*, Vol. 2: *c. 1757-c. 1970*, Cambridge, 1984. See the section on Eastern India written by B. Chaudhuri. Also see B. S. Das, *Studies in the Economic History of Orissa: From Ancient Times to 1833*, Calcutta, 1978.

28. There was the road link between Calcutta and Orissa which, except in the dry season, was not fit for wheeled vehicles. There was also the danger of being looted by bandits, particularly on the road between Balasore and Midnapur. The most common transport between the coastal districts of Orissa and Calcutta, before the railway was introduced in 1899, was the steamer or launch.
29. S. L. Maddox, *Final Report on the Survey and Settlement of the Province of Orissa, 1890-1900 (temporarily settled areas)*, 2 vols., Calcutta, 1900. See Vol. 1.
30. Ibid., Vol. 1, p. 132.
31. Fakirmohan Senapati, *Atmajibana Charita* (Oriya), Cuttack, 1927 (1st edn.), p. 21.
32. For an exposition of 'Internal Colonialism thesis', see Michael Hechter, *Internal Colonialism: The Celtic Fringe in British National Development, 1536-1966*, London, 1975. Also see Tom Nairn, *The Break-up of Britain*, London, 1977.
33. See Hechter, Introduction and Ch. 2.
34. 'The fate of Orissa is worst. You find all sorts of inconveniences here. Having railways, people from Bengal covered the distance which would take one day, in an hour. People of Orissa only got canals. Going by ferries, Oriyas would take one and a half days to cover the journey of one day. There is also the possibility that the ferries may end up in the sea. On the top of that, Oriyas have to pay tax to have this system of communication.' *Utkal Dipika*, 23 February 1878.
35. Extract from a letter from the Director of Public Instruction to the Secretary to the Government of Bengal. *General Report on Public Instruction in the Lower Provinces of the Bengal Presidency* (hereafter *GRPIB*), 1869-70, p. 62.
36. Gyanendra Mohan Das, *Banger Bahire Bangali* (in Bengali), Calcutta, 1931, Vol. 3 (microfilm, India Institute Library, Oxford), pp. 30-86. According to Das, as early as 1582, during the reign of Akbar, 9,000 Bengalis came to Orissa as Gomastas and Kanungos. 'Bengalis for spreading Dharma (religion), for pilgrimage, for trade and commerce, for spreading education and civilization, came and stayed in Orissa.'
37. It is not easy to find out the exact number of Bengalis in Orissa in different periods of time. I have taken the following figures from the Census as to the number of Bengali-speaking people in Orissa: in 1881, 28,953 people, and in 1891, 35,448. In 1901, out of a total population of 4,343,150 in the districts of Cuttack, Puri, Balasore and Angul, 40,096 were Bengalis. Out of a total population of 3,314,474 in the feudatory states, 66,544 were Bengalis.
38. *GRPIB*, 1870-71, p. 142.
39. L. S. S. O'Malley, *Cuttack District Gazetteer*, Calcutta, 1906. The educational reform was initiated by George Campbell in 1872, p. 188.

40. *Annual Report of Education*, 1870-71, Bengal Proceedings (P series), India Office Library and Records (hereafter, IOR), p. 51.
41. *Cuttack District Gazetter*, op. cit., p. 188.
42. Census of India, 1901, Vol. VI, *The Lower Provinces of Bengal and their Feudatories*, Part I, Ch. 11, pp. 299-300.
43. W. W. Hunter, op. cit., p.146.
44. *Report on Public Instruction in the Madras Presidency, 1882-1883*, p. 75.
45. Madusudan Das, who was one of the champions of Oriya nationalism, was the first Oriya graduate. He also had the distinction of being the first Oriya to obtain the law and Master's degree from Calcutta. Nabakishor Das, *Utkala Gauraba Madhusudan* (Oriya), Cuttack, 1951.
46. Out of 421 students who passed their B.A. from Calcutta University in 1886, only two were from Cuttack; out of 763 F.A. students, four were from Orissa. Quoted from Natabar Samantaray, *Odia Sahityara Itihasa 1803-1920* (Oriya), Cuttack, 1983 (2nd edn.), p. 168. In the three districts of Orissa, according to the 1901 Census, the total number of people educated (who could read and write) and pupils under instruction was 315,239 out of a total population of 4,151,239. *The Census Report of Bengal, 1901*.
47. In 1901, 40 Oriyas out of 10,000 were literate in English. In West Bengal the number was 180, in Central Bengal 362, and in East Bengal 82. *Census of India*, 1901, Vol. VI, *The Lower Provinces of Bengal and their Feudatories*, Part I, see the Subsidiary Table IV, p. 308.
48. *Letter from T. Walton, Magistrate and Collector of Puri to the Commissioner of the Orissa Division, 25 April 1871*. Education Department, Bengal Proceedings (IOR).
49. Report from the Inspector to the D. P. I. (12 March 1861), *GRPIB*, 1860-61, p. 123.
50. Prabhat Mukherjee, 'Employment of the people of Orissa in Government Service in the nineteenth century', *Orissa Historical Research Journal*, Vol. 7, No. 2, 1959, pp. 110-17.
51. *Cuttack District Gazetter*, op. cit., p. 186.
52. R. D. Banerji, *History of Orissa*, 2 vols., see Vol. 2, Calcutta, 1931. According to Banerji the early Bengali officials, in contrast to the later English-educated ones, in Orissa were dishonest and incompetent. To him the corruption of early British officers combined with the 'rapacity' and 'cruelty' of their Bengali subordinates in Orissa precipitated the 'Paik rebellion' of 1817. See Ch. XXVII and Appendix V.
53. Sala refers to the wife's brother but is usually used as a word of abuse.
54. Fakirmohan Senapati, op. cit., pp. 51-2.
55. *GRPIB*, 1872-3, p. 325.
56. *Utkal Dipika*, 27 January 1906, *Native Newspaper Reports*, week ending 10 February 1906.

57. *Letter from J. G. D. Patridge, Collector of Ganjam to the Chief Secretary to Government, 23 Feb. 1904*, Public and Judicial Department records (hereafter L/P&J) IOR, L/P&J/6/1905, file 401-34.
58. Extract from Madhusudan's autobiography quoted by Nabakishor Das, op. cit., p. 17.
59. Godavaris Misra, 'Ardha Satabdira Odissa O Tahinre Mora Sthan', *Godavaris Granthabali*, Vol. 1, Cuttack, 1960, p. 82. Nirad C. Chaudhuri, a Bengali, wrote in his autobiography about the arrogance of the Bengali bhadralok towards the Oriyas and Bengalis of eastern Bengal:

    He is no man—the Bengali of the East;
    The Orissan's worse, for he is a beast;
    None have tails, But it's wonderful to see
    How these creatures swing from tree to tree.

    The Autobiography of an Unknown Indian, London, 1951, p. 367. Hunter, too, wrote about the prejudices of Calcutta Bengalis towards the Oriyas. *Orissa*, op. cit., p. 139.
60. In Assam there was the similar controversy in the 1850s as to which language—Assamese or Bengali—should be taught in the school. This controversy created bitterness between the two communities. *East India Education (Bengal and N. W. Provinces), Education despatch of 19th July 1854*, [no place], 1859. India Institute Library. Amalendu Guha, *Planter-Raj to Swaraj: Freedom Struggle and Electoral Politics in Assam 1826-1947*, New Delhi, 1977. Also see Colin H. Williams, 'Separatism and the Mobilization of Welsh National Identity' in the book edited by him, *National Separatism*, Cardiff, 1982.
61. Mritunjay Rath, *Karmabira Gaurisankar*, Cuttack, 1925, p. 39.
62. Letter dated 18 September 1868, *GRPIB*, 1869, Bengal Proceedings (IOR), p. 44.
63. Letter dated 1 August 1869, *GRPIB*, 1869-70, pp. 60-2.
64. Statement of the Commissioner of the Orissa division, quoted by the Officiating Secretary to the Government of Bengal to the Director of Public Instruction, 8 November 1869, *GRPIB*, 1869-70.
65. *Utkal Dipika*, 10 July 1869.
66. Ibid., 24 July 1869.
67. Kantichandra Bhattacharya, *Udiya ek swatantra Bhasa nahe*, Calcutta, 1870.
68. *Proceedings of the Asiatic Society of Bengal*, June 1870, p. 209.
69. Ibid., p. 212.
70. As late as 1898, Rabindranath Tagore, the poet, lamented over the fact that Bengali could not become the written language of Orissa and Assam. In an article titled 'Bhasa Bichheda' (Bengali), published in the journal *Bharati*, he wrote: 'The way Bengali language was spreading in Assam and Orissa, if there were no obstructions, it would have brought two of its dialects (Upabhasa)—Oriya and Assamese—into its fold, by

breaking the small barrier that exists among them'. Quoted from *Rabindra Rachanabali*, Vol. 12, Calcutta, 1952, p. 549.

71. *Proceedings of the Asiatic Society of Bengal*, June 1870, pp. 119-20. The title of Beames's paper was 'On the relation of the Uriya to the other Modern Aryan languages'. Beames in his study of Indian languages had stressed the individuality of the Oriya language. Beames described Kantichandra's book as 'profoundly destitute of philological arguments'. Also see his *Comparative Grammar of the Modern Aryan Languages of India*, Vol. 1, London, 1872.
72. *Utkal Dipika*, Vol. 5, No. 9, 26 February 1870, pp. 35-6.
73. Two Bachelors of Arts, *The Oriya Movement: Being a Demand for a United Orissa*, Aska, 1919, p. 23.
74. *Memorandum to His Excellency The Right Honourable Charles Baron of Hardinge of Penhurst, the Viceroy and Governor General of India*, [no name and no date], L/P&J/6/1912, file 417.
75. Mayadhar Mansinha, *History of Oriya Literature,* New Delhi, 1962.
76. Ten years after the language controversy, Bipin Chandra Pal remarked: 'When I first went to Cuttack fifty years ago (1879) neither the classes nor the masses there had developed any separatist provincial consciousness'. *Memories of My Life and Times* (2 vols.), Vol. 1, Calcutta, 1932, p. 353.
77. Brajendranath De, 'Reminiscences of an Indian Member of the Indian Civil Service', *The Calcutta Review*, Vol. 133, No. 2, 1954. During the period 1894 to 1897 De was the Collector of Balasore; he mentions no heightened tension between the Bengalis and Oriyas. See Section X, pp. 87-96. Gopal Chandra Praharaj also mentions the decline of tension between the Oriyas and Bengalis in Cuttack towards the end of the nineteenth century. See Praharaj's incomplete autobiography published in *Praharaj Parikrama*, edited by N. Satpathy, Cuttack, 1970-1.
78. For a discussion of the relationship between language and nationalism, see Benedict Anderson, *Imagined Communities*, London, 1985, and Joshua A. Fishman, *Language and Nationalism: Two Integrative Essays*, Massachusetts, 1972.
79. In 1898-9, out of 18 societies in Orissa, fourteen were societies meant for improving Oriya language and literature. *Report on the Administration of Bengal, 1898-1899.* Some of the prominent associations were *Utkala-Bhasa Unnati Bidhayini Sabha*, Balasore, 1866; *Cuttack Debating Club*, Cuttack, 1869; *Utkal Bhasa-Udipani Sabha*, Cuttack, 1867.
80. Before the Cuttack Printing Company was established, there was only one press, Cuttack Mission Press, established and managed by missionaries since 1837.
81. See the *Third Annual Report of the Cuttack Printing Company* (for the year ending 31 August 1868), Cuttack, 1869. From 1 May 1867 to

31 August 1869, within sixteen months, fifteen literary texts in Oriya were printed. 18,200 copies of these texts were published.

82. For the discussion on the impact of printing on society see Elizabeth L. Eisenstein, 'Some Conjectures About the Impact of Printing on Western Society and Thought: A Preliminary Report', *Journal of Modern History*, Vol. 40, No. 1, 1968; Lucien Febvre and Henri-Jean Martin, *The Coming of the Book. The Impact of Printing, 1450-1800*, London, 1976; Ellen E. McDonald, 'The Modernizing of Communication: Vernacular Publishing in Nineteenth Century Maharashtra', *Asian Survey*, Vol. 8, No. 7, 1968.
83. Benedict Anderson, op. cit.

5

Home away from Home? The Spatial Politics of Modern Tamil Identity[1]

Sumathi Ramaswamy

> Home is a complex ideal.
>
> IRIS YOUNG

This essay explores the spatial politics of modern Tamil identity by considering two alternate home/land(s) that appear to vie for the attention and affect of the Tamil speaker. The first of these is the more familiar *Tamil nadu*, 'the land of Tamil', also variously referred to as *Tamil akam*, 'home of Tamil', *Tamil tecam*, 'Tamil nation', and *Tamil maanilam*, 'Tamil state' (Krishnan 1984). From the closing years of the nineteenth century, however, in the course of the upsurge of linguistic consciousness and mobilization that I have elsewhere glossed as 'Tamil devotion' (Ramaswamy 1997), this 'lived' home of Tamilnadu has had to contend with the 'lost' Tamil homeland of Lemuria (also known as *Kumarikkandam*, 'continent of Kumari', and *Kumari Nadu*, 'land of Kumari'). A former continent in the Indian Ocean stretching south of Kanya Kumari, this homeland had been catastrophically submerged as a consequence of a series of ocean floods which cruelly seized the ancestral birthplace of Tamil, so modern Tamil speakers are told (Ramaswamy 1999; 2000; 2004). Nationalism is predicated on the sentiment of belonging, as are modern regional identities. The citizenry is deemed to own and share critical elements within the nation-space, especially territory; from this collective ownership and possession, a sense of belonging to one another, and to that which is shared, is imagined to be generated. In this essay, by considering the relationship between the 'lived' and 'lost' homelands with which modern Tamil speakers are confronted, I suggest that loss, rather than possession, may be just as empowering for forging a sense of shared belonging. Taking my cue from Svetlana Boym's recent work (Boym 2001), I argue also that while apprehension of loss leads to a discovery of identity, this very process can be divisive at one level even as it is unifying at another.

Kumarikkandam surfaced to visibility in the Tamil life-world in the 1890s in the context of the dissemination in the Madras Presidency of metropolitan speculations about a 'lost continent' in the Indian Ocean that might have been the 'cradle of mankind'. This speculation—first aired in 1870 by the German biologist and Darwinian enthusiast Ernst Haeckel (Haeckel 1876)—was seized by a colonial bureaucrat, Charles D. Macleane, who, along with others, was struggling with what was by then characterized in colonial ethnological circles as 'the Dravidian Problem'. What was the origin and racial affinity of speakers of those Indian languages which could not be traced to Sanskrit and its Indo-European/Aryan 'family'? Why are they today confined to the southern half of the subcontinent? Setting aside a few decades of speculations about the Mongolian, Scythian, and Mediterranean origins of the Dravidians, Macleane suggested in 1885 in his influential *Manual of the Administration of the Madras Presidency* that the 'primeval home' of the 'ancestors of the Dravidas of this country and Ceylon' could well have been Lemuria, the very same continent identified by Haeckel as having formerly sprawled across the Indian Ocean (Macleane 1987: 33-4).

Macleane's *Manual* was published in the heyday of the colonial bureaucratic and ethnological preoccupation with classifying the diverse populations of the subcontinent into major racial categories such as Aryan, Dravidian, and Kolarian; determining their origins, homelands, and migrations; and ranking them in relation to each other on an evolutionary scale ranging from savagery through barbarism to civilization. By the 1880s, while there was general consensus that the Aryans were later arrivals to the subcontinent, there was much debate about who constituted the 'aboriginals' of India, as there was over the original homeland of one of these potential autochthons, the Dravidians. While Macleane's *Manual* did not put to rest these debates, it did add a new dimension by proposing a Lemurian homeland as the solution to the 'riddle' of Dravidian origins. This was a theory that was embraced—if only tentatively and in passing—by other colonial ethnologists and bureaucrats who wrote about the Dravidians in the next few decades, including influential men like Edward Thurston (1899; 1987) and Herbert Risley (1908). The official decennial Census reports of the Government of India of both 1891 and 1901 briefly aired the theory—not without disapproval—in their discussion of the origins of the Dravidians (Baines 1893; Risley and Gait 1903; Stuart 1893). And from 1909, history schoolbooks—written by men like Edmund Marsden (1909: 22-6)—incorporated the notion in their speculative discussions of the prehistoric movements of various races into the subcontinent. Indeed, well into the post-colonial period, numerous schoolbooks in both English and Tamil continue to discuss the possibility that Lemuria *could* have been the ancestral homeland of the Dravidians. So much so that as recently as 1981, a history textbook in Tamil published under the auspices of the Government of Tamilnadu for the 6th standard tells the students in the course of a discussion of the ancient Aryans and Dravidians that 'Some say that in the Indian Ocean several thousand years ago there was a vast land mass called Lemuriakkandam [Lemuria continent], and that that was the birth place of Dravidians' (Tamilnadu Textbook Society 1981: 20)

There are indeed several allusions in the pre-colonial Tamil literary corpus to an antediluvian land that was destroyed by the ocean's fury—allusions that find a renewed life in the twentieth century under the metropolitan sign of 'lost continent'. But it is with colonial bureaucratic writing that this antediluvian land is named 'Lemuria' and authorized as the possible Dravidian ancestral 'homeland'. This colonial authorization, however, is not accompanied by the deep wrenching sense of loss that is so characteristic of the Tamil yearning after Lemuria. In the colonial archive, the primeval inhabitants of the continent—soon to disappear into the ocean—are barely human, and certainly not the acme of world civilization as they are to Tamil's devotees. Lemurians might have been Dravidians, but in turn, Lemuria is offered as only one of their hypothetical homelands, and it was just as possible that they might have come into India from the north-west, and just as probable that they might not be the oldest peoples of the subcontinent. Most importantly, nowhere in this official archive is it suggested that

Lemuria is a *Tamil* homeland, the birthplace of the Tamil language, and the 'cradle' of Tamil culture and civilization.

All this came to pass from the latter half of the 1890s when the colonial imagination was seized by devotees of Tamil who used the metropolitan speculations about lost continents and submerged landbridges to fashion a deep prelapsarian past for their beloved language. Insisting that Tamil speakers were 'remnants of a pre-diluvian race' whose home was Lemuria, Tamil's devotees came increasingly to characterise the lost continent as the 'ancestral homeland', the 'Tamil homeland', and, most tellingly, the 'mother-land' (see, for example, Somasundara Bharati 1912; Appadurai 1941: 2-3). That this was a homeland that was forever lost to 'the swollen tides of the southern sea' (Somasundara Bharati 1967: 116) only added to the poignancy of the Tamil devotees' dilemma that they could never return to it and be reunited with it again. In this imagination, therefore, modern Tamil speakers are doomed to live in a state of perpetual exile. It is this state of being-in-exile that runs as an undercurrent through much of the twentieth century in Tamil devotional practice as Tamil speakers struggle, first as colonial subjects and then as national citizens, to accommodate their own regional sentiments and aspirations with a larger whole that is 'India'. As many have noted, this process of accommodation has been tendentious at numerous moments, especially during the middle decades of the last century when a powerful separatist surge distinguished Dravidian and Tamil nationalism from other movements of regional assertion in the subcontinent. Even after the 1960s when the separatist impulse had run its course, and the Tamil country ambivalently settled down to being a part of the Indian union, the yearning for an Elsewhere in the long-lost past where Tamil and its speakers had been born and had led a life of plenitude has not really ever abated. Lemuria is tantalizingly ever-around as a lost home/land that is the object of deep longing, even while Tamil's devotees call upon their fellow speakers to cultivate love and loyalty for their lived homeland of Tamilnadu/India.

There are many factors that made Lemuria's candidature as the ancestral Tamil homeland attractive to Tamil devotion. For one, it had been identified by metropolitan scientists as a vast and ancient continent, and as the birthplace of mankind: if Tamil speakers were the original inhabitants of Lemuria, this made them the most ancient peoples of the world, and the ancestors of all of humanity. As many a Tamil devotee insisted, with the sinking of the ancestral homeland, Tamilians fanned out to the rest of the world, settling and planting the seeds of civilization in the Indus Valley, Mesopotamia, Egypt, China, the Americas, even Europe. So, Lemuria allowed Tamil devotion to fashion a diaspora for Tamil and its speakers that was as widespread as it was ancient, stretching back to the very beginning of time.

Furthermore, the appropriation of Lemuria for the Tamil cause also enabled the recasting of Tamil speakers as an antediluvian people, allowing Tamil devotion to tap into all the symbolic potency—innocence, purity, and singularity—associated with prelapsarian bliss. Lemuria thus provides the ground on which antediluvian histories are written, further deepening the antiquity of the language and its speakers, the first in the subcontinent as well as in the entire inhabited world.

Perhaps most significantly, it is the fact that Lemuria had been deemed a former continent, lost forever to the ocean, that makes it so useful for the Tamil devotional project. The collective yearning for an unreclaimable past plenitude holds together a people otherwise riven apart by caste, class, and religious differences. Even within the community of Tamil devotees, which I have shown elsewhere has been radically divided over the meaning of Tamil and its relationship to the other languages, cultures and speakers of the subcontinent (Ramaswamy 1997), most unite around the consensus that Tamil is an antediluvian language whose origins can be traced to the lost homeland of Lemuria. Loss, therefore, is enabling in Tamil India, and is a sentiment that has to be continually fed and stoked. As Marilyn Ivy has noted in another context, 'the loss of nostalgia—that is, the loss of the desire to long for what is lost because one has found the lost object—can be more unwelcome than the original loss itself. . . . Modernist nostalgia must preserve . . . the sense of absence and lack that motivates its desire' (Ivy 1995: 10). Thus, Tamil devotion's complex and variegated labours of loss cannot actually afford to find the lost homeland, or to close the gap, to present the absent. To do so would mean the end of its project, its own logic for existence. As Susan Stewart (1993: 144) writes perceptively:

> the nostalgic is enamored of distance, not of the referent itself. Nostalgia cannot be sustained without loss. For the nostalgic to reach his or her goal

of closing the gap between resemblance and identity, *lived* experience would have to take place, an erasure of the gap between sign and signified, an experience which would cancel out the desire that is nostalgia's reason for existence.

Yearning for—and mourning—the lost homeland becomes an end in itself, therefore, for a people who imagine themselves in perpetual exile.

Loss in this sense may be empowering, but there are also dangers in pursuing a project whose object of desire is an Elsewhere that can never be attained. This is especially so when the Elsewhere falls outside the territorial boundaries of the nation-state which is the lived homeland, not to mention the ground of practical politics.[2] From the start, the relationship of Lemuria to the lived homeland of Tamilnadu/ Tamilakam, itself a small part of 'India', is plagued by ambiguity in the Tamil devotional imagination. Some of Tamil's devotees suggest that all of what we know of as 'India' today had been part of Lemuria, spatially reiterating the claim that Dravidians (and hence Tamilians) had been the original peoples of the subcontinent before they had been driven south by the 'Aryan invasion'. Others are content to include in Lemuria only peninsular India, that region of the subcontinent that colonial ethnology had so closely identified with Dravidian speakers; still others insist that only Tamilnadu had been part of the erstwhile homeland. If there is any consensus at all among Tamil's devotees on this matter, it is over Kanya Kumari, which everyone agrees is one remnant of the former antediluvian world to survive the catastrophic ravages of the ocean floods. As I have suggested elsewhere, Kanya Kumari therefore acts as a critical *lieu de mémoire*, in Pierre Nora's terms, standing on the threshold, as it were, between two places, that which is imagined to have been lost, and that which survived the catastrophic disappearance of an entire continent (Ramaswamy 2000).

The discursive ambiguity over Lemuria's relationship to the Indian subcontinent is visibly—and visually—underscored in the numerous maps of the lost homeland that come to be produced in the Tamil country from the early years of the twentieth century (Ramaswamy 1999). I discuss here only four instances from a larger cartographic archive that tellingly point to the dilemmas of belonging to a lived—and present—homeland, and yearning simultaneously for a lost—and absent—one. So, a 1946 map shows the Indian subcontinent as many colonial maps would have it, as extending from the borders of Afghanistan in the west to Burma in the east, and from the mountains in the north to the ocean to the south (Fig. 1).[3] Extending in a southerly direction from today's land's end, however, is the 'ancient Tamil realm' whose southern borders (indicated by dotted lines) extend to Madagascar in the west and Australia in the east at the moment of the lost homeland's greatest reach before its progressive disappearance into the 'southern ocean'. The map appears to suggest that Lemuria included what we recognize today

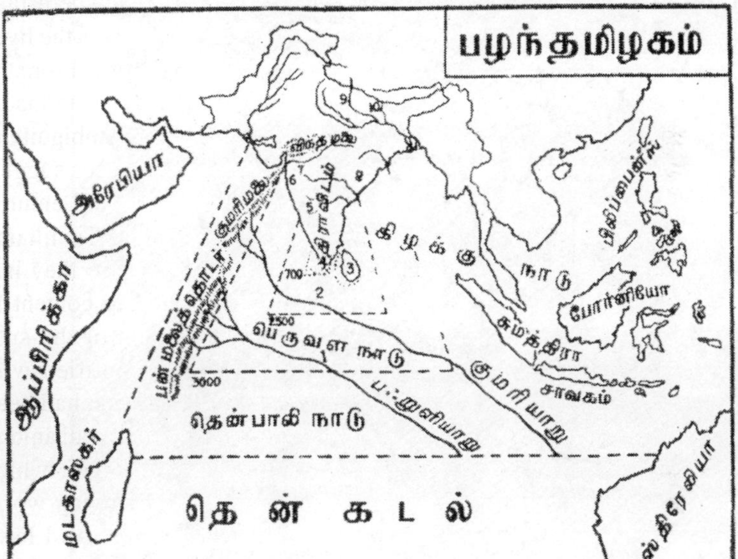

Fig. 1. Pulavar Kulanthai, Palaiya Tamilakam (Ancient Tamil Homeplace). This map in Tamil shows the modern Indian coastline superimposed on the ancient submerged land mass of Lemuria (designated here by the outermost dotted lines), reaching at its greatest extent to Madagascar in the west and Australia in the east. The dotted lines marked 3000, 2500, and 700 represent the progressive loss of land to the ocean. Figures 1 and 2 represent the lost cities of Tonmaturai and Tenmaturai on the banks of the rivers Pahruli and Kumari, whose sources lay in the mountain ranges along the western edge of Lemuria. From Pulavar Kulanthai, *Iravana Kaviyam* (1946; reprint Erode: Vela Patippakam, 1971).

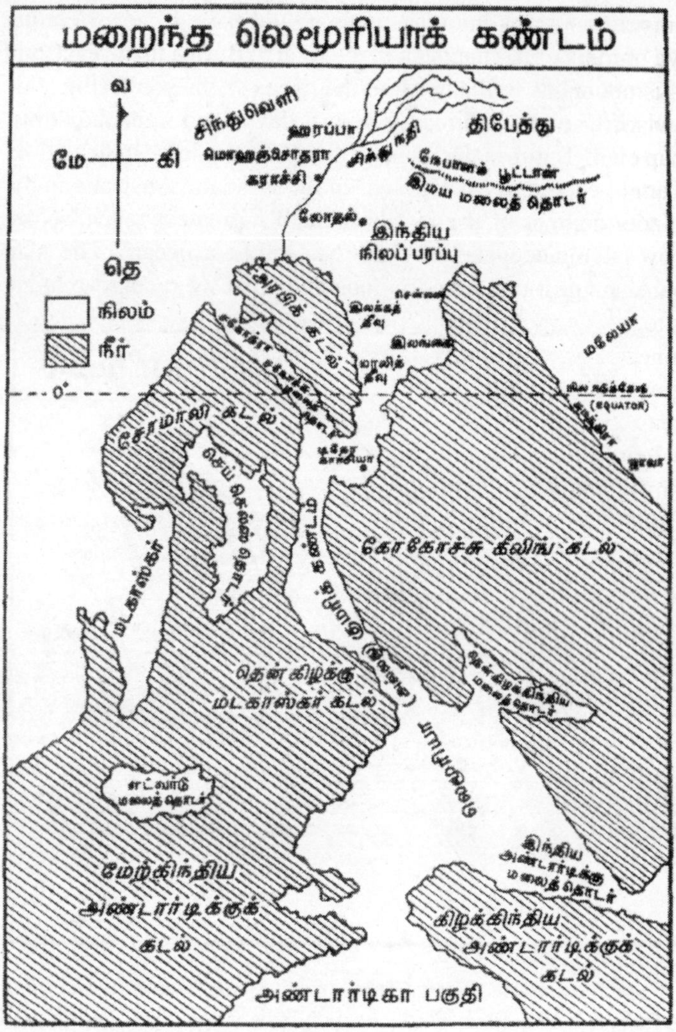

Fig. 2. R. Mathivanan, Marainta Lemuriakkandam (Vanished Lemuria Continent). This map in Tamil shows the reconstructed Indian peninsula to the north with a land bridge connecting to the large landmass of Lemuria in the south, terminating in Antarctica. The shaded portions represent the oceans surrounding Lemuria. From M. Ramachandran and R. Mathivanan, *The Spring of the Indus Civilization* (Madras: Prasanna Pathippagam, 1991).

as peninsular India, although the status of regions north of the Vindhya mountains—the heartland of the present-day Indian polity—is not entirely clear (Pulavar Kulanthai 1971).

Likewise, the relationship of 'India' to Lemuria is ambiguous in a 1991 map entitled 'Lost Continent of Lemuria' (Fig. 2). It is the work of the Tamil scholar R. Mathivanan, who has also written extensively on the Indus valley civilization as Tamil in its origins, created as it was by Tamilians who had fled from a submerged Lemuria. In Mathivanan's map, Lemuria (also named 'Kumarikkandam') snakes its way to the south to the continent of Antarctica, while to the north it is connected to a land mass named 'India'. The borders of India as a recognizable polity, however, are completely dissolved in this map, and even its integrity as a distinctive subcontinent—so important for the Indian nationalist imagination—is under question (Ramachandran and Mathivanan 1991).

In a 1981 map tellingly entitled 'India in 30,000 BC' an alternate version of the subcontinent is offered (Fig. 3). This map is the work

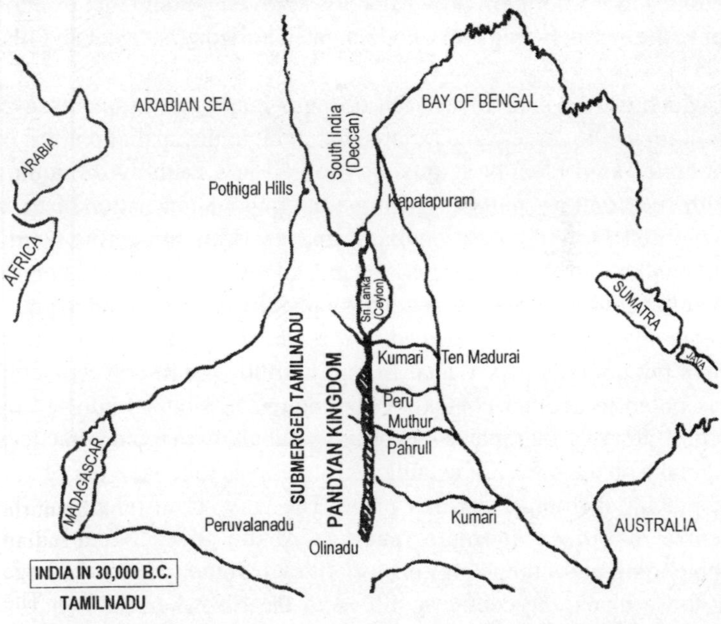

Fig. 3. N. Mahalingam, India in 30,000 BC: Tamilnadu. From N. Mahalingam, editor, *Gems from the Prehistoric Past* (Madras: International Society for the Investigation of Ancient Civilization, 1981).

of a well-known Coimbatore-based industrialist, N. Mahalingam, and has been reproduced over the years in many different contexts, including on the World Wide Web. It identifies Lemuria as the 'submerged Tamilnadu' and as the 'Pandyan kingdom', and shows it as a vast land to the south that supplements India, whose significance is further reduced through an erasure of its all-important northern plains and mountains. Very little of the subcontinent seems to have actually been a part of the lost homeland, which might have included, at best, what we know of today as Tamilnadu and Kerala (Mahalingam 1981).

My final example is from a school textbook of 1951 for Class VI (Fig. 4). The focus of this map—as indeed in all the other maps I have discussed here—is not India, but 'Kumarikkandam that has been seized by the ocean'. As in Mahalingam's map, 'India' is visually—and powerfully—supplemented by a vast territory to its south—the lost homeland; today's lived homeland of Tamilakam (which, importantly, also includes the present state of Kerala) is reduced to the northern provinces of a sprawling realm that extends far to the south, fading into a undelineated horizon (Sivasailam Pillai 1951).

Much can be said about each of these maps, but in this essay I limit myself to three observations that point to the spatial politics of modern Tamil identity as this was forged in a cauldron brimming with the contrary pulls of an imperializing Indian nationalism, a separatist Dravidian nationalism, and an accommodating Tamil nationalism. First, these maps—as indeed the discourse on Lemuria over the course of the last century—radically de-centre India, and it frequently comes to be placed at the vanishing point of the map, *there* but not quite. As Walter Mignolo, following Rudolf Arnheim, has noted in another context, a commonplace strategy adopted by contestatory cartographies—especially subaltern mapping practices that take on the power of established states—is to rewrite the centre, displacing it from its familiar place. The very act of relocating the centre mobilizes alternate readings of the space occupied by contending and competing territorialities (Mignolo 1995: 219-33). In these maps, the centre is shifted to the Elsewhere of Lemuria, whose space is invariably filled in with rivers (such as the Kumari and the Pahruli), mountains (such as Panmalai Atukkam and Kumarimalai), regions (Peruvalanadu and Olinadu), and cities (like

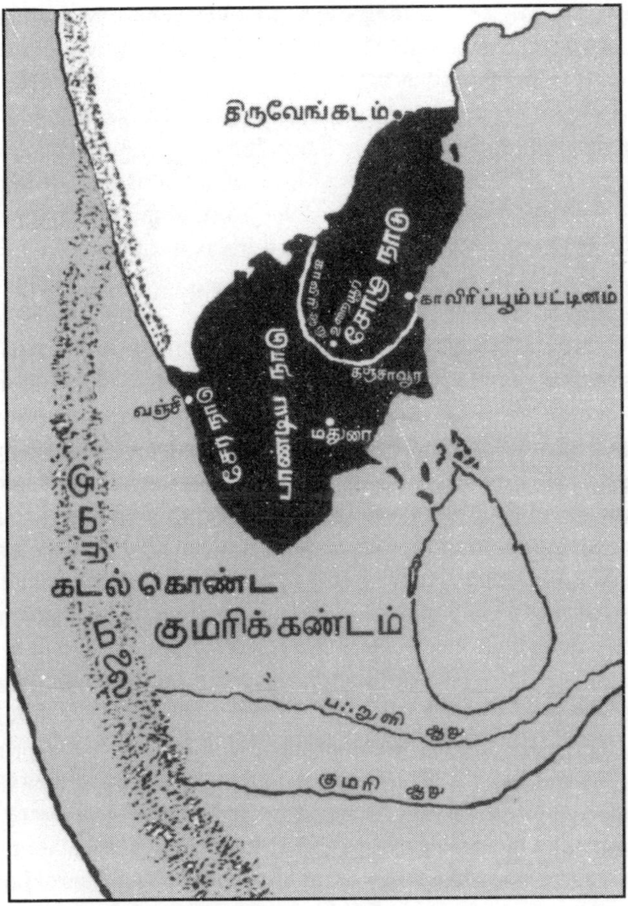

Fig. 4. Sivasailam Pillai, Katal Konta Kumarikkandam (Ocean-seized Kumarikkandam). This map in Tamil shows the Indian peninsula (the blackened part represents postdiluvial Tamilakam), south of which stretches antediluvial Kumarikkandam (shaded in gray). From Sivasailam Pillai, *Putumuraik Kalakat Tamilppattam* (*Mutar Puttakam: Mutar Parattirku*), revd. edn. (Tirunelveli: The South India Saiva Siddhanta Works Publishing Society, 1951).

Ten Madurai and Kapatapuram) which exist only in the antediluvial geographies of the Tamil life-world. The space outside the lost homeland, however, is left blank, as India's known geography is erased and replaced by the geography of Elsewhere. As is well known, in modern cartographic practices, blank spaces suggest unknown and even uninhabited places—*terra incognita*. So, in these maps, it is Lemuria that is the known and inhabited territory—and the centre of the known world. India, on the other hand, is reduced to a blank nothingness. All the same, because India and one of its regions, the Tamil country, is still the lived homeland of the Tamil devotees, it cannot be entirely done away with, and it appears on these maps to remind the reader that this is what postdiluvial Tamil speakers had to settle for, *after* the loss for ever of their beloved ancestral homeland.

The radical de-centring of India (which from the Indian nationalist perspective ought to be perceived as the true homeland of all loyal citizens) is also accompanied by the dissolution of its known boundaries. The clear delineation of borders is one of the primary agendas of modern state cartography, if not its *sine qua non* (Thongchai Winichakul 1994). In the subcontinent, both the British colonial and the Indian state have been dedicated to this enterprise over the past two hundred and fifty years, producing maps that transformed 'India' from an inchoate space into a known and identifiable geo-body (Edney 1997). Yet the Tamil maps of Lemuria question the very territorial integrity of the Indian nation-state, and point instead to a time when its present, and even historical, boundaries had not mattered at all. Even more subversively, they suggest that India's present borders circumscribe a territory that is far more limited in area and reach, in contrast to the ancestral Tamil homeland, which reaches in several instances, as I have noted, all the way to Antarctica. Once again, the modern Tamil reader of these maps is reminded that his lived homeland is a mere remnant—and a paltry one at that—of a much larger lost homeland, a continent no less.

Not the least, through various cartographic strategies, the Tamil devotee's maps of Lemuria remind today's Tamil speakers of the enormity of their loss. So, in 1927, M. S. Purnalingam Pillai's *Tamil India* included three maps (printed on the same page) entitled 'Puranic India before the Deluges', 'Puranic India after the Deluge', and 'Tamilaham 1st *c.* AD' (Purnalingam Pillai 1945). Others, such as Pulavar Kulanthai in 1946, drew maps in which the lost homeland of Kumarikkandam is superimposed over the lived homeland of India. Still others—such as the 1951 school textbook—use cartographic strategies like hatching and shading to show the lost homeland as a vast supplement to the lived land. Regardless of the strategy used, the consequence is generally the same, namely, to visually persuade the reader of these maps to consider the loss of land over time that the verbal narratives that accompany these maps frequently expand upon. So, typically, Tamilians (who are generally the intended audience for these maps) are told that once upon a time, their ancestors had lived on the vast and sprawling Lemuria. After its catastrophic loss, Tamil kings had established their rule over postdiluvial *Tamil akam*, the 'Tamil realm' which extended from Tirupati Hill to land's end, and from coast to coast. Frequently, maps of (postdiluvial) Tamilakam, often labelled 'Tamil Nadu' but including within its boundary the present-day state of Kerala, accompany these discussions. Almost invariably, the reader of these narratives and these maps is brought down to the present when 'Tamil Nadu' has become even more emaciated, with the progressive loss over the centuries of its western and northern areas to its neighbouring domains of Andhra Pradesh and Kerala. To paraphrase Thongchai, '. . . the agony [of loss of territories] is visually codified by a map. Now the anguish is concrete, measurable and easily transmittable' (Thongchai 1994: 152).

And yet the fact remains, as I have already noted, that loyalty and attachment to the lived homeland of Tamilnadu, itself a part of India, has also to be generated, especially if Tamil's devotees want their fellow speakers to rally together to protect and nurture their language—or what was left of it after the ravages of time and after the onslaughts made on it by rival languages and their patrons. Here is where the structure of loss in which Lemuria is embedded proves to be critical, for, as Tamil speakers are reminded again and again, the fact that what they are left with is a remnant of their lost homeland is all the more reason that what is left—fragmentary though it might be—has to be guarded and cherished. The lived homeland, in other words, becomes 'a memorative sign' of the lost homeland. In Jean Starobinski's suggestive reading, the memorative sign is 'related to a partial presence which causes one to experience, with pleasure and pain, the imminence and impossibility of complete restoration of [all our former life] which emerges fleetingly from oblivion. Roused by the "memorative sign," the conscience comes to be haunted by an image of the past which is at once definite and unattainable'

(Starobinski 1966: 93). So, during the 1940s and 1950s, the very decades that saw the birth of independent India and the reconfiguration of its internal political geography, everyone from the Tamil school-going child to the literate adult citizen was reminded that even though modern Tamilians could never have Lemuria, they should work hard to ensure that what was left of this remnant—namely, Tamilnadu—should not be lost to the neighbouring states of Kerala and Andhra Pradesh. Particularly satisfying to all concerned was the final incorporation—not without sacrifice of lives and the loss of other territory—of Kanyakumari (which for the past few centuries had been part of neighbouring Travancore) into Madras state in December 1956. The one serious irredentist consequence of Tamil fantasies about a lost antediluvian homeland, the redeeming of Kumari was politically important because it had served as the postdiluvial southern boundary of the Tamil realm. Symbolically, of course, its significance was no less, because, as I noted earlier, the Cape had been transformed into a *lieu de mémoire*, a place where memories of the lost homeland are more acutely experienced (Ramaswamy 2000).

In the imagination of the lived homeland as a memorative sign of the lost homeland, naming practices play a very important role. Hence, the metropolitan Lemuria is re-christened very early on as Kumarikkandam or Kumari Nadu, thus establishing a direct connection with the remnant of Kanyakumari, but also with the important 'Tamil' goddess who reigns over land's end. Even more dramatically, from very early on, Lemuria is frequently referred to as 'Tamilakam' and 'Tamilnadu', nominally transforming that latter from a mere region into a vast continent. Such a naming suggests also that the lost continent was intimate Tamil territory, and that the postdiluvial Tamilakam, and the modern state of Tamilnadu (itself named as such only in 1968), were formerly parts of the antediluvian homeland. Those Tamil devotees who are Indianist in inclination even name the lost homeland 'India', establishing a nominal connection between the nation-state and Lemuria. The lived homeland is thus subsumed by the lost.

The politics of loss thus works to establish a productive tension between lost and lived homelands in twentieth-century Tamil India. The two are intimately linked precisely because the one—the lived—

is imagined to be the fragment of the whole that is lost. Because that which is lost is lost forever, this means that the fragment becomes even more precious, and has to be protected and cherished, to the point of giving up one's life for it, if need be. A critical division of labour animates this productive nexus between lived and lost homelands. The former becomes the object of loyalty and of pragmatic love, in other words, of patriotism; the latter is the focus of insatiable yearning or sentimental love—of nostalgia.

In recent years, much has been written on this most elusive of sentiments which lies 'at the very core of the modern condition' (Boym 2001: xvi). In *The Future of Nostalgia*, Svetlana Boym reminds us that 'nostalgia is a longing for a home that no longer exists or has never existed', and that 'Nostalgic love can only survive in a long-distance relationship' (Boym 2001: xiii). Not surprisingly, nostalgia has found a flourishing home in Tamil India, whose relationship to the lost Lemuria is, irrevocably, 'long-distance'. Similarly, the feminist scholar Iris Young notes that 'nostalgia is a flight from having to come to terms with [an originary] loss, by means of constant search for a symbolic substitution for a lost home' (Young 2000: 54). The symbolic substitution for the lost Kumarikkandam, I have noted, is the lived homeland of Tamilnadu/India. It comes to stand in for the lost home/land. Young also distinguishes usefully between remembrance and nostalgia, suggesting that while the latter accompanies the fantasies of a lost home, the former attempts to preserve and nurture what one holds. 'Nostalgic longing is always for an elsewhere. Remembrance is the affirmation of what brought us here' (Young 2000: 66). In other words, the lost homeland returns to present consciousness through nostalgia and a narrative mode that resembles fantasy, while the lived homeland is remembered through linear recollection and the realist genre of history (Ramaswamy 2004).

Not least, following the philosopher Edward Casey, I propose that the lost homeland inhabits 'an absolute past, a past that was never a present. Such a world with such a past . . . cannot be recollected as such' (Casey 1987: 367). It can only be recollected, instead, as nostalgia—as longing, yearning, mourning. The lost homeland is a 'world vanished in the shadows of an absolute past' (Casey 1987: 381). It is thus not a threat to the lived homeland of the here-and-now. On the contrary, as I have suggested here, returning to haunt the present as irrevocable loss, Lemuria paradoxically functions to remind modern Tamil speakers of what they do possess and hold—their lived homeland of Tamilnadu, even India. This, then, is the logic of the fascination with this lost world in today's Tamilnadu, a logic that is rooted in labours of loss that are passionate, nostalgic and bittersweet. As Casey observes, 'In being nostalgic, we are moved by a past world that is the more potent for being absent or "vanished" ' (Casey 1987: 378-9). As a lost home-place that is both discursively definite but also fabulously unattainable, Lemuria's potency for Tamil's devotees derives from the fact that their labours of loss have transformed it into a site where they witness the 'baffling combination of the sweet and the bitter, the personal and the impersonal, distance and proximity, presence and absence' (Casey 1987: 379). This, then, too, is the allure of Lemuria for Tamil's devotees, as a place-world that is there—but not really—to remind them of the pristine origin of their beloved language and land in a moment of absolute plenitude and perfection that is now forever lost, and hence safe and secure from the ravages of time—and of history.

NOTES

1. An earlier version of this paper was presented at the 'Conference on Regions and Regionalism' at the University of Pune, Pune, in December 2001. I am grateful to Anne Feldhaus, Rajendra Vora and other participants at the conference for their comments.
2. I am mindful here of Anthony Smith's observation that the nationalist spatial vision has to be ultimately tangible and practical. 'It demands a terrain on which nations can be built' (Smith 1986: 184). But note also his follow-up observation: 'But the vision also contains an unearthly note, an element of archaic mystery, particularly where the environment yields up vestiges of a pre-history that antedates the community' (ibid.).
3. This map is appended to *Iravana Kaviyam*, an epic poem by Pulavar Kulanthai. Proscribed soon after its publication by the then Congress government, the poem celebrates the 'demon' Ravana as the ideal Tamil king and proposes that his kingdom was once part of Lemuria. The ban on the poem was lifted soon after the DMK was voted into power in 1967, and the text was republished in 1971.

REFERENCES

Appadurai, K. 1941. *Kumarik Kantam allatu katal konda tennadu* (*Kumarikkandam, Or the southern land seized by the ocean*). Chennai: The South India Saiva Siddhanta Works Publishing Society.

Baines, J. A. 1893. 'Ethnographic Distribution of the Population', in *Census of India, 1891: General Report*. London: Indian Government.

Boym, Svetlana. 2001. *The Future of Nostalgia*. New York: Basic Books.

Casey, Edward. 1987. 'The World of Nostalgia', *Man & World* 20: 367-84.

Edney, Matthew H. 1997. *Mapping an Empire: The Geographical Construction of British India, 1765-1843*. Chicago: University of Chicago Press.

Haeckel, Ernst. 1876. *History of Creation: On the Development of the Earth and its Inhabitants by the Action of Natural Causes* (*A Popular Exposition of the Doctrine of Evolution in General, and of That of Darwin, Goethe, and Lamarck in Particular*). New York: D. Appleton and Company.

Ivy, Marilyn. 1995. *Discourses of the Vanishing: Modernity, Phantasm, Japan*. Chicago: University of Chicago Press.

Krishnan, P. 1984. *Tamil Nulkalil Tamil Moli, Tamil Inam, Tamil Natu* (*Tamil Language, Tamil Community, and Tamil Nadu in Tamil Literature*). Madras: Ilantamilar Patippakam.

Macleane, Charles D. 1987 (1885). *Manual of the Administration of the Madras Presidency*. Reprint edition. Vol. 1. New Delhi: Asian Educational Services.

Mahalingam, N., ed. 1981. *Gems from the Prehistoric Past*. Madras: International Society for the Investigation of Ancient Civilization.

Marsden, E(dmund). 1909. *History of India for Senior Classes*, Part I: *The Hindu Period*. London: Macmillan.

Mignolo, Walter. 1989. 'Comments on Harley's Deconstructing the Map', *Cartographica* 26 (3): 109-13.

Pulavar Kulanthai. 1971. *Iravana Kaviyam* (*Epic Poem on Ravana*). Reprint edition. Erode: Vela Patippakam.

Purnalingam Pillai, M. S. 1945. *Tamil India*. Reprint edition. Tirunelveli: The South India Saiva Siddhanta Works Publishing Society.

Ramachandran, M. and R. Madhivanan. 1991. *The Spring of the Indus Civilization*. Madras: Prasanna Pathippagam.

Ramaswamy, Sumathi. 1997. *Passions of the Tongue: Language Devotion in Tamil India, 1891-1970*, edited by V. Bonnell and L. Hunt, *Studies on the History of Society and Culture*. Berkeley: University of California Press.

———. 1999. 'Catastrophic Cartographies: Mapping the Lost Continent of Lemuria', *Representations* 67: 92-129.

———. 2000. 'History at Land's End: Lemuria in Tamil Spatial Fables', *Journal of Asian Studies* 59 (3): 575-602.

———. 2004. *The Lost Land of Lemuria: Fabulous Geographies, Catastrophic Histories*. Berkeley: University of California Press.

Risley, H. H. and Edward Gait. 1903. 'Caste, Tribe, and Race', in *Census of India, 1901: Report*. Calcutta: Office of the Superintendent of Government Printing.

Sivasailam Pillai. 1951. *Putumuraik Kalakat Tamilppattam* (*Mutar Puttakam: Mutar Parattirku*) (*New Kazhagam Tamil Reader for Class Six*). Revised edition. Tirunelveli: The South India Saiva Siddhanta Works Publishing Society.

Smith, Anthony D. 1986. 'Legends and Landscapes', in *The Ethnic Origins of Nations*. Oxford: Basil Blackwell.

Somasundara Bharati, S. 1912. *Tamil Classics and Tamilakam*. Madras: [n.p.].

———. 1967. 'The Pre-deluge Pandinad and Her Southern Frontier', in *The Papers of Dr. Navalar Somasundara Bharatiar*, edited by S. Sambasivam. Madurai: Navalar Pusthaka Nilayam.

Starobinski, Jean. 1966. 'The Idea of Nostalgia', *Diogenes* 54: 81-103.

Stewart, Susan. 1993. *On Longing: Narratives of the Miniature, the Gigantic, the Souvenir, the Collection*. Durham: Duke University Press.

Stuart, H. A. 1893. 'Caste, Tribe, And Race', in *Census of India, 1891: Madras*. Madras: Government Press.

Tamilnadu Textbook Society. 1981. *Intiya Varalaru: 6* (*History of India for Class Six*). Madras: Tamilnadu Text Book Society.

Thongchai Winichakul. 1994. *Siam Mapped: A History of the Geo-Body of a Nation*. Honolulu: University of Hawaii Press.

Thurston, Edgar. 1899. 'The Dravidian Problem', *Madras Government Museum Bulletin* 2 (3): 182-97.

Young, Iris M. 2000. 'House and Home: Feminist Variations on a Theme', in *Resistance, Flight, Creation: Feminist Enactments of French Philosophy*, edited by D. Olkonski. Ithaca: Cornell University Press.

6

The Place of Mumbai: Circles of Urban Identity in the Nineteenth and Twentieth Centuries

Jim Masselos

Any attempt to contextualize the role of a great city brings into play myriads of ideas, interpretations, attitudes and feelings. Here I am concerned with those which coalesce around two main sets of issues. One is the city's place in a state polity and national governance. The other is the issue of its surrounds, the countryside around it. Is a great city an integral part of both state and countryside or does it exude a character all its own? Similarly, is it of the region in which it is located, inextricably interconnected with that in which it is sited or is it distinctively separate from this and other parts of the territories which constitute the national realm.

In talk about great cities mutually conflicting points are often made. One is the apparent truism which sees them as separate from the state or nation in which they are located: New York, for instance, is not USA and is distinct from its surrounds. Much the same is said of London, Sydney, Tokyo and other large urban complexes. On the other hand, there is a converse truism—that each city has a specific character as being American, British, Australian or Japanese. Each is a part, and perhaps even a determining part, of the dominant culture of the region and of the nation in which it is situated. The view can be extended to argue that cities epitomize the nation; they are the nation.

Another set of concerns focuses on geographical environment. Are the city and its suroundings interconnected or separate? One approach sees the city and countryside as distinctively different—and by extension even as polar opposites. The idea is so frequently expressed that the contrast has become a cliché—although a useful one. The differences are apparent when rural and agrarian pursuits of the countryside are juxtaposed against activities associated with or dependent on cities—like factory production, trade, office work and cultural matters. While the spatial location of the economic divisions of labour and of commercial networks go far to provide urban conglomerates with characteristics distinguishing them from countryside settlements,[1] the identity that attaches to each is reliant on how they are perceived.

There is nothing simple or straightforward here. Contrasting perceptions aggregate around the notion of city and country. To them attach tropes of approval and disapproval, and both city and countryside arouse negative and positive attitudes. Ashis Nandy, for instance, sees a dynamic Indian polarity where the colonial metropolis is 'the pivotal fantasy and counterpoint to the village', a place of escape from the confines of tightly constricted caste and economically bound village society.[2] Raymond Williams delineates opposed stereotypes derived from European experience but ones still resonant in South Asian contexts:

> On the country has gathered the idea of a natural way of life: of peace, innocence, and simple virtue. On the city has gathered the idea of an achieved centre: of learning, communication, light. Powerful hostile associations have also developed: on the city as a place of noise, worldliness and ambition; on the country as a place of backwardness, ignorance, limitation.[3]

It is easy to conjure up other oppositions. All involve stereotypes—one dimensional images frozen in a single moment that do not incorporate ideas of change over time. Thus another urban axiom may be forgotten, that summed up in biological metaphors of the city as a complex organism which changes and grows, which multiplies and has a diversity evident in its social mix of ethnicities, classes, communities and even nationalities.

Cities may thus be the subject of widely differing approaches. How they apply to Mumbai's varied and dichotomous relationship with its limited and extended environs—physical, political and mental—is the concern of what follows. Put differently, what follows deals with issues of urban identity and identification, with how the city identified itself and how its identity was formulated.

FORMAL STRUCTURES OF ASSOCIATION AND SEPARATION

Currently Mumbai has a national identity as the capital and dominant city of Maharashtra. It is formally part of the structure of the government and administration of the Republic of India as it is also an integral part of the national financial structure. An enormous megalopolis driven by a thriving engine of economic and technological achievement, it has the premier role within the Republic as the nation's primary machine of wealth and productivity. It is thus integrated within the modern nation-state and its economy.

Basically there is little new in the structure of its relation to wider state entities. A similar pattern has formally existed virtually from the time of its foundation. Under its original name, Bombay, the city was for a long time, going back into the early years of colonial rule, the capital, what was then known as a Presidency. When it was founded by the British East India Company, it had no surrounding territory outside the tiny islands on which it was sited and was for a short time subordinate to the trading post at Surat. Thereafter it became pre-eminent in the region and as the Company's economic interests expanded so did its territory. In the late eighteenth century it not only acquired non-contiguous land in Gujarat but also won the adjacent island of Salsette to the north of what was becoming the single continuous strip of land known as the Island of Bombay. For much of this time Bombay operated as a city-state dependent on coastal and international trade and shipbuilding enterprises, justifying the settlement and a British presence on the west coast of the subcontinent. From here, after the conquest of the Maratha nation in the second decade of the nineteenth century, the city ruled its surrounds as the capital of what was known first as the Presidency of Bombay and later in the twentieth century as the Province of Bombay.[4]

From the beginnings of British occupation the logic of the settlement at the southernmost tip of the seven low lying islands had meant it was physically separate from the land across the harbour which was alien territory under the inevitably hostile Maratha power. The location of the settlement reinforced one of its primary purposes, its function as a trading factory. It needed both protection from attack and easy access to the trading routes that gave it reason for existence. So, from the first moments of their occupation the British, as was necessary for a small and vulnerable foreign trading operation, developed Bombay by constructing a fort and various walls and ramparts—all of which were progressively extended until finally demolished in the mid-nineteenth century. The result was a town physically and mentally separate from its mainland neighbourhood environs. A specific ethos for Bombay was thus coalescing from early in its history—an ethos of being apart from its contiguous hinterland and one which expressed the foreign power's trading and political interests.

Whether this ethos, a function of location and the early needs of a trading company, would survive into the nineteenth and twentieth centuries when contiguous territories were acquired was neither inevitable nor predetermined. During the nineteenth century while its role as an administrative centre of an expanded Presidency and its economic functions gave Bombay significant links with its hinterland, its island location ensured that a sense of spatial differentiation was maintained even in terms of the region over which it ruled. On the other hand the administrative re-organization of the territories conquered by the British brought the city within the parameters of what became their Indian empire. While Bombay retained some rights of direct access to decision makers in London, it was subordinated to the governor-general in Calcutta. Bombay was part of the state polity established by the British raj and was integrated into the structure of the imperial state which ruled over India. The city was thus at the meeting point of overlapping circles of British power. It was subsumed within the circle of the two world systems, the global economy and the global imperium, which the British Empire operated; it was within the circle of the power structures Britain applied over its subcontinental empire, and it was part of the circle of British administration of the region of the Presidency. In the shadow of the overlap was Bombay's distinctiveness, or at least a part of it.

Other particularities ensured that Bombay, even under a unifying British structure of administration, would have a distinctive place apart from the rest of British India. Though integrated within state structures, Bombay was also a formally separate entity.

Its separateness had legal underpinnings. Given the accident of its acquisition as part of the marriage dowry of Charles II to Catherine of Portugal, the British received manorial rights which meant that all-India legislation regarding urban change could not apply to Bombay Town and Island. Any initiative which specifically affected it demanded separate legislation. Thus, an ambiguous legal situation existed in Bombay's relations even with the suburban areas that grew on neighbouring Salsette Island from the late nineteenth century, since that territory had been acquired by conquest not by deed. The two required different legislation: the Suburban districts came under all-India purview while Bombay Town and Island had its own specific laws.

Thus, Bombay under British rule, while part of the structures of imperial control through a governor who headed an administration covering both the city and the presidency region, was at the same time formally separate. Moreover, from the 1870s the establishment of an elected municipal corporation gave it further particularity, legally, structurally and perceptually.

The motto of the corporation, *urbs prima in Indis*—the first city in India, summed up the situation. The motto underlined the city's place within British India and asserted its pre-eminence. Other sobriquets crept into talk about the town as the second city in the Empire and the Queen of Asia,[5] but it was the motto rather than the epithet which became the cliche. City corporators intoned it in speeches; it appeared in print polemics; and travel writers used it as the starting point for praise or satire. Whichever, the distinctiveness of the city was affirmed as was its geo-political positioning.

The notion of a pre-eminent city was one which appealed strongly to its articulate ruling classes: its British administrators; its independent-minded European merchants, and other non-officials; and its Indian public men—social and political leaders, intellectuals, journalists, teachers and others. The last two groups used the corporation to assert ideas of urban pride and urban patriotism. Only the best was suited to Bombay just as Bombay outdid India's other cities in civic affairs. And by using arguments about city pride in various debates a degree of Indian and anti-imperial sentiment could be inserted into the public discourse in a manner which made it virtually impossible for it to be considered seditious or threatening to the regime. At its core Bombay's relationship with the dominant regime could have a subversive undertext, carrying notions of separation and independence. Conjoining circles could be separated whilst retaining an appearance of interconnectedness.

Such ambiguity was exemplified in the strong reaction against government attempts in the 1880s and early 1900s to force on Bombay a standard time common to all of India. The underlying point of the opposition was to defend the city against what was perceived as an attack on its special character. One set of arguments contended that standardizing time would interfere with people's daily routines and religious observances, another set was far more emotional in insisting that what might be good for Madras or Calcutta or even the countryside was not in the least good for Bombay. Bombay's own needs were adversely affected by the proposed measure, to say nothing of the hurt to its *amour propre*.[6]

The first attempt to impose a standard time, which was to be the time current in and, even worse for Bombayites, known as Madras time, evoked strong feelings of urban pride. A newspaper editorial sardonically noted that Bombay's inhabitants accepted it

> was true . . . that the sun evinced a preference for rising first on Madras, and it was even admitted that this should qualify the Stygian adjective sometimes applied in that Presidency. But like the people in the virgilian Hades, the people of Bombay also knew a sun of their own, or believed they did, and intended to keep on knowing it too; and would only condescend to meet the arguments against them by saying that if they were half an hour behind the rest of India every day, they gained half a century on the rest of India every year.[7]

Some two decades later Pherozeshah Mehta confounded the government's second attempt to impose a (different) standard time by appealing in the corporation chambers to notions of what was special about the city and its separateness from the countryside. 'The Government were mistaken', he fulminated, 'in trying to deal with a large and populous city like Bombay in the same way as they dealt with the mofussil. Bombay stood upon quite a different basis altogether because with its population of 10 lacs it could not be treated as if it were a portion of the mofussil.' He continued: 'It is not fair and proper that the population of this City should be driven like a flock of dumb cattle. . . .' And then Pherozeshah the Ferocious, the Lion of Bombay, reiterated the idea: 'Perhaps it is a matter of mere sentiment and prejudice, but I will always take a pride in standing up for the integrity, the dignity and the independence of the immense population of the City of Bombay. (Loud applause.) The Corporation is a representative body of the citizens of Bombay . . .

[and] was created for the purpose of representing and looking after and watching and guarding the interests, the wishes and the sentiments of the whole population of the City.'[8] These wishes, interests and sentiments, Pherozeshah asserted, were different from those of people elsewhere in India as was their city. It may have been part of an imperial whole but it was also its own being.

As to standard time, the matter was resolved in a way that resolved nothing, not the dislike of standard time nor the need for conformity. Certainly not resolved was the urban paradox—of integration and separation—which was at the heart of the issue. Neither supporters nor opponents were satisfied with what came into effect. Government offices, railways and European businesses operated on Standard Time, while municipal offices, schools and other agencies, and most Indian businesses used Bombay Time. Appointments were fixed according to BT (Bombay Time) or ST (Standard Time), a practice that caused some confusion. Only after Independence did Bombay cede its temporal identity and, for the greater national good, accept Indian Standard Time. At that time and on this matter at least, the urban paradox of overlapping circles of urban identity and of external power were brought into benign conjunction.

Conflicting notions of the corporation's place under the raj forcefully emerged in other controversies. During Civil Disobedience, for instance, the issue of differentiation in the corporation chambers is easiest seen in an ongoing dispute over whether the Congress flag (according to the government), or the national flag (according to Congress),[9] should fly over the Corporation building. Since attempts to pass resolutions permitting its hoisting were defeated or adjourned during the 1930s[10] the Corporation perforce accepted its place in the imperial structure yet the underlying issue was clear to officialdom: hoisting was 'an affront to Government and an open manifestation of anti-Government tendencies'.[11]

Even after Independence the conjunction of circles was not invariably benign, and differentiation could surface. When in the first decades Congress controlled the municipality, as well as state and national governments the overlapping circles were essentially, but not always invariably, in conformity but when different parties were in office there could be dissension. Again, when a particular issue was strongly supported within the city but not outside it, the city could become a cockpit for conflict, a source of opposition and a site of contestation as happened after 1956 when the Nehru government made Bombay the capital of a combined Marathi- and Gujarati-speaking state. The Samyukta Maharashtra movement opposed the move, leading to heated dispute and major riots. The outcome was that the decision was rescinded in 1960 and Bombay became the capital of a new Marathi-speaking state, Maharashtra. While this ensured that Bombay was integrally part of the Marathi region, the city nevertheless continued to be subject to the play of divergent forces.

The organizational structure of national parties could reinforce differentiation between one or other of the circles. After the establishment of linguistic states Congress, India's dominant political party until the 1990s, continued the structure of regional organization which Gandhi had set up during the Non-Cooperation campaign of 1920 in that both Bombay and Maharashtra each retained separate Congress committees. The politics of urban difference, the representation of a separate urban entity, was thus recognized and retained. Similarly and paradoxically, the party that did represent Marathi interests, the Shiv Sena, had a similar effect following on its inability to achieve a sizeable base of support outside Bombay until a couple of decades after its formation in 1967. Its potency derived from its championing of Marathi interests and attitudes within the city. A spectacular demonstration of its ability to do so was in 1969 when it campaigned against the central government's attempts to resolve the Maharashtra and Mysore state border dispute. The consequence was an outright affirmation of disagreement by blocking the entry of the Deputy Prime Minister, Morarji Desai, into the city from the airport, and by the week long riot that followed.

Such action was only one in a line of issues put forward by one or other of these and other parties and pressure groups driven by city distinctiveness and the numerous and even contradictory interests within it. On occasions they could be in conformity with the various formal power structures which had their effect on the city but at other times they could be in disjunction, and in very forceful opposition.

Perceptions of Urban Difference

Apparently less paradoxical was the city's positioning in terms of its specific relationship with its geographical surrounds. A sense of its distinction from the countryside was clearer.

To return to pre-Independence years, raj preconceptions of the difference between town and country were inscribed in Indian English vocabulary. A structural distinction between Presidency town and territory was mediated through the use of the word *mofussil* (or *mufassal*) though probably more frequently in northern rather than western India. The idea of separation came from an original Arabic meaning of 'separate, detailed, particular', which transferred into Hindi and thence to Indian English.[12] *Mofussil* classified all the country outside the Presidency town, or by association all areas outside any large town, as the *mofussil*, as upcountry. All that lay beyond either of the three Presidency towns, Calcutta, Madras and Bombay, was *mofussil*. By extension the term could distinguish the principal station or town from its surrounding district so that, for those living in Poona (Pune) or similar large towns, what lay outside their boundaries was also *mofussil*. In all its variations the term reflected a sense of separation between city and an undifferentiated countryside.[13]

Its use may have been less common in other Indian languages. Although the word, *mofussil*, does not seem to have been used much in Marathi, an equivalent differentiation (but from the perspective of the countryside) may have been conveyed in the early nineteenth century by the word *khedegaon* (or similar cognates), which referred to villages collectively or was a comprehensive term for villages and hamlets,[14] thus by implication setting village India mentally apart from the town or city. There was clearer distinction in the use of another word which also made the transition into Indian English. *Des* (or *desh*) could mean a country or tract, but also a province or division of a country.[15] Early nineteenth-century usage gave it a definition which separated it from Bombay city to encompass 'the Maharashtra, and by contraction Maratta desh, [including] the Kokun [Konkan], but the term is more generally applied to the whole Maratta country east of the Syhadree range'.[16]

Awareness of difference was evident elsewhere. It was there in those who travelled to Bombay from the Marathi hinterland, to something distinctively different from what they were used to. The journey intensified the disjunction. Before the advent of railways major effort was required to get to Bombay. Take the case of young D. K. Karve's attempt to reach Bombay for an exam.

> We therefore decided to go to Bombay by a ship that was going to sail from a creek, six miles from Murud. The time of departure was fixed at midnight,

and we all went to the boat in the evening with our kits and put up at a Dharmashala on the bank of the creek. At about 9 p.m. a storm broke out and it began to rain cats and dogs. The creek was soon flooded and it was not possible for the boat to sail. It was no use waiting there, as stormy weather continued till next morning. We therefore returned to Murud, although it was not at all easy to wade through the flooded creek near our village. It was not then possible to reach Bombay in time.[17]

His expedition aborted, Karve had to make other arrangements and it was some time before he completed a journey to the city. There the weather again affected him: 'During the monsoon season the coastal steamers suspend their services; if I had wanted to see him [his dying father], I would have had to undertake a long journey on foot, so my brother and my mother did not write to me about his illness at all.'[18]

Others, of course, completed journeys to Bombay on the coastal shipping of the day, a mode by which generations of Indians had moved up and down the western shoreline with relative ease. It was easier than the alternative, the journey by land, which was probably more common. Most people travelled by cart or other similar conveyance, some even walked—whichever the method the Konkan's bridgeless rivers had to be crossed and the journey was necessarily difficult and could take days to complete.[19] Railways did not entirely remedy the situation as it was not until late in the twentieth century that a railway line finally drove southward through the Konkan.

On arrival, the city itself was an experience. The chasm between village or small town and the city is captured in Lakshmibai Tilak's memory of wonderment during her first visit.

I . . . was having the greatest fun! I was utterly bewildered by the six- and seven-storeyed buildings, the trams and the streets. From the time I arrived at the station I was stupefied, and did not know where I was going. I was continually looking all around me. Before we reached home Tilak [her husband] had to warn me three or four times to watch my step. Home! We had not even a house yet. We spent the night at a hotel, and next day arranged to rent a room somewhere in Girgaon near the Prarthana Samaj. In this room Tilak and I set up house. He brought in the things, and I undertook to arrange them, but I was so enchanted by the astonishing sights of Bombay that on merely hearing strange street-cries I kept running out to look.[20]

Her sense of strangeness has its parallel in other accounts, though not necessarily her elation. Decades after Lakshmibai, Sangabai

Parbhu Sinoran began annual visits to Dr Ambedkar's death commemorations at Dadar with a trepidation later dissipated: 'I used to be so scared of this city when my husband used to bring me here. But even after my husband died almost 15 years ago, I continued to come here with my daughters and now even my grandchildren.'[21] For others, the journeying to Bombay could be ordinary and routine, as the narrator in a Dalit short story assumes when he begins a conversation with a fellow passenger in a train to Bombay.

> 'Where are you going, Saab?' Startled, he looked in the direction of the voice. The man standing near him had asked him the question.
>
> 'To Bombay.' The words escaped his lips unexpectedly. He must say something more, so he asked, 'And you?'
>
> 'I too am going to Bombay.'
>
> He didn't feel there was anything special about it. Every day thousands of people go to Bombay.[22]

As it turns out, the two of them are escaping to Bombay, one from riot and massacre, and the other from caste discrimination and village violence.

People went to Bombay for a variety of reasons—refuge, pilgrimage, work, marriage among them. Whatever their motivation, what they went to had something which was not in what they had left. While their movement, the fact of the journey, indicates the city's links with surroundings that could be near or far, it also indicated the divide between town and country. They were different universes, even if such journeyings interlinked them.

European travellers arriving in Bombay in the time of the raj likewise stepped into another universe and were equally overtaken by what they encountered. It was the more overwhelming given the contrast with the journey out from Europe. That journey was a time away from cares and usual behaviour, when friends were easily made and as easily forgotten after landfall, when the norm became nightly parties and fancy dress balls. Maisie Wright in 1928 noted the boarding of five maharajas on her ship at Marseilles, as well as 'some' provincial governors returning from leave, and a bishop:

> Now a full programme of social events was organised, competitions for deck games, camp-fire concerts round an electric fire on deck at night, and a gymkhana. I danced every night and wore all my new evening frocks. . . . After calling at Aden, we had a fancy-dress dance, which I enjoyed very much. My table-companions came in kilts made from bath towels with

sporrans of sponge-bags and two dangling shaving brushes, but they were drunk by dinner-time, so I kept out of their way. . . . I made a new friend named Robert who was dressed as a pirate. . . .[23]

The journey out began as a charade, a time as distinct from what was left behind as what was ahead. It became an extended threshold, where the physical passage matched a moment of transition in persona. On the journey ordinary people turned into rulers. Aldous Huxley en route to Bombay sensed the transformation:

The young man who goes out from a London suburb to take up a clerkship in India finds himself a member of a small ruling community; he has slavish servants to order about, dark-skinned subordinates to whom it is right and proper to be rude. Three hundred and twenty million Indians surround him; he feels incomparably superior to them all. . . . He may be ill-bred, stupid, uneducated; no matter. His skin is white. Superiority in India is a question of epiderms.[24]

The physical crossing of arrival was marked by a mass of porters cascading onto the ship, a flurry of noise and a bustle that was overwhelming. Bombay was unlike anything experienced before.

I gazed down from the deck on to the quay, fascinated by the sight of swarms of coolies with legs like black sticks carrying enormous trunks and crates on their swollen heads. After a time I saw that their heads were not swollen but swathed in turbans. . . . I was so puzzled by these incredible men that I forgot I had to land here. I had always dreaded this moment. How does one 'land'?[25]

Once achieved, the move from ship to dock produced more thresholds, reinforcing the sense of difference.

The noise in the dock is maddening. The Customs, the police, the health-officers, all mob the voyager with undreamed-of formalities. . . . Then, again, the dispersal of the luggage, which must be fished out at another spot amid the yelling horde of coolies who rush at the trunks and use the portmanteaus as missiles, till at last we are in the street.[26]

And then outside, through into a whole new city and country. Like Lakshmibai, European travellers marvelled at the crowds and the strangeness of the people, often detailing the kinds of people noticed. What the new arrival saw for the first time was not only city but something that stood for India as a whole. For a short time Bombay constituted, represented, all of India. The two, city and subcontinent, were conflated into a single notion, something that would not have occurred to Lakshmibai or other Indians making their journey to Bombay: for them Bombay perhaps represented something modern, prosperous and grand. But it was not for them, as it was initially for the European arrival, a quintessentially Indian artefact. Lady Strachey wished she had kept 'a more minute recollection of my first Bombay impressions; they were very vivid at the time, and I remember being struck with surprise that all accounts of India that had fallen in my way were so meagre, when materials new and strange were in such abundance.'[27]

Nor were European travellers always impressed, certainly not William Shepherd who expected in 1857 to come to 'the grand city of Bombay'. The 'unfinished looking streets, heaps of unremoved rubbish, bricks, rabble [*sic*], want of footpaths, want of form, shape, and neatness, impress us with the idea that we are in the outskirts of it. Not a bit of it; we are *in* Bombay.'[28] In the following century Aldous Huxley was equally unhappy about Bombay's splendid Indo-Gothic buildings: 'Architecturally, Bombay is one of the most appalling cities of either hemisphere. It had the misfortune to develop during what was, perhaps, the darkest period of all architectural history.'[29] Huxley saw Bombay as being distinguished but not with the approbation others gave it.

Just as he saw the city through his own aesthetic prejudice, other Europeans looked at the city not with fresh eyes but with preconceptions carried from England. They saw what they were conditioned to see but that was not necessarily or entirely Orientalist. Maria Graham at the beginning of the nineteenth century, in talking of exotic people and antique sculptures, was guided by the picturesque idiom of late eighteenth-century English art theory and by a concurrent, if somewhat contradictory, neo-classical sensitization to Roman and Greek antecedents.

> Leaving the bunder we crossed the esplanade, which presented a gay and interesting scene, being crowded with people in carriages, on horseback, and on foot. A painter might have studied all the varieties of attitude and motion in the picturesque figures of the *koolies*. . . . While the better sort of native women in their graceful costume, reminding one of antique sculptures, are employed in drawing, filling, or carrying water from the neighbouring wells. . . .[30]

Almost a hundred years later Prince Karageorgevitch was more sensationally ethnographic in his impressions of the 'incredibly mixed crowd', the almost naked 'natives' who were distinguished from Parsis in their distinctive costumes, the 'Hindoos, clad in thin bright silk, and rolls of light-hued muslin on their head' and even the English soldiers. Like many who preceded him he too noted the various types of carriages and conveyances and the variety of shops and bazaars.[31] Aware of the expected, Aldous Huxley into the twentieth century was phlegmatic: 'The brown skins, the bare feet, the nose-rings, the humped bullocks—all these things were foreseeable, seemed obvious and familiar from the moment of landing. The really odd, unexpected thing about Bombay was its birds.'[32]

The experience of the first encounter produced a necessarily limited and shallow focus on movement, people, costumes and streetscapes. But European travellers instinctively interpreted the scene in terms of that sense of class and place inherent in English social life. Place provided important comparisons; for Lytton it was with Europe: 'I think I never in my life saw a town so picturesque as Bombay—I do not even except Venice.'[33] For Ruby Madden it was Australia: 'The fashionable part where Gov. House and everybody lives and reminds me so of Darling Point [Sydney].'[34] More perceptive were eyes sensitized to the manifestations of class in their own societies: in dress and costume they easily read the signs of status differentiation. Maria Graham noted the 'better sort' of woman, Karageorgevitch distinguished superior Indians from the half naked 'natives'; both showed awareness of difference within Indian society, a sense of social position whose structural underpinnings had nothing to do with the exoticism of Bombay but with wealth and standing—or their absence. Bombay could hence be understood within terms of a continuum of social praxis already experienced outside and far from it. It could be seen as much the same social universe even if apparently utterly alien in its manifestation.

There was, as might be expected from travel memoirs, curiosity about people and an eye for curiosities—a quickness to capture the quirks of custom which is after all part of what travellers' accounts are expected to unveil. But the exotic activities noted were not only of Indian groups but covered the curious habits of Britons in their raj habitat. Even for someone fresh from England like Maisie Wright British rituals of acquaintanceship seemed inbred:

Lois takes me in hand to initiate me into the Indian ways as we drive out to leave visiting cards in the little boxes inscribed with the names of the owners which are attached to gates and walls. Then I have to sign the visitors' book of His Excellency the Governor. . . . I realise now that some British people may live in this country for years and yet know very little about India or Indians. Here in Bombay the Europeans live in their own quarters, such as the Fort or Colaba, they shop in British shops like the Army & Navy Stores and spend their leisure time in clubs from which Indians are excluded, so the only Indians they meet are their servants.[35]

Philip Steegman was equally sardonic about how social acceptability was mediated through the foibles of European expatriates:

There are two kinds of letters of introduction: those which distantly suggest to the Important One that the writer would be grateful for a little attention to So-and-So, and those which invoke racy memories of palmy days to stir the Important One to be kind to a friend. I had a mixed bag; but I soon realised that India is no ordinary country, where citizens of other worlds might wander unimpaired, receiving and returning hospitality and making little distinction between one friend and another.[36]

Being in India was not merely about recording the customs of locals; it was also about coping with the customs of compatriots, all of which made the visit to Bombay singular indeed.

Just as journeying into Bombay in such narratives had a sense of the special, leaving it had similar drama. It too was about transition and breaking through boundaries. It was at this point that Bombay receded as representing India and the idea of India being out there became paramount. Any departure was complicated, requiring effort and planning, though not as much once the railways came on steam. Before, in the century's early years, almost military logistics were needed to mount Maria Graham's tour to Poona.

Our company consists of one lady, two gentlemen, and three children, besides ourselves, but our attendants are near two hundred; we are obliged to carry tents, furniture, cooking utensils, and food, so that our train cannot consist of fewer persons. Besides, we must have koolis to carry our baggage, lascars to attend to and pitch our tents, servants to dress our food, others to take care of the horses and the beasts of burthern, and hamauls for our palankeens. Having sent on the baggage and servants the preceding day, we embarked at the bunder in the fort of Bombay, and after a three hours sail we reached Panwell. . . .[37]

The size of the entourage marked the nature of the difference between the country and the town she had just left. An army of servants was necessary to obviate the difficulties expected to be encountered upcountry. Her account went on to describe the places where they camped, and she began to note distinctions: 'The natives of Panweel,' she thought, 'have a more martial air than those of Bombay.'[38] All was part of being in a qualitatively different environment.

Later, railways made travel out of Bombay easier. Europeans nevertheless still thought they needed help in coping with the pandemonium of stations and journeys. It was *de rigueur* to have servants, even if only one or two. Thus Steegman in going to Delhi 'set about the fearful business of engaging a bearer for the journey, for railway travel in India is said to be fraught with dangers. I spent curious hours in my room interviewing relays of Mohammedans and Hindoos of every age and size, all ready to devote their lives to me.' Once selected, his bearer 'suddenly leapt to life. He seized all my clothes and trunks and made chaos. After dinner he directed the pile of my luggage on to a rickety bullock-cart amid a babble of high-pitched shouts. When all was ready, the cart creaked away. . . . After a final drink in the hotel, I followed in a taxi and was soon lost to Bombay.'[39] The departure retained its mystique, a venture into unknown India, away from what had become a familiar and now tamed, but still distinctively separate, city.

For Lakshmibai, the departure had less trauma as far as the station was concerned but what marked her journey was the women's compartment in which she travelled: 'The carriage was filled with rich Gujrathi women of the Bhatiya caste. (Bhatiya also means she-cats.). . . . No one would give me room to sit down. Amongst all these she-cats I was like a little mouse.'[40] But although she had no servant she was accompanied by an uncle who put her in her compartment and 'came to ask after me at every station. I told him that everything was all right, but the opposite was the truth.'[41] For her and her uncle, the journey, as for the European, equally constituted a transition of unknown potentiality.

These accounts do not cover all the kinds of experience people had but they highlight some obvious points about the ways in which Bombay was understood. As the place of entry and departure Bombay was a hub which operated much like some present-day airports, a transition point for other destinations. But Bombay had more character than any airport terminal. The descriptions present two perspectives. The first encounter of Bombay for the European, because it was the beginning of the Indian experience, was constituted as India. As observers became more familiar with it they realized it had its own identity so that what they saw was in terms of Bombay itself rather than of some portmanteau notion of India. The city became an entity in its own right, with its own qualities. What was outside was quintessential India. For Indian travellers what was quintessential about Bombay was that it represented an idea of city, whatever the specific content. The experience of arrival and departure mediated responses to the place itself and helped heighten perception of a separate urban identity as a capital, a place of opportunities and strange things, a centre. In all this, Bombay managed to create a character of its own, avoiding being subordinated to what came from outside, from Britain and the rest of the world, or from other parts of India. Nor did the imperium impose a dominant character on the city, its grand Indo-Gothic buildings notwithstanding. Europeans were barely visible in the city outside their ghettos. Bombay, though a through point was also a place in its own right, a presence of juxtaposed phenomena. After all, outside the European space were the temples, mosques and agiaries, the bazaars and markets, the schools and colleges, the factories, docks and workshops—all those things that made a city, to say nothing of all its housing and the people in them.

Ideas of arrival and departure were important in constructing and maintaining a notion of Bombay as a singular entity, the city as a special place, a space on which ideas and values might be inscribed. These could be contradictory as was demonstrated during the outbreak of plague in the late 1890s and the concurrent onset of a severe famine. As many inhabitants as could do so fled from the city for healthy sanctuary elsewhere. Paralleling that exodus was a large movement of people flocking into the city, famine-stricken, destitute, in search of employment and food. At the one and same time the city was both a sanctuary and a place of death as was the countryside which was alternately also a place of life or of death. The movement of people made the contrast evident and sharpened the division. Within the city itself neither the municipality nor the Presidency government were able or willing to cope with the influx of famine victims and attempts were made to extern them, to return them to their towns and villages in the countryside, to get them out of a city in which they were considered to be a source of infection.[42]

This was of course an exceptional moment but there were other such moments as when the British rulers externed people who challenged their authority. During the Civil Disobedience movement the Bombay provincial government externed from Bombay city 1587 political opponents between 1933 and 1936.[43] People with criminal records or associations were also regularly deported from the city. City distinctiveness was thus asserted in no uncertain manner by excluding those whose activities the government disliked or considered a bad influence. And it was not just the government that compelled people to move out of the city. Whenever serious riots broke out a large number of people fled the city. At least 150,000 people left Mumbai after the 1992/3 riots.[44] As one refugee, Selvan, explained at the railway station: 'Even if things settle down, I don't think I will come back. I can't live here knowing that Bombay is capable of so much violence.'[45]

More the norm was an annual exodus of mill workers and other labourers from the city during the summer months. Workers returned home to their villages in the countryside to escape the heat and help with the harvest. Though the actual proportion of the industrial labour force which did so is unclear their number was considerable. But there was reverse movement as others, probably members of the same family, would go to the city at the same time to work in the place of the absent worker.[46] The return to the city showed the links between town and countryside and their interdependence but the movement equally showed the distinction which operated between the two. When finally a worker stopped working entirely and went home to his family he was a different person, as suggested in Waman Hoval's story about a dock worker, Bayaji, who retires to his village but encounters caste Hindu attempts to re-subordinate him within the social tyrannies of village life.[47] The city metaphorically could thus come to the village but the village could assert itself to maintain its own traditions and prejudices.

Conclusion

The entry into and the departure from Bombay set it apart for Indians as much as for Europeans. Movement in and out demarcated its distinctive space away from its surrounding regions on land or its linkages by sea. As the city grew, the trajectory of the railway journey itself, the geography of the route, may have reinforced the sense of entry and the special quality of arrival. The two railway lines out of the city both moved through Bombay Island, traversed Salsette Island, and then finally reached the mainland. As the settlement of the city expanded northwards from the original fort centre and onto what became suburban areas in Bandra and Sion/ Chembur, the extent of the journey through distinctive urban space likewise increased. The crossing onto Salsette Island initially provided a sense of movement into something different. When suburbs became city precinct, absorbed into it, the moment of difference occurred at the point of entry at the mainland border.

Later, in the final decades of the twentieth century when the city had grown into a megalopolis and urban settlement had spread extensively throughout Salsette Island and even onto the mainland, the railway journey helped maintain a sense of city identity among its inhabitants themselves. Daily journeys could take two or three hours each way as people traversed up to 50 or more miles from where they lived to where they worked. The railway became the city's backbone enabling it to function as an integrated unit, giving it some sense of being a single place, no matter how widespread and extended that was. Thus arrival and exit in the twentieth century merged with the daily commute to help define the city as an entity on its own, regardless of whatever factors may have bound it to the outside.

In conclusion, this chapter has presented two ways of looking at Mumbai's relations with its region. One has been to use the metaphor of circles of power: those circles—the urban entity, the state and nation—conjoined, overlapped or superimposed one on the other at different times and according to circumstance or issue. They could be in dissonance or consonance. Whichever, the city retained a distinctiveness which did not detract from its place within wider entities. It was issue and circumstance which determined the content of that identity, and the attitudes which attached to it at one moment or another. The second approach has been to use the circumstance of travel, of entry into and exit from the city to discern urban integrity through the notion of border and boundary, of within and without. While a journey asserted linkage, it also signalled difference; there was a continuum but there was the disjunction of the threshold. The city was thus a space on its own, but that space could be contextualized in a variety of ways according to time and predisposition, and values and ideas. Some of those ideas and activities were about relations with the external. The city was apart and interconnected.

NOTES

1. Fernand Braudel considers the market to be the determining characteristic between town and country. See Satish Chandra's discussion in his *Fernand Braudel on Towns*, Occasional Papers Series: 11, Urban History Association of India, New Delhi, 1992, pp. 3-4.
2. Ashis Nandy, *An Ambiguous Journey to the City: The Village and Other Odd Ruins of the Self in the Indian Imagination*, Oxford University Press, New Delhi, 2001, p. 12.
3. Raymond Williams, *The Country and the City*, Paladin, St. Albans, 1975, p. 9.
4. For a more extensive discussion see my 'Changing Definitions of Bombay: City State to Capital City', in Indu Banga (ed.), *Ports and their Hinterlands in India (1700-1950)*, Urban History Association of India, Nehru Memorial Museum & Library, and Indian Institute of Advanced Studies series, Manohar, New Delhi, 1992, pp. 273-316.
5. The Queen of Asia epithet derived from Sir Richard Temple, an 1870s Governor of Bombay, see George W. Clutterbuck, *India: or Bombay the Beautiful*, The Ideal Publishing Union, London, 1897, p. 18.
6. For a fuller discussion see my 'Bombay Time', in Meera Kosambi (ed.), *Intersections: Socio-cultural Trends in Maharashtra*, Orient Longman, Hyderabad, 2000, pp. 161-86.
7. *Bombay Gazette*, 12 March 1883, p. 2.
8. Speech of 23 April 1906 reprinted in J.R.B. Jeejeebhoy (ed.), *Some Unpublished & Later Speeches & Writings of The Hon. Sir Pherozeshah Mehta, M.A., LL.D., K.C.I.E., Bar-at-Law*, The 'Commercial' Press, Bombay, 1918, pp. 177-8.
9. Home Dept. Special letter of 2 August 1930 to Bombay Commissioner of Police in Maharashtra State Archives, Home Dept. Special, 750 (28) 1930, p. 157.
10. For resolutions moved in August 1930 see Maharashtra State Archives, Home Dept. Special, 750 (28) 1930, p. 243; in July 1931, see ibid., p. 361; and in December 1935 see Maharashtra State Archives, Home Dept. Special, 800 (27), Pt1/1935, pp. 47, 93 and 167.
11. Minute by G.A.T., 27 June 1931 in Maharashtra State Archives, Home Dept. Special, 750 (28) 1930, p. 374.
12. Henry Yule and A. C. Burnell, *Hobson-Jobson . . .*, Munshiram Manoharlal, Delhi, 1979, reprint of 1903, 3rd edn., p. 570.

13. See H. H. Wilson, *A Glossary of Judicial and Revenue Terms* . . . , Eastern Law House, Calcutta, 1940, p. 554.
14. Baba Padmanji, *A Compendium of Molesworth's Marathi and English Dictionary*, Education Society's Press, Bombay, 1863, p. 113; and *Molesworth's Marathi-English Dictionary*, Corrected Reprint, Shubhada-Saraswat, Poona, 1975.
15. Baba Padmanji, *A Compendium of Molesworth's Marathi and English Dictionary*, Education Society's Press, Bombay, 1863, p. 219.
16. Capt. John Clunes, *Itinerary and Directory for Western India, being a collection of routes through the provinces subject to the Presidency of Bombay, and the Principal Roads in the Neighbouring States* . . . , H. Townsend, Bishop's College Press, Calcutta, 1826, p. 167. Molesworth gave it a similar meaning in Marathi as 'the middle country, the country bounded by the Sayhadri range, the Balaghat hill, the Carnatic, and the Godavari river', op. cit., p. 425.
17. D. K. Karve, *Looking Back*, Hindu Widows' Home Association, Poona, 1936, p. 15.
18. D. K. Karve, *My Life Story*, 1915, transl. in D. D. Karve, *The New Brahmans: Five Maharashtrian Families*, University of California Press, Berkeley and Los Angeles, 1963, p. 29.
19. See, amongst others, D. G. Karve, *Ranade the Prophet of Liberated India*, Aryabhushan Press, Poona, 1942, p. x.
20. Lakshmibai Tilak, *I Follow After: An Autobiography*, trans. E. Josephine Inkster, Oxford University Press, Bombay, 1950, pp. 44-5. The Marathi originals for the translation appeared in the mid-1930s.
21. Interviewed in Kishore Rathod, 'Lakhs flock to Chaitya Bhoomi', *Mid Day*, Mumbai, 7 December 2001, p. 4.
22. Avinash Dolas, 'The Refuge', trans. Y. S. Kalamkar, in Arjun Dangle (ed.), *Poisoned Bread: Translations from Modern Marathi Dalit Literature*, Orient Longman, Hyderabad, 1992, p. 219.
23. Maisie Wright, *Under Malabar Hill: Letters from India 1928-1933*, ed. John Wall, BACSA, London, 1988, pp. 1-2.
24. Aldous Huxley, *Jesting Pilate: The Diary of a Journey*, Flamingo, London, 1994, reprint of 1926 edition, p. 4.
25. Philip Steegman, *Indian Ink*, Cobden Sanderson, London, 1939, p. 2.
26. Prince Bojidar Karageorgevitch, *Enchanted India*, Harper and Brothers, London and New York, 1899, pp. 3-4.
27. Lady Strachey, *Memoirs of a Highland Lady*, 1898, p. 417, reprinted in R. P. Karkaria, *The Charm of Bombay: An Anthology*, D. B. Taraporevala, Bombay, 1915, p. 107.
28. William Ashton Shepherd, *From Bombay to Bushire, and Bussora; including an account of the present state of Persia, and Notes on the Persian War*, Richard Bentley, London, 1857, pp. 9-10.
29. Huxley, *Jesting Pilate*, p. 6.

30. Maria Graham, *Journal of a Residence in India*, Archibald Constable and Co., and Longman, Hurst, Rees, Orme and Brown, Edinburgh and London, 1812, p. 2.
31. Karageorgevitch, *Enchanted India*, op. cit., p. 4.
32. Huxley, op. cit., p. 6.
33. Letter to Queen Victoria in his *Personal and Literary Letters*, Vol. 11, pp. 6-7, reprinted in R. P. Karkaria, *The Charm of Bombay: An Anthology*, D. B. Taraporevala, Bombay, 1915, p. 112.
34. Helen Rutledge (ed.), *A Season in India: Letters of Ruby Madden. Experiences of an Australian Girl at The Great Coronation Durbar, Delhi: 1903*, Fontana/Collins, Sydney, 1982, p. 39.
35. Wright, *Under Malabar Hill*, p. 3.
36. Steegman, *Indian Ink*, p. 3.
37. Graham, *Journal of a Residence in India*, pp. 59-60.
38. Ibid., p. 60.
39. Steegman, *Indian Ink*, pp. 12-13.
40. Lakshmibai Tilak, *I Follow After*, p. 45.
41. Ibid.
42. For a detailed discussion see my 'Migration and Urban Identity: Bombay's Famine Refugees in the Nineteenth Century', in Sujata Patel and Alice Thorner (eds.), *Bombay: Mosaic of Modern Culture*, Oxford University Press, Bombay, 1995, pp. 25-60.
43. Reply of C. W. A. Turner to question from P. D. Kulkarni on 9 September 1936 in *Bombay Legislative Council Debates*, Vol. 45, 1936, p. 196.
44. For a fuller discussion see my 'Postmodern Bombay: Fractured Discourses', in Sophie Watson and Katherine Gibson (eds.), *Postmodern Cities and Spaces*, Blackwell, Oxford, pp. 199-215.
45. Interview in *Indian Express Sunday Magazine*, Bombay edition, 17 January 1993, p. 2.
46. See the discussion in Morris David Morris, *The Emergence of an Industrial Labour Force in India: A Study of the Bombay Cotton Mills, 1854-1947*, University of California Press, Berkeley and Los Angeles, 1965, pp. 97-100.
47. Waman Hoval, 'The Storeyed House', translated by M. D. Hatkanagalekar in Dangle, *Poisoned Bread*, pp. 155-62.

PART II

Regions in Imagination and Ritual

7

Religious Geography and the Multiplicity of Regions in Maharashtra

Anne Feldhaus

In their path-breaking *Mental Maps*, Peter Gould and Rodney White (1986: 82-3) tell of a conversation overheard somewhere in London. A young woman was enthusiastically telling a friend about her recent vacation in Majorca. When the friend asked, 'Where is Majorca?' the woman who had travelled there replied, 'I don't know exactly. I flew.' The people I plan to discuss here have, I think, a clearer idea than this woman did of where they go when they travel, and perhaps also of where they are the rest of the time.

I shall discuss some words and actions of some people who live in small areas of western India. Because these people's words and actions seem to me to give the areas a coherence and meaning they would not otherwise have, I call the areas 'regions'. A region, that is, is a part of the earth that has coherence and meaning in some respect for some people.

In recent years, a number of humanists and humanistically inclined social scientists have focused their attention on what they call 'place'. For some theorists the place *par excellence* is the domestic residence, the home, but the notion of place can also be extended to include a region. The philosopher Edward Casey, whose work I find particularly helpful, prefers to think of a region not as a large place, but as an area in which a number of different places are connected with one another. He defines region as 'a concatenation of places that, taken together, constitutes a common and continuous here for the person who lives in or traverses them' (Casey 1993: 72).

The kind of geographical awareness involved in a sense of a region as place is not merely knowledge *about* the region. It is not merely the ability to list and describe all the places in the region. At a more fundamental level, a sense of place forms one's cosmology and orientation to the world. Such a geographical awareness, which depends ultimately upon bodily experience, can be the immediate result of administrative arrangements, of physical geography, or of images and stories.

For an example of administrative arrangements providing people's basic orientation, look at the grid of most of the American landscape. In the nineteenth century, the western two-thirds of America was divided up into rectangles, large, small, and medium-sized, oriented to the cardinal directions. Besides organizing the farms, townships, counties, and states of the American West and Midwest, this grid also provided the basic, common-sense orientation of the people who lived within it. The geographer John Brinkerhoff Jackson (1994: 3-4) says that, still today, he has 'been in homes in Kansas where they refer to the southwest (or northwest) burner on their stove. They tell you that the bathroom is upstairs, straight ahead south.' In the Desh, the Deccan Plateau area of Maharashtra, orientation is more often based on rivers than on the cardinal directions. People speak not so often of 'west' and 'east' as of 'up' (*var*) and 'down' (*khālī*). 'Up' and 'down' mean 'upstream' and 'downstream' on the rivers that flow across the Deccan from north-west to south-east, joining the ocean in the far-off Bay of Bengal.

Beyond this sort of basic orientation, a sense of place also involves the emotions. A person cares about places, likes them or dislikes them, longs to go to them, to return to them, to leave them, or not to leave them. In some cases, the sense of region as place includes a sense of the place as one's own, as home, as a place that one belongs to and that belongs to one in some important way. Beyond this, awareness of where one is (or where one comes from) can, and sometimes does, become an important element in understanding who one is. Not only can such an awareness provide a basic cosmology or orientation to the world and a focus for one's affections, but it can also become an important element of a person's identity.

In such cases, a sense of region as place can give rise to regionalism or nationalism. For, besides being a place writ large, or a 'concatenation' of places, a region can also be a nation writ small, or what Eric Hobsbawm has called a 'proto-nation'. However, not every 'proto-nation' necessarily becomes a nation. The fact that a sense of place is important for the development of nationalism does not mean that a sense of place or region, a sense of home, or a geographically based sense of personal—or even community—identity has a political teleology.

When most of us think about pilgrimage in Maharashtra, we tend to think of the Vārkarī pilgrimage to Pandharpur at Āṣāḍh Ekādaśī, the largest, best-known pilgrimage in this part of the world. In their most important annual pilgrimage, Vārkarīs accompany palanquins that travel from all corners of the Desh to Pandharpur, the site of the principal temple of the god Viṭhobā. In the late 1940s, Iravati Karve accompanied the most famous Vārkarīs palanquin, that of the thirteenth-century saint Jñāneśvar, as it made its two-week journey from his *samādhi* temple at Alandi to Pandharpur. When Karve took part in the Vārkarīs' pilgrimage, the Samyukta Maharashtra movement (the movement for a United Maharashtra) was well under way. Karve's experience of the pilgrimage seems to have been coloured by the politicized regionalism that people like her were very conscious of at the time, and that brought the Samyukta Maharashtra movement its ultimate success. In summing up her account of the pilgrimage, Karve stated:

> So, I was getting to know my Maharashtra anew every day. I found a new definition of Maharashtra: the land whose people go to Pandharpur for pilgrimage. When the palanquin started from Poona, there were people from Poona, Junnar, Moglai, Satara, etc. Every day people were joining the pilgrimage from Khandesh, Sholapur, Nasik, Berar. As we neared Pandharpur, the pilgrimage was becoming bigger and bigger. All were Marathi-speaking people—coming from different castes, but singing the same songs, the same verses of [the] Vārkari cult, speaking to each other, helping each other, singing songs to one another.

For Karve, the pilgrimage to Pandharpur was a way to experience Maharashtra, a way of 'getting to know' it. The pilgrimage was a way to think about Maharashtra, to give it a 'new definition'. And it was a way to deepen her own identification with the region ('my Maharashtra'). Iravati Karve was an influential person. Her essays were widely read. Her experience of the Vārkarī pilgrimage must have captivated her readers' imaginations and strengthened the Samyukta Maharashtra movement. The pilgrimage became for others, too, a way of thinking about Maharashtra, and it helped them to articulate their demand for the founding of the state.

However, the region defined by the Vārkarī pilgrimage is an exception. It is the one religiously-defined region that closely approaches congruence with modern Maharashtra State. Unlike the Vārkarī pilgrimage, the other pilgrimages and religious-geographical imagery I have studied have not yet had effective interpreters like Karve, nor have they contributed to the formation of major modern political entities. They nevertheless enable people to experience and think about regions. They help people to make sense of their world, and to be at home in it.

Here I present a number of examples of religious images and pilgrimages that I believe do this for some groups of people in Maharashtra.[1] I will discuss, first, several regions formed by different kinds of religious ideas and practices related to rivers, and, secondly, regions defined by numbered sets of places that are scattered throughout them; in the conclusion, I will show how the very variety of these regions prevents them from having the political effectiveness that I believe the Vārkarī pilgrimage to have had.

RIVERS

In the course of their forest exile, the five Pāṇḍavas decided to perform a sacrifice at a place called Pandeshvar that is now located on the Karha River. At the time of the Pāṇḍavas, the temple did not exist, the Karha River did not exist, and there was no water at Pandeshvar. Searching for the water that they needed for their sacrifice, two of the Pāṇḍava brothers, Arjun and Nakul, found an ascetic brahman sage meditating on a nearby mountaintop. The brothers knocked over his water pot (his *karhā*), and the water from the pot flowed down the mountainside and across the plateau toward Pandeshvar. With the furious ascetic hot on their heels, the two brothers ran downstream along the route that the water was taking. Each time the ascetic came too close, they would toss a grain of rice behind them. The grain of rice would turn into a Śivaliṅga, and the ascetic would stop to worship it. Thus were founded the Śiva temples of the many villages along the upper reaches of the Karha River.[2]

This story, which is widely told in Purandar taluka of Pune district, is a story about the founding of a region. The story shows how a set of places came to be connected to one another. The connection among these places came into being because the two brothers ran from one place to another. In another sense, the places came to be connected because they are similar: each has a temple with a Śivaliṅga that the brothers installed and that the ascetic sage was the first to worship. And, most fundamentally, the places are connected because the water of the Karha River flows from one of them to another (Map 1). Rivers are the only element of the landscape that themselves move. As they flow from one place to another, they connect the places that they move between. Because they move,

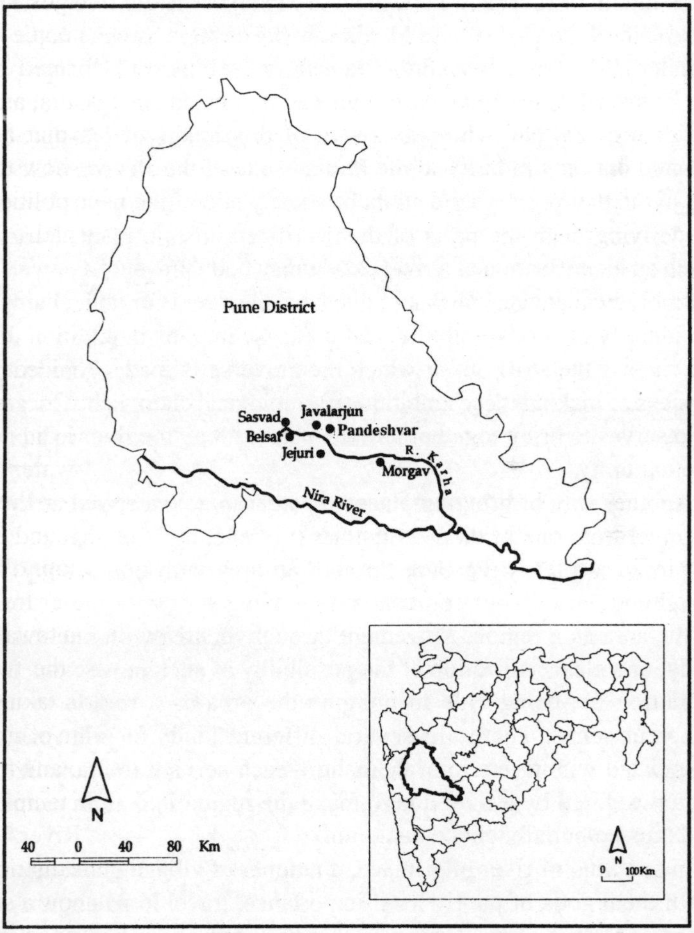

Map 1: The Karha River

providing a physical link among places, rivers allow people to bring spatially separate places together in their imagination.

The story of the origin of the Karha River is but one example of the many ways in which people in Maharashtra use rivers to imagine, conceptualize and experience regions. Let me present three more examples: one is a verbal image and the other two are pilgrimages.

The Marathi version of the *Godāvarī Māhātmya* by Dāsagaṇū identifies eight 'organs' or 'limbs' (*aṣṭāṅga*) of the Godavari River: Brahmagiri (at Tryambakeshvar) is the Godavari's head; Punatambe is its mouth or face; and Puri, 'near . . . Paithan', is the river's neck. The heart of the Godavari is Manjarath; the navel is Śaṅkha *tīrtha* (at Nanded). Manthani, in Andhra Pradesh, is the hips, and Dharmapuri the knees, while Rajamahendri is the eighth limb, the feet. A brahman resident of Paithan who was aware of this image of Dāsagaṇū's pointed out its similarity to the Puruṣasūkta of the *Ṛgveda* (10.90), the hymn that portrays the strata of society and of the natural world as deriving from the parts of the sacrificed cosmic giant, Puruṣa. Such an identification of a river as a human body presents a powerful cosmological image, one that implies that the river is organic, human. To identify the body with the Vedic Puruṣa implies in addition that the river is the stuff out of which the universe is made. And in the process of making these ambitious cosmological claims, the imagery also serves to bring together various places along the river in a conceptual unity.

Another way of bringing places together in a conceptual unity is to travel from one of them to another (to travel by land, that is, and not in an airplane). Passing through an area with one's body, or imagining oneself—or someone else—doing so, gives one a sense of the area as a region. Movement through an area with one's own body, or a clear realization of the possibility of such movement, is a condition for being able to imagine the area as a region in any coherent sense. There are several different kinds of pilgrimages associated with rivers in Maharashtra, each serving to dramatize a region watered by a river and to make the region into a circulatory, and thus potentially conceptual, unit.

In one kind of river pilgrimage, a number of village gods, almost all of them gods of purely local importance, travel in palanquins to some one place along a river so that they can all be bathed at the same time. In the converse kind of pilgrimage, people carry water from a river to the temple of a god. One ritual of the first type (gods to water) takes place at Daund, a railway junction and taluka headquarters on the Bhima River in eastern Pune district, on the eleventh day of the bright half of the month of Āṣāḍh (June-July). This is the day known as Aṣāḍhī Ekādaśī, the culminating day of the Vārkarī pilgrimage to Pandharpur. On this day in 1998, twelve palanquins from different villages in Daund taluka and neighbouring Baramati taluka (Map 2) formed a procession at the far side of the railway tracks, away from the river. The palanquins held brass masks or other portable images of goddesses and Śaiva gods. The procession travelled slowly through the underpass beneath the railway lines, onto the main street of Daund, down that street past the main square and into the market area, and finally to the river. There the people accompanying each of the palanquins removed the god's image from its palanquin, washed the god, took baths in the river, and performed *pūjā* to the god before setting off to return home.

Even though the deities in the various palanquins that came to Daund that year for the procession and bath in the river are all goddesses or forms of Śiva, several people who offered me interpretations of the festival understood it in terms of the cult of Viṭhobā of Pandharpur, a god usually identified with Kṛṣṇa or Viṣṇu. These interpreters saw the Bhima River as linking Daund with Pandharpur. Flowing past Daund to Viṭhobā's distant town, a town that is the goal of hundreds of thousands of pilgrims on the eleventh day of Āṣāḍh, the river enables the villagers and gods who come to Daund to connect their ritual with the larger pilgrimage that reaches Pandharpur on the same day.

In addition, though, the Daund pilgrimage has another religious-geographical function. It dramatizes the small region constituted by the places from which the gods in the palanquins come to Daund. The procession of the palanquins from the various places brings together important gods as well as representative citizens, the men and women who have brought the gods. The procession of the people carrying the gods in the palanquins makes the region they all come from visible, both to the participants and to observers. No one but me, as far as I know, has designed a map like this one, but the palanquin procession to the river forms a map of a different sort. This map represents the region not on paper but by means of the images of the gods and the bodies of the people it brings together.

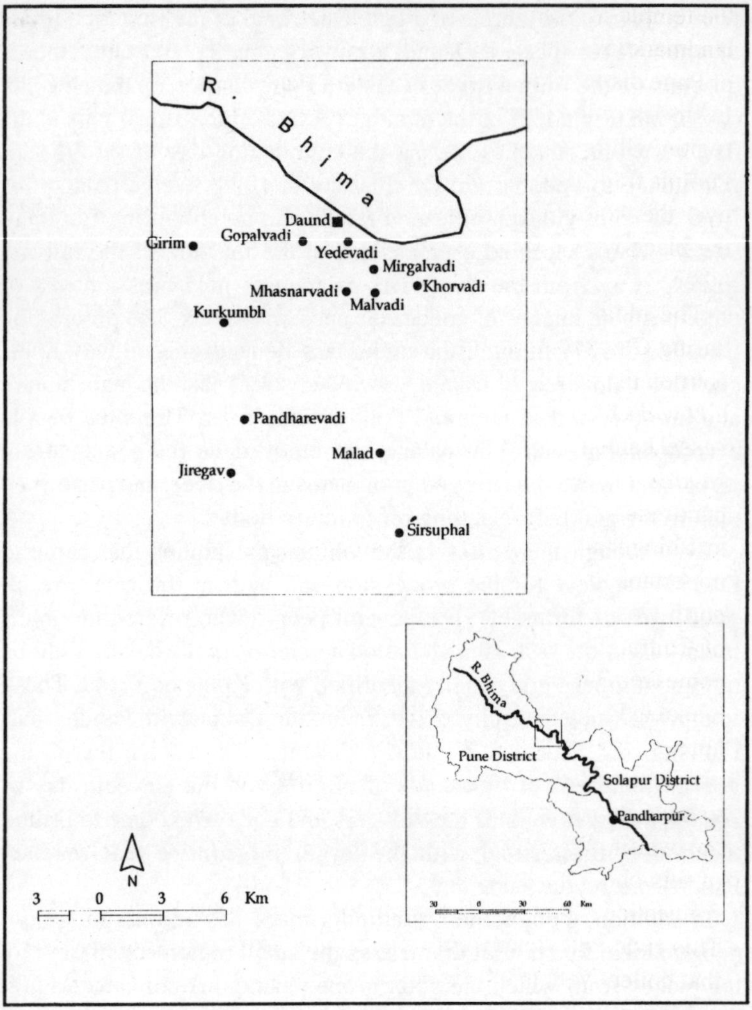

Map 2: The Daund Pilgrimage

THE PILGRIMAGE TO SHINGNAPUR

In the converse sorts of pilgrimage festivals, people carry water from a river to a god. The most elaborate example in Maharashtra of this kind of festival is the annual pilgrimage to Shingnapur in the month of Caitra (March-April). Visible for a great distance in all directions, the temple at Shingnapur is arguably the most prominent religious landmark in Satara district, important also for the south-eastern half of Pune district and for many people in Solapur district and beyond. In stories of the Dhangar shepherds and other rural residents of this region, Shingnapur takes the role that the heaven Kailās has in Purāṇic traditions: it is the place from which Śiva watches and rules over the world, the place where he lives with his wife Pārvatī, and the place where they play dice or parcheesi and quarrel with each other.

The most prominent feature of the pilgrimage to Shingnapur during Caitra is the fact that people carry water there in *kāvaḍ* to pour on the god, who is called Śambhu Mahādev. At its most basic, a *kāvaḍ* consists of a pole slung over the shoulder with a water vessel hanging from each end; at their most elaborate, at Shingnapur, *kāvaḍs* remain contraptions for carrying water. In addition to hundreds of small ones, there are also many large *kāvaḍs* that come to Shingnapur for the festival. Six of them, considered especially important, are the last to be carried up an extremely steep cliff on the north-west face of the mountain, on the afternoon of the twelfth day of Caitra. The cliff is called Muṅgī Ghāṭ. All six of these *kāvaḍs* come from the north-west of Shingnapur, four of them from Purandar taluka in Pune district. The most important of these, almost everyone agrees, is that of Bhutojī Telī from Sasvad; this *kāvaḍ* has the privilege of being the very last to climb Muṅgī Ghāṭ and the very last to have its water poured over the god in the temple, at midnight on the twelfth day of Caitra. The second-most-important *kāvaḍ* is a rival of this one, in that the men who carry it claim to have even closer connections than the Sasvad group's to the original Bhutojī Telī. This rival *kāvaḍ* comes from a group of five villages near Sasvad that collectively call themselves 'Pañcakrośī'.

Men attached to the Sasvad *kāvaḍ* and to its rival from the neighboring group of five villages identify themselves in terms of, and see their ritual as expressing, a kind of fierce Śaiva bhakti. Their trip, which they make on foot, cross-country, in the hot month of Caitra, has a distinct ascetic element. This is especially true for the leaders, who must make the trip in their bare feet and without eating. The theme of renunciation is also present, to be seen in ritual acts commemorating Bhutojī's practice of burning his house down behind him and not looking back as he set off for Shingnapur.

The element of physical difficulty and even danger reaches its climax in the final ascent of the mountain, up an extremely tall, sheer cliff. To get the heavier *kāvaḍs* up this cliff, the men carrying them—all young, strong wrestlers—must struggle and strain, slipping and scrabbling all the way. Most of the large *kāvaḍs* are pulled up from above by ropes, as well as being pushed from below by the young men, but the last *kāvaḍ* reaches the top without the help of ropes, each of the men pushing up with his head on the buttocks of the man before him. A piece of cloth attached to the vertical pole of each large *kāvaḍ* serves as a kind of sail, the men explain, and Mahādev (Śiva) provides the wind that fills the sail and helps propel the *kāvaḍ* to the top.

Nowadays the *kāvaḍs* are carried empty up the cliff, but even so the big ones are extremely heavy. In former days, the men say, there used to be water in them, and Bhutojī Telī is said to have carried his up loaded with sand. Some say he got his name from '*bhūt*', 'ghost'—for his ghost-like power to get the heavy contraption up the precipice. Nowadays even empty *kāvaḍs* sometimes fall back down from partway up, and occasionally men get hurt. At the foot of the cliff is a shrine to a young man who died there, trying to get one of the large *kāvaḍs* up to the top of the hill.

As the men who bring these *kāvaḍs* are climbing up Muṅgī Ghāṭ on the twelfth day of Caitra, other groups of pilgrims, many of them also carrying *kāvaḍs*, are already leaving. Most of these pilgrims come from the east and north-east of Shingnapur, from various places in Marathvada (Map 3). These people arrive and leave by a different route, the road that leads north-east from Shingnapur to Natepute and Malshiras. These other pilgrims, who leave on (or before) the Bāras, include three groups and individuals who have especially important ritual roles in the festival. These three are a weaver from Khamasvadi who brings a long cloth called a *dhaj* that gets suspended between the pinnacles of the two main temples at Shingnapur; a horseman, Kāḷ Gāvḍā from Malegav, who has the ritual right to climb the temple steps on his horse and to enter the temple in his shoes; and a group of men who bring from Bhatangali a tall pole (*kāṭhī*) that plays the role of Śiva's bride. Before the *kāvaḍs* that climb Muṅgī Ghāṭ arrive, all these men have already played their roles in the festival.

The story about this festival that participants and observers most

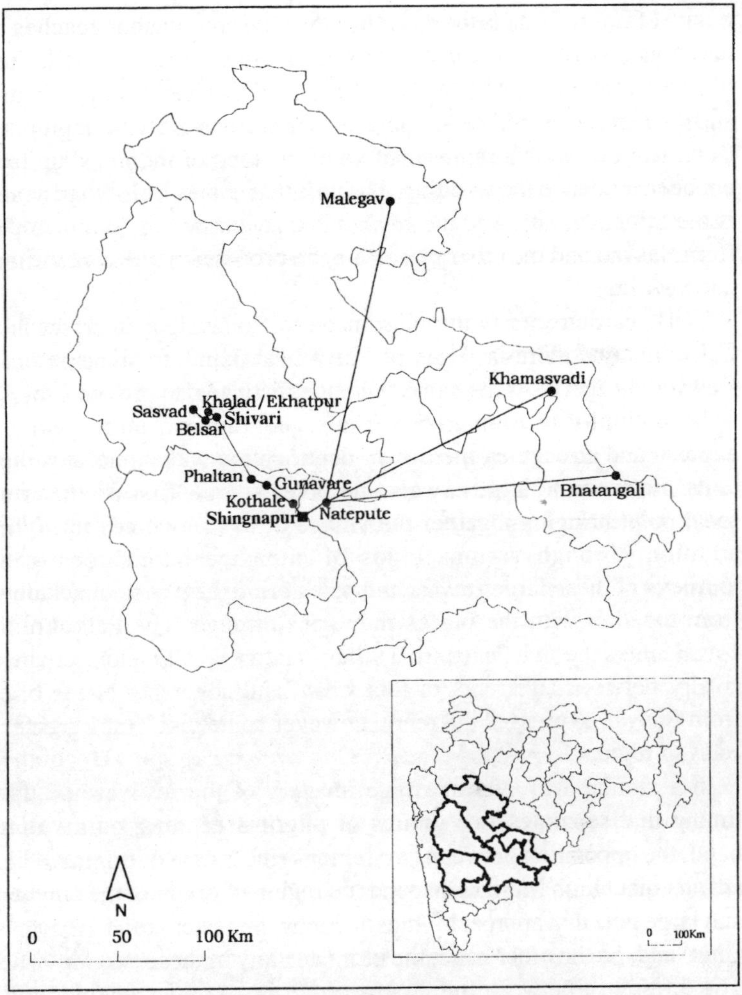

Map 3: The Pilgrimage to Shingnapur

readily articulate—to the small extent that they tell any story at all—is that of Śiva and Pārvatī's wedding. Once, when Śiva and Pārvatī were playing parcheesi (*sārīpāṭ*) in Kailās, Śiva lost repeatedly to Pārvatī. A poor loser, he left Kailās and came to Shingnapur. Eventually Pārvatī found him there, and they were married again. In the context of this story, the *kāvaḍs* come to Shingnapur to celebrate the god's wedding. The wedding takes place on the eighth day of the month of Caitra. This is the day when the *dhaj* appears, hung between the pinnacles of the two main temples at Shingnapur, and it is the day when the principal *kāvaḍs* 'set out' in the evening from Sasvad and the Pañcakrośī villages. The *dhaj* is the turban of the bridegroom, Śiva. Kāl Gāvḍā is a representative of the king of Indore, who had not been invited to the wedding. The pole that comes from Bhatangali is the bride, Pārvatī. And the *kāvaḍs* that get carried up Muṅgī Ghāṭ from Sasvad and the other places are the procession, the *varāt*, after the wedding.

Thus, participants in the pilgrimage to Shingnapur interpret the Caitra festival there in terms of Śaiva bhakti and, to some extent, wedding imagery. At the same time, the festival also provides them an opportunity to dramatize various geographical units, and to express and strengthen their own identification with some of these units. Each of the large *kāvaḍs* and poles serves, first of all, as a focal point bringing together the village or town it comes from. In addition, through various kinds of intensive interactions, the journeys of these large *kāvaḍs* and poles bring the places they come from together with the places they pass through. The Pañcakrośī *kāvaḍ* unites the five Pañcakrośī villages into a small region, and the rivalry between adherents of this *kāvaḍ* and adherents of the one from Sasvad expresses the unity, however contentious, of a greater Sasvad region.

In a similar way, the marriage imagery of the festival and the timing that separates two groups of pilgrims express, on the one hand, the opposition between two regions (the region of origin of the *kāvaḍs* that climb Muṅgī Ghāṭ and the region of origin of the *kāvaḍs* and large pole that approach Shingnapur by the eastern road, Bhavānī Ghāṭ) and, on the other hand, the ultimate unity of these two regions. The difference between the groups of *kāvaḍs*, in the view of some men who explained it to me, is not simply that the *kāvaḍs* come from different areas, and not even simply that they reach the top of the hill at Shingnapur by different routes. The two groups also represent the two parties of the wedding that the festival celebrates, the wedding of Mahādev and Pārvatī, or Śiva and Śakti.

That the *kāvaḍs* that climb up Muṅgī Ghāṭ, those that come from Sasvad and other places to the west, should be identified as the ones forming the groom's party, those on 'Śiva's side', fits well with the fierce Śaiva loyalty of the men who bring them to Shingnapur. That the *kāvaḍs* from the east should form the bride's party, those on 'Śakti's side', fits with the fact that the Bhatangali *kāṭhī*, which plays the role of Pārvatī in the wedding at Natepute, comes from that side. The designation 'Śakti's side' also fits with the fact that the major goddess temple at Tuljapur, the temple of the goddess Bhavānī lies to the east of Shingnapur. Indeed, as I have mentioned, the road leading eastward from Shingnapur is called 'Bhavānī Ghāṭ'; Tuljapur is one of the places that the Bhatangali *kāṭhī* visits on its journey home.

The notion that the ebb and flow of the pilgrims at Shingnapur corresponds to the bride's and groom's sides of a wedding party is an example of an opposition that is at the same time a powerful image of and occasion for unity. Like the rival Bhutoj Telī *kāvaḍs* of Sasvad and the Pañcakrośī villages, the 'Śiva's side' and 'Śakti's side' pilgrims at Shingnapur constitute the poles of an opposition that is contained within a higher unity. On the level of theology, Śiva and Śakti, though opposed, are interdependent and complementary. On the level of social relations, each wedding brings together two families that are previously not related to each other. Indeed, bringing two unrelated families together is the very point of a wedding, as well as the source of much of the tension it involves. On the level of geography, the idea that people come from two different 'sides', Śiva's and Śakti's, means that at Shingnapur two regions come together in a unity that encompasses them both.

For most participants who think about the festival, the name of that whole is simply Maharashtra. One of the men who explained to me the distinction between the *kāvaḍs* from Śiva's and Śakti's 'sides' said, at one point, 'Mahādev is the family god of Maharashtra.' Although he saw the wedding festival as being organized in such a way as to keep pilgrims from two different parts of Maharashtra separated, he also realized that the festival brings those two different parts of Maharashtra together: it brings pilgrims from both parts to the same place to celebrate a festival of unity.

Numbered Sets of Places

My next example illustrates a phenomenon that is found at the all-India level as well as at the regional level. This phenomenon is that of pilgrimage places grouped in numbered sets. My example is the eight places known as the Aṣṭavināyak. The Aṣṭavināyak is a set of temples all located within 100 km of Pune and dedicated to Gaṇapati (Map 4). How old the eight places are is not clear, nor is it clear when they were brought together as a set. All appear to have been pre-existing holy places that became prominent in the seventeenth and eighteenth centuries, a number of them through their connection

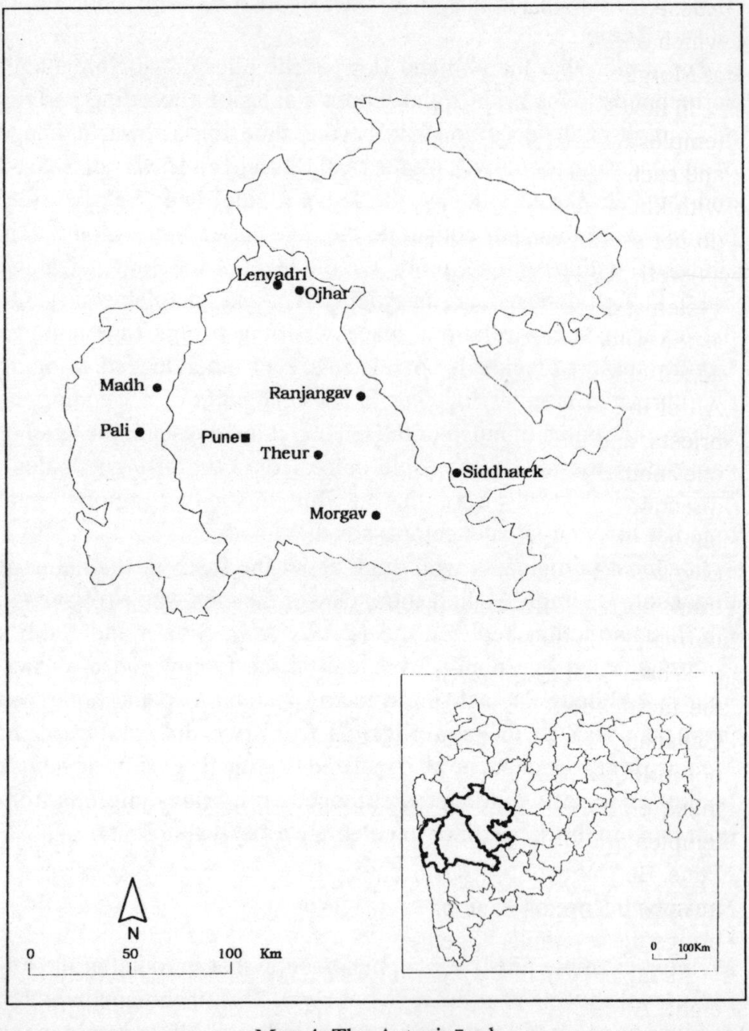

Map 4: The Aṣṭavināyak

with the seventeenth-century Deśastha brahman holy man Morobā Gosāvī (1610-59) of Cincvad, a village near (and now an industrial suburb of) Pune. The present popularity of the Aṣṭavināyak sites and their pilgrimage is in large part a product of modern means of transportation and communication. Today pilgrimage to the eight temples is a popular form of middle-class outing from Pune. There is no particular pilgrimage festival during which people travel *en masse* to the Aṣṭavināyak temples. There is no particular order in which one should visit the places, except that—according to priests at Morgav, at least—it is best to start with Morgav.

In fact, it is not particularly clear what coherence the Aṣṭavināyak temples have as a set. Each place's Gaṇapati has a different name, and each place has its own story, telling about Gaṇeś's interactions with kings, gods, and/or demons. These stories, for the most part, do not seem to be coordinated with one another. In other respects as well, the Aṣṭavināyak temples are not particularly unified or systematically related to one another. Not all the temples were built at the same time or by the same person, and they continue to be added onto and improved in an apparently uncoordinated fashion. All of the places have brahman priests, but some also have Gurav priests, and the brahman priests are not, as far as I know, related to one another in any formal, organized way. The temples face different directions: most of them face toward the east, but not all. Some, but not all, of the Gaṇeś images in the temples are 'self-formed' (*svayambhū*), uncarved rocks. In one of the temple images, Gaṇeś's trunk curls to his right; in the others the trunk turns to the more normal, left side.

What is it, then, that brings the Aṣṭavināyak together? In part, it is the fact that all the places are dedicated to the same god: Gaṇeś, Gaṇapati, or Vināyak. But there must be hundreds of thousands, if not millions, of temples and shrines to Gaṇeś in India. Why have these eight been chosen to belong to this set? These particular temples are all located within a reasonably accessible distance of Pune. But, here too, within the area covered by the Aṣṭavināyak there must be hundreds of temples and shrines to Gaṇeś. So what is it that brings these temples together?

As far as I can tell, what brings the temples together is the number eight. Along with Gaṇeś's name Vināyak, the number eight, *aṣṭa*, also appears in their name. The number eight is what defines the set of temples. It makes the set finite, bounded, and therefore specific. And, to the extent that the numbered set is finite, bounded, and specific, the area throughout which it extends is a coherent region.

In visiting the Aṣṭavināyak places, the pilgrim ends up criss-crossing this region. From Morobā Gosāvī's seventeenth-century travels between Cincvad and Morgav to the weekend outings of contemporary day-trippers, the feet and wheels of pilgrims have moved back and forth across the Pune region, connecting the Aṣṭavināyak places and bringing them together as a set. In recent decades, the Maharashtra Tourism Development Corporation, the State Transport bus system, and numerous private bus companies have facilitated and accelerated the process, turning the area around Pune into a circulatory region defined, in one respect, by travel to the Aṣṭavināyak places. However, it is not only, and not even primarily, through the mechanism of pilgrimage that the Aṣṭavināyak contribute to the formation of their region. Many more people in the Pune region are aware of the Aṣṭavināyak than have ever been to any of the places. Many who have gone on pilgrimage to one or more of the Aṣṭavināyak temples have not, or not yet, managed to travel to all of them. Nevertheless, the existence of the Aṣṭavināyak as a numbered set makes possible a sense of their area as a region. Even without travelling to all of them, residents of this region can think of the eight of them as a unit by saying the name 'Aṣṭavināyak' or by looking at the combined holy picture that is multiplied many times over on living room walls, on refrigerator doors, and in household shrines throughout the region.

By representing the Aṣṭavināyak as a group, the picture also represents as a whole the region throughout which the eight places are distributed. It serves as a reminder, to family members and to visitors in the many households in which it is displayed, of where they are and what that 'where' includes. It fosters in people of the Pune region, whether they have visited the Aṣṭavināyak or only heard of them, an awareness of how their world is anchored. And, when the many people who place the Aṣṭavināyak image in or near their household shrines perform *pūjā* to the image, they worship the whole set of Gaṇapatis at once. To the extent that the Aṣṭavināyak represent the region in which they are found, such people's *pūjā* of the Aṣṭavināyak image also, at the same time, pays homage to the region.

CONCLUSION

These, then, are just a few of the many regions I have discovered in my investigation of Maharashtra's Hindu religious geography. The regions I have identified overlap, criss-cross, and exclude one another, becoming salient in different religious contexts. Almost all these regions are found within more or less the area of the modern state of Maharashtra. However, only a few of them get identified as 'Maharashtra'. Often the regions have names other than 'Maharashtra', or they have no name at all.

What, then, is Maharashtra? In one sense, the reader might conclude that Maharashtra is a network of overlapping regions that interweave to form a richly textured whole. And yet, I hesitate to affirm that the regions I have studied form a 'network' or are 'interwoven' in the sense that any person or group makes significant connections among them. For the regions are, by-and-large, mutually oblivious. They coexist, next to one another or superimposed on one another, without any person or group of people necessarily connecting them in their minds. When different regions overlap in a single area, one region becomes important in one context, another in another context.

Take, as an example, Jejuri. A town that lies 50 km south-east of Pune on the old highway and the railway lines that lead from Pune to Satara, Jejuri is most famous as the site of an important temple of the god Khaṇḍobā, family god to people of many different groups in Maharashtra.[3] Jejuri lies on the bank of the Karha River; it is one of the places along the upper reaches of the Karha that not only the river connects, but also the story of the river's origin that I began with. Jejuri is one of the early, important stops on the route of the large *kāvaḍs* that travel from Sasvad, the Pañcakrośī villages, and other places in Purandar taluka (in which Jejuri itself also lies) to Shingnapur. And it is the starting point and end point of a pilgrimage in which the goddess Jāṇāī travels to her original place, 100 km south of Jejuri, around the time of the Hoḷī festival.[4]

In addition, Jejuri is a major, overnight stop on the route of Jñāneśvar's palanquin, the most famous of those that travel to Pandharpur on the Vārkarī pilgrimage. Situated close to Morgav, the principal member of the Aṣṭavināyak temples, Jejuri also falls within the triangle formed by Maharashtra's three-and-a-half principal goddess temples, a set analogous to the Aṣṭavināyak.[5] But it lies outside the region formed by the Eleven Mārutis (yet another analogous set), outside the region formed by the story and pilgrimage festival of Maḷāī,[6] and outside the region of the pilgrimage in which a bedstead and palanquin travel to Tuljapur for the Navarātra and Dasarā festival.[7] Besides, Jejuri is completely irrelevant to the pilgrimage traditions of the Mahānubhāv sect, which centre on the Godavari River Valley and Vidarbha, two parts of Maharashtra that lie far to the north of Jejuri.[8]

Thus, while Jejuri surfaces in various regions formed by different religious images and pilgrimages within the modern state of Maharashtra, there are many other religiously defined regions to which it has no particular connection. In addition, the various regions in which Jejuri does participate are not necessarily connected to one another. The overnight stay of the Vārkarīs in Jejuri causes congestion that hardly anyone living there can fail to notice. Yet the passage of the Shingnapur *kāvaḍs* through town causes less of a stir. People can live in Jejuri without being aware of the Shingnapur festival, without knowing the story of the origin of the Karha River, and even without taking cognizance of the pilgrimage festival of Jāṇāī, which starts from their town. Most people in Jejuri are probably aware of Morgav and the Aṣṭavināyak set of placeṣ, many know of the three-and-a-half principal godḍesses of Maharashtra, but hardly anyone in Jejuri knows about the palanquin and bedstead that travel to Tuljapur in time for the Navarātra festival. Finally, many people in Jejuri know that goddesses come in sets of seven sisters located at different places, but almost every citizen of Jejuri, when asked, would come up with a different list of the seven sisters and their locations.[9]

In other words, a number of different regions intersect in Jejuri, but they do not necessarily meet there. There is no one person or group that puts them together into a single imaginary unit. And this is the situation in many other places in what is now Maharashtra, as well as for Maharashtra as a whole. Together the many regions form a congeries, with the residents of each normally aware of, and acting in terms of, their own region but not the others—even though these other regions are sometimes ones in which, by someone else's definition, they live. Rather than a network, then, Maharashtra as a whole is better represented as an overlapping, ragged, unfinished patchwork of regions.

The complexity of the picture, the vast number of religiously sanctioned but by-and-large mutually oblivious regions that fill up and spill out of the area now known as Maharashtra, would be enhanced even further were we to take into account Maharashtra's non-Hindu religious-geographical and pilgrimage traditions—Jain, Christian, Jewish, Buddhist, and Muslim—or Maharashtra's tribal areas and former small kingdoms, or the districts and talukas of the modern state, or earlier adminstrative divisions, or the multitude of regions that people have experienced, imagined, and conceptualized but to which no one has given a name.

Still, the area that came into being as the State of Maharashtra in 1960 corresponds more closely to the region covered by the Vārkarī pilgrimage than it does to any other of the religious-geographical regions that I have found. Of the many regions that could have attained existence as a political unit, this is the one that has in fact done so. True, the Aṣṭavināyak region corresponds to the heartland of the Peśvā kingdom, and the Mahānubhāvs' Godavari Valley corresponds to the kingdom of the much-earlier Yādavas, while at least one modern author with Hindu-nationalist leanings has pointed out the correspondence of the Eleven-Māruti region to the core area of Shivaji's power.[10] Nevertheless, for the most part the pilgrimages, concepts, and images I have found have not affected the political aspirations of the people who participate in the pilgrimages or hold the concepts and images in their minds. And yet these pilgrimages, concepts, and images have provided, and do provide, an important means for people to experience, to imagine, and to conceptualize a variety of regions—including some that get called Maharashtra.

Thus there are many religiously-defined, meaningful regions that coexist within or overlap with the one that happened to become the state of Maharashtra. The fact that the region defined by the Vārkarī pilgrimage became a political unit is the exception that proves the rule. Through their large number, great variety, and lack of systematic order, the many religiously sanctioned regions of Maharashtra illustrate the vast array of possibilities from among which the political and administrative units of modern India have been chosen. But the many religiously meaningful regions of Maharashtra also inspire hope, both for the rest of India and for other fragile, fissiparous areas of the contemporary world. For these regions show that people can value a region in religious terms without feeling the need to make it into a politically separate entity.

In places around the world where regionalistic and nationalistic political movements have arisen—as ever-smaller units of Eastern Europe, Central Asia, Africa, and Indonesia aspire to nationhood, and as ever-smaller areas of north-eastern India aspire to become states within a federally organized modern nation—scholars can look back at imagery, concepts, and pilgrimages like those I have presented and can interpret them as expressions of proto-nationalism. But what of the cases where political movements do *not* arise? Although an understanding of the roots of potential regionalistic and nationalistic political movements is one of the contributions of a study such as mine, another, more timely contribution is to point out the multiplicity of intersecting, overlapping, but often mutually ignorant regions that can co-exist in one large place.

The fact that people attach religious meanings to regions makes those regions important, but it does not make them nations, nor does it mean that they necessarily become political or administrative units. For religious meaning does not automatically bring with it political consequences. When a part of the world to which people attach religious meanings does become a nation-state, the meanings can strengthen the bonds that hold the people together. When people attach different religious meanings to the same part of the world, the meanings can ignite the bombs that the people hurl at one another. But there is also still a chance, even now, that religious imagery can enrich the lives of individuals and small communities without engendering bloodshed and hatred. My work seeks to illustrate that possibility.

NOTES

1. These and other examples are discussed in greater detail in my *Connected Places: Region, Pilgrimage, and Geographical Imagination in India*, New York: Palgrave/Macmillan, 2003. I am grateful to Nikhil Shejwalkar for making the maps.
2. Some of the villages along this river have names that connect them with this story. The place where the sage ran out of *bel* leaves for worshipping the Śivaliṅgas is called Belsar (*sar* comes from the verb *saraṇe*, 'to give out', 'to be expended'). As Arjun and Nakul came close to Pandeshvar, they heard Yudhiṣṭhir calling out impatiently, 'Arjun! Where are you?'

—'I'm nearby (*javaḷ*)!' Arjun replied. And thus the place that Arjun had reached by then is now a village called Javalarjun—the village just upstream from Pandeshvar.

3. See Günther-Dietz Sontheimer, *King of Hunters, Warriors, and Shepherds: Essays on Khaṇḍobā*, edited by Anne Feldhaus, Aditya Malik, and Heidrun Brückner. New Delhi: Indira Gandhi National Centre for the Arts/Manohar, 1997.
4. See Chapter 3 of *Connected Places* (note 1, above).
5. The most common list of these places includes Kolhapur, Tuljapur, Mahur, and Saptashringi. For additional information on the three-and-a-half goddesses (and also the Eleven Mārutis), see Chapter 4 of *Connected Places* (note 1, above).
6. See Chapter 3 of *Connected Places* (note 1, above).
7. Ibid.
8. See Chapter 6 of *Connected Places*.
9. For more on the seven sisters in Maharashtra, see Chapter 4 of *Connected Places*.
10. Annabuva Kalgavkar, *Akrā Mārutī*, Caphal: Shriram Devasthan Trust, 1973.

8

Celebrating Allegiances, Ambiguated Belonging: Regionality in Festival and Performance in Sringeri, South India

Leela Prasad

When you board the night bus from Bangalore to Sringeri, get tossed around sleepily while the bus steadily climbs the winding, often rain-soaked roads of the Western Ghats, and wake up at dawn to look out at the misty green valleys of areca palms and rice fields and deep forests, you know you are in the hill regions of the *malnad* in Karnataka, the land of rains. At Chikmagalur, the district headquarters, about four hours before Sringeri, the bus would have nearly emptied, leaving just dishevelled pilgrims, and occasional residents returning home, to journey bumpily upward into the Ghats. It would have stopped many times, often at one-house 'villages', dropping off or picking up milkmen, school bound children, or those shuttling to work. Once, it is said, Krishnaraja Wodeyar, the Maharaja of Mysore, was so overcome by the tranquil beauty of Sringeri, and by the friendly fish that rush to meet you as you wash your feet in the Tunga River, that he took off his gold ring and slipped it on to the pouting nose of a fish. And even today you hear that, if you're lucky, you can see the fish with its royal nose-ring, a fleck of gold in the holy Tunga. And indeed this was one of the first Sringeri stories I was to hear during my many years of fieldwork.[1]

Sringeri, with a population of about 4000 people, is a small town in north-western Karnataka in Chikmagalur district (2001 Census of India). The *malnad*, of which Sringeri is a part, takes its name from *male* (hill) and *nāḍu* (land); it receives on an average 100 to 400 cm of rain every year. One rarely visits Sringeri—or leaves it—between June and September when the rains can be torrential. The *malnad* is one of those regions that are not marked on a map, but charted very tangibly in popular imagination. It lies east of the Sahyadri range and includes the talukas of Sringeri, Koppa, Narasimharajapura, and sometimes Mudigere (Map 1). The *malnad* is roughly 650 km long, and 55-65 km wide, with heights ranging from 150 to 900 m above sea level (Das 1984).

The town of Sringeri is defined by the ever-flowing Tunga River that curves around it, and by two main streets that run parallel to the river. The streets form an L-shape, meeting at the arched gates of the famous 1200-year old *maṭha*, believed to be the southern of four Advaitic centres in India founded by Shankara. The *maṭha*, associated primarily with the Vijayanagara empire, but also patronized by other dynasties and diverse communities, consolidated its position between the fourteenth and sixteenth centuries. Various royal endowments helped establish *agrahāras* (brahman settlements) around the *maṭha*, settlements that give Sringeri and its vicinity their geographical character. Politically Sringeri was administered as a *jāgīrdāri* by the *maṭha* until its independent status

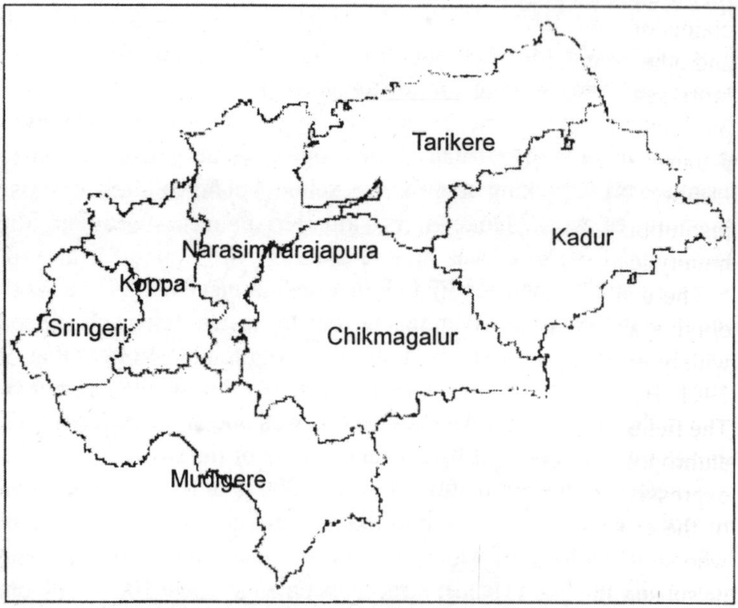

Source: http://www.kar.nic.in/district_glance.asp/distname=Chikmagalur

Map 1. Map of taluks of Chikmagalur district.

was abolished in 1959. After the land-reform acts of the 1960s and the 1970s, the *maṭha* was left with roughly sixty acres from the several thousands it used to have. Today the *maṭha* continues to be regarded as an interpreter of the Dharmaśāstras and Dharmasūtras by many of its mostly south Indian followers.

In this paper, I draw on my ethnographic fieldwork to examine three specific moments of collectivity in Sringeri to show how they display markedly different senses of regional identity. These three moments are located in the public celebrations of the nine-night goddess festival of *navarātri* in September-October, the spring *rāmanavami* festival in Sringeri, and the performance tradition of *āśīrvāda* (ceremonialized blessing). I ask the following questions: what affiliations are invoked, what spatio-cultural intersections are drawn, and what cultural histories are remembered in these moments? What divergences of community identity become evident when cultural conceptualizations of 'region' are held up for scrutiny? Arjun Appadurai, Frank Korom and Margaret Mills remind us that claims about cultural ownership do not always indicate straightforward identifications of practitioners. Often in performance, such claims of ownership go beyond caste and gender to reflect regional and other forms of community identity (1991: 13). How have recent large-scale changes in the socio-political landscape of Sringeri, particularly the land-tenancy reforms, and Sringeri's growth as a tourist centre in the 1980s, affected configurations of regional identity? How does the presence of a historically powerful religious institution with a pan-regional reach affect constructions of community identity in its immediate vicinity?

The question of how social and political processes mediate the elusive and concrete expression of collective identity has been widely explored in the social sciences and humanities (Anderson 1991, Herzfeld 1985, and Ramaswamy 1997 are recent examples). The fields of folklore, ethnography of communication, and symbolic anthropology especially have been interested in the ways in which expressive traditions reflect 'group identity' (Abrahams 1993). One of the early formulations of collectivity was by Emile Durkheim, who suggested that collectivities emerged from a common morality or subscription to a sacred order (1915). This view gradually came to be challenged by the understanding that ritual or festive events, rather than only reaffirming a 'mechanical solidarity' (Durkheim

1893) or regenerating on a human level a transcendent order (Eliade 1957, for example), also could contain immense 'anti-structural' potential (Turner 1969). The carnivalesque, it has been suggested, can in fact be a revealing index of alternative community identity formation (Bakhtin 1968, Falassi 1987). Community or place maps are redrawn outside festive contexts also. While most pilgrimages demarcate cultural spaces through devotional narrative, personal experience stories, and packaged tourism, pilgrimages inspired by religious nationalism stake claims to places by excluding entire communities (van der Veer 1994). Dislocations triggered by colonialism (Butalia 1998) and by migration, forced or voluntary, create new formulations of self and community that are understated by terms such as 'exile', 'refugee', or 'diaspora' (Gupta and Ferguson 1997, and Prasad 1999).

THE *MALNAD*

In common parlance, the *malnad* is contrasted to the *maidan* (plateau), the erstwhile Mysore kingdom to the south-east of Sringeri. When I used to describe my travel through *maidan* areas to friends in Sringeri, I would be gently reminded, '*avaru bēre* (they are different)!' *Malnad* residents articulate this difference in a discourse around *namma malnāḍinalli* (in our *malnad*) that characterizes the *malnad*'s foodways, social customs, and language use, but the highlight of this discourse is *malnad* hospitality, or *upacāra*. Residents explain that travel to Sringeri was difficult in the old days with the thick mountainous forests, long spells of heavy rain, and inadequate transportation. *Malnad* homes, which on account of land-owning patterns in the region were virtually single-home villages, became the loci for elaborate traditions of hospitality toward visitors. Dance dramas, like *yakṣagāna*, provided occasions for local families to socialize, and visiting performance troupes would stay with a family for weeks. A long-standing tongue-in-cheek opposition is made by Sringeri residents between *maidān oarṭu* (the *maidan's* coarse manners) and *malnāḍ upacāra*. But yet another differentiation is made by Sringeri residents, between a *malnad* identity and a Sringeri identity. Protesting against recent criticism that they have relegated hospitality to the services of the Shankara *maṭha*—which offers *prasāda* as free food and subsidized lodging to visitors—Sringeri residents unanimously cite a uniquely Sringeri performance tradition called *āśīrvāda* as a marker of Sringeri *upacāra*. *Āśīrvāda* performances are speech-events that occur at the end of religious celebrations or festive life-cycle occasions. They involve an extempore recitation in Kannada by a priest or a male elder in the community who is called upon to deliver a speech. This speech, through various improvised narratives, is an expression of thanks to guests, hosts, and deities, and a commentary on the framing event that includes instruction on moral being.

Not surprisingly, the three moments I describe in this paper are part of other discourses of self-representation in the Sringeri area.[2] There flourishes, as in most regions of India, a genre of stories, kept alive by contestation, about the origins and character of the area—what one may loosely call Sringeri's *sthaḷa purāṇa,* or legends of the place, like the one I recounted at the beginning of this essay. The most ubiquitously cited, however, are variations of the story of Sringeri being the place where Shankara saw a snake shielding a frog.[3] A close friend in Sringeri narrated this story, which I heard often:

> When Shankara first came to Sringeri, he saw, on the sandy banks of the river, a cobra and a frog, and, as you know, cobras prey on frogs. The frog was struggling in labour, and the cobra had spread its hood to protect the frog from the sun's glare. Shankara, beholding this sight, thought, here is a place where even sworn enemies live as friends. And with this vision, he established the Sringeri *maṭha*.[4]

As for many Sringeri residents, for my friend such stories locate Sringeri's historical beginnings in the establishment and growth of the Shankara *maṭha*. The story is told in Sringeri that Shankara, after defeating Mandana Mishra[5] in debate, renamed him Sureshvaracarya and appointed him the first head of the *maṭha*. Oral accounts trace from Sureshvaracarya an unbroken lineage of gurus of the *maṭha*. Just as Shankara is believed to have established four *maṭhas* in the four directions of India, in Sringeri he is credited with setting up four temples around the main Sharada temple. In the east is the Kāḷa Bhairava temple, the Kāḷikāmba temple is to the north, the Durgāmba temple to the south, and the Kere Āñjanēya temple to the west by the *kere* (lake).[6] The popularity of this narrative is apparent from its reproduction in varying detail and emphasis in verbal accounts, commercial paintings, tourist brochures, museum depictions, state and district gazetteers, and popular songs. Equally popular but not sharing the same breadth of visual representation is the legend of the rain-bearing sage, Rishyashringa. The story goes that the sage Vibhandaka, who performed his penance in these regions, was seduced by the celestial courtesan Menaka, who took the form of a deer when their child was about to be born, and then returned to her heavenly home. The child, born with the horn of a deer, was called Rishyashringa, or 'the one-horned, born of a sage', and was endowed with the power to bring rain wherever he went. The hill where he lived and performed penance came to be known as Rishyashringagiri, and thus Sringeri got its name. Six miles from Sringeri, in the town of Kigga, is a temple dedicated to Rishyashringa, where the Śivalinga has a single horn. On a hill in the town of Sringeri, there is a prominent Śiva temple called the Malahānikareśvara temple which consecrates the place where Rishyashringa's father, the sage Vibhandaka, merged with a linga while he was immersed in penance. They say in Sringeri that you never visit the Kigga temple without visiting the temple on the hill.[7]

Although the region in which Rishyashringa lived is not specified in Valmiki's *Rāmāyaṇa*, which refers to the legend[8] (Sawai 1992), the point is that larger-than-local texts can underwrite 'local' history. These mega-narratives present a history of Sringeri that privileges one representation over others. Popular songs, incessantly booming from cassette shops, showcase images of Sringeri abstracted from these legends for visiting tourists and pilgrims, images that situate Sringeri in a spiritual, ancient past and a peaceful present. In fact, the main roads of the town, Bharati Street and Harihara Street, could be thought of as metaphors of mega-narratives. Bharati Street is characterized by innumerable small hotels and lodges; stores that stock pre-recorded audio cassettes, photo film, *japa mālās*[9] and other religious paraphernalia; and roadside vendors who sell fresh flowers, tender coconut, and puffed rice to feed the fish in the river. Like the inner structures that 'master stories' eclipse, most of these small stores are the newly-constructed fronts of centuries-old houses, which often have courtyards, cattle sheds, private temples, and living quarters beyond the frontage. For instance, Srungagiri Xerox, a tiny, 50 sq. ft. photocopy and memento store, is the main but undetectable entrance to a house that actually sprawls for a quarter mile behind the store, and is complete with an areca garden that stretches to the northern bank of the Tunga, a twenty-room lodge, and four apartments. It is always thrilling to discover the intricate interior behind a store front: the low-roofed, wooden-beamed rooms with shelves built into beams close to the ceiling, the narrow corridors leading to storage areas and dining halls, the engraved solid wooden doorways, an open well usually fitted with an electric pump, the elaborate *dēvara-mane* or *pūjā* room, the kitchen with separate areas for festive and everyday cooking, and the bathing area with its deep *haṇḍe*, the wood-burning copper pot for heating water.

These inner structures obscured by storefronts remind one in their hiddenness of the barely-narrated pre-Shankara period of Jain settlements in Sringeri. Largely written about as the story of defeated heterodoxy, this period, of which little is really known or documented, is not generally perceived as belonging to Sringeri's show-case items. Pervasive instead, in most depictions of Sringeri, is the complete romanticization of its character. For one, its location in thickly-forested, mountainous country makes Sringeri available for claims that it is 'preserved from civilization'. A publication of the *maṭha*, *The Greatness of Sringeri*, declares, 'When peace eludes you, when the world is too much for you, when the fever of life torments you, come to Sringeri', where 'peace is palpable, tangible!' (1991: 6). Most of this literature is from the perspective of devout adherents of the *maṭha* who, drawing from their devotion to particular gurus, focus on the religious activities of the *maṭha* and glorify it (Rao 1968; Aiyar 1968; Subbaratnam 1968).

However, historical writing on the pre-Shankara period speculates that prior to Shankara's arrival in Sringeri around the eighth century, the Jains who lived in these parts enjoyed the support of regional rulers (Kamat 1991: 25) and were settled '. . . in the patronage of traders, merchants and officers of the state . . .' (Thapar 1978: 75). Lewis Rice, a British official known for his work on the stone and copper-plate inscriptions in the old Mysore area, presents evidence that suggests that around 350 BC Jains moved into the Mysore region to escape a famine in northern India (Rice 1983 [1897]). Reconstructions of Shankara's times depict the mediation of relations between Shankara and non-Advaita believers as proceeding from *vāda*, philosophical debate and argument.[10] Through debates, ideological positions were mapped onto physical geographies: defeat resulted in displacement, and victories awarded territorial rights.

Oral accounts in Sringeri claim that the Jains, having lost in debate, moved out of Sringeri, where they had been long settled with their streets and temples, to live on the outskirts in new settlements. While, ostensibly, reconstructions portray debates as contests of knowledge, they contain the implicit assessment that debates constitute an appropriate forum for making and effecting statements of power. A college lecturer in Sringeri, himself an adherent of the Sringeri *maṭha* and greatly respected in the region, pointed out to me that it was possible that Shankara had a political agenda as he established the Sringeri *maṭha*. Reflecting on the *Vidyāraṇya Śaṅkaradigvijaya*, he noted that the places surrounding Sringeri—Narsimharajapura Venuru, Karkala, and Mudubidre—had indeed been Jain pilgrimage sites. Further, he said:

> Vidyaranya's book tells us this much: Vedic brahmans lived in this region, and they used to perform Vedic rituals and sacrifices. In other words, this was a region where the *karma kāṇḍa*[11] school of thought flourished. Now why would Shankaracarya come here? We know that Shankara's objective was to oust the *karma kāṇḍa* school and bring the *jñāna kāṇḍa* school to power. After all, that was his mission, wasn't it? So, from this perspective, it isn't very surprising that he chose Sringeri as the site of the *maṭha*. . . . This snake-and-frog story that you hear, all that came much later. We don't find any textual reference for that story. . . . It's an oral tale,[12] that's all. Shankaracarya deliberately chose this spot to establish the *maṭha*.

The added presence of Tantric sects like the Kāpālikas and the Pāśupatas,[13] against whom the Jains competed for religious dominance (Ramesam 1971; Venkataraman 1990) further argues against an idyllic, unpopulated vision of Sringeri. Scholars have noted that Shankara himself met opposition both from the well-established Jains and from these iconoclastic sects. His encounters with the Kāpālikas are poeticized in texts like the Sanskrit *Śaṅkaradigvijaya*,[14] the legendary biography of Shankara, which recounts: 'In the Karṇāṭa country, Shankara conquered the Kāpālikas through fire generated by his chanting of the syllable hum', and 'the followers of the Pāñcarātra doctrine . . . claiming that immortality belongs to those who recognize five basic differences, were defeated by the very excellent disciples of the sage (Shankara)' (translated in Sawai 1992: 146-7). Critical assessments of this competition for religious high ground make it clear that the Sringeri in which Shankara chose to establish the *maṭha* was occupied by diverse sects who competed with each other on many levels, and that the Jains were the most powerful community in the region at that time. This knowledge that Jains once lived in the area and were compelled to leave it is not denied in Sringeri today, but it does not shape most formulations of 'Sringeri's past'.

The First Moment of Collectivity: *Navarātri* and Royalty

It is believed that Vidyaranya, the twelfth guru of the *maṭha*, helped Harihara I and his brother Bukka[15] to establish, around 1350, what became one of the most powerful and expansive Hindu kingdoms in Indian history, the Vijayanagara empire (Thapar 1966).[16] Although scholars are uncertain whether Hakka and Bukka were independent rulers, or ministers in the court of the last of the Hoysala kings who ruled in the Karnataka region prior to the Vijayanagara kings, it is generally held that the brothers sought Vidyaranya's counsel to overthrow the Muslim conquerors of southern India (Devi 1990; Shastry 1982). Soon after their victories, acting on Vidyaranya's advice, they founded the nine-gate city of Vijayanagara in the shape of a *śrī cakra* (a tantric diagram whose nine triangles symbolize the universe) with a temple at its centre. Hakka's coronation is believed to have been personally conducted by Vidyaranya. According to Devi (1990: 11) the *Vidyāraṇya Vṛttānta* notes,

> Vidyāraṇya seated himself upon the throne before the coronation of Harihara and received from him with libations of water a gift of a lakh and a quarter, territory both above and below the Ghats in the kingdom of Karnataka, which he [Hakka] had obtained (from the earlier ruler or rulers) for the maintenance of the maṭha and the choultry [resthouse] at Sringeri as well as the agrahāra [brahman residential locality] and Paramahamsa choultry. Then seating Harihara on the throne Vidyāraṇya performed his coronation.[17]

The durbār itself vividly symbolizes Sringeri's once-intimate ties to royalty. According to historical records as well as popular belief, the Sringeri durbār has its origin in the *guru dakṣiṇā* that Harihara and Bukka offered to Vidyaranya in return for his help in establishing the Vijayanagara empire (Thapar 1966). The story goes that when the brothers were asked by Vidyaranya what they would give as *guru dakṣiṇā* to him, they offered him their entire empire. When Vidyaranya, a sannyāsī, pleased with their devotion, declined (or as some versions go, he accepted the empire nominally and returned it immediately), they insisted that for at least ten days in the year he should symbolically rule as emperor. This came to be the tradition of the *navarātri* durbār at the Sringeri *maṭha*. The Vijayanagara kings are reported to have themselves lavishly celebrated *navarātri* in Sringeri (Kulke 1985).

Historians cite several inscriptions recording that Harihara and his brothers reciprocated Vidyaranya's help by visiting the *maṭha* in 1346 and donating nine villages to it. These were deemed, like all subsequent land grants, *sarvamānya* (exempt from duties and taxes). Called the Śṛṅgapura grant by historians, and recorded in a stone inscription preserved in Sringeri, this is the first known land-grant received by the *maṭha* (Row 1927; Shastry 1982; Devi 1990; Venkataraman 1990). The Śṛṅgapura grant led to the formation of the Śṛṅgapura *agrahāra*, the first of many brahman settlements in the area. Between the fourteenth and the eighteenth centuries many land grants and other endowments were made by various rulers. In all, these endowments totalled to an annual revenue of 3003 pagodas,[18] and hence Sringeri came to be known as *mūru sāvira mūru varahada sīme*, or 'property of three thousand and three varahas'. The patronage of the *maṭha* came to be, for rulers, an important means of maintaining the cordial relations perceived necessary to augment positions of power. The Sringeri *maṭha*, in its turn, reciprocated by offering religious services, and also by deploying its religious authority to 'validate' the political position of the patron-king. Many instances are recorded of the astute politics and patterns of patronage involving the Sringeri *maṭha* shown by the fine-tuned transactions between the *maṭha*, the Keḷadi kings, and the Maratha and Muslim rulers (Shastry 1982; Stein 1999; Wagoner 1996).

Sringeri remembers in a singular way during *navarātri* its historical transition from a pilgrimage centre to an area with a powerful political presence. The pan-Hindu festival of *navarātri* is celebrated by the worship of the goddess (*devī*) for ten days, each day dedicated to a different aspect of her. Each day, prayers, sacred recitations, and rituals are performed along with elaborate traditional feasts in accordance with the aspect being invoked. On the fifth day, the goddess is worshipped as Lalita, the supreme goddess; on the seventh, as Sharada, the goddess of learning; on the eighth, as

Durga, warrior and protector; on the ninth, as Kali, the battle-hungry destroyer of demons; and on the tenth and final day, as Vijayalakshmi, the victorious goddess who bestows wealth. Public festivity during *navarātri* is the domain of the *maṭha*, where the principal deity of the *maṭha*-temple complex, Sharada, is bedecked in silk, flowers, and jewellery of gold and silver inlaid with precious stones, many of which are gifts from rulers and kings over the centuries. Visitors throng to Sringeri from all over south India to witness the magnificent *alaṅkāra* (adornment) of the goddess. For each of the ten days, the adornment is specific to the aspect of the goddess being represented. In addition to the special worship in the temple that includes recitations from the Vedas and other sacred texts, fire sacrifices, and festive meals, the *maṭha* organizes chariot processions during which the goddess rides grandly out into the streets of Sringeri every evening. There are nightly music concerts where well-known musicians are invited to perform, and durbārs, or royal courts, held only during the *navarātri* nights, when the guru is attired in his special regalia.

Residents of Sringeri participate in the *maṭha's* festivities in many ways, but most typically by at least a daily visit to the temple. Except for a few hours in the early afternoon, the temple complex is packed with people seeking *darśana*, socializing, or attending the evening concert or the durbār. Residents, who dress festively to come to the *maṭha*, take this opportunity to catch up with friends from neighbouring towns, to participate collectively in special worship at the various other temples of the *maṭha* in the town, and often, to sponsor a *pūjā* at the main temple. In the evening, hours before the durbār which concludes the day's activities, the chariot procession (Plate 1) seating the smaller image of the goddess journeys along this street, accompanied by the students of the *maṭha's* Vedic school, who chant sacred verses, and by musicians who play the nadaswaram. The procession is led by the *maṭha's* bedecked elephants, which, as they lead the way, are fed coconuts and bananas by many in the assembled crowd. Residents who live along the route of the procession light the lamps of their domestic shrines from the lamp on the chariot. During my visits to nearby villages and towns, people told me that they would visit the *maṭha* at least once during *navarātri*, even if it was their only visit to the *maṭha* in the year. For some, there is the additional attraction of the *jātre*, the travelling street fair, that comes

Plate 1. *Navarātri*, October 1996. Crowd gathers for the chariot procession organized by the Shankara *maṭha*. ©Leela Prasad

to Sringeri during *navarātri*. Carts and temporary stalls, some of which are set up on people's doorsteps, sell *kaḷḷepuri* (spiced puffed rice), clothes, fabric, 'imitation jewellery', small mirrors, combs, foodstuffs, flowers, 'Bombāi mithāi' (cotton candy), toys, cassettes, household wares, and worship items—the temporary universe of the travelling fair clusters into the main street that leads to the temple. During my fieldwork, after sober hours in the temple, I used to look forward to the razzle-dazzle of the marketplace, and with my mother—who had for years wanted to experience a Sringeri *navarātri*—I would enthusiastically window-shop for small things.

The *navarātri* festival, as oral accounts reveal, provides an occasion to the residents of Sringeri, irrespective of caste, gender, age, or social standing, to express cultural ownership of the festival despite the fact that the organizational control of the public festivities still remains with the *maṭha*, and that participation is pan-regional, with pilgrims from all over south India attending. Residents speak of the festival unequivocally as theirs, and *navarātri* is considered a marker of community identity in a way that no other festival celebrated in Sringeri is. This community identification can perhaps be likened to the cohering force behind what Joyce Flueckiger calls a 'folklore group', a transient collectivity which assembles in the context of a performance and breaks up after the performance is over (1996: 177). However, everyday discourse about the *maṭha* among residents makes the *navarātri* celebration a more complex formulation of community identity in Sringeri. While ethnographic confidentiality does not allow me to disclose the identities of people who shared their opinions about the *maṭha* with me, many times these evaluations were critical of some of the policies and personages of the *maṭha*. At the same time, people were generally cognizant of the complex position of the *maṭha*, especially since it had seen significant socio-political transformations in the 1960s and 1970s. Individuals in Sringeri also pointed out that the *maṭha* had obligations as a social institution, obligations that were likely to clash sometimes with local priorities. During my stay in Sringeri, I realized that the phrase 'the *maṭha*' did not always mean the *same* structure of pontifical authority. With this term individuals could refer to a politically active institution, an institution represented by particular persons or symbolic of historical periods, or a geopolitical entity. Thus, one could ask: what is the nature of the linkages between the festival and the residents that makes it possible for them to suspend—or more accurately, to negotiate—this ambivalence toward the *maṭha*? Further, how does the public festival of *navarātri* emerge as marker of a common Sringeri identity when, in fact, local cultural demarcations between insiders and outsiders continue to be observed during the celebrations?

If the *maṭha* was an important player in the wider region's politics, it was of course central to the daily lives of those who lived in its proximity. The growth of the *maṭha* into a *jāgīrdāri* which granted to it autonomy in virtually all areas of government argued for mutual interdependence between the *maṭha* and the residents of the *jāgīr*. This interdependence was heightened during festive occasions: the *maṭha's* festivals were as much the community's responsibility, and, in fact, it was expected that the *maṭha* would call on local participation when festivals were organized. No lodging being available at the *maṭha*, visitors stayed with Sringeri families for even as long as a month or two, given the arduous journey back. 'It did not matter if one was *paricita*, or *aparicita*, acquaintance or stranger' (Shenoy 1995). The *navarātri* festival provided residents of the Sringeri *jāgīrdāri* the opportunity to perform the famed *malnad upacāra*, or traditions of *malnad* hospitality, and simultaneously display the Sringeri *jāgīrdāri's* centrality. Thus, although everyday discourse about the *maṭha* among residents is marked by an ambivalence towards the now-impersonal *maṭha*, with many generations-long relationships strained, the *navarātri* celebrations reinvoke the political role of the *maṭha* as an important player in history, and put on display Sringeri's once privileged position on the politico-cultural map of the wider region.

How do geographic boundaries get redrawn in the upbeat discourse of *navarātri*? In fact, the (regional) 'border' or *sīme* (also the word for region) appears to be an elastic construct in Sringeri's cultural geography. Residents recall how the festival used to draw hundreds of people from the district of Dakshina Kannada (southwest of Sringeri), who trekked for miles through the *malnad* forests and mountains (Shenoy 1995; Bhat 1994). The nearest town in Dakshina Kannada district is about 70 km south of Sringeri. One resident, illustrating the local imagination of this 'distance', explained that even until the early 1950s, Koppa, just 25 km north of Sringeri, was considered far enough for people to be differentiated as being *Koppada sīme avaru* (from the region of Koppa). A jocular threat among government employees and schoolteachers in Sringeri used to be: *tappu māḍidare, Koppakke hākri*! (make a mistake, and you will be posted to Koppa). Hosanagara, again, 50 km north-west, was thought of as being 'very far'. In spite of this conceptualization of distance (shaped by the scarce transport, the *malnad* forests, and the torrential rains), *navarātri* in Sringeri brought people from the 'far regions' of Dakshina Kannada. Today, the wide availability of bus services and packaged pilgrimage tours that include Sringeri in a long list of must-see towns has diminished Sringeri's exclusive cultural status, but the celebration of *navarātri* restores, in some measure, its sense of distinctiveness in the region.

THE SECOND MOMENT OF COLLECTIVITY: *RĀMANAVAMI* AND LOCALITY

If the *navarātri* festival is centralized in the *maṭha* and invokes Sringeri's glorious connection to the historic Vijayanagara empire, *rāmanavami* celebrations in Sringeri are diffused across neighbourhoods and households, and bring epic imagination to local spaces. Nine days after the Kannada new year day, *ugādi* (which usually occurs in April), is *rāmanavami*, a pan-Hindu festival that commemorates the birth of Rāma. During *rāmanavami*, brahmans in the villages of Sringeri taluka and nearby *agrahāras* of Vaikunthapura, Vidyaranyapura, and Sachidanandapura form Rāma Sēvā Samitis that organize celebrations over ten days. While the festivities are independently conducted, they sometimes share cooking vessels and items of worship, all of which are stored in the house of the elected president of the Brāhmaṇa Mahāsabhā (Brahman Council). The festivities are synchronized to facilitate the sharing, but take place more or less within a few days of each other. The celebrations that I attended in Sringeri in 1995 began with the installation of the image of Rāma, as traditionally pictured with Sītā, Lakṣmaṇa, and Āñjaneya. The site that year was the main hall of the Girls' Middle School (Plate 2), a three-minute walk from where I lived. I was told that year after year, for the nearly seventy-five years of this tradition in the town of Sringeri, the Rāma Sēvā Samiti had to cope with the difficulty of finding a suitable venue for the celebrations. It is a predicament that many people metaphorically sum up in terms of

Plate 2. *Rāmanavami*, April 1995. Community *Satyanārayaṇa pūjā* in the Girls' Middle School, Sringeri. ©Leela Prasad

Rāma's own exile in the forests for fourteen years. 'It is fated that our Rāma should also have to wander', an older resident said to me during one of the days of the celebration. The images were worshipped twice every day in the main hall, which was covered with educational posters, maps, well-known pledges and poems, and slogans like 'Each One, Teach One'. But it was the evenings that transformed the quiet hall. Men, women, and children of all ages packed the hall for the *bhajane*, community devotional singing, for the speeches and announcements, the final *ārati*, and the *prasāda* which was distributed. Each day's worship and *prasāda* were either individually or collectively sponsored.

During the ten days of the celebrations, Sanskrit prayer lessons were also offered, recitation competitions were held (where children memorized and recited sections from a popular rendering of the *Rāmāyaṇa*), and concerts were organized. The *bhajane* were sung with gusto, as everyone seemed to know the songs and wanted to sing. It was a grand occasion for socializing—everyone knew each other, and there were no tourists—and I remember enjoying the boisterous chatting that drowned out the speeches in spite of the public address system. In fact, it was during one of these speeches that my husband, Prasad, and I, immersed in the chatting and the eating, were caught by surprise when the speaker introduced us as 'special participants' of that year's celebrations. As the audience clapped—we knew many in the gathering—we clumsily tried to acknowledge the gesture.

One cannot miss the intensely 'local' flavour that permeates *rāmanavami* festivity. One is immediately struck by the alternative space—physical and cultural—that the celebrations occupy in Sringeri when compared to the *maṭha*-organized *navarātri* festivity. The long-established temple-complex lends to the *navarātri* festival a predictable stability of locale that seems to elude Sringeri's Rāma. That the *rāmanavami* celebrations every year have to be held in a different place, acquired through a process of protracted negotiation, is interestingly worked into a narrative of *sañcāra* Rāma, the 'wandering Rāma', analogous to the travails that beset the legendary Rāma in his exile in the forest. This amusing narrative, shared almost as if to authenticate the *rāmanavami* celebrations through the Rāma story itself, is an inside story about the celebrations.

The sense of locality is underscored by the fact that residents of Vidyaranyapura, barely 5 km away, have their own *rāmanavami* celebrations, and are invited as guests to the Sringeri celebrations. There are Vidyaranyapura Rāma *bhajans* and there are Sringeri Rāma *bhajans*, and when the Vidyaranyapura group sang 'their' songs at the Sringeri celebrations one evening, they were formally felicitated for their participation. At other times, Vidyaranyapura residents are not in any way considered *apart* from the Sringeri community, and among the area's *agrahāras*, there is considerable traffic, trade, and interdependence. Similarly, although the district census report mentions Nemmar as one of the villages 'which more or less functions as a subcentre of Sringeri', being situated so close to it (Das 1984: 256), when musicians from Nemmar were invited to Sringeri in the 1995 celebrations, they were thanked for gracing the Sringeri celebrations, having come all the way from 'outside'.

Interestingly, while Vidyaranyapura and Nemmar, like other villages in Sringeri taluka, conduct separate *rāmanavami* celebrations, the cooking vessels and items of worship that they use in the celebrations are drawn from a common store whose caretaker is the Sringeri Brahman Council. Along with Sringeri, these towns share an autonomy from the *maṭha* as far as *rāmanavami* celebrations go, an autonomy which is claimed through statements such as, 'We don't have any *sambandha*, any connection, with the *maṭha*. This is our own thing' (compare Flueckiger 1996). The position of autonomy from the *maṭha* has perhaps less to do with material independence of the Brahman Council (since the *maṭha*, as a matter of fact, contributes provisions or space for the concluding community meal), than with an articulation of locality in which the *maṭha* is not considered quite so local. Considering that during the *navarātri* celebrations the *maṭha* is perceived as local, the shift in organizational control and management of festivity is a way of retaining optional loci of cultural identity (what Richard Bauman [1972] calls 'differential identity').

The Sringeri-ness of the *rāmanavami* celebration is more fine-grained: 'Sringeri identity' generated during *rāmanavami* is primarily a brahman collectivity. My brahman family friends, particularly a well-respected elder, repeatedly and enthusiastically invited one of my neighbours and close friends who was not a brahman to the celebrations, but she did not attend them. Given that she only smiled when I asked her, and I did not think it appropriate to push the question, I can only ask whether the region's predilection for caste distinctions in some way dissuaded her from participation in an event barely three minutes from where she and I lived, an event she had herself identified as a Sringeri thing? Thus, the discourse about 'localness' that frames Sringeri *rāmanavami* is a good example of how local practices can presume 'larger-than-local' ones (Shuman 1993). Or, should one also add, smaller-than-local? The *rāmanavami* festival of Sringeri, like scores of other traditions, confounds the analytic categories of 'folk' and 'classical' in the identification of genres or even communities, and is hard to fit into such dichotomous vocabulary. Drawing simultaneously on Karnataka-wide traditions of celebrating the festival and on Sanskritic traditions of worship, and incorporating practices unique to Sringeri, the *rāmanavami* celebration is still seen by the community as a Sringeri tradition, where 'Sringeri traditions' constitute a viable discursive category.

So the question arises, what does the redrawing of such spatio-cultural boundaries affirm? For one, while it unsettles the idea that geo-political identity implies an invariant regional consciousness, it demonstrates that allegiances to place are constantly configured—and erased. While perhaps this is not a startling insight for Indian situations, what the Sringeri festivals reveal are the *dynamics* of the making of region-based constructs. They help us recognize that temporal and spatial contextualization is necessary for us to understand the deep-rooted heterogeneity of Indian regions.

THE THIRD MOMENT OF COLLECTIVITY: SRINGERI *ĀŚĪRVĀDA* (CEREMONIALIZED BLESSING) AND *MALNĀḌ UPACĀRA* (HOSPITALITY)

Malnāḍ upacāra keḷa bēka? As for the *malnad's* lavish hospitality, does one need to ask? *Malnad* hospitality, especially of the *jāgīrdāri* days, was exemplified by such luxuries as the famous *abhyañjana*, or oil baths, provided to visitors to the Kuthgodu home, 6 miles from Sringeri, or by the generous meals that the goddess Annapūrṇā is believed to provide her pilgrims in the neighbouring town of Hornad irrespective of the time of day or night they arrive, or by the feasting and entertaining of guests for weeks during the long monsoons of the *malnad*.[19]

And indeed, for many months, gratefully enjoying as I did the rich welcome I received at every home I visited and lived in, it was easy to be swayed by that popular perception of *malnad* culture. Gradually, my visits to Sringeri over the years educated me to the fact that *Sringeri upacāra* was far from the unproblematic cultural category that the regional label makes it to be. In Sringeri narrations, the term was used ironically by 'outsiders' (meaning people from the *maidan*, or from Bangalore and Mysore) to refer tongue-in-cheek to the supposed shrugging off of hospitality by Sringeri residents onto the Shankara *maṭha*. For those who identify with the Sringeri area, however, Sringeri *upacāra* is exemplified, not perhaps by a material enactment of hospitality, but by the tradition of *āśīrvāda* which involves an extempore recitation in Kannada by a priest or a male elder at the end of a ceremony like *pārāyaṇa* or an *upanayana* hosted by a family in a home, a temple, or a rented space (Plates 3 and 4). This poetic speech is an expression of thanks to guests, hosts, and deities, a commentary on the framing celebratory event, and most

Plate 3. *Ā-sīrvāda*, December 2001, performed at the end of an *upanayana*. Sanskrit scholars reciting mantras during the *ā-sīrvāda*. ©Leela Prasad

Plate 4. *Ā-sīrvāda*, December 2001. The distribution of *tāmbula* (betel-nut leaves) and fruit among women after the conclusion of the *ā-sīrvāda*. ©Leela Prasad

importantly, an instruction on everyday conduct. *Āśīrvāda* performances last for about thirty minutes and take place after the festive meal. While I analyse the performance contexts and "texts" of *āśīrvāda* speeches elsewhere in detail, in general, I observed that these exegetical speeches are intricately layered: they cite *śāstra* and *sūtra* texts, they abstract stories from the epics, *purāṇas*, and regional narratives, and they weave local history and politics with social commentary. Eclectic sources are improvised to outline idealized models of conduct. In one *āśīrvāda* performed at the end of an evening Durga *pūjā* in 2004, the host couple made a short formal statement after the festive meal thanking everybody for having attended and asked to be excused for any lapse. They then invited a well-versed scholar-priest (who also maintains the Kanyakumari temple unique to the region) to deliver the *āśīrvāda* speech. Alternating between praise, prayer, and story, in his speech explaining the contextual meanings of the Durga *pūjā*, the scholar linked several narrative sources dialogically to underscore the relevance of *devī* worship in daily life. In such a way, *āśīrvāda* performances, in their attempt to situate *śāstric* texts in practised contexts, seek to clarify ambiguities, outline symbolic geographies, and confront the exigencies that characterize everyday life. Speeches display a spectacular interplay of voice, textual allusion, and poetic mood. The reflexivity of *āśīrvāda* speeches is demonstrated by a repetitive attention to their 'function' of explication through variations of the statement, 'This is the meaning'.

Why do Sringeri residents point to the speech-oriented *āśīrvāda* tradition as illustrating *malnad* hospitality (*upacāra*) traditions that are characterized by material comforts? Local exegesis suggests that *āśīrvāda* brings closure to an event, but does so on a note of remembrance and continuity in which guest-host relations are praised and dramatized. But apart from the poetics of the performance, there are economic and political reasons for the local tradition to affirm allegiance to a larger-than-local one—thus demonstrating the creative adaptability of regional consciousness. The abolition of the *jāgīrdāri* affected the *maṭha's* economic base, necessitating a dependence on pilgrims. This dependence was fostered by the *maṭha's* institutionalization of hospitality through subsidized accommodation. Land reform acts of the 1960s and 1970s limited the resources available to Sringeri families. Improved transportation to Sringeri (which brought visitors in great numbers), and changing lifestyles, which circumscribed the length of visits, dramatically altered the capacity of Sringeri families to perform *upacāra* on the generous scale of the past.

A close family friend, a much-respected elder of Sringeri (now no more), paraphrased the dilemma in terms of appropriate performance of *ātithya*,[20] which is not only a prominent Indian idiom but one that is tremendously reinforced by the *malnad's* reputed traditions of hospitality. In his words, 'If we say to a visitor, "Okay, you could stay at the *maṭha*", it means we turn over hospitality to the *maṭha*. On the other hand, if we insist they stay with us, we will be obstructing a pilgrim's wish to bathe in the Tunga and eat *prasāda* at the *maṭha*.' In answering the question, 'What constitutes appropriate conduct?' the *āśīrvāda* tradition is seen as presenting the 'essence' of *malnad upacāra* as not simply the indiscriminate expression of generous hospitality, but the sensitive and subtle imagination of the wishes of guests. *Āśīrvāda* celebrates guesthood, poetically delineates it, but reminds the audience more generally of the supreme importance of the context in matters of conduct. And thus, caught between contested discourses of the past and discourses about a contested present, through *āśīrvāda* the Sringeri community redefines the region's *upacāra* tradition in order to reclaim its belonging to the *malnad*. Narrations of visitors' critiques of Sringeri's *upacāra* are especially interesting for the manner in which they position the *āśīrvāda* tradition between competing and complementary discourses of regionality and locality.

Conclusion

In this paper I have considered how celebrations of Sringeri festivals index different senses of regionality, and how Sringeri discourse about a performance tradition reveals that Sringeri identity is a contextually changing collectivity. Each collectivity is moored in configurations of the past and in the ways that these configurations work in the present. The fluidity of what or who constitutes past/present is important in understanding who belongs now and who does not—not always are these in linear relationships.

While these juxtapositions of community identity that derive and diverge from conceptualizations of geographic and cultural space no doubt emphasize the highly particularized political and economic moorings of collective identities, it is just as important to explore how regional identities are defined by a variety of insider/outsider configurations. The *navarātri* festivity expresses a Sringeri identity (whatever it is for each individual) for socially and economically disparate individuals as much as *rāmanavami* is a Sringeri celebration for even the non-brahman communities, though they rarely participate in the public celebration. *Rāmanavami* can be a 'Sringeri celebration' but not 'our celebration'. In the same vein, for the brahmans of the Sringeri area, belonging to the *maṭha* can hardly be taken for granted, given the *maṭha's* history of empowering and disempowering sub-castes. The rhetoric of regionally anchored community identity, then, says little about the ironies embedded in it; and although Benedict Anderson would say, '. . . communities are to be distinguished not by their falsity/genuineness, but by the style in which they are imagined' (1991: 6),[21] close readings of collectivities reveal who is not part of them.

NOTES

1. I had visited Sringeri with my parents during my childhood, but it was only during doctoral research in 1994-5 that I took up residence in Sringeri. Since then, I have been to Sringeri on both extended and brief visits. My paternal grandfather, a district judge, had lived in Sringeri from 1950 to 1955. These ties to Sringeri, my identity as a Telugu-speaking brahman, and my fluency in Kannada, facilitated my research in the mostly-brahmanical community of Sringeri, and also helped me adjust to life in Sringeri.
2. When I say 'the Sringeri area', I translate from local usage to mean Sringeri and its immediate vicinity that extends to neighbourhoods about ten miles around.
3. In fact, 'Shankara stories' are a well-known corpus. Audiocassettes like *Śāradā-Śaṅkara* (Advaith Audio, Bangalore, 1995) contain songs that narrate Shankara stories. These stories, which support the belief that he was an incarnation of Śiva, usually centre on the events surrounding his renunciation, the miracles he performed during his journeys as a *sannyāsī*, his commitment to Advaita or non-dualism, and his brilliance as an orator who defeated many scholars from different schools in philosophical debate.
4. A Śivalinga on the bathing *ghāṭ* on the banks of the Tunga within the

temple complex marks this spot, and a frog and cobra are carved in the stone beside it.

5. Shankara's encounter with Mandana Mishra, a reputed advocate of the Karma Mīmāṃsā school (characterized by its adherence to Vedic ritual and sacrifice), is one of the well-known stories about Shankara's philosophical victories. As most people familiar with the Smārta tradition know, the debate was refereed by Mandana Mishra's wife, Ubhayabharati, herself a learned scholar and believed to be an incarnation of Saraswati, the goddess of learning.
6. The *Guruvaṃśakāvya*, a Sanskrit work written sometime between 1735 and 1739 by Kāśī Lakṣmaṇaśāstrī, a Vedic scholar in the *maṭha*, details the history of successive gurus of the Sringeri *maṭha* from the times of Shankara to 1734, and states that Vidyaranya, the thirteenth-century pontiff and administrator, established these temples (Sawai 1992).
7. Such 'rules' of pilgrimage play a significant role in charting sacred geographies based on kinship or other intimate or competitive relations between deities. Local stories explain these connections. In Tirupati, for example, a domestic quarrel between Lord Venkateswara and his consort Padmavathi explains why there are two temples, his on top of the Tirumala hill and hers in the city below. The pilgrimage is not considered complete unless a pilgrim visits both temples.
8. Rishyashringa is mentioned in Valmiki's *Rāmāyaṇa* as the sage who was pivotal in performing the *putrakāmeṣṭi* sacrifice for King Daśaratha, who desired children. Rāma and his three brothers were born to Daśaratha and his wives following this sacrifice.
9. Rosaries made of basil stem, crystal, or the *rudrākṣa* seed.
10. Even in Vedic times, debate was an established genre of refutation with an elaborate system of rules that had as much to do with proving doctrines as with perpetuating power relations between contestants (Heesterman 1984).
11. 'School of ritual' as opposed to Shankara's 'school of knowledge', distinguished by its uncompromising commitment to the observance of ritual.
12. In the conversation, the Kannada term used is *danta kathe*, which literally means 'tooth tale'.
13. Such sects generated much controversy through their 'extreme non-conformity' of religious practice, including, it is believed, human sacrifice (Thapar 1992), which the Buddhists and the Jains—and also Shankara—opposed (see also Ramesam 1971).
14. While the literal translation is 'Shankara's Conquest of the World', the military metaphor is misleading, since debate seems to have been the primary means to achieve victory. There are numerous, variously authored hagiographic works called the *Śaṅkara Vijaya*, the oldest of which is agreed to be *Mādhavīya Śaṅkaravijaya*, or the *Śaṅkara-digvijaya*, whose authorship is debated but ascribed by adherents of

the Sringeri tradition to Vidyaranya, the twelfth guru of the *maṭha* in the fourteenth century (Tapasyananda 1978). Yoshitsugu Sawai notes that the text has been attributed to indeterminate author(s) of the eighteenth century (1992).

15. It is a matter of speculation among historians as to where the two brothers Harihara (commonly known as Hakka) and Bukka originally belonged. While some scholars argue that the brothers were from neighbouring Andhra Pradesh, others (Nilakanta Sastri 1955, for instance) claim that Harihara and Bukka were of local origin, and were ministers in the erstwhile Hoysala kingdom.
16. There are no contemporary historical sources that can inform us about Sringeri in the years between the establishment of the *maṭha* in the eighth century and the emergence of the Vijayanagara kingdom. There were three successive Vijayanagara dynasties after the kingdom's establishment in the early fourteenth century, until the combined Muslim forces of Bijapur, Golkonda, Ahmednagar, Bidar and Berar in the northern Deccan overthrew the last Vijayanagara king, Sadashivaraya, in the battle of Talikota in 1565 and destroyed the capital, Hampi. The rule of Krishnadevaraya (1509-29) is considered the pinnacle of Vijayanagara glory. During this period, the Sringeri *maṭha* was able to consolidate its vast holdings and acquire a high profile.
17. Ever since, the gurus of the *maṭha* have held the title of *Karṇāṭaka Siṃhāsana pratiṣṭāpanācārya*, or the '*sannyāsīs* who are founders of the throne of Karnataka'.
18. A gold coin of that time with the figure of a pagoda on one side. While most recent texts refer to *pagodas*, studies of Vijayanagara coinage use the more general term of *varaha*, which is a gold coin weighing 52 grams. Various figures of gods and goddesses are imprinted on them, and the term *pagoda* refers to one such coin, which has the figure of a pagoda on it. A gram of gold was worth about Rs. 400 in 1996, and in contemporary reckoning, a *pagoda* would be about Rs. 21,000. In 1818, a *pagoda* was worth Rs. 3.50 (Dirks 1987).
19. The rhetorical question has even been treated in writing about the region, as in the fiction of Gorur Ramaswamy Iyengar and U. R. Ananthamurthy.
20. *Ātithya*, derived from *atithi*, 'guest', is the Sanskrit word for hospitality. There exist in Sanskrit numerous treatises (most well-known of which are the *gṛhyasūtras*, 'domestic codes') that describe in great specificity the duties of a householder with regard to the hosting of guests. With these emphases, it is no surprise that the guest is accorded a very high place in everyday social engagement in Hindu culture.
21. Two salient critiques of the concept of community that examine the historical and disciplinary implications of the concept are Abrahams 1993 and Noyes 1995.

REFERENCES

Abrahams, Roger. 1993. 'After New Perspectives: Folklore Study in the Late Twentieth Century', *Western Folklore* 52: 379-400.

Aiyar, R. K. 1968. 'Sri Shankara Bhagavatpadacharya', in *Sringeri Vignettes*, ed. K. R. Venkataraman. Tiruchirapalli, Tamil Nadu: Sri Vani Vilas Press, pp. 29-45.

Anderson, B. 1991 [1983]. *Imagined Communities*. New York: Verso.

Appadurai, Arjun, Frank Korom, and Margaret Mills, eds. 1991. *Gender, Genre and Power in South Asian Expressive Traditions*. Philadelphia: University of Pennsylvania Press.

Bakhtin, M. 1968. *Rabelais and His World*. Cambridge: M. I. T. Press.

Bauman, R. 1972. 'Differential Identity and Social Base of Folklore', in *Toward New Perspectives in Folklore*, ed. Americo Paredes and Richard Bauman. Austin: University of Texas Press, pp. 31-41.

Das, B. K., ed. 1984. *Census of India, 1981. District Census Handbook, Chikmagalur District, Karnataka*. Bangalore: Government Central Press.

Devi, Konduri S. 1990. *Religion in Vijayanagara Empire*. New Delhi: Sterling Publishers.

Dirks, N. 1987. *The Hollow Crown: Ethnohistory of an Indian Kingdom*. Cambridge: Cambridge University Press.

Durkheim, Emile. 1915. *Elementary Forms of Religious Life*. London: Allen and Unwin.

———. 1893. *The Division of Labor in Society*. New York: Fress Press.

Eliade, Mircea. 1957. *The Sacred and the Profane: The Nature of Religion*. New York: Harper.

Falassi, A., ed. 1987. *Time out of Time: Essays on the Festival*. Albuquerque: University of New Mexico Press.

Flueckiger, Joyce B. 1996. *Gender and Genre in the Folklore of Middle India*. Ithaca: Cornell University Press.

Gowrishankar, V. R. n.d. *Navarātri at Sringeri*. Sringeri: Sri Sharada Peetham.

Gupta, Akhil and James Ferguson. 1997. *Anthropological Locations: Boundaries and Grounds of Field Science*. Berkeley: University of California Press.

Heesterman, J. C. 1984. *The Broken World of Sacrifice: An Essay in Ancient Indian Ritual*. Chicago: University of Chicago Press.

Herzfeld, M. 1985. *Poetics of Manhood: Contest and Identity in a Cretan Mountain Village*. Princeton: Princeton University Press.

Kamat, S. U. 1991. 'Religions and Cults and their Backgrounds', in *Encyclopedia of the Folk Culture of Karnataka*, ed. J. S. Paramashivaiah. Vol. 1. Madras: Institute of Asian Studies, pp. 23-30.

Kulke, H. 1985. 'Maharajas, Mahants, and Historians: Reflections on the Historiography of Early Vijayanagara and Sringeri', in *Vijayanagara—City and Empire: New Currents of Research*, Vol. 1, ed. A. L. Dallapiccola and S. Zingle-Ave Lallement. Stuttgart: Steiner Verlag, pp. 120-42.

Nilakanta Sastri, K. A. 1955. *A History of South India*. Oxford: Oxford University Press.

Noyes, Dorothy. 1995. 'Group', *Journal of American Folklore* 108: 449-78.

Prasad, Leela, ed. 1999. *Live Like the Banyan Tree: Images of the Indian American Experience*. Philadelphia: The Balch Institute for Ethnic Studies.

Ramaswamy, Sumathi. 1997. *Passions of the Tongue: Language Devotion in Tamil India, 1891-1970*. Berkeley: University of California Press.

Ramesam, N. 1971. *Sri Śankaracharya*. Ponnur, Andhra Pradesh: Sri Bhavanarayanaswami Temple.

Rao, T. R. 1968. *Sringeri Revisited*. Vijayawada: T. R. Rao.

Rice, B. L. 1983 [1897]. *Mysore: A Gazetteer*, revd. edn., Vol 1. Westminster: Archibald, Constable and Co.

Row, B. R., ed. 1927. Introduction to *Selections from the Records of the Sringeri Mutt*. Mysore: Government Branch Press.

Sawai, Yoshitsugu. 1992. *The Faith of Ascetics and Lay Smārtas: A Study of the Śaṅkara Tradition of Sringeri*. Vienna: Institute for Indology, University of Vienna.

Shastry, A. K. 1982. *A History of Sringeri*. Dharwad: Karnatak University Press.

Shuman, Amy. 1993. 'Dismantling Local Culture', *Western Folklore* 52: 344-64.

Subbaratnam, K. V. 1968. 'The Educational and Cultural Activities [of Sringeri]', in *Sringeri Vignettes*, ed. K. R. Venkataraman. Tiruchirapalli: Sri Vani Vilas Press, pp. 56-61.

Tattvaloka (publisher). 1991. *The Greatness of Sringeri*. Bombay: Tattvaloka.

Tapasyananda, Swami. 1978. *The Śaṅkaradigvijaya of Madhava-Vidyāraṇya*. Madras: Ramakrishna Mission.

Thapar, Romila. 1992. *Interpreting Early India*. New Delhi: Oxford University Press.

———. 1978. *Ancient Indian Social History: Some Interpretations*. Hyderabad: Orient Longman.

———. 1966. *A History of India*, Vol. 1. New York: Pelican.

Turner, V. 1969. *The Ritual Process: Structure and Anti-Structure*. Ithaca: Cornell University Press.

van der Veer, Peter. 1994. *Religious Nationalism: Hindus and Muslims in India*. Berkeley: University of California Press.

Venkataraman, K. R. 1990. *The Throne of Transcendental Wisdom.* Sringeri: Sri Sharada Trust.

Wagoner, P. 1996. ' "Sultan among Hindu Kings": Dress, Titles, and the Islamicization of Hindu Culture at Vijayanagara', *Journal of Asian Studies* 55.4: 851-80.

9

Celebrating a Region through Historical Commemoration

Daniel Jasper

If one travels to Mumbai today, the first space one encounters will almost certainly be named after Shivaji Maharaj, the founder of the Maratha Empire. The international airport is now known as Chhatrapati Shivaji International Airport. The domestic terminal, just a few kilometers away, is called Chhatrapati Shivaji Domestic Airport. The main train station, formerly known as Victoria Terminus, is now called Chhatrapati Shivaji Terminus. When one detrains at Dadar Station in central Mumbai, Shivaji Park, with its imposing equestrian statue of the king, is nearby. In south Mumbai, the main road that leads from the Gateway of India, a structure erected to celebrate the arrival of George V and Queen Mary in 1911, is called Shivaji Marg. This road leads past the Chhatrapati Shivaji Museum, once known as the Prince of Wales Museum.

In recent years the presence of Chhatrapati Shivaji has become increasingly prominent in Mumbai. The two airport terminals were officially renamed by Prime Minister Atal Behari Vajpayee on 31 March 1999. One year earlier, the Victoria Gardens in central Mumbai were renamed Veermata Jijabai Udyan after Shivaji's mother. A statue of her with Shivaji as a child now prominently occupies the centre of the park. The colossal Victoria Terminus was renamed after Shivaji in 1996. An equestrian statue of him was erected behind the Gateway of India in 1960, the year of the founding of Maharashtra State.

The large number of visual reminders of Shivaji is not limited to Mumbai. Shivaji is prominent throughout Maharashtra. From the major cities of Mumbai, Pune, Kolhapur, and Satara to small towns and villages, reminders of Shivaji are strategically placed. Throughout the state of Maharashtra, there are over 600 statues of him (Masselos 2001). Roads and housing societies bear his name; his picture inspires millions in public buildings and private homes; plays, lectures, and films about him are frequent. In short, the commemoration of Shivaji is central to public culture in Maharashtra.

As the boyhood home of Shivaji and the seat of the ensuing Peshwa dynasty, Pune is strongly associated with the Shivaji legacy. In addition to many statues, the city is home to a number of sites associated with his rule. In 1988, for example, the Pune Municipal Corporation unveiled a replica of Lal Mahal, Shivaji's boyhood home. The ground floor of Lal Mahal is dedicated to Shivaji's mother, Jijabai; the upper floor celebrates Shivaji's political career. The large room contains eleven unsigned paintings depicting different scenes from his career. In the centre of this room is a large topographical map of Maharashtra, with some of the sites associated with Shivaji's rule prominently identified.

The wide-scale commemoration of Shivaji indicates the near universal celebration of him as a heroic figure representative of a golden age. In present-day Maharashtra, Shivaji serves as the historical focal point that unites Maharashtrians into a common cultural-political entity. Both state and popular actors forge a region out of a shared sense of place and a common history, creating an area linked through a narrative of social and political unity.

Political leaders demarcate public spaces through renaming prominent places, installing statues, and preserving historic sites. This identifies Shivaji with shared space, reinforcing his prominence in the area. Political elites also play a role in framing the interpretation of Shivaji's regime, most significantly through official publications and school texts. While the elites deploy resources to frame debates about interpretations of history, popular actors reinterpret this history in individual ways.

In this paper, I look at popular commemorations of Shivaji to address the ways in which people forge a collective Maharashtrian regional identity. I focus on the celebration in Pune of the festival of Shivaji's birth. In analysing this celebration I emphasize two related points: the variety of actors who appropriate the history (as actors with differing ideological positions embrace the celebration of Shivaji to lend legitimacy to their projects, there is a wide range of interpretations of Shivaji's life and rule) and the ways in which a common narrative emerges out of this diversity and establishes the political and cultural foundation of Maharashtra as a unified region.

In Pune and in other towns, villages, and cities of western Maharashtra, the most prominent commemorations of Shivaji are celebrations of the annual Shivaji festival. For one day each year, the entire population of a city can step outside their everyday lives to collectively pay homage to a glorious past. As a public ritual, the Shivaji festival is a political act in which social actors compete for control over the use and meaning of the past.[1] Through commemorations of Shivaji, a wide range of actors debate the significance of Shivaji's rule. By collectively celebrating Shivaji, these actors reinforce his central position as the cultural and political foundation upon which Maharashtra is based.

The Shivaji festival was begun in 1896 by the nationalist leader Lokmanya Bal Gangadhar Tilak.[2] During its early years, it was a relatively formal affair with a common anti-colonial message. Committees of prominent citizens organized events in one large public space in each town, most often a temple. The festivities, typically lasting one or two days, most often included speeches by historians, leading citizens, and political leaders who emphasized the genius of Shivaji. There were often youth competitions such as essay writing, drawing, and athletic contests, each of which emphasized the youthfulness of Shivaji when he began his campaigns.

The Shivaji festival today is vastly different. The commemorations are no longer well-organized and contained celebrations designed to articulate a unified, collective voice. People today make of the commemoration what they want, and so there has been a proliferation of activities and meanings associated with it. The festival today is much more popular than it was in the late nineteenth and early twentieth centuries. Large numbers of people participate, and many different images of Shivaji are presented. Yet, there is a striking uniformity to an underlying narrative that holds these disparate meanings together.

Out of the multiple images and meanings of Shivaji that have been put forth in the field of Shivaji commemoration, a narrative unity emerges. This unity is represented through a repetitive stock of themes that characterize the celebrations. The most common themes present Shivaji as the manifestation of political awakening, as the embodiment of an ethno-regional identity, and as a figure who demonstrates the importance of religion for the development of character and leadership. On the political front, Shivaji is seen as the father of political awakening in Maharashtra, and as the leader who first established a government responsive to the people. These political developments are rooted in Shivaji's connection to the land, seen through his mastery of the terrain in developing tactics of guerrilla warfare. Shivaji's connection to the land also delineates the territory inhabited by those who inherited his legacy and regime. In this way, Shivaji has come to signify the linguistic and ethno-regional identity of Marathi-speakers in the state of Maharashtra. The final theme is the importance of Hinduism in understanding Shivaji's character. While some present Shivaji as the political culmination of an egalitarian bhakti revival, others present him as a conservative Hindu inspired by the epics or as a follower of Ramdas. Both perspectives, however different in other respects, place a great deal of emphasis on Shivaji's religious life as the explanation of his achievements. These perspectives on Shivaji's religious life give him a religious aura and make him a god-like figure.

The Shivaji Festival in Pune

In 1999, the year in which I observed the Shivaji festival, the main day of the festival was 17 April, but the associated programmes stretched for a week on either side. The events of the Shivaji festival are varied and show clearly that the field is populated by a wide range of actors. Individuals and voluntary organizations take part, political parties have a prominent place, and state agencies sponsor government-sanctioned 'official' programmes of commemoration.

During the main day of the festival, the municipal corporation sponsors a morning parade through the old part of the city. The central core of the city is sanctified as the parade proceeds along significant thoroughfares. Beginning near the central market in the crowded shopping district, the parade is symbolically anchored on one end by commerce. From the market, the parade proceeds along Shivaji Road and over Shivaji Bridge. It culminates at the Shri Shivaji Military Preparatory School, anchoring the other end in state power represented through military training. At the school, the mayor leads other politicians in garlanding the grand equestrian statue of

Shivaji. After the equestrian statue is garlanded, a host of politicians deliver speeches, each speaker presenting himself as the inheritor of Shivaji's regime and the upholder of his legacy.

As the marchers make their way through the old city, they carry pictures and yell out cheers. Someone who stumbled across this procession would be hard-pressed to know that its purpose was to commemorate Shivaji. It seems more of a generic celebration of Maharashtrian political glory. Pictures of Shivaji are carried, but so are pictures of other prominent Maharashtrian political leaders from the past, most notably Mahatma Phule, Dr. Babasaheb Ambedkar, and Lokmanya Tilak. Similarly, chants are called out to celebrate Maharashtra's historical leaders: one person will call out a name through a bull horn, the marchers will respond '*ki jai*' (victory to). 'Shivaji Maharaj' is called out often, but no more frequently than 'Mahatma Jotirao Phule'. The parade, presided over by political leaders, becomes a celebration of prominent political figures from Maharashtra. The politicians and their supporters who lead the procession are placing themselves at the front of this historical line of political leaders. Shivaji represents the ground upon which all of these leaders have been able to blossom.

The image of Shivaji as the father of political consciousness and activity in Maharashtra has developed over a number of years. During the anti-colonial period, Tilak, M. G. Ranade, and others emphasized the political maturity of Maharashtra through representations of Shivaji. Similarly, leaders of the Samyukta Maharashtra Movement positioned themselves as the successors of nationalist leaders as well as of Shivaji. Each of these political figures reinforces the idea that Maharashtra shares a common unfolding narrative of political awakening that begins with Shivaji.

During the day the most notable activity of the Shivaji festival is the installation of small shrines—called *pandals*—containing statues and/or pictures of Shivaji. This practice is common to many religious celebrations in Maharashtra, most prominently to the Ganesh festival. The pandals for the Ganesh festival are elaborate constructions presenting themes from current events that are judged for their creativity and originality. Compared to the Ganesh pandals, the pandals for the Shivaji festival are much more modest, often just a small table with a picture or statue of Shivaji and perhaps a couple of other images. The larger pandals more closely resemble the pandals of the Ganesh festival: they are large constructions that each depict a scene from Shivaji's life. The number of shrines is directly proportional to the population density: in the old sections of the city, there may be four or more on a single corner; in the newer, outlying parts of the city, they are likely to be only at major intersections or the entrances to housing societies.

These Shivaji shrines are the most prominent feature of the Shivaji festival. They are everywhere, and thus they indicate the degree to which the festival has become popular among nearly all communities in Maharashtra. The universal acceptance of the Shivaji festival is seen in the cantonment and other sections of Pune that are home to sizeable Muslim and Christian populations. In 1999, these areas too were populated with pandals, and Muslim and Christian youth were likely to have assisted in installing them. In these religiously diverse areas, themes of religious pluralism and interfaith respect were common. In Nana Peth, for example, a part of the city that is home to members of several religious communities, one pandal presented Shivaji as a religious leader involved in interfaith dialogue with Christian and Muslim clergymen; behind them were images of a Hindu temple, a mosque, and a church.

The pandals are installed mostly by *mitra mandals* (societies of friends), ubiquitous throughout Pune and other urban areas. They are usually housed in a storefront or small shack where the male youths of a neighbourhood gather. Most mandals are directed on a full- or part-time basis by older adult males. Some sponsor athletics, job training, social service, or cultural programmes, but for the most part they are gathering places where boys read the papers, drink tea, and chat. Many political parties have developed networks of mitra mandals staffed by organizers, as a means of developing a cadre of party workers.[3] Many of the more elaborate and crowded pandals are set up by political parties in the old parts of the city. The shrines are surrounded throughout the day by the young men of the mitra mandal, who spend their time dancing, talking, setting off fire-crackers, and taking pride in their installation.

The mandals differ in the size of their membership, financial resources, and political connections, all of which are manifest in the Shivaji shrines that they build. The smaller ones might have a simple card table holding a single bust or picture and some burning incense. The larger ones are more likely to construct a structure with multiple and elaborate images, often depicting a battle or court scene. These structures serve as stages for lectures or concerts that begin before and extend beyond the date of the festival.

As is the case with other public festivals in Maharashtra, the pandals are coupled with extensive music systems. The sound systems are constantly in use, and the volume is high. What is so striking about the battling sound systems during the Shivaji festival is the relative uniformity of what one hears. With rare exceptions, the audio programmes are of two types: either the soundtrack of a current blockbuster Hindi film, or a tape of a *powada* performed in Marathi.

Hindi film music is the most frequent form of music played during most public festivals. With its association with escapist entertainment and choreographed dancing, Hindi film music signifies the desire for merriment. The prominent place of film music points to the importance of the entertainment element in the Shivaji festival, as it does with other public celebrations. Shivaji is thus symbolically linked with other figures and events that mark the calendar of public rituals throughout the Indian subcontinent.

Not all mitra mandals, however, play film music during the Shivaji festival. More commonly, *powadas* are broadcast. These Marathi-language epic ballads reinforce the regional nature of Shivaji celebration: he is a Maharashtrian hero celebrated through a Maharashtrian folk tradition. Powadas narrate stories from Shivaji's life that most people are familiar with, reinforcing both the key events of Shivaji's life and the proper interpretation of those events. As narratives of martial greatness, powadas also indicate that one must struggle to maintain and protect a Maharashtrian identity.

During the 1970s, almost all political parties began to use powadas to broaden their base of supporters in Maharashtra. As tape recorders became more prevalent, it was an easy, cheap, and effective way of getting the message out.[4] By appropriating a regional cultural form, the parties were also establishing their populist credentials, sending the message that they were 'of the people'. This renewed interest in the powada, and the concurrent expansion of the entertainment industry, helped foster the development of celebrity shahirs who sing the powadas. Walking throughout Pune on 17 April 1999, not only could one hear the same four or five performers throughout nearly the entire city, but one could hear each of them performing his most famous ballad, which without question narrated one of the more dramatic episodes from Shivaji's life. The killing of Afzal Khan, Shivaji's escape from Agra, and the battle between Shivaji and Shaista Khan were prominent.

Because of the constant and ear-numbing levels of sound, it is easy to forget that the festival is primarily a visual experience. Music grabs the attention, but it is the pandal that draws people in. Other than the size of the shrines, the most common distinction among them is the amount of colour that they contain. The statues are made of either copper or clay, with many of the clay variety being brightly painted or covered with red powder, signifying religious devotion. The shrines are often graced by one or many saffron flags that represent Shivaji's kingdom. The painting and adorning of the statues draws on the practice of elaborately decorating clay statues of Ganesh during the Ganesh festival. It is also a way for the mitra mandals to distinguish their pandal from others, since the statues of Shivaji are nearly all the same. Nearly all pandals display a simple bust of Shivaji, though a few have small life-sized statues of him standing with a drawn sword.

At many of the shrines, paintings sit behind the statues. Shivaji is pictured atop a horse, sitting on his throne, or holding his sword Bhavani.[5] All of these are common images that can be bought from road-side picture sellers the year round. While these are familiar images that refer to various episodes in the life of Shivaji, the significance of each is different. Riding on horseback, the great warrior Shivaji is leading his troops into battle. The stately Shivaji sits upon his throne surveying his holdings and delivering justice to the poor farmers. When Shivaji is shown in a military pose, his sword signifies strength derived either from courage of facing down a larger power; when the sword is shown being blessed by the goddess, it signifies strength derived from religious observation.

Images of Shivaji are often coupled with pictures of other historical figures. Most common are his lieutenants Tanaji Malusare or Netaji Palkar, his son Sambhaji, and the religious leaders Sant Ramdas and Sant Tukaram. As with the pictures of Shivaji, these images have different symbolic meanings. With his lieutenants, Shivaji is a leader of men, with the charisma to inspire courage and loyalty that lift his followers above their stations in life. They, in turn, are the devout followers who do what is expected of them.

Sambhaji shows that Shivaji's authority was of a traditional sort, passed down from father to son. Similarly, Ramdas signifies the importance of accepting one's god-given position. Tukaram, on the other hand, signifies the rejection of the caste system by questioning its religious basis. As a low-caste devotee of Vithoba, Tukaram was one of a long line of saint-poets who saw religious merit as being the result of reverent devotion, not birth.

Often images of more contemporary leaders join Shivaji, Tilak being the most prominent. When asked why, people gave two types of responses. The most common credited Tilak with establishing the Shivaji festival as an important public ritual in Maharashtra; this was often followed by an impromptu analysis of the role of festivals in challenging colonial authority. Other respondents emphasized that Tilak was a 'great man' (*mahapurush*) who deserves to be honoured and celebrated just as Shivaji does. In both of these frameworks, Tilak represents an activist form of populist politics. When coupled with Ramdas, he represents a politics rooted in a conservative theology.

Of interest is the complete absence of images of M. G. Ranade. Like Tilak, Ranade was instrumental in reviving an interest in Shivaji as part of an anti-colonial nationalist politics.[6] Though he had less success, Ranade preceded Tilak in bringing attention to the decaying state of historical sites associated with Shivaji. While Tilak editorialized and delivered speeches about Shivaji, Ranade delivered lectures to the Bombay Branch of the Royal Asiatic Society and published an English-language historical monograph on the Maratha power. Ranade addressed his analysis of Shivaji's regime to elite audiences, while Tilak took his directly to the people, and it is the populism of Tilak's politics that is celebrated, while the elite focus of Ranade is left aside. The absence of images of Ranade during the Shivaji festival, however, does not indicate that his liberal interpretation of Shivaji has fallen completely out of favour. Ranade helped to popularize the symbolic link between Shivaji and Tukaram, a connection that is still commonly celebrated. However, this relationship today is seen more as proof of Shivaji's Hindu personality and less as the manifestation of liberal politics that Ranade saw in it.

In the music played, there is a common repertoire of ballads; on the pandals, there is a common repertoire of images of Shivaji.

Whereas these images signify vastly different interpretations of who Shivaji was and what made him great, each is seen as representative of a different episode in his life. The meanings of these different symbols are not contested, nor is their accuracy. Mandals are free to include whatever images they see fit. Certain images are commonly placed together, such as Tilak and Ramdas, but there are no hard and fast rules. As a hero for all, Shivaji can be commemorated in any way that people see fit. There is, however, a theme to these images. The theme is that Shivaji's greatness was manifest in three distinct realms: warfare, where he popularized guerrilla tactics and militant direct action; statecraft, where he simplified the administration; and religion, where he was a model of devotion.

In the evening hours of the festival, the energy becomes kinetic, shifting from the sidewalk shrines to street theatre. Processions start from locations throughout the old city, making their way toward Shaniwar Wada, a palace built in 1736 by the Peshwa Baji Rao.[7] On floats pulled by trucks, tractors, or bullocks, groups of children and adolescents act out scenes from Shivaji's life. Some of the more elaborate floats might also employ cavalry on horse- or camel-back, or an elephant leading Shivaji to his coronation.

While there is a terminus there is no starting point, nor are there fixed routes for the processions. The floats begin the journey from wherever the group gathers, and gradually make their way through the winding streets and narrow alleys toward the Wada. Each group, however, is conscious of its own stature: the smaller productions take more direct routes to arrive earlier in the evening, while the larger floats travel a circuitous route through the prominent streets. Lacking a choreographed route, and with the state of the infrastructure in the older parts of Pune, the processions are slowed down by numerous traffic jams and bottlenecks. If too large a crowd gathers on the narrower streets, the floats are unable to pass until a few rows of spectators have been cleared out of the way.

Although the floats move slowly, they do, in fact, move. The audience, on the other hand, is stationary; people sit on the curb, or stand in doorways and windows to watch as the procession passes in front of them. But the scenes on the floats are not static: the youths are performing Shivaji's life and career. With each float choosing its own episode, and no co-ordination among the floats, it would seem that there is no narrative coherence for the spectator whatsoever. But only rarely would someone not know after only a fraction of a second what scene is being enacted. The floats do not need to be pedagogical, because everyone already knows the stories. Instead, the performances reinforce pre-existing interpretations of the past and proclaim the greatness of Maharashtra.

This uniformity is striking primarily because of how a mere handful of stories have become emblematic of Shivaji's life. One of the more important themes is that of doing one's duty: in other words, accepting one's dharma. Shivaji learns about duty and other concepts of proper behaviour as a boy, when his mother reads him the *Ramayana* and *Mahabharata.* This signifies not just religious duty, but also the duty of obeying one's parents, which is only a small step removed from doing God's will. The popular story is that Jijabai encouraged Shivaji to set out on his campaigns, and the goddess Bhavani appeared to provide him guidance.

The importance of duty can also take on a more directly politicized connotation. The conservative approach that accepts a hierarchical caste order is portrayed through Shivaji's accepting guidance in statecraft—specifically, state-building—from Ramdas. When Shivaji is represented as offering his kingdom to Tukaram, duty is defined as devotion. Instead of being ascribed, status is achieved through piety and abnegation.

Many of the stories emphasize justice, reinforcing not just the idea of responsive government, but also the role of the individual as citizen. Shivaji's coronation symbolizes the establishment of a state with local control where administration is attuned with the working people. Shivaji's coronation as representative of the triumph of the people is embraced by a variety of political parties in Maharashtra. Parties of the Left and the Right claim legitimacy for their political programmes by linking them with Shivaji's coronation as a symbol of responsive rule. In this context, however, Shivaji represents not only the power of the state, but also the power to outwit and defeat an illegitimate regime. Shivaji went to Agra to present himself at the Mughal court, but was rebuffed. His protests at this landed him and Sambhaji in jail. Shivaji arranged for them to be carried out of their imprisonment hidden in crates of sweets. He was able to outrun the pursuing guards all the way back to Pune because farmers and other common people hid him the entire way.

One of the most popular stories is Shivaji's killing of Afzal Khan, the much larger Bijapuri general, in hand-to-hand combat. In the early years of the festival, the embrace of the Afzal Khan episode was seen as emblematic of the communal nature of the festival: the story represented Hindu-Muslim opposition. Today, the story represents treachery, or rather what becomes of those who are treacherous. The emphasis is placed on Afzal Khan striking first: as he and Shivaji met for a peace conference, Afzal Khan embraced Shivaji in a bear-hug, ready to plunge a dagger into him; thereupon, Shivaji disembowelled him with a weapon known as tiger-claws.

If the Afzal Khan episode represents the justice meted out to the treacherous, the Shaiste Khan episode shows the justice faced by opportunists. This Khan, instead of siding with his indigenous brethren, was in the employ of the foreign, Mughal power. In his pursuit of Shivaji, he seized the Lal Mahal Palace in Pune, and effectively closed down all entrances to the city. Shivaji and his men had to sneak into Pune, and then into Lal Mahal. The last part wasn't difficult because Shaiste Khan was distracted by dancing girls. Shivaji chased Shaiste Khan. Although he fled through a window, Shivaji was able to cut off his hand before he escaped.

As Shivaji is commemorated in the contemporary celebrations of the Shivaji festival, he is represented through a relatively fixed set of symbols. Celebrants draw on these symbols and combine them in unique ways to portray a variety of visions of who Shivaji was and what his significance is in the modern world. The 1999 festival was a cacophony of voices heralding radically different kings, and yet, out of all of these voices came a singular message. As king, Shivaji was a devoted protector of his people, the natural inhabitants of Maharashtra. The guerrilla warfare that Shivaji and his armies practised is more than a military strategy. Through emphasis on the role of hill forts and an intimate knowledge and connection with the terrain, Shivaji becomes tied to a bounded physical space. Marathi becomes the 'natural' language of this territory. Maharashtrians are thus defined as a unique ethnic group, culturally distinct from other groups not only linguistically, but more importantly through the cultural practices unique to this region.

Another essential cultural trait of Shivaji's greatness is his Hinduism, as a central defining trait of the self. Through devotion and deference to religious authority, manifest from childhood, Shivaji's temporal authority is legitimized. Shivaji is seen as a decidedly Hindu king, and it is this Hindu nature that allows his political success.

Whether Shivaji's greatness was the result of conservative or progressive sensibilities is irrelevant. The important thing is that he is seen as the founder of political consciousness in Maharashtra. He is the symbolic father of a long line of Maharashtrian political leaders who populate the entire political spectrum. Shivaji's daring political feats present him as the father of political awakening in Maharashtra: he was able to envision an alternative political dispensation. In current Maharashtrian popular culture, Shivaji is linked to other prominent figures of political awakening, most notably Mahatma Phule and Lokmanya Tilak. It comes as little surprise, then, that nearly all politicians in Maharashtra try to demonstrate their close connection with Shivaji.

Taken together, the themes of Shivaji representing political awakening, ethno-regional identity, and religious identity, coalesce to present Shivaji as the salvation of Hindu Maharashtra. There is little difference between a pandal during the Shivaji festival and a temple. His icons are treated in the same way that temple icons are. The figures and pictures are dotted with vermilion, incense is burned, and the icon is offered coconuts and other ritually marked foods.

In sum, then, the Shivaji festival is a day of collective public commemoration in which large numbers of people involve themselves in celebrating his legacy. Because it is a relatively unorganized festival, individuals and groups are able to put forth their own interpretations and to make connections between Shivaji and others as they see fit. Despite the relative openness of the celebrations, however, a narrative coherence is evident throughout the festival. Certain stories and connections have come to be emblematic of Shivaji's glory, and these are repeated throughout the city and throughout the day. Within this set of stories, individual groups emphasize those stories that support their ideological perspective. But rather than a cacophony of competing perspectives, these different approaches in effect reinforce each other as parts of a singular narrative of Shivaji as the embodiment of the Maharashtrian spirit.

NOTES

1. On the political implications of public rituals, see Davis 1986 and Newman 1997.
2. On Tilak, and his embrace of the Shivaji legacy, see Cashman 1975, and Samarth 1975.

3. On the importance of *mitra mandals* for political parties, see Heuze 1995, for example, on Shiv Sena *mitra mandals* in Mumbai.
4. On the importance of cassettes for political mobilization in north India, see Manuel 1993.
5. Shivaji's sword is named after a goddess popular in Maharashtra.
6. Tucker 1972.
7. The palace was destroyed by fire in 1827. Today only the walls, and the grass which they surround, remain.

REFERENCES

Benei, Veronique. 2000. 'Teaching Nationalism in Maharashtra Schools', in *Everyday State and Society in Modern India*, edited by C. J. Fuller and Veronique Benei. New Delhi: Social Science Press.

Cashman, Richard. 1975. *The Myth of the Lokmanya*. Berkeley: University of California Press.

Davis, Susan G. 1986. *Parades and Power*. Berkeley: University of California Press.

Heuze, Gerard. 1995. 'Cultural Populism: The Appeal of the Shiv Sena', in *Bombay: Metaphor for Modern India*, edited by Sujata Patel and Alice Thorner. Bombay: Oxford University Press, pp. 213-47.

Manuel, Peter. 1993. *Cassette Culture*. Chicago: University of Chicago Press.

Masselos, Jim. 2001. 'Solid Identities: The Statuary of Memory', Presented at the Ninth International Conference on Maharashtra, Saint Paul, Minnesota, 6-10 June.

Newman, Simon P. 1997. *Parades and the Politics of the Street*. Philadelphia: University of Pennsylvania Press.

Samarth, Anil. 1975. *Shivaji and the Indian National Movement*. Bombay: Somaiya Publications.

Tucker, Richard P. 1972. *Ranade and the Roots of Indian Nationalism*. Bombay: Popular Prakashan.

10

Inhabiting Times and Producing Spaces

Sanjay Palshikar

In a famous interview with the editors of *Herodote*, Foucault says that region is a fiscal, administrative, military notion. His interviewers agree and point out that 'since geography grew up in the shadow of the military', it is natural that 'certain spatial metaphors are equally geographic and strategic... The *region* of the geographers is the military region', its Latin root, *regere*, means 'to command', 'a *province* is a conquered territory', and '*field* invokes the battlefield' (Foucault 1980: 68-9). In what follows I plan to use the term 'region' in the foucauldian spirit, that is, as a form of domination, or as a set of spatial strategies. In so doing, however, I do not want to set up an opposition between time and space. On the contrary, I would like to show how their complex interrelationship constitutes our daily practices.

An attempt of this kind has no doubt been facilitated by the paradigmatic shifts within geography, from the positivism of the 1960s to Marxism to post-modernism, bringing about transactions between geography and social sciences. Immanuel Wallerstein and others have pointed out that the study of social reality was for a long time compartmentalized into separate disciplines and that, as a result, 'treatment of space and place was relatively neglected in the social sciences'. Space was either regarded as the platform 'upon which events unfolded', something 'essentially inert', or as the context of events, influencing them in a marginal way (Wallerstein et al. 1997: 25-6). Progress and change were identified with the temporal dimension, and in this the philosophy of consciousness played a crucial role. For it was this strand of modern philosophy which gave us the notion of history and proposed one of the most influential self-understandings of our times, namely, that we are constituted in and through history, and, more tantalizingly, that we are history-making creatures.

From this celebration of the temporal and the corresponding neglect of the spatial, characteristic of much of social science until recently, 'space' has emerged as one of the principal categories of social theory. Doreen Massey (1992) cites a number of scholars—from Berger, Jameson, and Braudel to Homi Bhabha and Laclau—whose work and pronouncements stress the importance of 'space'.[1]

This turn in favour of the spatial, however, should not lead to 'a facile substitution and replacement', or to 'anti-history' (Soja 1989: 23), and some scholars have warned against such tendencies. Avoiding absolutization of any one element, we need to view time and space in their interrelationship, producing a range of political possibilities. Edward Soja has argued for such a perspective in what he calls 'spatialized ontology'. He says, '[T]he temporality of social life, from the routines of day-to-day activity to the longer-run making of history . . . is rooted in spatial contingency in much the same way as the spatiality of social life is rooted in temporal/historical contingency' (Soja 1989: 130).

Admittedly, this is rather abstract and needs to be fleshed out, a programmatic statement, a gesture in a certain direction. There are many complex ways in which time and space relate to each other. Here I look at how certain ways of constituting temporality construct a region. I believe that the activity of constructing a region, whether overtly political or not, is an activity of domination. With this orientation informing my account, I will focus on how our time-related practices and activities make 'a particular geo-social space stand out in relief'.[2] I hope to make this argument a little less abstract by giving a few illustrations from modern Maharashtra. Each of these examples will involve modes of temporality, for example, time as recall, as nostalgia, or time as history. They all contribute to region-construction in the sense indicated above.

My first example is a Marathi novel from the early 1960s by Jaywant Dalvi, *Saare Pravaasi Ghadiche*. The narrator, Apu, settled with his family in Bombay, visits his native place in Konkan after many years. He reminisces about his childhood there and tells us about the people from his village (not many of whom have survived the ravages of time), his school, his parents, his beedi-smoking grandmother, etc. We are not told the name of the village, but that does not matter, because it can easily stand for many such places in Konkan—with its palm trees, ghosts, heavy rains leaching the already barren land, emaciated cattle, itinerant *dashavatari* performers, powerful local deity, eccentric people, mad people, illicit relations involving widows and temple women, gossip, drunken brawls, and inveterate litigants fighting court battles over the ownership of a tree or two. The time is the pre-Independence period, when the school head-master was also the postmaster of the village, corporeal punishment was the universally accepted form of instruction, school children were made to sing the glory of King George V, untouchability was practised in a most unconcealed manner, and the landlords exercised paternalistic authority over the villagers. It is clear from Apu's narration that there is hardly anything in village life—whether it was the spectacle of exorcism, or the family feuds—that his sensibilities today would approve of or rejoice at recalling. But evidently, the very act of recall is valuable for the narrator and for the author. Therefore the superstitious and narrow-minded villagers, given to slander and bitterness, and cynical to the core, are presented as uncomplicated and spontaneous, if somewhat coarse. This sets up a contrast between the authentic villagers with their genuine warmth and today's impersonal urban life.

The world recalled in the novel is the world of an upper-caste boy, now an adult. Only one Muslim, Ibrahim the butcher, figures in this world. Through the device of remembrances the author has sought to give an authoritative description of a certain space and, through that, claim it for all upper-caste Hindu readers. There are several such novels on Konkan (as also on other parts of Maharashtra), some of which are popular and highly acclaimed. As a result of these works, Konkan is not a free subject of thought and imagination.[3]

True, authors from other backgrounds too can appropriate for themselves Konkan (or any other region), and we have examples of well-known novels, like Hamid Dalvai's *Indhan*, to suggest that this is indeed possible. But such examples are far too few. Moreover, the problem of literary appropriation is not easy to deal with, involving, as it does, complex issues of aesthetic criteria.

In a recent article on Muslim Marathi literature, Fakruddin Bennur (2001) speaks about the literary work on Konkan by Muslim writers of the 1950s. He says that though Muslim Marathi literature is four to five hundred years old, a literary movement started only in 1990 when the All India Muslim Sahitya Parishad was established. The fact that Muslim (or Dalit) writers have felt the need for a separate platform speaks of the stifling nature of elite Marathi literature and literary criticism. Movements like these have the potential to contest the established literary criteria, but given the cultural capital that the established Marathi writers have, and the thinness of the reading public among Muslims, one can see how difficult the campaign is going to be. And campaign it will be, because a given literature is not just the sum total of purely aesthetic activities carried out quietly by several writers in seclusion from one another. It is a movement in which considerable energy is invested. Muslim writers will have to make a concerted effort at the organizational as well as the intellectual level. Till then, the imagination of the established writers must act as a constraint on them. In short, the contest over Konkan (or Marathwada, for that matter) has barely begun and regions of Maharashtra still remain annexed to the elite imagination.[4]

My next illustration comes from the writings of Acharya Atre, a hugely popular speaker and journalist of his time. I want to specifically draw attention to his editorials and speeches (Atre 1997) during the Samyukta Maharashtra movement demanding the formation of a linguistic state of Maharashtra, made up of all the Marathi-speaking areas including Bombay. Of importance is his selective invocation of the history of Maharashtra. Shivaji and his achievements, his personal integrity, character, and the Ram Rajya he ushered in are central to Atre's account of Marathi identity. He takes to task leaders from Gandhi and Nehru to Balasaheb Kher and Morarji Desai for their disrespect towards this *mahapurush*, Shivaji. The Delhi government is like Aurangzeb and the local Congressmen are traitors like Suryaji Pisal. In what Atre reveres and what he condemns, he uses figures and events from Maratha history selectively. He invites his readers and audiences to believe in the goodness of those times when the Maharashtra Dharma of fierce self-respect, integrity in public affairs, and martyrdom was followed. He claims that the Samyukta Maharashtra Samiti, spear-heading the agitation, is actually carrying on the task that Shivaji started and that the formation of Maharashtra will be the only appropriate way of honouring his memory.

Atre's appeal to revive Maharashtra Dharma is significant for two reasons. The notion of 'Maharashtra Dharma' has a rich and complex history going back to at least the writings of Sant Ramdas, Shivaji's illustrious contemporary. Since the nineteenth-century revival of the notion, the Maharashtra Dharma has often been associated with a certain account of 'Maratha history', namely that Shivaji successfully challenged the oppressive and foreign reign of Muslim rulers and re-established the rule of dharma. Atre's invocation of the Maharashtra Dharma has unmistakable allusions to that reading of Maharashtra's history. But more interestingly, the Samyukta Maharashtra agitation, of which he was an important leader, was laying claims on Bombay, a place marginal to the Maratha history. Atre's rhetorical strategy was often successful in making people overlook that marginality and instead focus on the common Marathiness. In inviting every Marathi person to share in the glory of the Maratha past, leaders like Atre were forging a larger community and simultaneously, by situating that community spatially, making a particular territory 'stand out' with significance.

My third illustration is a calendar which claims to be 'a symbol of India's cultural tradition' and also 'India's largest selling publication'. This is *Kalnirnay*, published from Bombay since 1973. Starting with a modest 10,000 copies, Sumangal Publishing Company today sells over 8 million copies of *Kalnirnay*. The website of the Company describes the calendar as a 'unique blend of almanac, magazine, recipe book and a visual source of day-to-day information'. The focus, we are told, is the housewife (a claim we will have to return to later), and the reverse of the calendar's pages are filled with 'useful tips on first aid, food preservation, gardening, stitching, cookery', home remedies, rail and bus time tables, important local phone numbers and pin codes, auspicious days and times for marriage, yoga and astrology, and reflective articles on life and culture by well-known Marathi writers.

The first issues of the calendar were plain, the quality of printing ordinary, and the layout unimpressive. The squares of dates, now crammed with information, used to be bare and empty. Very few days of the year were highlighted as birth or death anniversaries of important national or regional figures. The advertisements were mostly from the Pune–Nasik area and the only products advertised were the 777 washing bar, Rawalgaon toffees, and Manikchand *jarda*. Soon more anniversaries of 'national' figures started appearing and also greater details of ritually auspicious timings, phases of the moon, festivals big and small. Today the calendar gets advertisements from Parle, the ubiquitous Hindustan Lever, and the equally ubiquitous Kachhua brand mosquito coil. The important days of the Jews have increased in numbers,[5] but enough care has been taken to display festival days of all other major religions. (In fact, the 2003 issue of *Kalnirnay* gave dates from the Islamic calendar as well, a practice discontinued the next year.) The anniversaries of great leaders and heroes are carefully representative—the proprietor told me that he wanted the calendar to be acceptable to all, and not hurt or offend any group or community; so you have Annabhau Sathe, Phule, and Ambedkar, as well as Vasudev Balwant Phadke, Hedgevar, and Savarkar. Even then it is possible to allege a certain bias. For example, it took the company a full seven years to start showing Ambedkar's birth anniversary on its calendar, and the print-prominence of bold type still eludes Nehru.

Instead of quibbling over these things, it is more helpful to look at some other features of the calendar. And the most striking one is that it straddles the divide between the 'Western' and 'Indian' and between the 'modern' and the 'traditional'. By making a clever use of such typographical devices as colour, font-size, and symbols, *Kalnirnay* not only presents the modern calendar and the almanac on the same page[6] but also tries to achieve an equivalence of sorts between the two. While the days and dates given in bold type in Devanagari script follow the modern calendar, the colour of the squares indicates the Hindu lunar month. Inside each square is given in small print the lunar day (*tithi*) corresponding to the phase of the moon, and the specially designed symbols indicate full moon and new moon days. While the attempted equivalence (and synthesis!) between 'West' and 'East' is in conformity with a strand in the self-understanding of modern India, the simplification of the almanac has its own significance. Presented here without credits to any *shastri* or any religious authority, and thus secularizing it, the simplification increases its accessibility. What we have here then is a modern version of a traditional practice.

Related to this is another feature of the calendar: how it absorbs into a new spatiality the many scattered places of religious and spiritual significance, thereby making the devotional map neatly coincide with the politico-administrative map of Maharashtra. This it does by giving loads of information about religious figures, deities, and festivals from the smallest places in Maharashtra. It is well-known that there are innumerable centres of pilgrimage or yatra where, on certain days every year, devotees from the surrounding areas congregate and in some cases the idols are taken around ceremoniously in a procession. The full-moon days usually see several such *yatras*, some of which are quite famous, such as the Pandharpur Yatra, or the Gangapur Yatra. But there are many others which are local affairs. For example, a place called Kalamb in Yawatmal district has Sri Chintamani Yatra in the lunar month of Magha every year; or take the Moreshwar Yatra at Sindkhed in Akola district in the month of Chaitra; or the Sant Gulabkaka Yatra at Kaatel, Buldhana, in the month of Shravan. They all find a mention on the pages of *Kalnirnay*. Similarly the various local religious figures, remembered and revered mostly by the local people: the calendar informs us about their birth and death anniversaries. Not just about Sant Dnyaneshwar and Tukaram and the Akkalkot Swami but also one Nanaji Maharaj from Kapshi in Wardha, or Sant Marotrao Malegaokar from Nagapur in Nanded district. Not many people from other parts of Maharashtra will have heard of these holy figures. So where did the publishing company get to know about them? Partly through surveys and partly through petitions from people of the respective areas. This is interesting: imagine people from Dhule district approaching the company and requesting it to display on the calendar the day of Madhusudan Maharaj's death anniversary, or people from Hinglajpur coming with a similar request about Sri Jwalamukhi Devi Yatra. It is interesting because it takes these celebrations beyond the local, unselfconscious, apolitical religious events which they must have been for decades, going on unaided without modern devices like the television or the calendar. Now the devotees and the organizers of these events want to announce them at a place like the page of a calendar from where the wider public of Maharashtra can get to know about it. It is similar to what happens in cities, where followers of a leader who may not have had the good fortune to be regarded as a national hero lobby with the local authorities for naming a square or a lane after their leader. It is an attempt to stake claims to certain space, and every successful claim of this sort also entails being drawn into a larger identity. There may also be what David Harvey calls 'interplace competition' involved here, an attempt on the part of the organizers of these events to compete with other places for recognition as a cultural centre.[7]

These processions and yatras are place-specific, though not necessarily autonomous of the wider region. What the *Kalnirnay* calendar is doing is that, by effecting their 'formal subsumption'[8] under a representation of the culture of Maharashtra (and, indeed, under 'Indian culture'), it is constructing a region called Maharashtra. This is not the first or the only construction, of course; it is just a construction with the specificities it has: its attempted all-inclusiveness, the co-existence of the religious with the secular (as it highlights days of secular importance along with ritually important days and timings), the religious being mainly caste Hindu, and so on. The astrological column is of some significance in this respect. The advice on coping with planetary influences is entirely non-ritualistic and this-worldly. It counsels patience, caution, moderation, pragmatism; warns against acting illegally; warns against trusting anyone blindly; its major concerns are money, health, and convivial domesticity. At the centre of this domesticity is the 'housewife', and the calendar's web-site explicitly says that the focus is on her. This is significant for many reasons. While T. N. Madan (1987) has drawn attention to the non-hierarchical principle of auspiciousness and the important place of women within the cultural practices governed by it, Frédérique Marglin (1985) has pointed out the affinities between the almanac, the cycle of seasons, and the menstrual cycle.[9] For a world-view which regards women, fertility, and renewal as the core of a spiral growing towards the public realm, the idea of cycle of time is laden with meanings. Clearly, *Kalnirnay's* avowed focus on the 'housewife' is an allusion to those meanings; but what the calendar does is, far from organizing all the information around this core, to use these associations for laying out details of the public realm, a largely men's world—the dates, the holidays, the rail and bus timetables. The cyclical world of domesticity and the lunar months is clearly subordinated to contemporary urban concerns.

There is enough evidence besides the astrological column to suggest that it is the urban middle classes, their needs, tastes, and concerns which are at the centre of the content of this calendar. The intergenerational ties have grown weaker in the case of families from these classes, making the traditional modes of cultural reproduction unviable. These classes, strongly drawn to modernity, still want to hold on to something from their 'traditions'. Here is a calendar giving them recipes, tips on how to get rid of stubborn stains, or how to starch your clothes, thoughtful write-ups by respected literary figures on topics like the future of the Marathi language, or how to cope with stress; here is a calendar incorporating within itself an easy-to-follow lunar calendar for easy-to-observe (and increasingly optional) rituals. And all this comes with the banner of unproblematic Indian nationalist identity—unproblematic because it is smugly comprehensive in its celebration of all the leaders and public figures from a wide ideological spectrum. It is these emphases, this style, and these preferences going into the construction of the region which is what is specific about it.

There is another noteworthy feature as well. In the process of accommodating all the leaders, sants, heroes, deities, festivals, acharyas, sects, and pilgrimages, and calling them by the name of the Indian culture, the *Kalnirnay* calendar produces something undifferentiated, something internally continuous. Pierre Bourdieu says, 'Just as the [Enlightenment] map replaces the discontinuous patchy space . . . by the homogeneous, continuous space . . . so the calendar substitutes a linear, homogeneous, continuous time for practical time, which is made up of incommensurable islands of duration each with its own rhythm.'[10] At one level *Kalnirnay* represents linear time progressing evenly from one week to the next, from one month to the next. But it also gives you a whole time cycle by incorporating the annual festivals and yatras which occur year after year, succeeding each other in an orderly, predictable manner.

Behind each religious figure remembered, or yatra taken out, there is history, and this history is tied to the history of the place. By putting all such celebrations on the small squares of dates, the calendar flattens them into a collection of indistinguishable dots or moments. Their specificity erased and preserved, all these places and their histories are integrated into the cultural landscape of Maharashtra. This 'formal subsumption' can lead to 'real subsumption' when the scattered activities are brought together ideologically for identity politics. This occurrence should not surprise us, since 'the final victory of modernity is not the disappearance of the non-modern world but its artificial preservation and reconstruction'.[11]

The process of making an ethnic or national identity out of a bundle of heterogeneous times[12] is entirely compatible with the construction of region. The big companies making cosmetics and soaps, present on the pages of the calendar through their advertisements, contribute to an alignment between the various levels of identity formation. They seek to generate the same pan-Indian desires, anxieties and objects of desire everywhere, the floating markers of modernity, no matter who you are and what you are being solicited to become.

In *Grundrisse*, Marx remarks on 'the annihilation of space by time' (Marx 1981: 524). The remark figures in the context of his discussion of the means of transport creating the 'physical conditions' of exchange. About fifteen pages later (539), in the section on the relationship between circulation time and the determination of value, he virtually repeats the remark, observing that 'while capital must on one side strive to tear down every spatial barrier to . . . exchange, and conquer the whole earth for its market, it strives on the other side to annihilate this space with time, i.e. to reduce to a minimum the time spent in motion from one place to another'—circulation time is a barrier to the self-realization of capital. The example of the calendar we are looking at suggests that this process of time annihilating space is supplemented by that of time creating space in the sense of changing our relations with certain spaces, thereby altering the significance they have for us. In an article on the hegemonic spatial strategies of Hindu communalism in India, Satish Deshpande has put Foucault's idea of heterotopia to promising use. Though heterotopias are real, physical places, they are not 'products of nature: considerable ideological labour is needed to transform a given site into a heterotopia'. Spatial strategies perform the task of 'articulating the physical-material and the mental-imaginative aspects of social space' (Deshpande 1998: 250-1). It is in this sense of transforming the physical entity called Maharashtra into a spatial entity whose cultural-historical significance has hegemonic consequences that one can speak of space being 'created'. It is to this transformation, an essentially ongoing and open-ended process, that the *Kalnirnay* calendar contributes through its time-related practices: dates and days, almanac, rail and bus timetables, astrological forecasts, yoga. All these are modes of ordering and regulating time, coping with it, through different ways of dividing it, signifying it, prospecting it, calibrating it, and, as in yoga, slowing it down to an agreeable rhythm.

All three examples taken here are representative of trends and tendencies in contemporary Maharashtra. Let us start with the calendar. *Kalnirnay* is not only phenomenally successful by itself, but it has also spawned many similar calendars. *Mahalaxmi*, more popular in southern Maharashtra, is one. *Sainirnay*, published from Bombay—its name sounding similar to *Kalnirnay* but at the same time making itself distinct by invoking the memory of the widely revered holy figure of Sai Baba—is another. Then there is a calendar, again published from Bombay, called *Maharashtra Darshan* (its 2002 edition had the pictorial theme of the brassware used traditionally in Maharashtra, but now increasingly confined to ceremonial or museum value) and also one started by a well-known Marathi newspaper published in Pune. Some of these are poor imitations of *Kalnirnay* while others have tried to improvise upon the model. But they all try to combine elements of a modern calendar, an almanac, and details of local religious festivals and celebrations scattered across the geography of the state. In the case of my second illustration—that of a 'regional novel'—I have already said that this is a well established genre within modern Marathi literature and that even the Konkan region has figured in the works of reputed writers. And finally, Maratha history. It will not be an exaggeration to say that there is almost an obsession in modern Maharashtra with the stories of Shivaji. He has enjoyed such unqualified admiration that arriving at a factually or historically authentic account of his life and reign is almost impossible. Shivaji is an icon, a superman with an element of the divine, a hero for everyone across the ideological spectrum.

So whether you look at the numbers involved, or spread, or preponderance in contemporary public life, these are significant activities representing strong cultural trends. What is common to them, in my view, is that they all have to do with the temporal dimension of our individual and collective life, whether in the mundane sense of having to do with days and dates, or in the sense of dealing with the auspiciousness of time, or in the sense of nostalgia and history. And they all contribute to region-making.

Yet the region-making in each case is such that the significance conferred on a space cannot be shared by everybody and at the same time cannot be easily disregarded by anybody. Apu's Konkan is not the Konkan of Ibrahim the butcher, nor can Muslims feel comfortable in a Maharashtra that has come into being riding high on the rhetoric of completing the task that Shivaji started. Not every user of *Kalnirnay* can be interested in knowing how to make soya curry or have anxieties about the future of Marathi. It may be argued that they need not, that they can read novels for entertainment, or use a calendar for information on public holidays. Surely, we are not talking here of subjects being involuntarily constrained by structures. The point, rather, is that when some ways of imagining space circulate with prestige and with a stamp of authenticity, this has consequences for social relations in that spatial context.

If, for a certain space to be a region, the minimal requirement is that it be shown to have a homogeneity or internal coherence, then what such practices and activities do (consciously or otherwise) is to accomplish such a coherence through their selective representations of Maharashtra (or Konkan). It is important to note that the two dimensions—space and time—are not simply juxtaposed or nominally connected in these activities. In each one of them, the process of constituting past, present, or future is intrinsically connected with conferring a certain space with significance. But if we ask, for whom has this space been rendered significant, we realize that it cannot be for all. It is for somebody, and not everybody, that the space 'stands out in relief', and thus becomes a region. But I have something more in mind: I propose that we understand region-making as a complex of intellectual and institutional practices that Foucault calls knowledge/power. This, I think, will be a promising line to follow. True, to make the idea more convincing, we need to demonstrate the articulations between these temporal practices and what is more narrowly called political-administrative processes in contemporary Maharashtra. That would be the task of a detailed empirical enquiry which the theory-inspired impressions and perceptions presented here urge us to take up.

NOTES

1. What is meant by 'space' here is close to what Doreen Massey (1984) means: it includes distance, movement, specificity of places, and the symbolism associated with them and with space. I thank Sasheej Hegde for having introduced me to this author.
2. This is an expression used by Satish Deshpande (1998).
3. Obviously, I am adapting Edward Said's remark that 'because of Orientalism the Orient was not (and is not) a free subject of thought or action' (Said 1978: 3). Said goes on to say that this does not mean that 'Orientalism unilaterally determines what can be said about the Orient, but that it is the whole network of interests inevitably brought to bear on . . . any occasion when that peculiar entity "the Orient" is in question. How this happens is what this book tries to demonstrate.'
4. As an illustration of what I mean by making efforts at the intellectual level, see Bennur's serialized write-ups on Muslim Marathi literature in the Marathi periodical *Parivartanacha Vaatsaru*, June 2001 to March 2002. It is significant how often Bennur appreciates this or that Muslim author for avoiding shrillness of tone or his restrained tone and language. In effect, he is arguing for a certain style—and, by implication, for an aesthetic criterion.
5. It is tempting to speculate about the reasons for this increase. Surely market calculations could not have been the main reason, given the fact that the Jews form a small minority in the population of Maharashtra. Significantly, there is a tendency among rightist politicians in Maharashtra to eulogize Israeli Jews for their indomitable nationalism. But it would be simplistic to draw conclusions on the basis of this tenuous link.
6. Norbert Elias has observed that calendar time is an example of a synthesis by means of which the three sequences—natural, social, and those belonging to an individual life span—can be related (Elias 1992: 16). He has also remarked that people in the West have now got so used to the Gregorian calendar that they 'do not mind very much if they live in areas where Easter . . . does not coincide with spring, with a new young green breaking through the dark earth, or where Christmas coincides with the spring rains' (ibid.: 198). In the context of *Kalnirnay*, it can be argued that it provides, unintentionally perhaps, some links between socio-cultural activities and the rhythms of nature by presenting the almanac and the calendar together on the same page, a relationship which has otherwise become tenuous.
7. Harvey says, 'Interplace competition is not simply about attracting production. . . . It is also about attracting consumers through the creation of a cultural centre, a pleasing urban or regional landscape, and the like. Investment in consumption spectacles, the selling of images of places,

competition over the definition of cultural and symbolic capital, the revival of vernacular traditions associated with places, all become conflated in interplace competition' (Harvey 1993: 8).

8. The term 'formal subsumption' figures in the *Grundrisse* of Marx in the discussion of the first phase of labour's subordination to capital. The second phase is called 'real subsumption', a term which I use a little later in this discussion. I am hinting at the analytical possibility of distinguishing the stages by which the scattered, local cultural/religious events come to be drawn into the politics of communalism.
9. In this connection, Seemanthini Niranjana's comment (2001: 109) is worth noting. She says: 'the possibility of women becoming visible subjects in the domain of auspiciousness need not, of course, entail that the significance of the spatial has been grasped . . . while Madan dwells upon the imperatives and intricacies of relating auspiciousness to the flow of time, its relation to space remains largely undeveloped.' She goes on to say that in Marglin too 'the spatial is never theorised', though she takes the notions of auspicious-inauspicious to be inextricably linked to time.
10. Quoted by David Harvey (1990: 253).
11. MacCannell (1976: 8), quoted by Harvey (1993: 12). The comment has its relevance in the case of the examples considered earlier as well—the novel and the use of history for contemporary politics.
12. The expression 'heterogeneous time' is *not* an allusion to Partha Chatterjee's 'The Nation in Heterogeneous Time', *The Indian Economic and Social History Review*, XXXVIII.4, 2001.

REFERENCES

Atre, Prahlad Keshav. 1997. *Zalach Pahije!* Thane: Dimple Publication.

Bennur, Fakruddin. 2001. 'Muslim Marathi Sahitya Chalval: Viparyas ani Vastusthiti', *Samaj Prabodhan Patrika*, No. 156, July-September.

———. 2001-2. 'Muslim Marathi Sahitya Parichay', *Parivartanacha Vaatsaru*, 1-15 June, 1-15 July, 1-15 August, 16-31 August, 16-31 December 2001; and 16-31 January, 16-28 February, 1-31 March 2002.

Dalvi, Jayawant. 1981 (1964). *Saare Pravaasi Ghadiche*. Bombay: Majestic.

Deshpande, Satish. 1998. 'Hegemonic Spatial Strategies: The Nation-Space and Hindu Communalism in Twentieth-Century India', *Public Culture*, Vol. 10, No. 2, pp. 249-83.

Elias, Norbert. 1992. *Time: An Essay*. Oxford: Basil Blackwell.

Foucault, Michel. 1980. *Power/Knowledge*, ed. Colin Gordon. New York: Pantheon Books.

Harvey, David. 1990. *The Condition of Postmodernity: An Enquiry into the Origins of Cultural Change*. Oxford: Blackwell, 1990.

———. 1993. 'From Space to Place and Back Again: Reflections on the Condition of Postmodernity', in *Mapping the Futures: Local Culture, Global Change*, ed. Jon Bird, Barry Curtis, Tim Putnam, George Robertson, and Lisa Tickner. London/New York: Routledge.

Madan, T. N. 1987. *Non-Renunciation: Themes and Interpretations of Hindu Culture*. New Delhi: Oxford University Press.

Marglin, F. A. 1985. *Wives of the God-King*, New Delhi: Oxford University Press.

Marx, Karl. 1981. *Grundrisse: Foundations of the Critique of Political Economy*, Harmondsworth: Penguin Books.

Massey, Doreen and John Allen, eds. 1984. *Geography Matters! A Reader*. Cambridge: Cambridge University Press.

Massey, Doreen. 1992. 'Politics and Space/Time', *New Left Review*, No. 196, pp. 65-84.

Niranjana, Seemanthini. 2001. *Gender and Space: Femininity, Sexualization and the Female Body*. New Delhi: Sage Publications.

Said, Edward. 1991. *Orientalism: Western Conceptions of the Orient*. London: Penguin.

Soja, Edward. 1989. *Postmodern Geographies: The Reassertion of Space in Critical Social Theory*. London/New York: Verso.

Wallerstein, Immanuel et al. 1997. *Open the Social Sciences: Report of the Gulbankian Commission on the Restructuring of the Social Sciences*. New Delhi: Vistaar Publications.

PART III

Regions in Politics

11

Caste Politics through the Prism of Region

Suhas Palshikar

This paper is about politics. It seeks to understand politics by looking at two important axes around which politics in India—and contemporary politics, more so—seems to revolve: caste and region. Of these it is caste that is given the most attention. 'Region' as a factor has only assumed significance in the 1990s. After the disintegration of the 'Congress framework' of politics, observers began to note the 'regionalization' of politics (Nigam 1996; Palshikar 2003; Rangarajan 1999). The rise of regional and state-based parties to prominence is an expression of this regionalization. But apart from the dramatic proliferation and rise of regional parties, a less noticed but more interesting aspect of regionalization has been related to 'all-India' parties. The Congress, Bharatiya Janata Party (BJP), and Communist Party of India (Marxist) (CPI-M), have themselves become regionalized in terms of their strategies and practices.

Regionalization refers to five factors. (i) Issues are/have become region specific. Although the press may continue to project issues in all-India terms, these make sense only when translated into regional contexts. This applies equally to the 'secular-communal' divide and to 'globalization'. (ii) Leadership is structured and ratified regionally. Parties may still project towering 'national' leaders but state-level leadership is more relevant, and only through this kind of leadership do people relate to 'national' politics. (iii) Regionalization further means that social forces are constituted at the regional level, so that the support base of parties can be identified only at the state level. Whether one can describe the base of parties at the all-India level by adding up their state bases, however, is somewhat doubtful. (iv) In electoral and mobilizational context, a set of choices exists at the state level. People, as voters and as groups, have to choose from among the state level choices. (v) Following from the above factors, political competition takes place at the level of region. Consequently, the outcome makes sense only at the regional level. It is in this sense that the 'theatre' of politics has shifted to the states—away from the 'all India' theatre.

Before turning to the question of how this regionalization links up with caste, let us briefly explore the concept of 'region'. The territoriality expressed by the term 'region' often has a flexibility and indeterminacy with regard to its physical boundaries. In this sense, 'region' refers to a wide range of territorial configurations: a locality, a subregion, a state, a supra-state region, etc. In our discussion of caste below, we shall be considering all these units. Secondly, region can bypass territoriality and convey a broader and perhaps more fluid element of space. Thus understood, region would refer to a non-territorial, non-physical sphere just as it would refer to a physical territory. We bring this element of region into the discussion because caste can be seen both as interacting with territory and as providing space for following a certain kind of politics. It needs to be seen how caste as social space interacts with region as territorial space.

A further point may be raised at this introductory stage. How does a region become politically sustainable? It is possible to think of many factors, but the point is that territoriality needs to be translated into a political factor. Language, culture, economy, etc. provide a base to territoriality to sustain politics. It may be argued that caste is not only yet another base, but one which potentially combines other factors—particularly economy—as a factor in politics. Thus we can imagine a complex relationship between caste and region, a relationship of interdependence. Caste is expressed regionally, region becomes politically sustainable on the basis of caste; caste is bound up by territoriality and in constituting social space caste takes the form of a region.

We hope to understand politics in the post-Congress phase by exploring the tension and relation between caste and region. The post-Congress phase is charaterized by coalitions, but an alliance of regional parties does not seem to be a possibility. On the other hand, caste emerged in the 1990s as a possible framework within which politics would be organized, even though it now appears that politics of backward castes—or OBC politics as it is popularly known—seems to be stagnating. The expressions of regionalism are vocal in some areas but muted in others. Moreover, apart from region and caste, another contending framework of politics has emerged—Hindutva—showing signs of accommodating both region and caste. With this background, we probe the meaning of regionalization and elaborate the link between caste and region in contemporary Indian politics. In short, the paper deals with the overlap between the two axes—caste and region—and how this overlap affects the nature of these axes even when they are operating independently of each other.

Caste, as a system of vertical division, sustains itself on the basis of localization. Caste hierarchy may invoke the ideologies of *chaturvarnya* and of purity-pollution, but the hierarchy works only when it is concretized in a local situation. Studies on jati by sociologists and social anthropologists have always pointed out how the hierarchical ranking of jatis makes sense in the context of the village or locality. Similarly, the cultural and ritual life of members of a jati is organized in the village or locality. It is only with reference to other castes in a locality that the higher or lower status of a caste can be experienced. Anthropological studies, thus, look at the extent of intermixing among castes and the finer ethic followed in the course of such intermixing within a locality to assess the extent of separation and commensality among castes. A statement that 'carpenters dine with ironsmiths' does not carry any meaning unless it is specified as to where this interdining took place. In other words, jati as a unit of social relations, ritual status and cultural universe is firmly based within the framework of well-defined spatial units. As much as the vertical, the horizontal separateness of a caste, too, has a locality as a point of reference.

This explains why there are distinct 'pockets' of various castes. Most castes are specific not only to a certain state but also to a particular area. This means that a caste which has a concentrated existence in one area may also constitute a numerically significant group in that area. In a study of north India, Schwartzberg has shown how caste concentration takes place at the village and district level. He shows that more than 50 per cent of Ludhiana's population is Jat, and that Chamars and Majahabis have separate pockets in Punjab. The same applies to UP, Bihar, Orissa, etc. He argues that in the case of both peasant castes and Dalits, exclusivity seems to be the rule. This means that if in one village Jats are the largest group, other peasant castes would almost be non-existent. Similarly, in districts where Majahabis are numerous (e.g. Amritsar), other Dalit castes are rarely seen (Schwartzberg 1968: 99-106). This study gives an indication of the strong link between caste and locality or sub-region. In the case of peasant castes, the regional base is considerable, while non-peasant castes are often confined to smaller pockets. This pattern is evident in state after state. In Tamil Nadu (TN), Vanniyars belong to North and South Arcot, Salem and Chingleput (Hardgrave 1965: 40); Thevars to Ramnad (Beteille 1992: 105-6); Nadars earlier belonged to Tirunelveli (Hardgrave 1970: 105-6). Similarly, Izhava subcastes belonged to different parts of Kerala—Tiyyars to the north, Izhavas to the central parts, and Tandans to the south (Mencher and Unni 1976: 122). The Vokkaligas of Karnataka are concentrated in the Mysore region (Srinivas 1962: 32). In Maharashtra the Agris are concentrated in one district of Konkan, Raigad; the Leva Patils in Jalgaon district of north Maharashtra; and the Vanjaris in Nasik, Ahmednagar and Beed districts. The Malis of Rajasthan belong to the Jodhpur region (Jenkins 1993: 640), and most smaller castes are concentrated in specific areas (Lodha 1999: 3346). The case of the Jats of western UP is too famous to require mention. In Bihar, the Bhumihars have a concentrated strength in the south while the Rajputs live in the western parts (Frankel 1989: 53). The Kammas belong to the Andhra region and the Reddis to Rayalseema (Elliott 1970: 149). One can extend this list of examples. M. N. Srinivas observed in 1957 that 'this kind of relationship between a caste and a region is widespread in India . . .' (Srinivas 1962: 72). More specifically, as Washbrook observes in the context of TN, most endogamous jatis extended over no more than a few adjacent villages (Washbrook 1989: 223).

This association of many castes with specific territorial 'pockets' has produced two political results. One is the rise of 'locally dominant' castes. Srinivas's early use of the term 'dominant caste' was specifically with reference to a small locality or village or group of villages. In his 1955 essay, 'The Social System of a Mysore Village', Srinivas mentions that the concept of the dominant caste is 'important for understanding intercaste relations in any *local area*' (Srinivas 1987: 77, emphasis added). Elaborating on the concept in 1957, he uses the phrase 'locally' dominant and then adds,

'Occasionally a caste is dominant in a group of neighbouring villages if not over a district or two, and in such cases, local dominance is linked with regional dominance' (Srinivas 1987: 96). As far as 'local dominance' is concerned, there seems to be a direct link between domination and numerical preponderance. A large population, though, has one other implication. Often a caste has numerical advantage when it also has a high degree of control over resources—land. Thus economic power and size combine to produce patterns of local domination. If one carefully follows Srinivas's account of a locally dominant caste in Mysore, two inferences follow: (a) the political effect of the caste-region interface is not a result of colonialism but simply an outcome of local hierarchy based on caste and (b) like the dominance of one caste, the subordination of others is a result of 'localization'. Castes that are 'trapped' by circumstances into a locality face subordination. For some, localization produces opportunities for domination, whereas for others, localization portends subordination.

Another, more commonly noted political result of caste pockets relates to electoral politics. Localized pockets have come to mean that candidates of a particular caste get elected from certain areas. Our study of Maharashtra gives ample evidence of this. The Maratha–Kunbi caste cluster, which is spread across the state, manages to send the largest number of MLAs to the state legislature, irrespective of political upheavals. In 51 constituencies, the elected candidate has been a Maratha for six consecutive elections since 1978. In 19 other constituencies too, a candidate of the same caste has been elected since 1978 (these exclude constituencies reserved for SCs). Thus, in one-fourth of the constituencies, the caste of the MLA has been the same since 1978. More specifically, Agris always get elected from Raigad district, Leva Patils from Jalgaon district, Telis from Wardha and Bhandara districts, Lingayats from Solapur and Kolhapur districts, Malis from Amravati district, etc. (Data collected by the Department of Politics, University of Pune; see also Thite 1996). It is clear that there exists a tendency among parties to match caste by caste in the selection of candidates. But the case of Maharashtra suggests that local caste pockets have an important implication for the phenomenon of regionally dominant castes. It is only through such localized pockets that smaller and non-dominant castes get an opportunity to stake their claims to power. If smaller, non-dominant castes are not concentrated in one area, they are not likely to get any representation on their own strength. In Uttar Pradesh (UP), the Kurmis and Binds have formed their separate parties, Apna Dal and Pragatisheel Manavsamaj Party respectively, and it has been observed that in 1999 Apna Dal did get a large number of votes in 5 Lok Sabha (LS) constituencies, although no candidate of the party was elected. The Binds, one of the more backward castes, rallied behind their caste candidates and made their presence felt in 7 LS constituencies (S. G. 1999: 2912). This clearly shows that the Kurmis and Binds can draw upon their localized demographic 'resource' to at least protest the domination of the Yadavs, just as Maratha domination in Maharashtra can be contested in a few pockets of non-Maratha castes.

Construction of Regionally Dominant Castes

Localized concentration leads to localized domination and possibilities of representation. On the other hand, throughout the twentieth century, certain jatis evolved into castes spread over a large territory. This gave rise to the regionally dominant castes. From the 1950s onwards, politics in most states centred around one (or two) regionally dominant caste(s). In most cases, middle level (often peasant) castes sought to contest the ritual superiority, material ascendance and political domination of Brahmans, Kayasthas and Thakurs. In the first half of twentieth century, the middle-caste protests took the form of non-Brahman movements in Maharashtra and in the south. In the second half of the twentieth century, the middle castes extended their claims to state power at the regional level. In both these phases, the middle castes sought to transcend locality and assume a 'regional' presence.

The non-Brahman movements in Maharashtra and the south were concerned with creating 'regional' non-Brahman identities. In Maharashtra, the invocation of Shivaji and Maratha rule was crucial in bringing various peasant castes together. The movement also facilitated the emergence of Maratha politics on a larger scale geographically (Omvedt 1976: 184-206). In Tamil Nadu, the non-Brahman movement was built upon the collapse of caste and region. The Brahmans were excluded from Dravid identity (Hardgrave 1965). In Karnataka, the Vokkaliga 'caste' came into being by the fusion of various peasant jatis such as the Morasui, Hallikar, Halu, Nonabad, and so on (Srinivas 1962: 5). In Gujarat, Kanabis of different areas came together in 1931 to constitute themselves as 'Patidars', although Saurashtrian Kanabis are still looked down upon by the Gujarat Patidars. Also, the Leva and Kadvi divisions of Patidars are supposed to refer to sub-regional differences. Yet, from 1931 onwards, the 'Patidar' identity has evolved as a regional or state-level identity (Pocock 1972). Similarly, despite internal tensions, in Gujarat kshatriyas have been organizing themselves as one group. Rajputs, in the forefront of this kshatriya mobilization, are regionally differentiated. Gujarat Rajputs, being mostly tenants or landless, sought to align with Kolis and Bariyas (also landless) as kshatriyas. Saurashtra Rajputs, being land owners, resisted the claims of non-Rajputs to kshatriya status. However, over the years, the kshatriya group of castes in Gujarat as a whole has provided a counterpoint to Patidar politics. The Kshatriya Sabha took an initiative in bringing together Rajputs and Kolis and shaping their politics (Kothari and Maru 1970). The Jats are probably the most regionally structured caste. Various *khaps* of the Jats span specific villages, and at meetings of all the *khaps*, the *Sarvakhap* meets to discuss common matters. But alongside *khaps*, Jats of western UP and adjoining Haryana are also organized through the All India Jat Mahasabha, which always extended support to Charan Singh (Pradhan 1966; Gupta 1997: 49-58; Hasan 1998: 131).

It can be argued that in many states the rise of the non-Brahman movement and the rise of middle-level castes as dominant follow a similar pattern. A protest against castes ranking high in the hierarchy gives an impetus to these processes. But these processes gain momentum when small, localized, endogamous jatis overcome their localization by seeking either in mythology or history a link with a larger territorial unit. They ignore or underplay the details of ritual separation, and instead amalgamate large groups into their new boundaries, often expanding traditional identities. This development is accompanied by the formation of territorial or even 'all-India' associations—Mahasabhas or Mahasanghas—of the newly-evolved caste group. A moderately reformist posture follows concerning intra-caste practices, particularly marriage practices. Since the process is ideologically rooted in opposition to upper castes, the claims of such 'castes' relate to share in power, opportunities for material uplift, and the amelioration of tradition-inflicted disabilities. Central to this whole process is the journey from locality to region (mostly state). Once a caste crosses the threshold of locality, the chances of realizing its political aims become very real. A geographical expansion allows the concerned caste to make claims on the bases of representation and caste injustice. Besides, association with a larger region allows access to other strategies like regional ideology, cultural-historical claims, etc. In fact, most dominant castes, as also proponents of non-Brahman movements, claim that the heritage of that region belongs to them; they are the true and authentic bearers of symbols associated with the particular region; they represent the culture of that region; etc. So it is the non-Brahmans who are the Dravids, the Marathas who are the bearers of the symbol of Shivaji, the Patidars who exemplify the essence of Gujarati culture, and the Jats who represent the true kisans.

Linguistic States

If a caste claims that it represents the regional culture better than others, it follows that there will be a strong connection between such dominant castes and regionalist movements. Today we can talk about dominant castes in the context of states because in most cases these have been constituted as linguistic states. They are not solely geographical-administrative entities, but socio-cultural and political units also. Hence the link between dominant castes and states.

One can come across many different patterns of relations between caste and regional identity. These include assertions by upper castes, convenient collaboration between upper and middle castes, the rise of contending middle castes, the exclusion of upper castes, etc. Probably the latest example would be Uttaranchal, where caste played an indirect role. When the union government decided to implement the policy of reservations for OBCs, stiff opposition came from upper castes of Uttaranchal. It was argued that this region did not have OBCs—at least not in large numbers. For the anti-reservation movement, the issues of separate identity of hill people distinct from plains people came to the forefront (Pradeep Kumar 2000). Without much exaggeration, it could be said that the formation of Uttaranchal is an instance of upper-caste assertion where 'regional' distinctiveness was indirectly claimed on the basis of a different caste composition of the population. Historically, such upper-caste assertion may be detected in the regional nationalism of Orissa. When the Oriya-speaking territory was part of Bengal, Brahmans and Karans came together to shape Oriya opposition to Bengali domination. In 1912, this same social force invoked Oriya nationalism to protest against Orissa's annexation to Bihar (Mohanty 1990: 336-7). Since the creation of Orissa state, the upper castes have generally retained their hold over the state's politics, culture and economy.

As far as collaboration between upper and middle castes is concerned, Maharashtra is a very good example. Although the non-Brahman movement had considerably villainized Brahmans, the Samyukta Maharashtra Movement (for a united Maharashtra state) saw the Brahmans and sections of Marathas collaborating and mobilizing the masses on the basis of regionalist sentiments. This collaboration had a major long-term effect. While the formation of Maharashtra state ushered the Marathas into positions of power, the sharpness of non-Brahmanism was almost lost. The Brahmans, of course, were not in a position to make a comeback to politics, but nor were they hounded out of politics in particular or the public domain in general. On the contrary, Brahmans continued to dominate culture, education, and the media, under the benign auspices of 'Maharashtra Dharma' (Vora and Palshikar 1990; Vora 1999). More tangentially, the regional assertion led by Brahmans and Marathas displaced the focus of the non-Brahman movement, considerably weakening the anti-caste discourse. Instead, Maratha domination became legitimized in the name of non-Maratha lower castes, identified in the 1960s (in Maharashtra) as Bahujan Samaj (majority of masses). The caste-region nexus in Maharashtra, thus, exemplifies the process of one caste legitimating its claims by usurping the claims of other, smaller castes of that linguistic region.

Just as the Gujarati-Marwari baniya was the cause of Marathi Brahmans and Marathas coming together, the prominence of Tamil Brahmans resulted in the unity of Telugu Brahmans and non-Brahman castes in Andhra. Although initially the non-Brahman Telugus joined the Justice Party, they were not taken in by the anti-Brahman rhetoric. Instead, their anti-Brahman sentiment got directed against Tamil Brahmans, allowing co-operation among Telugu-speaking people on a regional-linguistic basis. This weakened the non-Brahman movement in Andhra. It has also been argued that the co-option of elite Reddys into the Congress facilitated a less acrimonious relationship between Brahmans and Reddys (Elliott 1970: 150-3). The examples of Maharashtra and Andhra show that regionalism can intervene in the competition between upper castes and middle castes. Secondly, these examples suggest that regionalism can help a smooth transfer of the state-level political apparatus to middle castes. Often, in this 'smooth' transfer, radicalism is lost and the claims of lower castes get short shrift through symbolic gestures and tokenism.

Starting with limited collaboration between upper and middle castes, Maharashtra and Andhra Pradesh witnessed the rise and assertion of middle castes. A similar assertion was witnessed in UP once the Jats of the west became politically organized. As we mentioned earlier, this Jat assertion took the form of a demand for 'backward' status. From this, Charan Singh also attempted to project himself (and therefore, Jats) as representative of backward groups. However, because of a strong association between Jats and land, their leaders (Charan Singh earlier and Tikait later), harped on the farmer identity of Jats in particular and of Gujjars as well (Byres 1988; Gupta 1997: 89-98; Hasan 1998: 131-8). Interestingly, during Tikait's farmers' agitations, a stage came when activists of Bharatiya Kisan Union proposed that they should ask for a separate state for western UP (quoted in Gupta 1997: 74). Thus, the Jats are an example of middle-caste assertion at the regional level. Politics in Haryana is another instance of Jat assertion at the state level, while in Rajasthan Jat assertion took the form of a concerted effort to claim backward status. The Jats of Rajasthan deviated from pro-Congress politics to vote for the BJP in 1999, for the sole purpose of getting their backward status recognized. The Jat Mahasabha decided to vote for the BJP once Vajpayee promised to concede their demand. Accordingly, Jats of Rajasthan except Bharatpur and Dholpur have been included in the list of OBCs (Lodha 1999: 3347).

Many states have witnessed keen competition between two castes or caste-clusters; the contending castes usually belong to a middle status. In Rajasthan, the competition between the Jats and Rajputs has been rather neatly transformed into a bipolar party situation. Gujarat and Karnataka are two other examples of contending middle castes, but politics there is not organized so neatly. The Patidars of

Gujarat rose to prominence in the course of the national movement. The Patidar caste also gained control over resources, and sought to displace the Brahmans and baniyas from political power. However, in Gujarat politics has been characterized by Congress efforts to attract kshatriyas, the Swatantra Party's efforts to forge an alliance of Patidars and kshatriyas, a Patidar alliance with Brahmans and banias in opposition to reservation, and growing affection among kshatriyas for the Congress (Shah 1990). These developments led in the 1990s to the emergence of the BJP as a Patidar force. Karnataka witnessed a tussle between Vokkaligas and Lingayats right from the time of the creation of a Kannada-speaking state. The Mysore area was dominated by Vokkaligas, but they felt that if the other Kannada-speaking areas were brought together, the Lingayats would get an upper edge. Therefore, two Kannada-speaking states were demanded. This has been recorded by the State Reorganization commission (Srinivas 1962: 32-3). Thus, here is an example of a large caste-cluster opposing a unified linguistic state for fear of losing its numerical advantage. Vokkaligas dominated Mysore politics between 1947 and 1956 (when a Kannada-speaking state came into being). From 1956 to 1972, although Lingayats did get the upper hand, political dominance was shared by these two contending caste-clusters (Manor 1989: 338-48). Ambedkar noted that linguistic states would only lead to consolidation of the 'upper' castes, jeopardizing the interests of the scheduled castes. In Punjab, for instance, the scheduled castes were not very supportive of the demand for a separate state of Punjab organized on linguistic communal lines. Even scheduled-caste Sikhs kept away from that demand, fearing that a reorganized Punjab would facilitate domination by Jat Sikhs (Nayar, 1966: 50-1).

Tamil Nadu manifests a pattern of caste-region relationship that is quite distinct. It did not throw up any single dominant caste, although Vellalas and Nadars benefited the most from the Dravid non-Brahman movement. Second, the non-Brahman movement dealt with the issue of regional identity right from the beginning (in the second decade of twentieth century). Non-Brahmanism was identified with Dravidianism. While attempting to unite all non-Brahman castes on the Dravid platform, the Dravid movement refused to recognize Brahmans as part of Dravid society. Just as this movement sought to effect a fusion of many non-Brahman castes, it also aspired to build a 'southern' identity opposed to the 'north'. In 1937, the movement led by Periyar waged an anti-Hindi agitation. The logical culmination of an anti-Hindi, anti-north, Dravidian and non-Brahman thrust was reached in 1939, when the Justice Party demanded an 'independent' Dravidsthan (Hardgrave 1965: 10-35).

Thus, caste-region interaction in Tamil Nadu strengthened an exclusionary regional nationalism. Further, it also sought to delegitimize the superiority of Brahmans. However, this exclusion did not last long. Once the regional claims were realized through the formation of Madras (now Tamil Nadu) State and non-Brahman claims were translated into an extensive policy of reservations, Brahmans were incorporated as members in Tamil society. Brahmans are accommodated as ideologues and legitimizers of the regional legacy of the Dravid movement. It is indeed ironical that a strong non-Brahman movement, through its regionalism, allowed the re-entry of the Brahman caste both into the elite and into the political arena in general (Washbrook 1989: 207-8, 253-5).

In the 1990s, the political assertion of the Vanniyars marked the political scene in Tamil Nadu. The Vanniyars have a long history of separate political organization. In spite of the efforts of the non-Brahman movement to bring together all non-Brahman castes, Vanniyars were organized as the Tamilnad Toilers' Party and the Commonweal party. Although the DMK supported the latter in 1952 with a view to defeating the Congress, Kamraj was successful in bringing both Vanniyar parties into the Congress fold (Hardgrave 1965: 40-5). Another backward caste, the Thevars, backed the Forward Bloc for a long time (Beteille 1992: 107). These details suggest that in spite of the very vocal non-Brahman movement, Tamil politics did not throw up a single middle caste around which state politics could be organized. Even the predominant castes in a given district do not account for more than one-fourth of the population of that district. Probably this peculiar situation led to sustained recourse to militant regional nationalism, particularly by the Dravid parties. However, as Washbrook observes, this Dravidianism 'neutralized many of the caste based issues of conflict that dominated Tamil Nadu politics in the first half of the twentieth century' (Washbrook 1989: 207-8). Perhaps those contradictions which Dravidianism sought to push under the carpet of regionalism have resurfaced in Tamil Nadu with Dalit–OBC conflicts and the

Hinduization of some backward castes. In the absence of any particular caste group as central to politics, Tamil politics took on an exclusionary character: exclusion of Brahmans, Aryans, north Indians and, less explicitly, even Adi Dravids.

Two Ruptures

Demography, agrarian relations, and the political economy of the post-Independence period all combined to produce strong linkages between region and caste. In particular, the different patterns of caste relations gave substance to the region as a political category in states like Andhra Pradesh, Tamil Nadu and Karnataka. These developments established region-specific dominant castes in most parts of India. This feature came under stress at two stages when certain types of caste politics attempted to cross regional boundaries. Both these ruptures in the established pattern of caste-region equation came as opposition to upper as well as newly dominant castes in various regions. In the interplay of caste and region, Dalits and OBCs were and are often excluded or marginalized. Therefore these sections attempted to breach the happy coincidence of caste and region by pursuing the project of all-India 'Dalit politics' and 'OBC politics'.

At the intellectual level, Ambedkar was the first to grasp the implications of 'linguistic states' in terms of the consequent marginalization of Dalits. But even before this issue came up, Ambedkar had realized the need to mobilize Dalits at an all-India level if they were to stake claims to political power. Thus, in the 1940s, abandoning the Independent Labour Party, he formed the Scheduled Castes Federation (SCF). On the one hand, through the SCF, he sought to intervene in the negotiations for India's freedom and to wrest a minimum share in power. On the other hand, the SCF was also visualized as a major opposition to the upper-caste dominated Congress in the period immediately after Independence. The failure of the SCF notwithstanding, it is important to note that Ambedkar saw the unfolding of a process of conflict between SCs and upper castes and also believed that a united all-India instrument of SCs could alone take on the task of contesting upper-caste claims. Although he once again veered to a more broad-based party in the form of the Republican Party of India (RPI), this party came to be identified as a Dalit party and could not sustain the all-India claims which Ambedkar had always insisted upon. In the mid-1980s, Kanshi Ram formed the Bahujan Samaj Party, primarily a party of Dalits. The BSP has made its presence felt outside UP, in the Punjab, Rajasthan, Madhya Pradesh, etc., and hopes to spread to Maharashtra and Karnataka also. In this sense, the BSP manifests an all-India ambition and an awareness that upper-caste domination has to be fought at the all-India level. Thus, the initial lead by Ambedkar and the later formation of the BSP challenge the caste-region nexus. They seek to problematize the caste question at the national level and force a solution through intervention in national politics. The approach of the BSP is more instrumentalist than Ambedkar's. The BSP believes that only in a period of instability can Dalits force their entry into the network that controls the national state apparatus. Therefore, the unity of Dalits at the all-India level and unity between Dalits and other disadvantaged castes are seen as strategies for shifting power away from the Brahmanical (*manuvadi*) sections of society towards the masses.

In the 1960s, Lohia argued that 'backward castes' constitute a majority and should be given a fair share in power. This was reminiscent of the arguments of the non-Brahman movement in the south and in Maharashtra. Although backward-caste politics gradually emerged in UP and Bihar, it was only in the 1990s that it became an issue at an all-India level. After the agitations against reservations in Gujarat and Bihar in the 1970s and 1980s, the agitation in many north Indian states on the issue of reservations for backward castes underlined the simmering conflict between the privileged and the underprivileged. Since the controversy over the recommendations of the Mandal Commission, sections of backward castes have shown a renewed awareness about reservations and sharing power. This has resulted in the large-scale mobilization of backward castes, dramatically catapulting their representatives into positions of power.

These developments had two effects. First, the political discourse in the country as a whole changed considerably. 'Social justice' became the central term around which this discourse was constructed. Such a construction facilitated the entry of the caste question onto the all-India political scene, rather than letting it remain state-specific. The backwardness of certain castes and their consequent political disadvantage was no more seen in state-specific contexts; instead it was conceived as a phenomenon following from Brahmanical Hindutva and the domination of national politics by upper castes. The remedy was to take over power in Delhi. 'OBC' (as the backward castes came to be known) claims were quickly recognized by the various political parties. In particular, the BJP exhibited remarkable adaptability by introducing changes in the social composition of its key workers in Maharashtra, Madhya Pradesh and UP. Most other parties, too, underwent the process of 'Mandalization', the Congress probably being the slowest and most reluctant. However, even the Congress manifested awareness of this factor in Rajasthan, Gujarat, and Madhya Pradesh. In other words, OBC politics did not throw up any all-India instrument—any party claiming to be representative of OBC interests—instead, it forced certain changes in political parties and in politics in general. The social composition of many legislatures changed between 1990 and 2000. Reservations for OBCs became less controversial and also became part of the policies adopted by various parties. At least at the formal level, parties conceded the claims of OBCs in terms of share in power. The politics of the backward castes became an all-India phenomenon. But did Dalit politics and OBC politics actually break the caste-region association?

In the case of Dalit politics, one can witness a steady fragmentation in the post-Ambedkar period. This fragmentation takes place at three levels: Dalit politics is fragmented among the various factions of the Republican Party. Secondly, it does not have a 'national' identity—it is too state-specific. Thirdly, the Dalit community is often fragmented along caste lines. The RPI could never project itself as a united party of Dalits. Various rival RPI parties emerged. The absence of a single effective political instrument resulted in the fragmentation of Dalit votes also. On the other hand, concrete political issues faced by Dalits took a state-specific turn. In Maharashtra, for instance, the issue of 'renaming' a university after Dr. Ambedkar remained an emotive issue for Dalits for over a decade (1979-91). In states like Bihar, atrocities by various middle castes became the main concern of Dalits. In Tamil Nadu, frustration with Dravid politics, non-accommodation in the regional identity, and conflicts with lower OBCs (Thevars and Vanniyars) have been shaping Dalit politics. The long history of Marxist-Leninist agrarian struggles in Andhra Pradesh has produced a marked Dalit radicalism. Such state-specific situations are inevitable because of differences of levels of Dalit consciousness and differences in the political economy at the state level. This means that the arena of conflict and the response vary from state to state. The main adversaries of Dalits are also not necessarily common. The voting preferences of Dalits are also likewise shaped at the state level. Dalits in Rajasthan, Gujarat, MP, and Maharashtra tend to vote in favour of the Congress; those in West Bengal and Kerala prefer the Left. In UP, the BSP has established itself as the main party of Dalits. At one stage (1999) the BJP-led alliance got more Dalit votes than does the RJD of Laloo Yadav in Bihar, probably because of the JD faction led by Ramvilas Paswan, who allied with the BJP. Similarly, in Karnataka too the BJP alliance gets more Dalit votes than the Congress. (These observations are based on voter surveys conducted by the CSDS, Delhi, in 1996, 1998, and 1999. I have been associated with these surveys as part of the research team and the co-ordinator for Maharashtra.)

A further complication regarding the Dalit situation needs to be noted. While ideologues of Dalit politics prefer to project themselves as one social force, Dalits do not constitute a unified social force even at the state level. For various reasons, state-specific reasons not the least, internal stratification among Dalits is a reality. In Maharashtra, the Mahars are seen as politically advanced, and Matang and Chamar Dalits resist 'Mahar domination'. The Mala–Madiga dispute in Andhra Pradesh reached such a proportion that the state government decided to divide reservations between these two communities (Balgopal 2000). The Dalits of Bihar, other than the Paswans, do not look upon Ramvilas Paswan as their leader (Louis 2000: 980). In Karnataka, the large group of Madigas (radical and left-oriented) demand that the reservations for Dalits should be split, with a fixed quota to Holeyas and other Dalits, to allow Madigas to enjoy 90 per cent of the reservations (Assadi-Rajendran 2000: 1612). Further, in one instance of violent conflict between Holeyas and the dominant land-owning groups, other Dalits did not come forward in support of the Holeyas (ibid.: 1610). In UP, Jatavs are seen as politically powerful and as getting all the advantages. The Balmikis and Pasis feel deprived (Pradeep Kumar 2001: 3507). In West Bengal, the Namsudras and Rajbanshis have their 'pockets' in Faridpur, Khulna, and Jessore and in the north Bengal districts of Cooch Behar, Jalpaiguri, and Dinajpur, respectively (Bandyopadhyay et al.: 51-75). These two communities are seen as taking advantage of the reservations. All these details suggest the difficulty in organizing an all-India Dalit political force. Only by intervening in the state political process do Dalits stand any chance of affecting politics.

The case of the OBCs is not very different. To begin with, the 'OBC' category, though a convenient shorthand for a large mass, is not very definitive. It includes, formally, castes listed by governments in the state lists as other backward classes. As such the question, 'Who are the OBCs?' is itself a controversial one. Inclusion or exclusion in the OBC list is often a matter of politics for those castes who have attained adequate political skills. The Jats in Rajasthan and the Vokkaligas and Lingayats in Karnataka have pressed for inclusion in the list of OBCs. This gives the mass called OBCs an amorphous character and, moreover, produces tensions within, between the more and the less deprived sections. Needless to say, all these factors develop against the backdrop of state-specific situations. Except on the general issue of reservations (for OBCs), the OBCs cannot be mobilized on an all-India level. In the 1990s, on the heels of the Mandal controversy, many OBC organizations rallied round the issues of reservations. However, when it came to organizing the nuts and bolts of OBC politics, state-specific situations asserted themselves. Thus the Janata Dal, which sought to bask in the glory of its pro-Mandal stand, witnessed internal bickering: the Orissa unit under Biju Patnaik distanced itself from the Mandal platform, while the Karnataka unit under Hegde made its displeasure about 'Mandalization' known. Both state units felt it unnecessary to have V. P. Singh as a campaigner.

Much mobilization on the Mandal platform took place in UP and Bihar. The politics of backward castes did not become articulated in a substantial manner in Orissa and Andhra Pradesh. It did not have much relevance to Tamil Nadu since that state has had a long history of non-Brahman politics. In Karnataka, the Congress under Devraj Urs had earlier mobilized the OBCs. Therefore, in the 1990s the Mandal platform did not evoke much enthusiasm there. In Maharashtra, the small OBC castes cannot match the strength of the Maratha-Kunbi caste cluster. This leaves the states of UP and Bihar as the main theatre of OBC politics. In a sense, the so-called all-India claims on behalf of OBC politics are based on politics in north India where the caste issue has emerged onto the political scene rather late. Thus the phenomenon of OBC politics is much more relevant to UP and Bihar than to other states.

The internal stratification among OBCs is another matter where state-specific issues come to the forefront. As noted above, the identification of certain castes as OBCs is itself state-specific. This is borne out in the case of the Jats, and more effectively in the case of the Lingayats of Karnataka. The state government went on appointing commission after commission to resolve the issue of whether Lingayats were backward or not (Natraj 1990: 182-5). Even when the issue of identification is resolved, the question of the share of different castes and caste groups continues to pose a challenge. In the field of reservations, most states seem to be veering to the strategy of classifying OBCs into two or three groups and assuring them of separate quotas of reserved seats. This classification, again, takes place in the context of state politics, as has been exemplified by the decision of the BJP-led UP government (Pradeep Kumar 2001). Besides reservations, the question of 'share' involves claims to power. Various backward castes not only want to be included in the apparatus of power, they hope to use power to their advantage and, if possible, gain controlling shares in power. Negatively put, backward castes push for the exclusion of the upper castes so that the complexion and content of power may change substantively. These claims bring a double conflict into focus. There is a conflict between the already-established dominant caste and the aspiring caste or caste-group. The constellations of these conflicts are again state-specific because the ideological battle line of upper *vs* backward translates differently in each state. In Maharashtra, for example, when Maratha domination is sought to be challenged, Kunbis, included in the list of OBCs, would pose a problem. The 'Maratha' caste cluster includes Kunbis. Thus, the battle is between the dominant caste and a section of OBCs *vs* other OBCs. In Karnataka, the OBCs compete with Lingayats, who themselves have been claiming inclusion in the list of OBCs. The political economy of each state produces patterns of dominance in accordance with which these battle lines get defined. The other conflict involves the aspiring castes themselves. When the Brahmans were displaced, on the whole, only one caste (or caste bloc) sought to replace them at the state level. With democratization penetrating larger sections in the contemporary period, a peculiar development has taken place. Just as the established dominant caste is about to be displaced, more than one claimant emerges to stake claims to power. This does not allow any single caste to become stable in power. The recent history of UP and Bihar shows that among the OBCs, when one caste surges ahead 'on behalf' of OBCs, its representational claims are de-legitimized by competitors from within the OBC fold. The Yadavs of UP and Bihar who claimed in the 1990s that they were leading the OBC revolution, have been challenged by non-Yadavs in both states. Both these conflicts are reflected in the party preferences of the OBCs. Backward castes in different states vote differently, and within a state they are often divided among different parties.

These claims and counterclaims, in fact, further regionalized politics during the 1990s. The unprecedented rise of regional parties in the 1990s was singularly unassociated with 'regionalism'. Caste occupied the centre stage of political discourse and regional parties became the vehicle of this often incoherent and fractured discourse.

The discussion so far suggests that the two 'ruptures' have been, in fact, ideological formulations that sought to challenge upper- and middle-caste domination by unifying the lower castes. This kind of formulation has not been able to assert itself as a concrete principle around which politics is organized. The objective caste situation varies from the presupposition that all 'lower' castes have same experience of political exclusion or marginalization. Also, the subjective identification of various castes with the politics of being 'lower'-caste varies both caste-wise and state-wise. As a result, instead of being able to rupture the caste-region nexus, both Dalit politics and OBC politics have yielded to this nexus and become regionalized.

Conclusion

Our review of the operation of caste shows that states as socio-linguistic regions are convenient units for caste to operate. Although many instances can be shown where small castes intervene in the local political process, the effective role of caste can be detected at only the state level. At the same time, castes cannot assume all-India identities, and caste alliances cannot be easily forged at the all-India level. The political salience of caste increased only after castes transcended their local identities and by forging new 'mega' caste identities became significant players at the regional level. However, this process probably stops at the regional level. The efforts of the Kurmis to forge an alliance with Kanbis and Kunbis did not succeed. The Yadavs of UP and Bihar follow separate politics from each other. Even in the case of the Jats, the Jat Mahasabha exists but Jat politics in Punjab, Rajasthan, Haryana, and western UP cannot be clubbed together. Thus patterns of caste politics cannot be replicated in different regions, nor can they become all-India in their reach or spread. In this sense, caste as a factor in contemporary politics has become well-entrenched at the regional or state level. As we shall see, it retains its existence and relevance at the local level while, as the preceding section argued, the existence of caste at the all-India level is more ideological than concrete.

The relevance of caste at the regional level flows from the following four factors:

1. Social relations of hierarchy are identifiable at the regional, sometimes even sub-regional, level. The fact that somebody is a Brahman simply places that person in an ambiguous position of superiority outside the region where that person belongs; but in the region where s/he belongs, a fine tuning will be made depending upon whether that person is, say, a Chitpavan. To take a concrete example, being a 'Maratha' carries meaning only in Maharashtra. The Marathas are simultaneously farmers, warriors, ex-landlords, etc. Rather than their ritual status either as kshatriya or shudra, the historically-constructed and materially-experienced identity as 'powerful' will be quickly brought into focus. Regional associations also allow myths, prejudices, and stereotypes to operate as markers of ranking. These do not make sense outside of that region. Therefore, for most castes, a hierarchical ranking is relevant only in a specific region. Social relations based on these assumptions of hierarchy shape social attitudes about claims of power by different castes, giving way to competition or caste conflict. Thus, when non-Brahmans of Maharashtra were claiming separate representation in the early twentieth century, the Brahmans derided them by asking what business ordinary agriculturists had in the legislature! All the same, the Brahmans

accepted—though unwillingly—Maratha entry into the political arena. In contrast, the claims of Dalits are not so silently accepted. Conflicts at the village level take place when Dalits in a village try to capture the panchayat.

2. Historically, many middle castes and sometimes even lower castes seek upward mobility in their ritual/social status. Studies of caste point out that this happens when a caste achieves material strength. It must be noted that the process of gaining upward mobility is strictly region-based, not merely because a particular caste in one region attains material strength, but also because claims are made and accepted or legitimized regionally. Such 'mobile' castes even change their caste names and this is accepted in the given region. Transformations from Kunbi to Maratha or Kanbi to Patidar are legion. Similarly, the mobility of Nadars (erstwhile Shanars) of Tamil Nadu has been well documented (Hardgrave 1969). Other examples include the Awadhias, Mahatos and Jhanuks taking Kurmi identity; Gwalas and Gopes becoming Yadavs, Padayachis of Tamil Nadu becoming Vanniyar kshatriyas, etc. (Pradeep Kumar 2001: 3505-6). Such mobility facilitates horizontal unity among castes. These developments are an 'internal' matter of the concerned regions and often indicate the emergence of regionally powerful caste groups. Thus, changing definitions of caste status give rise to patterns of competition in each region.
3. As noted earlier, in the course of competition among castes, regionalism or sub-regionalism can be easily invoked. Regionalism serves one of two purposes. It can project one caste or caste group as inheritor, protector or representative of regional identity and pride. This way, an assault on that caste or caste group is shown as an assault on regional pride and self-respect. Implicitly, this also means that the advancement of the interests of that caste constitutes regional advancement and therefore, the demands of the caste group can be transformed into demands for regional development. To be sure, regionalist politics is shaped by many factors. What we are suggesting here is that once caste and region are identified, the interests of caste can be projected as regional interests. Alternately, regionalism can be invoked to construct a broad social alliance of different castes. In this second formulation, distinct caste identities are superseded by the

ideology of regionalism. This often helps the already dominant castes.

4. Apart from the ideology of regionalism, region can provide yet another advantage to the dominant castes. Each seeks to legitimize its dominant position on the basis of some ideological argument. Region, as the social unit having a common cultural-linguistic context, forms the basis from which justification of domination can be adduced. Alternatively, arguments by the dominant caste make sense within the region. Thus, Jat claims of being kisans or Haryana Jat claims to a martial tradition appeal to the people in those respective regions rather than to outsiders. Similarly, Lingayat claims to reformism in orthodox Brahmanical Hinduism become relevant only in the Kannada-speaking region. The ideology of 'Maharashtra Dharma' justifying the Brahman-Maratha leadership, and the Bhadralok ideology of elite domination also have similar region-specific appeals. Thus the region is the unit at which caste domination is legitimated. In the 'dominant caste thesis', the emphasis on numerical strength has deflected attention from both the contents of domination and the ways of attaining domination. Mere numerical strength would not lead to domination; claims of 'high' status usually accompany numerical strength. But a high ritual status is not the only ideological component. 'Dominant' castes employ a more complex set of ideological arguments in order to win their position, and we argue that the region provides a helpful arena for working out these arguments.

It follows that any counter-hegemonic assaults on the dominant caste would emanate from a similarly regionally-situated argument. In Tamil Nadu, the non-Brahman movement sought to delegitimize Brahmans by suggesting that they are not true Dravids. In Maharashtra, too, Phule's argument turns to this point when he argues that Brahmans—Aryabhats—came from outside (Iran). But more forcefully, Phule brings in the imagery of non-Brahmans as 'natives' by virtue of their association with agricultural activity. Both the claims of domination and the challenges to them are regionally situated.

Given the mutually-reinforcing relationship of caste and region in contemporary Indian politics, it is argued here that challenges to concrete instances of caste domination (as distinct from notions of caste superiority) can meaningfully rise at the regional level. This would further strengthen the links between caste and region. These links produce region-specific configurations of caste which fit the region's political economy. In the light of this argument certain trends may be noticed. These indicate the possible ways in which caste is likely to be constructed in Indian politics. In a way the following discussion engages caste itself as a 'region' or sphere.

In his introduction to *Caste in Indian Politics*, Rajni Kothari long ago pointed out the process of caste polarization (Kothari 1970: 14). He said, 'as one polarization is resolved in favour of one caste or caste category, new polarizations emerge . . .' (ibid.: 24). In many parts of the country, instead of neat polarization, 'more complicated and fragmented constellations of power' emerge (ibid.). Thus, on the one hand new 'dominant castes' have emerged on the scene; at least many new 'ascendant' castes have come to the forefront (kshatriyas in Gujarat, Khandayat in Orissa, etc.). On the other hand new equations have emerged. The most noted one is the BJP-led equation of upper castes and OBCs in Uttar Pradesh. In Maharashtra, the Charmakars and Matangs have been veering away from the Congress and RPI, preferring the Shiv Sena and BJP. The Bahujan Mahasangh in Maharashtra has been trying to forge an alliance of Dalits and OBCs. These new equations do not necessarily follow a similar pattern across the states, but a common factor is that in the emerging alliances traditional boundaries of ritual status are seldom followed. Alliances would be formed depending upon the perceptions about which caste or caste group monopolizes resources (including reservations). Besides, the choice of allies is often ad hoc, contingent upon who are perceived as adversaries. Underneath this contingent nature of alliances, there seems to be a consideration of two factors. One consideration is of material factors. Caste groups tend to ally when their material interests do not clash—or when they in fact complement—each other. The other consideration is share in power. When an alliance is likely to obtain some power for the caste (its elites), such an alliance becomes acceptable. Both these considerations go beyond simple alliances based on ritual status—alliances are not made simply because castes occupy a common status as shudras or Dalits.

Second, and partly following from the above, there is a disintegration of caste 'blocs' of Dalits and OBCs. We have discussed this point above. Not only do such blocs not materialize at an all-India level, they seem to be disintegrating even at the level of states. The trend seems to be moving in the direction of 'ethnicization' of caste (Fuller 1997: 12-27). One factor contributing to this process seems to be the pressure of modern reformist discourse delegitimizing the vertical structure of the caste hierarchy. In this background, caste survives, if not as upper-lower then, as 'different' groups having different cultures, rituals, 'histories', etc. Thus, caste becomes 'community' (ibid: 13-14). But the ethnicization of caste has other causes as well. One is that small castes still find no place in calculations for electoral purposes. They may be relevant in constructing caste 'blocs', but do not receive the benefits either politically or materially. In such a situation, organizing a single caste as one community becomes useful for gaining access to power and resources. It is not necessary for us to accept this logic, but that seems to be a factor influencing the process of the formation of single-caste organizations. Such organizations function simultaneously as socio-cultural associations, pressure groups pursuing immediate material concerns of the caste, and vehicles for caste elites to ride into the power structure (Palshikar 2000: 241-4). Although it is tempting to look at such caste organizations as a political resource, they imply localization. Such localized ethnicization is bound to entrap castes into local boundaries and the issues of culture, identity, and history rather than those of material advance and structures of domination.

Third, after reaching a high point through 'Mandalization', caste appears to be reaching a dead end in terms of its mobilizational potential. At one stage (in the 1950s), caste interests were advanced through regional mobilization. In the next phase (from the late 1970s), mobilization took place on the issues of reservations for OBCs (in Bihar and Gujarat) followed up by the Mandal issues and claims of the leaders of OBCs for power sharing. The 1990s have witnessed the acceptance of OBC reservations as state policy. During the same period, various parties incorporated OBCs, resulting in the changed composition of representatives. These developments have meant that the space to be occupied by the caste issue is bound to shrink except for further competition among OBCs for greater shares in power. At the local level, the provision enabling reservations for SCs, STs and OBCs in local government bodies has ensured that no effective mobilization can take place, and no party will take interest in such mobilization. This does not imply that caste has lost relevance, but that as an organizing principle of politics, caste may have reached its limits. Like region earlier, caste may have to search for catalysts that will revitalize the emotive and mobilization capacity of caste as a sphere of politics. In other words, the capacity of caste to construct new social forces and make politics revolve around them has become rather suspect.

This obviously raises doubts about the democratizing potential of caste as a sphere. The caste-region nexus meant that just as the domination of a caste or caste group would get established, it would be challenged by rival groups or by newly emerging lower sections. However, if our assessment that caste alliances are ad hoc and less mobilizational is correct, then the arena of caste politics is likely to lose the potential to democratize the Indian polity. Further, throughout the 1990s, the emphasis seemed to be on the 'presence' (of Dalits, OBCs, etc.) in positions of power. The twin thrust of controlling state power and diverting it to an agenda favouring the 'Dalit-Bahujans' was lost in the 1990s. Also, the need to construct a party as an instrument of Dalit-Bahujan interests was not felt because of the emphasis on 'presence'. These developments have deprived the arena of caste politics of democratizing possibilities. These issues obviously go much beyond the question of the caste-region nexus, but point towards the challenges faced by that core sphere of Indian politics, the politics of caste.

REFERENCES

Assadi, Muzaffar and S. Rajendran. 2000. 'Karnataka: Changing Shape of Caste Conflicts', *Economic and Political Weekly*, Vol. 35, No. 19, 6-12 May, pp. 1610-12.

Balgopal, K. 2000. 'A Tangled Web: Subdivision of SC Reservations in AP', *Economic and Political Weekly*, Vol. 35, No. 13, 25-31 March, pp. 1075-81.

Bandyopadhyay, Shekhar, Abhijit Dasgupta and Willem van Schendal, eds., 1954. *Bengal: Communities Development and States*. New Delhi: Manohar.

Barnett, Stephen. 1976. 'Approaches to Changes in Caste Ideology in South India', in B. Stein, ed., 1976, pp. 149-80.

Beteille, Andre. 1992. *Society and Politics in India.* New Delhi: Oxford University Press.

Byres, Terrence. 1988. 'Charan Singh (1902-1987): An Assessment', *Journal of Peasant Studies*, 15: 139-89.

Elliott, Carolyn M. 1970. 'Caste and Faction among the Dominant Caste: The Reddis and Kammas of Andhra', in R. Kothari, ed., 1970, pp. 129-71.

Frankel, Francine R. 1989. 'Caste, Land and Dominance in Bihar: Breakdown of the Brahmanical Social Order', in F. Frankel and M. S. A. Rao, eds., 1989, pp. 46-132.

Frankel, Francine R. and M. S. A. Rao, eds. 1989. *Dominance and State Power in Modern India*, Vol. I, New Delhi: Oxford University Press.

———. 1990. *Dominance and State Power in Modern India*, Vol. II, New Delhi: Oxford University Press.

Fuller, C. J., ed. 1997. *Caste Today*. Delhi: Oxford India Paperbacks.

Gupta, Dipankar. 1997. *Rivalry and Brotherhood.* New Delhi: Oxford University Press.

Hardgrave, Robert L., Jr. 1965. *The Dravidian Movement.* Bombay: Popular.

———. 1969. *The Nadars of Tamilnadu.* Berkeley: University of California Press.

———. 1970. 'Political Participation and Primordial Solidarity: The Nadars of Tamil Nadu', in R. Kothari, ed., 1970, pp. 102-28.

Hasan, Zoya. 1998. *Quest for Power: Oppositional Movements and Post-Congress Politics in Uttar Pradesh.* New Delhi: Oxford University Press.

Jenkins, Rob. 1994. 'Where the BJP Survived: Rajasthan Assembly Election, 1993', *Economic and Political Weekly*, Vol. 29, No. 11, 12 March, pp. 635-41.

Kothari, Rajni, ed. 1970. *Caste in Indian Politics*. New Delhi: Orient Longman.

——— and Rushikesh Maru. 1970. 'Federating for Political Interests: The Kshatriyas of Gujarat', in R. Kothari, ed., 1970, pp. 70-101.

Lele, Jayant K. and Rajendra Vora, eds. 1990. *State and Society in India.* Delhi: Chanakya.

Lodha, Sanjay. 1999. 'Elections 1999: Rajasthan—Caste and Two Party System', *Economic and Political Weekly*, Vol. 34, No. 48, 27 November, pp. 3344-8.

Louis, Prakash. 2000. 'Fractured Mandate for Social Change in Bihar', *Economic and Political Weekly*, Vol. 35, No. 12, 18-24 March, pp. 978-82.

Manor, James. 1989. 'Karnataka: Caste, Class, Dominance and Politics in a Cohesive Society', in F. Frankel and M. S. A. Rao, eds., 1989, pp. 322-61.

Mehra, Ajay K., D. D. Khanna and Gert W. Kueck, eds. 2003. *Political Parties and Party Systems*. New Delhi: Sage.

Mencher, Joan P. and K. Raman Unni. 1976. 'Anthropological and Sociological Research in Kerala: Past, Present and Future Directions', in B. Stein, ed., 1976, pp. 121-48.

Mohanty, Manoranjan. 1990. 'Class, Caste and Dominance in a Backward State: Orissa', in F. Frankel and M. S. A. Rao, eds., 1990, pp. 321-66.

Natraj, V. K. 1990. 'Backward Classes and Minorities in Karnataka Politics', in R. Roy and R. Sisson, eds., 1990, pp. 170-88.

Nayar, Baldev Raj. 1966. *Minority Politics in the Punjab*. Princeton: Princeton University Press.

Nigam, Aditya. 1996. 'India after the 1996 Elections: Nation, Locality and Representation', *Asian Survey*, Vol. 36, No. 12, September, pp. 1157-69.

Omvedt, Gail. 1976. *Cultural Revolt in a Colonial Society*. Bombay: Scientific Socialist Education Trust.

Palshikar, Suhas. 2000. *Politics of Marginalized Groups* (report submitted to UGC). Pune: Department of Politics and Public Administration, University of Pune.

———. 2003. 'Regional Parties and Democracy: Romantic Rendezvous or Localized Legitimation?', in Mehra et al., eds., pp. 306-35.

Pocock, D. 1972. *Kanbi and Patidar*. London: Oxford University Press.

Pradeep Kumar. 2000. *The Uttarkhand Movement: Construction of a Regional Identity*. New Delhi: Kanishka

———. 2001. 'Reservations within Reservations: The Real Dalit Bahujans', *Economic and Political Weekly*, Vol. 36, No. 37, 15-21 September, pp. 3505-7.

Pradhan, M. C. 1966. *Political Systems of the Jats of Northern India*. London: Oxford University Press.

Rangrajan, Mahesh. 1999. 'One, Two, Many Indias', *Seminar*, No. 480, August, pp. 26-9.

Roy, Ramashray and Richard Sisson, eds. 1990. *Diversity and Dominance in Indian Politics*. Vol. 2, New Delhi: Sage.

S. G. 1999. 'UP: Rise of Small Parties', *Economic and Political Weekly*, Vol. 34, No. 41, 8-15 October, pp. 2912-13.

Schwartzberg, Joseph E. 1968. 'Caste Regions of the North Indian Plain', in M. Singer and B. S. Cohn, eds., 1968, pp. 81-114.

Singer, Milton and Bernard S. Cohn, eds., 1968. *Structure and Change in Indian Society*. Chicago: Aldine Publishing Co.

Shah, Ghanshyam. 1990. 'Caste Sentiments, Class Formation and Dominance in Gujarat', in F. Frankel and M. S. A. Rao, eds., 1990, pp. 59-114.

Srinivas, M. N. 1962. *Caste in Modern India and Other Essays*. Bombay: Asia Publishing House.

———. 1987. *The Dominant Caste and Other Essays*. New Delhi: Oxford University Press.

Stein, Burton, ed. 1976. *Essays on South India*. New Delhi: Vikas.

Thite, Dinesh. 1996. 'A Study of Maharashtra Legislature: 1978-1995. Relationship between Caste and Power' (Marathi). M.Phil. Dissertation, Department of Politics and Public Administration, University of Pune (unpublished).

Vora, Rajendra. 1999. 'Maharashtra Dharma and Nationalist Movement in Maharashtra', in N. K. Wagle, ed., 1999, pp. 23-30.

Vora, Rajendra and Suhas Palshikar. 1990. 'Neo-Hinduism: A Case of Distorted Consciousness', in J. K. Lele and R. Vora, eds., 1990, pp. 213-43.

Wagle, N. K., ed. 1999. *Writers, Editors and Reformers: Social and Political Transformations of Maharashtra, 1830-1930*. New Delhi: Manohar.

Washbrook, D. A. 1989. 'Caste, Class and Dominance in Modern Tamil Nadu: Non-Brahminism, Dravidianism and Tamil Nationalism', in F. Frankel and M. S. A. Rao, eds., 1989, pp. 204-64.

12

Regions and Communities: Social Identities in Contemporary Punjab

Surinder S. Jodhka

After occupying the front pages of Indian newspapers for more than a decade, the movement for Khalistan, a separate homeland for the Sikhs, ended rather suddenly in the early 1990s. While it was never a popular movement, in the sense that a large majority of the Sikhs living in the Indian Punjab and outside did not directly participate in it, or openly endorse the idea of a separate Sikh nation, it affected almost every Sikh, wherever s/he lived. The prolonged violence and the presence of security forces in the state with extra-constitutional powers disrupted everyday life. The violent action in 1984 of the Indian armed forces on the most revered shrine of the Sikhs, the Golden Temple in Amritsar, to flush out Sikh militants, emotionally disturbed almost every Sikh. A large number of Sikhs were also killed and their properties looted during the riots in Delhi and other towns of north India that followed the assassination of Indira Gandhi supposedly in revenge for the attack on the Golden Temple.[1]

Another important consequence of the political disturbances of the 1980s was that they transformed the popular image of the Sikh community and of the territorial identity of the Indian Punjab. The political crisis, lasting for nearly fifteen years, affected, quite fundamentally, the status of Punjab in the Indian union. This had far-reaching implications for the state economy. From a region known for its vibrant and prosperous agriculture, the Punjab began to be seen increasingly as a 'troubled region'. Over the years, Punjab experienced a process of marginalization in the Indian federal economy (Jodhka 2001a).

The Sikhs had been a proud people: some used to even insist that they needed to be treated 'differently' by the nation because they had sacrificed and suffered more than 'others' for India's Independence from colonial rule. Apart from being in the forefront of the struggle for Independence and the sacrifices made directly by the people of Punjab, a large number of Sikhs also had to migrate across the newly drawn international border, leaving behind virtually everything they possessed, when the subcontinent was partitioned into India and Pakistan (1947), an experience they shared in common only with the people of Bengal.

Sikhs had also done quite well economically after Independence, which added to their self-pride. It was not only to the new agricultural technology that the success of Green Revolution in the 1960s was attributed. Credit was also given to the hard-working farmers of the Punjab. The success of the Green Revolution in the region solved one of the most vexing problems of newly independent India: the scarcity of food grains.

Another important implication of the crisis of the 1980s was, as the sub-text of the above paragraphs tends to suggest, a total identification of the region, the Indian Punjab, with the Sikhs. The Indian Punjab today has come to be seen, within the state of Punjab and outside, as a land of Sikhs. There is obviously some amount of justification for such an image. It was a section of the Sikhs who, under the leadership of the Akalis, launched the movement for a separate Punjabi-speaking state. Though the Akalis articulated their demand in terms of the general principle of cultural autonomy for the region based on language, there were some amongst them who had explicit communal or communitarian objectives (Nayar 1966).

A cursory look at the demographic history of Punjab, however, suggests something very different (Table 1). It was only relatively

TABLE 1: APPROXIMATE POPULATION OF DIFFERENT RELIGIOUS COMMUNITIES OF PUNJAB*

Year	Sikh Population (%)	Hindu Population (%)	Muslim Population (%)
1931	13	35	51
1951	36	61	01
1971	60	38	01

*These figures ought to be seen along with the geographical shrinkage of the region as discussed in the text below (for details of census figures see Brass 1974: 295-300).

recently, after its re-organization in 1966, that the Sikhs became a majority in the state. In pre-Independence united Punjab, the Sikhs, in pure demographic terms, constituted a small minority of the total population of Punjab. Geographically too Punjab has shrunk considerably. Further, there are many more people in India and in the subcontinent who speak Punjabi language and possess traits of Punjabi culture. Why has the Indian Punjab then come to be identified with the Sikhs?

The primary objective of this paper is to seek an answer to this puzzle. I will attempt to argue that for a historical and cultural notion of territory, one needs to look at regions in relation to 'communities'. The territoriality of a given region becomes meaningful only when it is claimed by a 'community'. While it is possible that in many instances such communities are themselves constituted by territoriality of the region or its linguistic distinctiveness, factors like religion, caste, and even class play important roles in the manner in which the politics of regional identity works. Thus, when seen in relation to the identity politics of communities, the territorial identity of regions could also be considerably fluid.

Though I primarily focus on the contemporary Indian Punjab, I also hope to show that this case could inspire new thinking about regions and the federal politics of contemporary India.

The Region and its Communities: Historical Background

Although the Punjab has had a distinct geographical and political identity for a long time, its boundaries have been quite fluid, physically as well as culturally. The total land area of the present-day Indian Punjab is only about 15 per cent of pre-Partition Punjab. Moreover, the boundaries of Indian Punjab were redrawn three times after the Partition.

Historically also scholars have found it difficult to precisely locate or demarcate the region. Commenting on the seventeenth-century history of the region, Chetan Singh, for example, writes that

> . . . though we have the word, viz. Punjab, with a specific meaning, the search for a corresponding historical reality . . . is likely to be disappointing if it envisages the existence of a Punjab with a well demarcated identity, elucidated in the works of generations of historians and firmly established by the passage of time. . . . The depiction of territorial boundaries of Punjab

has varied from time to time and from historian to historian (Singh 1991: 12).

Not only were the territorial boundaries of Punjab imprecise, its communities and their identities too were considerably fluid. As mentioned above, the Punjab had three important religious communities, Muslims, Hindus and Sikhs, and the province, unlike most other parts of the subcontinent, was also characterized by three separate but interconnected social systems. As Kenneth Jones points out (1968), the cultural values and, to some extent, the nature of social institutions varied from community to community.

However, it may be important to add here that while these categories as markers of religious distinctions and self-consciousness did exist, their identities and notions of difference were obviously very different from the way we understand them today. Moreover, the question of religious identity was perhaps of less significance to people in their everyday life than it appears to have become later. Much of the social life of individuals and groups was lived within the village, where the local social structure guided their everyday life.

Followers of the Muslim faith were the largest in the region. However, there were some regional variations in their concentration. They were concentrated more in the western districts of Punjab than the eastern parts. Most of them were agriculturalists. They owned much of the agricultural land in the western part of Punjab. Even in the eastern districts, Muslims were mostly landowners. They owned around one-fifth to one-fourth of the agricultural land in the eastern parts of the province (Talbot 1988: 18-20).

The social structure of Muslim society in Punjab was organized largely around kinship and tribal affiliations, but tribal political organization was stronger in the north-western areas of the province. Within these large tribal groupings, there were further divisions into clans consisting of endogamous kinship groups, the *biradaris*. These groups were not confined to the boundaries of a village, but spread throughout a district or a sub-region. The *biradari* panchayats supported their members during times of crisis and strictly regulated marriage alliances (Talbot 1988: 20). These panchayats also intervened whenever conflicts arose among their members, or of their members with the outside world.

Though almost every village of Punjab had a mosque of the orthodox Islamic nature, Sufism and Sufi *pirs* were also very popular in the region. Muslims were not the only ones who visited the Sufi *pirs*. The Sufi *dargahs* (places of worship where Sufi *pirs* lived or where their tombs are built) were popular with almost every community. The influence of Sufism on the region could be judged from the fact that the poetry of Sheikh Farid, one of the leading Sufi poets of Punjab, has found a place in the Sikh holy book, the *Guru Granth*. Even today in India people of different faiths visit the *dargahs* of Sufi *pirs*. Due to their charismatic qualities, the Sufi *pirs* commanded considerable influence in their own localities. The local rulers also patronized Sufi *dargahs* and gave them land grants. Over the years, some of them acquired large holdings and emerged as influential centres of power.

The other two communities of the region were the Hindus and the Sikhs. While the two communities had a rather obvious sense of difference in relation to the Muslims, distinctions among them were not so clearly marked. They together constituted a little less than half the population of Punjab. When the British made a census during the late nineteenth century, those recorded as Hindus were much larger in number than the Sikhs. The proportion of Hindus in Punjab in the late nineteenth century was a little more than one-third of the total population of Punjab. The Sikh population varied between 11 and 14 per cent.

Though a section of the Punjabi Hindus were affluent as money-lenders and traders, politically they had been a rather 'weak' community in the province, with leadership mostly coming from the Rajput princes. However, after the Mughal conquest the Rajput princes lost their position within their own community as well. From then on, the merchant castes of Khatris, Aroras, and Banias became the prominent Hindu castes of the region (Talbot 1988: 26).

Unlike in some other parts of the subcontinent, Hindus in Punjab did not have a strong and influential religious elite. The brahmans in Punjab were, in fact, an insignificant caste. Writing on social life in the late colonial period, Prakash Tandon, a Hindu Khatri, comments that the brahmans lived a 'frugal life' and it was rare to find an affluent brahman in the region (Tandon 1961:77). Most brahmans in his native village were treated as members of the menial castes. Like other menials, they too were mostly dependent upon the food they collected from their *jajmans*. Giving a vivid description of their social status, he writes:

> With us brahmins were an underprivileged class and exercised little or no influence on the community. Perhaps Muslims had so discouraged temples and external worship that the brahmins had no place left from where to exercise their authority. Our brahmins did not as a rule even have the role of teachers, because until the British opened regular schools teaching was done by Muslim mullahs in the mosques or by Sikh granthis . . . in the gurudwaras. Our brahmins were rarely erudite; in fact many of them were barely literate, possessing only a perfunctory knowledge of rituals and knowing just the necessary mantras by heart. (Tandon 1961: 76)

Despite being the smallest of the three major communities of Punjab, the Sikh religion, since its emergence in the fifteenth and sixteenth centuries, was an important factor in the social and political life of Punjab. Unlike Islam and Hinduism, Sikhism was the religion of Punjab. It grew and prospered here, while the Hindus did not have any major religious centre in the region.

The teaching of the Sikh gurus had a wide appeal in the region. Keshadhari Sikhs (those who kept unshorn hair) were not the only ones who believed in the doctrine of Sikhism. A large proportion of the Hindus in Punjab and Sindh also revered the Sikh gurus. Nanak, the first of them, and the other nine gurus were themselves from Hindu Khatri families. Though the teaching of Sikhism questioned many of the fundamental premises of the traditional Hindu faith, it was only later, during the late nineteenth and early twentieth centuries, that the boundaries between the two religious communities began to be clearly marked.

Apart from its ideological appeal, Sikhism had also been a religion of the rulers of Punjab. After the local Rajput rulers had lost power to the Mughals, the Sikhs gradually emerged as political leaders of the region, culminating eventually in the establishment of a Sikh kingdom under the leadership of Maharaja Ranjit Singh.

Given the diverse composition of his populace, Ranjit Singh's politics gave due representation to the members of Muslim and Hindu communities. However, his reign clearly had a religious flavour. Not only did he wear the external symbols of a Keshadhari Sikh, he also used Sikh ideology to legitimize his rule. He claimed that his kingdom represented the rule of the Khalsa and gave lavish donations to Sikh gurdwaras. It was he who decorated the famous Sikh shrine Darbar Sahib with gold and transformed it into, as it later came to be known, the Golden Temple (Deol 2000: 65). More important for the Sikh community has perhaps been the symbolic value of his rule during the later struggles for a separate identity and territorial autonomy. As Brass rightly emphasizes, 'The history of the growth and consolidation of Sikh power in the Punjab under Maharaja Ranjit Singh has provided Sikh leaders in modern times with a vast pool of symbols to draw upon to feed the modern sense of Sikh identity' (Brass 1974: 278).

British Colonial Rule in Punjab and Communities of the Region

The collapse of Sikh political power and the ascendance of British colonial rule in 1849 had far-reaching implications for the communities of the region. Perhaps the most important factor that affected the different communities was the gradual rise of new social classes amongst the three communities. The active role that the middle classes played in initiating social reform movements not only helped them consolidate their positions as new leaders of their communities but in many ways transformed the political consciousness of these communities. Given the focus of this paper, I shall confine my discussion to the reform movements among the Hindus and the Sikhs. The development of a separate Muslim consciousness in Punjab coincided with the nationalist politics and the emergence of the 'two-nation' theory, a subject too broad for this paper to deal with.

After making it a part of the colonial empire, the British introduced substantial changes in the administrative and legal system, as well as in the economy of the Punjab. This generated a much-enlarged structure of employment opportunities and economic mobility. During the initial years of their rule the British brought to the Punjab educated Bengalis from Calcutta to work in the subordinate bureaucratic positions in the province.

However, it did not take very long for an indigenous breed of *babus* to emerge. The urban Khatris and Aroras of the Punjab had all along worked for their rulers. They took to the new challenge rather easily and soon indigenous middle classes emerged in the region.

By the 1870s, the first generation of English-educated Punjabis had begun to participate in colonial rule. By the 1880s, they accounted for 80 per cent of the upper-level appointments (Banga 1989: 203). Though initially a large majority of these new *babus* were urban Hindus, a new middle class also emerged among the Sikhs and the Muslims around the same time.

When compared with the Western experience, the political and ideological implications of the rise of such a middle class in the region seem to have been very different. As is well known, it was the newly emerging middle classes in the West who initiated the process of secularization and propagated the doctrine of individualism. The rise of middle classes in the colonial context, particularly in Punjab, however, generated a different social dynamic. It was amongst these middle classes that communitarian consciousness became sharpest. They played a key role in articulating community identities in the region from the beginning, as Indu Banga (1989: 202) points out:

> Although a pan-Indian phenomenon, communitarian consciousness acquired a peculiar complexity in Punjab because each of its three religious 'communities', was important in its own way: Muslims constituted the majority, with 55 per cent of the population of the Punjab; at annexation, the Sikhs formed only about 12 per cent of the population, but they accounted for more than half of the 'aristocracy' in the province; and although less than 40 per cent in Punjab, the Hindus were a majority in the country.

The colonial administrative structure also deployed new categories of social aggregation and classification. The British thought of their populace in terms of religious communities and looked at them accordingly in the process of governance. They 'encouraged the members of each community to present their case in communitarian terms' (Grewal 1989). The role that census enumeration played in converting the fuzzy boundaries into well-defined communities was perhaps most obvious in Punjab. As Fox points out, these administrative discourses had far-reaching influences on the process of identity formation in the region (Fox 1985). The British, moreover, attributed to the religious communities certain racial qualities. The Sikhs, for example, were declared a 'martial community', and were given preference in recruitment to the colonial army.

ARYA SAMAJ AND HINDU CONSCIOUSNESS IN PUNJAB

Scholars of modern Sikh history and Punjab have done much work on the emergence of a separate Sikh identity in Punjab during the late nineteenth and early twentieth century (discussed below).[2] However, scholarly work on the rise of communal consciousness among the Hindus of Punjab has been comparatively less. One of the core arguments of this paper is that an understanding of the politics of Hindus in the region is as important as it is to understand the rise of a separate identity among the Sikhs. Such an understanding would be of great help in finding the answer to the question, why has the Indian Punjab come to be identified with the Sikh community?

As mentioned above, the Hindus had been a 'weak community' in Punjab. While the Sikhs, and before them the Mughals, had been rulers, leading groups of Hindus had only been traders or 'servants' of the local rulers. As Talbot writes, 'despite their economic strength, the Punjab Hindus always felt insecure. They had to be inconspicuous in order to survive in some of the frontier districts of Punjab, and often suffered high-handed treatment from the tribesmen' (Talbot 1988: 29).

The establishment of colonial rule further marginalized them in the provincial power structure. Given that the British rulers recruited a large proportion of their army from the Sikh and Muslim peasantry, colonial policies in Punjab were mostly designed to favour them. The Land Alienation Act of 1901, for example, was passed to appease the landed interests in the region and it directly harmed the interests of money-lending urban Hindus. The Act prohibited the transfer of agricultural land to the 'non-agriculturalist castes', mostly Hindu.

The growing activities of Christian missionaries and their increasing appeal, particularly among the low-caste Hindus, is widely viewed as the flash point that led to the rise of reformist movements among the Hindus of Punjab (Kapur 1986; Juergensmeyer 1988). The Arya Samaj spearheaded the Hindu religious revival in the region.

The Arya Samaj was founded by a Hindu brahman, Swami Dayanand Saraswati, in 1875 at Rajkot in Gujarat. Swami Dayanand Saraswati was a radical reformist. He pleaded for the promotion, purification and revival of Hinduism. Denouncing caste, idol-worship, and child marriage, and promoting of widow remarriage were, according to him, crucial. He laid emphasis on 'modernizing Hindu religious practices' by reviving the classical Vedic traditions and by giving up the rigidities of brahmanical rituals.

While Dayanand Saraswati did not find much of an audience in western India, where the brahman orthodoxy was well entrenched, his ideas found an eager audience among educated Punjabi Hindus. Brahmanical orthodoxy had always been quite weak in Punjab. Further, the urban Hindu elite would have also seen in the Arya Samaj a religious philosophy that was compatible with the egalitarian ideals of Sikhism and Islam. As mentioned above, the upper-caste Hindus were among the first to take to Western education and join the colonial bureaucracy, but felt a little uncomfortable with their religious resources. As Kapur writes (1986: 21): 'Their education had opened new opportunities for them, enhanced their social prestige within their own community . . . yet exposure to English interpretations of their society, their religion and their history undermined their ability to identify with their own traditions with dignity.' The Arya Samaj, thus, was seen as having the potential of filling in the gap and resolving their crisis of identity.

The Arya Samaj grew rapidly in Punjab during the last two decades of the nineteenth century, and its growing popularity gave a new confidence to Hindu Punjabis. They opened schools and encouraged the 'untouchable' castes to get educated. Initially an inward-looking reform movement, it gradually began also to attack other religions. Its initial target were Christian missionaries who had converted some of the 'untouchables' into their fold. However, as the Arya Samaj movement grew in popularity, its leaders also began to criticise Islam and the Sikh gurus. Using the traditional concept of ritual purification (*shuddhi*), they initiated a programme of bringing back into the Hindu fold those among the low castes who had begun to call themselves Sikh. This obviously provoked the Sikh leadership and began to widen the gulf between the Hindus and Sikhs, and proved to be a turning point in the history of communal relations and the process of identity formation in the region. Some of the Sikhs, who until then had worked along with the Arya Samajis, began to distance themselves from the movement.

Perhaps the most critical aspect of the Arya Samaj movement in Punjab was its construction of a Hindu identity in a pan-Indian nationalist mode. The promotion of such an identity required of the Punjabi Hindus a complete commitment to the Hindi language, seen as critical in building a new nationalist culture/consciousness, on the one hand, while on the other hand, distancing themselves from or even opposing any movement for the promotion of regional culture and regional identity, which included the Punjabi language.[3] From this point onwards, the dominant trend among the Punjabi Hindus had to be a singular identification with the Indian nation. The Indian nation, in such a consciousness, was itself constituted by Hindi and Hindu culture and identity.

The Sikh Reformers and Separate Identity

As mentioned above, during the initial years many urban Sikhs participated in the activities of the Arya Samaj with some degree of enthusiasm. However, as the Arya Samaj began to emphasize reviving Vedic Hindu traditions, which also included attacking and rejecting all the later religious movements, including Sikhism, Sikh reformers began to feel uncomfortable with its activities. The Hindu reformers in Punjab had always insisted that Sikhism was not a separate religion and that the Sikhs were a part of the Hindu society.

Thus, unlike the Hindu reformers, the Sikh reformers were, right from the beginning, oriented towards the 'external'. They reacted sharply to the claims of the Hindu reformers. Perhaps the most important statement asserting the distinctiveness of their faith was the publication of the famous booklet *Hum Hindu Nahin Hain* (We Are not Hindus) by Bhai Kahan Singh during the closing years of the nineteenth century. He argued in this booklet that Sikhism had always been a distinct faith. As the title suggests, the book addressed the Arya Samajis and other Hindu reformers who had been claiming that Sikhism was a mere 'sect' of Hinduism. The booklet, in fact, was published first in Hindi and only later in Punjabi. The Sikh reformers under the leadership of the Singh Sabhas also initiated various other activities, including the setting up of educational institutions. As a historian of the region puts it:

> The Singh reformers sought to redefine the Sikh faith and gave primacy to

Singh or Khalsa identity. They advocated the adoption of Sikhs' rites of passage, revived the doctrine of *Guru Panth*, took active interest in Sikh education, popularized their own understanding of Sikh religious literature, showed great concern for Punjabi in the Gurumukhi script, sought to underline the importance of the Sikh past, and evinced interest in numbers. (Grewal 1989: 197)

Harjot Oberoi, another historian, goes to the extent of saying that through these mobilizations, the new Sikh elite re-wrote the social grammar of Sikhism. It was an episteme shift—from an open and pluralistic *Sanatana* episteme to the homogenizing episteme of modern Sikhism:

> By founding a string of publishing houses, cultural bodies, schools, colleges, orphanages and clubs, the Tat Khalsa endeavoured to insert definition of religion and community into the day to day life of Sikhs. Through this process it became possible not only for a mass of people to experience themselves as Sikhs in the fashion desired by the Tat Khalsa, but also for non-Sikhs to visualise Sikhs as a distinct group. (Oberoi 1994: 416)

It is difficult to agree with Oberoi's thesis entirely, as he tends to give too much significance to a few individuals who, he thinks, could manipulate the minds of the community (Jodhka 1997; Deol 2000). However, this is not to undermine the fact that the late nineteenth century was indeed the beginning of a new trend in the life of all communities of the region and their self-identities.

By the second decade of the twentieth century, the Singh Sabha reformers had mobilized Sikhs to such an extent that they could launch a popular movement for the liberation of gurudwaras from the *mahants*. The *mahants,* who had become professional managers of many of the historic Sikh gurdwaras, had come to be popularly seen by the Sikh masses as corrupt and as practising brahmanical rites in the Sikh shrines.

Unlike the Singh Sabhas, which represented the urban and elite Sikhs, the 1920s movement for the liberation of gurdwaras was a popular movement and invoked participation of the masses. It was during this movement that the Shiromani Gurdwara Prabandhak Committee (SGPC) and the Akali Dal, the two most important Sikh religio-political institutions, came into existence. Further, it was during this movement that the Sikhs turned against the colonial rulers.

Though the Akali movement of the 1920s and the manner in which the colonial rulers dealt with it brought the Sikhs closer to the Indian nationalist movement, it also helped in consolidating their identity. The movement eventually succeeded in achieving its objectives. After a long drawn struggle, the colonial government conceded the Sikh demand. Under the newly enacted Gurdwara Act of 1925, the SGPC was recognized as a representative body of the Sikhs and was given control over the major historic gurdwaras. The SGPC was perhaps the first institution of its kind in the subcontinent with a democratic structure of its own based on universal adult franchise. All adult Sikhs were eligible to participate in its activity with a system of electing representatives (see Jodhka 2001b). This movement gave the community two very important institutions that had a very explicit political orientation and popular appeal and have since remained so.

However, despite the growing self-awareness of identity, there still was hardly any talk about territorial autonomy for the Sikhs until 1930. It was only when Partition began to be talked about as a possibility that the Sikh leadership began to wonder about the fate of their community, which was spread all over the province without a specific area of concentration. Although the Sikhs had always been small in numbers, they had never been a marginalized people. Not only had they been the rulers in pre-colonial Punjab, the colonial government also gave Sikhs a special status by including them amongst the martial communities and recruiting them into the army in big numbers. The Sikh aristocracy had also been duly accommodated in the new power structure.

Partition and institutionalization of modern nation states in the region, however, completely transformed political geography. The Sikhs had been against Partition, but could not remain aloof from its consequences. Not only were they comparatively small in number, the Sikhs were also dispersed almost all over Punjab. Given that the Partition was to be on a communal basis, a section of the Sikh political elite began to worry about the territorial rights of their community. However, they were not given any concrete choice in this regard, either by the British or by the new elite who were to acquire power from the colonial rulers. Their fate had virtually been tied with India. When communal violence broke out, almost all of them had to abandon their homes in western Punjab and move across to the Indian side of the partitioned Punjab. A large number of people were killed while crossing the border.

Post-Partition Indian Punjab was less than half of the colonial Punjab. The balance of communities too had changed. Muslims, who were the majority community in pre-colonial united Punjab, had been reduced to a small minority of less than 2 per cent in the Indian Punjab. Though numerically the Hindus benefited the most, the Sikhs too gained. The demographic advantage for the Sikhs was, in a way, more than that for the Hindus. For the first time in history Sikhs were numerically in the majority in some districts of Punjab.

The introduction of a democratic system of governance and adult franchise made demographic numbers much more critical than they had been before. While independent India was to be governed by secular principles and individuals were to be the bearers of rights, 'communities' of different kinds continued to be important agents in the new regime. Democratization required a certain degree of federalism and regional autonomy. The linguistic reorganization of the provinces was to take care of some of the cultural differences and political aspirations of regional communities.

Thus Independence and the introduction of a democratic system offered a set of opportunities to various cultural regions and communities. Linguistic reorganization became a way of accommodating the regional elite in the emerging power structure of the new nation-state. It is against this background that the Sikh leadership began to visualize the possibility of a province where they could feel a sense of autonomy.

Punjab as a Sikh Region

Starting with the social reform movements during the late nineteenth century, differences between the three major communities of the region had already become quite sharp. This process of boundary construction obviously required that communities represented themselves as culturally distinct from one another. Much before the republic accepted language as a legitimate source of cultural identity, the three communities of the region had already chosen to identify with three different languages, Urdu, Hindi, and Punjabi. The Muslims chose to identify with Urdu and the Hindus with Hindi. These were also the proposed languages of the two new nations,

Pakistan and India: neither Muslims nor Hindus thought Punjabi to be a source of their cultural identity. Both the Muslim Punjabi elite and the Hindu Punjabi elite chose to identify with the nation over the region.

Only the Sikhs 'owned' or made 'claims' over the native language of Punjab. Interestingly, a section of the Punjabi Hindus was willing to use Punjabi, but only if it was treated as a dialect of Hindi and was written in the *devanagari* script. The Sikhs, on the other hand, insisted that Punjabi was a fully developed language and had its own script, *gurmukhi*.

The question of language and regional/religious identities was obviously linked to the question of culture and power. Given that the new nation saw it as a legitimate marker of cultural difference, language became a source of political mobilization in post-Independence Indian Punjab. In the case of Punjab, the Sikhs had already won the game. By deciding to mobilize against Punjabi, and making claims to the 'national language' Hindi as their mother tongue, the Punjabi Hindus had, perhaps quite unwittingly, conceded to the Sikh claim to the region called Punjab.

The movement launched by the Akalis during the 1960s for a Punjabi speaking, Sikh majority state, the Punjabi Suba, was perhaps only a culmination of the process that began in the late nineteenth century. The distinction that the literature on the Punjabi Suba tends to make between the 'communal' approach of Master Tara Singh and the 'secular' credentials of Sant Fateh Singh because the former explicitly asked for a Sikh majority state and the later spoke only in linguistic/cultural terms is perhaps pointless. Such internal differences among the Akalis were of little significance for the process of identity formation when seen in a historical perspective. The Punjab and the Sikhs had already been identified with each other, both among Punjabis as also amongst outsiders.

It may however be useful to add that the later mobilizations by the Akalis and other political formations of the Sikhs asking for more autonomy for the state or claiming the status of a nation for the Sikh community were by no means a culmination of the same process. True, the militant movement of the 1980s, despite having failed, did succeed in further reinforcing the territorial identity of Punjab as a land of the Sikhs. This is reflected most sharply in post-1984 literature on the Sikh diaspora.[4]

Concluding Remarks

Regional consciousness and regional identities have often been viewed as residing in the territory. According to this understanding, territories provide the physical material for growth of cultural and regional consciousness. When compared with the territorial identity of the nation, such identities are seen as being 'natural' or 'authentic'. This is so because cultural regions of the subcontinent have been in existence for a much longer time and share a common history and tradition. The most widely accepted attribute of such regions in India has been language.

Against such a 'fixed' or 'essentialist' notion of cultural regions that defines them through the attribute of language, I have tried to argue in this paper that territoriality of a given region becomes a meaningful reality only when it is claimed by some group or groups of people. As mentioned above, while it is possible that in many instances such groups are themselves constituted by the region or its linguistic distinctiveness, they are not always exclusively demarcated by language. The other social processes involving religion, caste, and even class could play important roles in the constitution of such identities.

The contemporary Indian Punjab offers a good empirical example of such a process. Although, like many other provinces, the Indian Punjab too was reorganized as a separate state of independent India on the basis of language, it has over the years also come to acquire a strong identity as the land of the Sikhs. While Hindus and Muslims were numerically greater in the region, it was the Sikhs who saw Punjab as the land of their origin. Despite being much smaller in numbers when compared to the other two communities, the Sikhs were able to hegemonize the regional/territorial identity of the Indian Punjab quite successfully. The politics of Punjabi Hindus on the other hand was geared towards de-ethnicizing and de-regionalizing themselves. While this has certainly helped them to make claims to opportunities opened up by the new nation, it also helped the Sikhs to consolidate their claims over the region.

To explain away such processes purely in terms of communalist politics cannot take us very far. One needs to look at how and why regions/regional identities are appropriated by some and not by others. Constructivist formulations of ethnic consciousness or elite manipulation theories such as communalism tend to look at identities as being somehow false and hence to ignore the historical and sociological processes of their formation (Jodhka 2001c). We must recognize the fact that all modern communities are, in a sense, imagined. This includes nations. Such a recognition of diverse possibilities through which identities come to be formed would perhaps go a long way in making the Indian federal structures more open and accommodative.

NOTES

1. Various estimates of people killed during the Khalistan movement during the 1980s and 1990s put the figure to around 25,000 in the state of Punjab itself, with a majority of them being Sikhs. See, for example, Puri et al. (1999: 10); G. Singh (1996: 115).
2. Brass 1974, Oberoi 1994, Fox 1985, Kapur 1986, and many others.
3. This is not to suggest that all Punjabi Hindus participated in this project or distanced themselves from Punjabi language and culture. But this became the dominant trend among them. More importantly, perhaps, there have been no efforts at articulating a regional consciousness among the Punjabi Hindus.
4. Different studies have pointed to the construction or imagining of Punjab, and not India, as the homeland by Sikhs living abroad (Axel 2001; Tatla 2000). The following passage quoted in the recent study of Bryan Axel reveals this quite succinctly:

   > God gave the Sikhs their land, a rich and fertile land blessed with much sun and irrigation, the 'land of five rivers', the Punjab. . . . Maharaja Ranjit Singh gave the Sikhs their state, later handed in trust, first to the British then to the Hindu Raj—but the Sikhs never surrendered their ultimate sovereignty to any power other than their own. Today, after forty years abuse of their trust, the Sikhs are ready to create again their independent, sovereign state (Axel 2001: 211).

REFERENCES

Axel, B. K. 2001. *The Nation's Tortured body: Violence, Representation, and Formation of a Sikh Diaspora*. Durham: Duke University Press.

Banga, I. 1989. 'The Emergence of Hindu Consciousness in Colonial Punjab', in Chatterjee, ed., 1989, pp. 201-19.

Brass, P. A. 1974. *Language, Religion and Politics in North India*. London: Cambridge University Press.

Chatterjee, P. C., ed. 1989. *Self-Images, Identity and Nationalism*. Shimla: Indian Institute of Advanced Studies.

Deol, H. 2000. *Religious Nationalism in India: The Case of the Punjab*. London and New York: Routledge.

Fox, R. 1985. *The Lions of Punjab: Culture in the Making*. Berkeley: University of California Press.

Grewal, J. S. 1989. 'The Making of Sikh Self-image before Independence', in Chatterjee, ed., 1989, pp. 187-200.

Jodhka, S. S. 1997. 'Crisis of the 1980s and Changing Agenda of "Punjab Studies": A Survey of Some Recent Research' (Review Article), *Economic and Political Weekly* 32 (6), pp. 273-9.

———. 2001a. 'Marginalization of Punjab', *Seminar*, January. Annual Number, pp. 69-74.

———. 2001b. 'Minority Status for Sikhs in Punjab: What Does it Mean?', *Economic and Political Weekly* 36 (18): 1497-9.

———. 2001c. *Community and Identities: Contemporary Discourses on Culture and Politics in India*. New Delhi: Sage.

Jones, K. W. 1968. 'Communalism in Punjab: The Arya Samaj Contribution', *Journal of Asian Studies* 28 (1): 39-54.

Juergensmeyer, M. 1988. *Religious Rebels in the Punjab: The Social Vision of Untouchables*. Delhi: Ajanta Publications.

Kapur, R. A. 1986. *Sikh Separatism: The Politics of Separatism*. London: Allen and Unwin.

Nayar, B. R. 1966. *Minority Politics in Punjab*. Princeton: Princeton University Press.

Oberoi, H. 1994. *The Construction of Religious Boundaries: Culture, Identity and Diversity in the Sikh Tradition*. Delhi: Oxford University Press.

Puri, H. K., P. S. Judge and J. S. Shekhon. 1999. *Terrorism in Punjab: Understanding Grassroots Reality*. New Delhi: Har-Anand Publications.

Singh, C. 1991. *Region and Empire: Punjab in the Seventeenth Century*. New Delhi: Oxford University Press.

Singh, G. 1996. 'Re-examining the Punjab Problem', in *Punjabi Identity: Continuity and Change*, edited by G. Singh and I. Talbot. New Delhi: Manohar, pp. 115-38.

Talbot, I. 1988. *Punjab and the Raj 1849-1947*. New Delhi: Manohar.

Tandon, P. 1961. *Punjabi Century (1857-1947)*. New York: Harcourt, Brace and World.

Tatla, D. S. 1999. *The Sikh Diaspora: The Search for Statehood*. Seattle: University of Washington Press.

13

The Hindi Heartland: A Region Sacred to Hindus and Muslims

Rajendra Vora

The Hindi heartland of Uttar Pradesh (UP), Bihar, Madhya Pradesh (MP), Rajasthan, and Delhi elects 211 out of 543 members of the Lok Sabha and thereby determines the balance of political power in the country. This region is seen as a political region because of its distinctive political behaviour in the 1967, 1977, and 1984 elections (Rudolph and Rudolph: 1987: 180). The BJP is identified as a party of the Hindi heartland because of its speedy rise in the region in the past decade (Heath 2002: 240-2). The process of transfer of power from the upper to lower castes took a period of almost four to five decades after Independence in the Hindi belt, while it happened within one or two decades in the south (Jaffrelot 2003: 10). I argue in this paper that the Hindi heartland is also a sacred region, both for Hindus and for Muslims, and that the Muslims of this region have mistakenly adopted an ideology of minorityism. I further argue that there are two ways for the Muslims of this region to improve their political status: (1) to find an appropriate place in the caste-majoritarianism, and (2) to join the masses in their democratic struggle for survival.

Sacred Region

The Hindi heartland states are located in the Gangetic plain, which was the site of development of Indian civilization. It is a part of *Aryavarta*—which literally meant the territory inhabited by the Aryans. The term *Aryavarta* was applied to the northern Indian region between the Himalayas and the Vindhyas. Early Indian civilization (which in later periods came to be described as Hindu and Buddhist) developed in this area in the first millennium BC. It is believed that

Hinduism originated in the north among the Aryans who came from the north-west and settled in the Gangetic plain. Uttar Pradesh, one of the two most populous states of the region, is considered the heart of *Aryavarta*, the cradle of Indian civilization (Trivedi 1995: 50).

UP is supposed to be a holy land because some of the most sacred places of Hindus are situated in this state. Benares or Kashi on the banks of the holy Ganga is the place where death brings liberation. Kashi is believed to be the earthly manifestation of Shiva's Jyotirlinga and is said to be one of the seven cities that bestow *moksha* (Eck 1998: 165-6). Three other cities of these seven are situated in the state of UP: Ayodhya, Mathura and Hardwar. Ayodhya is a place of great antiquity and is believed to be the birthplace of Rama, while Mathura is the legendary birthplace of Krishna. Brindaban, near Mathura, is believed to be the place where Krishna spent important years of his life. Hardwar and Allahabad are two holy cities of UP where the Kumbha Mela is held every twelfth year turn by turn. (Ujjain in MP and Nasik in Maharashtra are two other Kumbha Mela centres.) Allahabad is known for the sacred confluence of the Ganga and Jamuna (and invisible Saraswati), while Hardwar is the place where the Ganga descends upon the plains. In the Kumbha Mela, which lasts six weeks, the most important day is the bathing day, when millions of pilgrims go to bathe in the river and witness the procession of bands of monks and sadhus who make their own way to the sacred waters (Pinch 1996: 143). The Kedarnath temple, which stands in the valley of the Mandakini at a height of 11,753 ft., and the Badrinath temple, in the valley of the Alaknanda at a height of 10,300 ft., are two major pilgrimage centres in the Himalayas in the state of UP.

There are two Jyotirlingas in MP, one at Ujjain on the banks of the Kshipra, and another at Omkareshwar on the banks of the Narmada. Ujjain is also a place where the Kumbha Mela is held every twelfth year. Rajasthan, besides being famous for the palaces of Rajput kings, is also known for the Nathdwara temple near Udaipur and the Brahmadeo temple at Pushkar near Ajmer. Gaya in Bihar is one of three most sacred centres of pilgrimage (*tristhali*), the other two being Kashi and Prayag.

However, the sacred region of Hindus is also a holy land for Indian Muslims. When the followers of Islam coming from the north-west conquered this region, and when the Delhi Sultanate (1206-1526) and the Mughals (1526-1757) established their rule, the region emerged as a 'hub of Indo-Muslim civilization' (Jones 1994: 48). If Varanasi (Banaras) and Allahabad (Prayag) are sacred cities for Hindus, Delhi and Agra are the most important cities for the Muslims. Delhi was the capital city of the Islamic conquest and remained the capital during the rule of the Delhi Sultanate, while under the reign of the Mughals Agra also came to prominence. Even after the fall of the Mughal empire Delhi continued to be the main cultural centre for Muslims (Jones 1994: 50-1). Its role as a pivot of Islamic thinking, education, and literature did not decline even in the nineteenth and twentieth centuries. Geo-historically, Delhi rather than Islamabad is better placed to play the role of the centre of inspiration for Muslims of the subcontinent (Puri 1978: 1707). In fact, UP, the heart of *Aryavarta*, is historically known as the centre of Muslim rule and culture in India. Here in UP are found Jaunpur, the capital of the Sharqui kings; Fatehpur Sikri, a city developed by Akbar the Great; Agra, known for the Taj Mahal built by Emperor Shahjahan; Bareilly, the place of the Rohillas; and Lucknow, the capital of the Awadh kingdom. UP is also a centre of Islamic learning. Aligarh Muslim University, Dar-al-ulum of Deoband (Saharanpur district), and Nadwat-al-ulum of Lucknow are located in UP. The Dar-al-ulum at Deoband had in 1994 enrolled 3,000 students, of whom around 500 came from fifteen countries. From Deoband to Mussoorie there are probably more *makatib* and *madaris* than in the capitals of some Muslim countries (Hasan 1997: 5). More than 6 lakh students were enrolled in the mid-1990s in UP's Islamic schools.

Apart from historic monuments like the Red Fort and Qutb Minar, many mosques and shrines or tombs are situated in the Hindi heartland region. They are found at centres of Muslim power such as Delhi, Agra, Jaunpur, Lucknow and Bhopal. Out of 7 Chishti *dargahs*, 6 are located in the north at places like Ajmer (Rajasthan), Delhi, Patna and Bihar Sharif (Bihar), and Aligarh (UP) (Troll 2003: 2).

Muslims of the Hindi Heartland

Scholars observe that Muslims belonging to the Hindi heartland have historically developed a distinct identity and that their political behaviour has remained different from that of their brethren from other parts of the country. Wright makes two broad categories of Indian Muslims—the coastal and the inland. The inland Muslims, according to him, are monument-conscious, living in the midst of their Taj Mahal and Red Fort. They have not been able to forget that once they were the rulers of this land (Khan 1997: 36). Mushirul Hasan finds that there is a 'profound difference in the way most Muslims in the north and the south perceive and relate themselves to the world they live in' (Hasan 1997: 9). Islam took forms that were not always in conformity with the Koranic ideals and precepts in Bengal, which was far away from the imperial power in Delhi-Agra, while the Islam south of the Vindhyas developed a tradition that accommodated some indigenous ways of worship. Scholars have also argued that the Hindi-heartland Muslims dominate Muslim politics in India. It is said that it would be 'absolutely necessary to know the dilemma faced by the Muslims of the great Ganga-Jamuna civilization' for a thorough understanding of the Muslim problem (Puri 1993: 2149).

The pre-Partition politics of Muslims was essentially and largely influenced by the position taken by the Muslims of the Hindi heartland. UP Muslims took the lead in the separatist movement and they were the main leaders of the Muslim League—with the exception of Jinnah, who came from Mumbai. In fact, many Muslims from UP went to Dacca to form the Muslim League in 1906. The secretaryship of the League was held by Aligarh and Lucknow leaders between 1906 and 1926. Wazia Hasan of Lucknow was responsible for getting concessions from the Congress for Muslims in the Lucknow Pact of 1916. During the Non-Cooperation movement Muslims from this region were in the forefront in collaborating with Gandhi and the Congress. When the Muslim League was at the peak of its separatist politics, UP Muslims were at the helm of affairs in the organization of the party (Robinson 1975: 5).

Separatist movements were started by the Muslim elites of the heartland who wanted to continue their dominance and at the same time to prevent the Hindus from gaining power on the basis of their (Hindu) proportion in the population (Brass 1975: 121). The demand for Pakistan arose basically among the Urdu-speaking Muslims of the north, and they were the people who migrated to Pakistan in great numbers. Except for some from Hyderabad, hardly any southern Muslims migrated to Pakistan (Engineer 1998: 63). The Muslims in the southern and western regions did not experience the 'social upheaval or economic dislocation' caused by Partition, and therefore their political orientations have remained different from those of the Urdu-speaking Muslims of the north (Hasan 1997: 9). Urdu is not spoken by Muslims south of the Vindhyas except those from Hyderabad. Therefore, when Hindi with the *devanagari* script was made the national language, the most affected section of Muslims was from the Gangetic belt. The Aligarh Muslim University is a 'distant institution' for the Muslims outside this region and, therefore, never became a symbol of hopes or aspirations. Muslims from other regions do not regard the Ulama of Deoband's Dar-al-ulum or of the Nadwat-al-ulum of Lucknow as the sole arbiters of their destiny. Even the Babri Masjid at Ayodhya for that matter does not carry emotional appeal for them. Their history and culture have taken a different course from that of Urdu-speaking Muslims of the Gangetic belt. The three most important religio-political organizations of the Muslims—the Jamiyat-ul-Ulama-e-Hind, the Jammat-e-Islami-e-Hind and the All India Muslim Personal Law Board—have their base among the Urdu-speaking urban Muslims of UP and Bihar (ibid.: 309). While the Muslims in southern states like Andhra Pradesh or Kerala have tried to achieve their political objectives through communal parties such as Majlis-i-Ittehad-ul-Muslimeen or the All India Muslim League, the Gangetic plain Muslims have relied on the Congress-like mainstream parties. The mainstream parties in turn depend upon the support of Muslim votes in the region. One of the reasons for the Congress dominance in north India before 1967, it is argued, was the support the party secured from the Muslims. Similarly, the Congress defeat in the 1977 elections in the northern states is ascribed, along with other factors, to the disenchantment of Muslim voters.

In fact, over-politicization of Muslims in the Hindi heartland has come under criticism from some well-meaning community leaders. Maulana Wahiduddin Khan has argued that 'the large dose of politics administered by their leaders to north Indian Muslims has led them to emotionalism and then to communal disaster'. According to him the feeling of insecurity is more intense among the Muslim community of the north, and recurring communal riots there are the indication of this feeling. South Indian Muslims do not suffer from such insecurity. Communal rioting occurs in south Indian cities only when north Indian leaders create tensions. And even when such disturbances take place, they are on a very small scale. Khan goes back to the origins of Indian Islam to find the reasons for this kind of difference, and points out that Islam was spread through merchants and traders in the southern region, in contrast to the north, where it was brought by rulers and soldiers. Therefore, the south Indian Muslims have never been swayed by 'emotional politics'. They have concentrated on non-controversial areas like trade and education instead of 'flexing their muscles' in politics, and thereby have established constructive traditions and not confrontational ones (Khan 1997: 96-7).

Communal Region

Notwithstanding its sacredness, the Hindi heartland turned into a region where communalism could take root and develop into a vigorous political movement resulting in inter-communal violence. Probably its sacredness itself became the cause of its communalization. The followers of two distinct religious traditions look to the region as their holy land, where places of worship, sacred rivers, sites of prayers, and religious monuments are located. The region is claimed by both communities as their own sacred region, to which only they have a right. Believers of one tradition, it seems, do not want to share the holiness of the region with those of the other.

Historically, Hindus and Muslims have lived together in this part of India for centuries. The mixing of Hindus and Muslims has been very deep, not only in the social and cultural spheres, but also in the religious domain (Burman 1996: 1211-15). The shrine of Nizamuddin Auliya in Delhi and the Muinuddin Chishti Dargah in Ajmer (Rajasthan) are examples of syncretism. But despite this centuries-long give and take, the region has become a hotbed of communalism since the second half of the nineteenth century. Historians have pointed out that the confrontation arose earlier in this part of India than elsewhere (Pande 1990: ix). Here both communities are increasingly using holy places to settle scores. Some places of worship get converted into the battlefields where communal battles are fought, while others are locked up for years, because both communities claim them as their own holiest places and insist that they should have exclusive rights over them. The secular authorities are approached to settle the religious disputes. In this sacred region, religious preaching gets converted into political sermons and religious processions end up in violent rioting, while mosques and the banks of holy rivers become platforms for inciting devotees against the followers of the other faith. Religious festivals are used as media of political mobilization, while sadhus and ulema, the holy men, indulge in power politics. Holy places are turned into forums of unholy politics. The Hindu Mahasabha was started at the Hardwar Kumbha Mela in 1915 and a Shankaracharya brought out a procession to support the cause of Ram Janmabhoomi liberation at the Kumbha Mela in 1986. The sacred region of Hindus and Muslims thus sheds its sacredness and transforms itself into a region of inter-religious enmity and communal violence. Why communalism chose this region to sow its seeds and why they grew vigorously in this holy land, has to be understood from both the historical and the social perspective.

It was from Muslim rulers that the East India Company captured power in northern India. A feeling of loss of power became one of the important aspects of the Muslim psyche for decades, and continues to be so. Brass has shown how the Muslims in the United Provinces in the late nineteenth and early twentieth centuries were more advantaged than the Hindus in urbanization, literacy, English education, and employment. He has argued that it was the Muslim upper class that formulated the political demand for equality with the larger Hindu population (Brass 1975: 121). It was this section that was in the forefront in the separatist movement. On the other hand, attempts were made to protect Islam from the challenge posed by Christianity and colonial modernity. These attempts gave birth to Islamic revivalism and tightened the hold of the ulema on the community. Modernity brought, along with other things, enumeration and representation, which grouped people into communities and developed internal cohesion among the followers of one faith. Modern politics introduced the phenomenon of organizing people around issues of 'common' interest that ultimately become the community's interests. In the politics of mobilization and competition, symbols and emotional appeals acquired more importance than material interests. When communal representation was introduced, through the Morley-Minto reforms of 1909 and through later reforms in 1919 and 1935, the colonial masters had legitimized communal politics. Economic tensions—for instance, those between Hindu peasants and Muslim talukdars and landlords in Awadh and Aligarh-

Bulandshahr, or those between Muslim artisans, shopkeepers, and petty traders, on the one hand, and Hindu bankers and big merchants, on the other, in towns of UP—provided the basis for competition and rivalry between the two communities in the political domain (Sarkar 1986: 60).

Because of its peculiar social composition and political history, the Hindi heartland proved to be fertile ground for the growth of organizations such as the Arya Samaj and the Rashtriya Swayamsevak Sangh (RSS), or, in later years, the Vishwa Hindu Parishad (VHP). Nearly 40 per cent of the Brahmans in all of India live in UP, and they form 10 per cent of that state's population (Hasan 1996: 87). On the whole, upper castes are more numerous in the north than in the south. Their proportion of the state population ranges between 13.6 per cent in Bihar and 24.2 per cent in Rajasthan. Such a large population has given them an advantage in furthering their status-quoist and upper-varna Hindu politics. They opposed, on the one hand, the rise of lower strata of Hindus and, on the other, the concessions to Muslims. They believed and took pride in the myth that Hinduism, as noted earlier, was born in *Aryavarta*, and they probably took upon themselves the task of defending its purity and sacredness from encroachment by Islam and Christianity.

The highest concentration of princely states of British India was in the Hindi belt—22 in Rajasthan and 67 in MP (Jaffrelot 2003: 8). The feudal set-up of the princely states was congenial to the growth of an ideology of maintaining Hindu social structure and Brahman-Rajput dominance, which in turn provided ground for the rise of Hindu communalism. The heartland emerged as the centre of Hindi literary culture, which insisted on Hindi language and the *devanagari* script and challenged the dominance of Urdu and indirectly that of Urdu-speaking Muslims. The partition of Bengal in 1905 and the divide-and-rule policy of the colonial government gave more than sufficient space for the development of communal tendencies, especially in the northern region, where other factors had already communalized the public sphere.

Controversial Issues

Controversies between Hindus and Muslims of this region flared up around religious issues in the beginning, and later some secular issues became 'sacred çows'. One of the very first controversies that divided the two communities was in fact around the cow, which is for Hindus the most holy animal, whose body they believe to contain numerous deities, while Muslims are supposed to sacrifice cows on the Bakr-id day. Hindu communalists started the cow-protection movement in 1888 and since then the issue has intermittently cropped up, resulting sometimes in severe communal riots. The cow emerged as a 'nurturing mother goddess' and a 'symbol of the Hindu nation' in the Hindi-speaking belt during the nationalist movement (Gupta 2001: 4295-6). Even today the controversy has not died down. The 'cow-belt' has been trapped in cow politics for more than a century. In the beginning of 2003, the killing of a cow produced a communal riot at Ganj Basauda in MP. The then Chief Minister of the state, Digvijay Singh, of the Congress party, even tried to project himself as a *gau-rakshak* (cow protector), taking a 'soft-Hindutva' line. He demanded a country-wide ban on cow-slaughter, perhaps in a futile attempt to pre-empt Uma Bharati, the leader of the Bharatiya Janata Party (BJP) in MP. The RSS sees the cow issue as a part of the global struggle against Muslim fundamentalism.

The Samajwadi Party (UP) and the Rashtriya Janata Dal (Bihar) are in a dilemma because their parties are seen as Yadav parties and the Yadav caste is identified with Krishna, who is believed to be the protector of cows, while both the parties seek the support of Muslims, the beef eaters. A resolution regarding a ban on cow slaughter has come up for discussion in Parliament more than once. The Union government, led by the BJP, promised to introduce the Bill again. The BJP wants to have a nation-wide ban on cow-slaughter and since 1996 its MPs have moved five Bills to that effect, but these have never been taken up for discussion. A National Commission on Cattle, constituted in 2001, has recommended a central law banning cow-slaughter (Kang and Bhaumik 2003: 30-8).

The conversion of Hindus to Islam has been a contentious issue since the conversion of Malabar (Kerala) during the Moplah rebellion in 1921. A conflict between Muslim peasants (Moplahs) and Hindu high-caste landlords had resulted in a communal outbreak. It was alleged by the Arya Samaj that Hindus had been forcibly converted to Islam by the Moplahs. The Hindi heartland experienced the repercussions of this event, which happened in the southernmost part of the country. The Arya Samaj started a *shuddhi* (purification to reconvert Muslims to Hinduism) and *sangathan* (organization) movement in the north to counteract Muslim moves. Swami Shraddhananda of the Arya Samaj extended the movement in 1923 to western UP to reconvert Malkana Rajput, Gujar, and Bania converts. He was murdered in 1926. Muslims began a *tabligh* (propaganda) and *tanzim* (organization) movement as a response to the *shuddhi* and *sangathan* movement of the Hindus. The Hindu Mahasabha incorporated the *shuddhi* programme and in its session held at Banaras in 1923 gave a call to start Hindu defence squads (Sarkar 1986: 216-17, 235). The Hindu nationalist organizations and parties have since then insisted on anti-conversion laws. O. P. Tyagi of the Bharatiya Jan Sangh had brought during Janata rule a private members' Bill (1978) to ban religious conversions by use of force, fraud, or inducement. Even though it was not passed, it generated a national debate on the issue.

On 19 February 1981, in the village of Meenakshipuram (Tirunelveli district, Tamil Nadu), around five hundred or so Harijans converted to Islam (Noorani 2003: 191). This conversion was attributed to the Tablighi-Jamaat, a revivalist organization, but the leaders of the organization denied the charge. Like the Moplah conversion, the Meenakshipuram incident also set in motion Hindu activism in the north. The VHP, which was started by the RSS in 1964 to counteract the activities of Christian missionaries with respect to the conversion of tribal people, came to the surface after the Meenakshipuram incident. Along with the BJP it held public meetings and organized demonstrations in various parts of UP to bring out the threat to Hinduism from the conversions (Hasan 1996: 90). It also started its campaign to strengthen unity among various castes and sects of Hindus. The Harijan conversion to Islam alarmed the Hinduist forces and also created a new space for them in the Hindi-speaking belt, especially UP. This was the time when the RSS and its affiliated organizations turned to Hindutva with a new determination and confidence and left behind the centrist politics of the late 1970s.

Muslims generally hold the view that their personal law should not be touched because it is given by God himself. It is so sacred that no government has the authority to make any change in it.

Whenever such attempts have been made, Muslims have opposed them tooth and nail. Yet the RSS and the BJP have emphatically argued a case for a uniform civil code and have condemned the separate personal law for Muslims. The Union government thought of modifying the personal law in 1961, but Zakir Husain, one of the most notable leaders of Muslims from the Hindi heartland, stopped it (Hasan 1997: 154-5). When in 1972 the change was again proposed, the Muslim leadership held a meeting at Deoband to oppose the move. At an all-India convention held for the purpose in December 1972, they formed the All India Muslim Personal Law Board to take care of activities with respect to personal law (Noorani 2003: 160).

A major controversy over personal law was triggered when the Supreme Court, in its judgement of 23 April 1985 in the Shah Bano case, held that a Muslim man must pay maintenance to his divorced wife until she remarried, and that, in case of conflict between Section 125 of the Criminal Procedure Code and Muslim Personal Law, the provisions of the former should prevail. Muslims regarded this as interference with the *Shariat* and their freedom of religion. All religious and political organizations of the Muslims condemned the judgement and organized protests against the interference, especially in the north Indian states. The upsurge was such that the Rajiv Gandhi government passed the Muslim Women (Protection of Rights on Divorce) Act in 1986. This Act was denounced by the Hinduist forces as another instance of appeasement of the Muslim community by the Congress. It invigorated the Hindu communal movement in the Hindi heartland to a very great extent. Rajiv Gandhi and his government thus bolstered the Muslim communal forces by yielding to their pressure and at the same time gave the Hindu communalists a cause to fight for.

In the sacred region of the north, a place of worship and prayer can itself grow into a controversy, as happened in the case of Ayodhya. The Mughal Emperor Babur built a masjid in 1528 on the site, Hindus claim, of Lord Ram's temple, which is claimed as the birthplace of Ram at Ayodhya. The VHP began a movement in the mid-1980s to liberate the Ram Janmabhoomi (Ram's birthplace), which had been locked in 1949 after Hindus had managed to put idols of Ram inside the masjid. The locks were removed by the government on 1 February 1986, and Hindus were allowed to go inside on the basis of the District Court's order. This was an attempt on the part of Rajiv Gandhi's government to please the Hindus, but in fact it gave strength to the VHP and BJP movement. The Babri Masjid Movement Co-ordination Committee held a mass rally in Delhi on 30 March 1987 to protest against the government's action to convert the masjid into a temple, and appealed to Muslims to continue their struggle for the restoration of the Babri Masjid (Noorani 2003: 254-7). The VHP and the BJP, for their part, organized agitations to mobilize Hindus for the unfinished task. One such ingenious agitation was the Rath Yatra (chariot procession) from Somnath in Gujarat to Ayodhya (September-October 1990). The route of the *yatra* was designed in such a way that it would pass through a maximum number of states of the Hindi heartland, the primary target (Davis 1996: 23). Finally on 6 December 1992 the masjid was demolished by the followers of the Hindu communalist organizations. The controversy has remained unresolved since then and has provided fodder to the communalism of both Hindus and Muslims of UP and of the region at large.

The place-of-worship controversy will not end even if the Ayodhya dispute is settled, because the VHP is using the slogan '*Ayodhya to jhanki hai, Mathura, Kashi baki hai*' (Ayodhya is just the beginning, Mathura and Kashi are also on the agenda). Aurangzeb built a huge masjid at Mathura. The VHP believes that it was built at the very birthplace of Krishna, and therefore should be demolished and replaced with a Krishna temple. Aurangzeb also built a masjid at Kashi (Banaras), on the site, it is claimed, of the Vishwanath temple. In its plan of 'correcting history', the VHP wants to demolish this masjid and in its place build a temple of Shiva (Khan 1997: 122-6). In February 1995 the VHP organized agitation in this regard (Basu 1996: 71).

The Kamal Maula Masjid at Dhar in MP is yet another disputed place of worship. Following communal tension in 1997, the entry of Hindus into the place, which is a Bhojshala for them, was restricted to just once a year, on the occasion of the auspicious day Basant Panchami. In April 2003, the Archaeological Survey of India (ASI) was ordered to throw open the disputed place for Hindus every Tuesday. For the BJP, this was a great victory (*Indian Express*, 9 April 2003). However, the ASI has allowed the place to be kept open between 1 and 3 p.m. on Fridays for *namaj* (*The Times of India*, 12 April 2003). For the time being the controversy has calmed down, but no one knows when or with what pretext it could erupt again.

The Urdu-Hindi controversy has divided Muslims and Hindus in the Hindi heartland to a very great extent. Even though both languages are essentially derived from the Hindustani of north India, due to the Hindi movement started in the late nineteenth century and the colonial government's policy of divide-and-rule, Urdu came to be associated with Muslims and Hindi with Hindus (Brass 1975: 128). Muslim members of the Constituent Assembly pleaded for adoption of Hindustani as the *lingua franca* of India, but their plea was rejected and Hindi was declared the national language (Noorani 2003: 291). After Independence Muslims tried to push the case of Urdu as the second language in states like UP. But UP had adopted Hindi as the official language under the Official Languages Act of 1951 and Urdu lost its place even as a second language. The Congress government, both at the centre and in the Hindi-speaking states, did not take any effective measures to enhance the status of Urdu—except in 1989 when the UP legislature, through an amendment to the above Act, decided to treat Urdu as the second official language of the state. But since this move has been challenged in a court of law by the Hindi lobby, nothing has been achieved. There is an overall decline of Urdu in UP (Pai 2002: 2705-8). Muslims in the Hindi heartland have failed to achieve their goal in this regard and their region has come to be known as the 'Hindi' heartland, where Sanskritized Hindi has acquired eminence. Bihari Muslims are in a better position because there the state government gave Urdu a second-official-language status in 1989 (Graf 1992: 219).

Besides these controversies, the politics of Muslims of the sacred region has revolved around the demands the community has made on the Indian state and the grievances it has put forward from time to time. The demands and grievances are basically oriented towards protecting Muslim religious, linguistic, and cultural identity. They want the Indian state to protect their fundamental rights regarding freedom of conscience and religion; freedom to manage religious affairs; conserving a distinct language, script or culture; and establishing and administering minority educational institutions. Controversial issues on which they have fought battles are essentially related to these rights, and the demands they have made on the Indian state also reflect basically these minority rights enshrined in the Constitution.

Along with demands concerning protection of places of worship, personal law, and Urdu, Muslims have made a related appeal to the government to maintain the minority character of the Aligarh Muslim University and to retain the word 'Muslim' in its name. This has been accepted. They wanted from the very beginning a Minority Board to look after the interests of minorities. In 1978 the Central Government appointed a Minority Commission (Noorani 2003: 181-3). The rights concerning minority educational institutions have not been touched by the government. Salman Rushdie's book *Satanic Verses* contains, according to the community, derogatory references to Islam, and therefore Muslims wanted a ban on it when it reached India in 1988. The government immediately imposed the ban. School and college textbooks, according to Muslims, should give due recognition to the contribution of Muslims. This was largely done, though since the coming of the BJP-led government at the Centre, official educational bodies are following an anti-Muslim line. A major grievance of the Muslims since the first riot in Jabalpur (1961) is that there is a bias in the law and order machinery of the government and that the life and property of the minority is not properly protected. Nothing substantial has been done to redress this grievance by the government.

Even though Muslims have expressed since 1961 their concern about how they are underrepresented in all walks of life, including government and legislative bodies, only in 1994 did they explicitly demand reservation of seats for Muslims in public employment and education and also in legislative and panchayat raj bodies (ibid.: 276-7). The national convention of the movement for the empowerment of Muslims held at New Delhi in 1999 has resolved to launch a movement to empower the community in the fields of education, employment, politics, administration, culture, health, and housing (ibid.: 283-4). This is the first time the community is going in a major way beyond religious demands and is trying to project what they want in order to improve their material conditions. This change in attitude has probably been prompted by the grave attack on their identity when the Babri Masjid was demolished in 1992. Muslim politics after Independence seems to be aimed at making government and parties accept these demands concerning the protection of the minority character and identity of their community.

THE POLITICS OF A MINORITY

In the 1937 provincial assembly elections in UP, Congress secured a majority by defeating the Muslim League, but when it came to forming a government, Congress went back on its promise to the League, and constituted a government on its own. At that time, the League realized what it means to be a minority. From then on, it pursued with a vengeance the project of creating a separate nation-state of Muslim-majority provinces. Muslims in Muslim-minority provinces of the north were staunch supporters of the League's idea of Pakistan, but most of them were left behind, after the 1947 Partition, in the Hindu-majority provinces, condemned to live the life of a minority. A very apt description of what the Pakistan project meant for Muslims was given by Maulana Husain Ahmad of Deoband Seminary: it was a 'death knell' (Hasan 1997: 65). Muslims who stayed behind in UP or Bihar were more vocal in their demand for Pakistan, probably because they saw in it 'a sort of countervailing sanctuary in case of persecution by the Hindu majority' (Talib 1979: 19). 'The Muslims of UP and Bihar were a minority and would remain so even after partition. . . . When the Muslim majority provinces went out of India . . . and Mr. Jinnah left for Karachi, these fools realized that they had gained nothing but in fact lost everything by the partition of India' (Engineer 1998: 60). These were the words of Maulana Azad, who more than anyone else had realized the risk involved in Partition, especially for the Ganga-Jamuna-belt Muslims. The separate Muslim electorates, which had made the Muslims' position in the colonial period enviable, were abolished after heated debate in the Constituent Assembly. The community took time to live without the support of the separate electorates and to come to terms with the political realities in an independent and partitioned country. The League and its politics having disappeared, its followers had no option but to accept the leadership of the composite nationalist school of Maulana Azad and Jamiyat-ul-Ulama-e-Hind, which had extended its support to the Congress at the outset.

Muslims, having thus realized that they were now a minority, decided to associate with the Congress, led by Jawaharlal Nehru, who had emerged as a symbol of secularism and proponent of the 'unity in diversity' thesis. Muslims entered into an unwritten contract with the Congress according to which the Congress was expected to protect their minority identity in return for electoral support. The contract remained unshaken until almost 1961-2. But after the communal riots in 1961-2 at Jabalpur and Jamshedpur (both in Hindi-speaking states), Muslims started rethinking. The cause of Urdu had also by that time got defeated due to the apathy of the Congress. Finally, after Nehru's death in 1964, Muslims opened alternative avenues, such as Muslim-Majlis-e-Mushawarat, formed at Lucknow in August 1964, to safeguard their interests. In the 1967 general elections, when opposition was united in the Hindi-speaking zone against the Congress, the Muslim community also tried to defect from the Congress to a certain extent. For the first time since Independence the Congress realized how much it depended on the Muslim vote. But with Indira Gandhi's arrival on the scene, Muslims went back to the Congress wholeheartedly. The National Emergency declared by Indira Gandhi in June 1975 was supported by most Muslim organizations, but soon they realized that the Emergency could also encroach upon their private space. Two programmes undertaken during the Emergency antagonized Muslims in the north: compulsory sterilization for birth control, and the slum-clearance drive, which was extended to Muslim localities in Delhi and Muzaffarnagar (Wright 1977: 1209-16).

In retaliation Muslims voted for the Janata Party in the 1977 parliamentary elections and contributed to the miserable defeat of Indira Gandhi in the Hindi-speaking states. This was the time when Syed Abdulla Bukhari, Shahi Imam of Delhi's Jama Masjid, emerged as the supreme arbiter, representing Muslims of this region. However, in 1980, he changed his colour and asked his community fellows to change as well by extending a helping hand to Indira Gandhi when she wanted it most, as usual in return for assurances. In this term of office, Indira Gandhi took a militant nationalist and pro-Hindu stance. This was clearly seen in the Jammu & Kashmir Assembly elections and also in the Delhi Municipal Corporation elections in 1983, as well as in her decision to take armed action against the Sikh terrorists hiding in the Golden Temple of Amritsar (Rudolph and Rudolph 1987: 44).

In the 1984 parliamentary elections, Rajiv Gandhi highlighted two themes—national unity and the need to save the nation from internal and external enemies. The Congress, for the first time since Independence, tried to distance itself from Muslims (Hasan 1996: 92).

From 1983-4 onwards we see a steady and sure growth of Hindu communal forces in the Hindi-speaking belt, with the Congress succumbing to their pressure every time. In February 1986, as noted earlier, the Congress government ordered the opening of the Babri Masjid to Hindus and in 1989 the UP government allowed the VHP to lay the foundation stone of the Ram temple at the disputed site in Ayodhya. The distancing of Muslims from the Congress started in 1984 was increased by these actions to such an extent that many of them voted for V. P. Singh's Janata Dal (JD) in the 1989 parliamentary elections. Shahi Imam also advised his community to support the JD, even though there was agreement between the JD and the BJP on several seats in the north. It has been observed that Muslims played a major role in 1989 in bringing about a new political landscape; whether their vote was decisive or not is a different proposition (Graf 1992: 235).

The division of the Muslim vote that started in the 1989 elections continued in 1991 and onwards. In almost all the elections held thereafter we observe a clear shift of Muslim voters away from the Congress in the Hindi belt. After the grand exit of V. P. Singh's Government, elections for parliament were held in 1991. Data based on two pre-election polls and one exit poll indicate that the Muslim vote was divided between JD and Congress in 1991. The exit poll conducted by *MARG* shows that 46.3 per cent of Muslim voters preferred the Congress, while 24.9 per cent chose the JD, and the Left Front got 16.7 per cent of the Muslim vote. In the 1993 UP Assembly elections, after the demolition of the Babri Masjid, Muslims decisively went towards the Samajwadi Party (SP) and Bahujan Samaj Party (BSP) alliance, and the Congress got only 20 per cent and JD 14 per cent of the Muslim vote (Sanjaykumar 1996: 318). This pattern of division of the Muslim vote has continued until the most recent parliamentary elections. In Bihar, from 1989 onwards the Muslim vote has been shared basically by the JD, the Rashtriya Janata Dal (RJD) of Laloo Prasad Yadav, and the Congress.

The Curse of Minorityism

This survey indicates that the social and political actions of Muslims of this region are guided essentially by the minority factor. Muslims account for 13.4 per cent of India's population and therefore form the largest minority in the country. The Muslim population of India (138 million) is larger than that of Pakistan or the entire Arab world (Zakaria 1995: 91). Khalidi makes a distinction between the Hindustan region (north) and the Deccan region (south) and points out that there is not a single district in these two regions where Muslims are in a majority. Rampur district of UP comes close to having a majority, with a 45 per cent Muslim population (Khalidi 1995: 7).

Muslims are a fragmented community regionally, unlike the Sikhs, whose population is concentrated in Punjab. In the sacred region the proportion of Muslim population is quite high, especially in UP and Bihar, the two largest states of the country. In UP Muslims account for 17.33 per cent of the total population, while in Bihar their proportion is 14.8 per cent. Considering that these two states are the most populous, the actual number of Muslims in these states comes to 3,68,97,669. In Rajasthan, MP and Delhi, Muslims account for 8, 4.96, and 9.44 per cent of the population respectively. Graf finds a formidable concentration of Muslims in the Ganges valley region, in which she includes UP, Bihar and also West Bengal. In UP, 20 constituencies out of 85 have a Muslim population between 20 and 45 per cent of the total population, and in 42 constituencies the Muslim population is around 10 per cent. In Bihar 9 out of 54 constituencies have more than 20 per cent Muslims, and in another 30 at least 10 per cent (Graf 1992: 226-7). Nevertheless, Muslims are a minority in the Hindi heartland and elsewhere, except in Jammu & Kashmir, and it is the Urdu-speaking Muslim community of the Hindi heartland that is the 'most rootless and alienated' and is 'suffering from a crisis of identity most acutely' (Puri 1978: 1711).

Muslims, it is said, experience the 'loss of their identity in the sea of Hindus who constitute almost 85 per cent of population' (Zakaria 1995: 91). However, Rudolph and Rudolph challenge the claim that Hindus are a large majority. If we take into account the proportion of Muslims along with other non-Hindus (Christians, Sikhs, Buddhists, Jains and Parsees) and the Scheduled Tribes, the figure comes to

38 per cent of India's population, so that only 62 per cent could be counted as Hindus, who again are fragmented on the basis of sect, caste, and language.

Rasheeduddin Khan goes beyond the mere numerical category and finds the very word 'minority' unsatisfactory, because according to him 'more often it conceals rather than reveals the human situation'. Minority status, he asserts, is a static frame of reference that 'generates a sense of fatalism'. It gives rise to tendencies such as separatism, inwardness, xenophobia, and preoccupation with one's own community. Instead, he proposes the category of 'segment', which subsumes both quantitative and qualitative attributes. For a community to be recognized as an all-India segment in his scheme, it must have 5 per cent population and be spread in at least one-third of the states and union territories. If we accept these criteria, only Hindus and Muslims can be recognized as all-India segments, and only Hindi and Urdu, again, as all-India segments. In that case, the Muslim problem becomes the problem of India—a national problem and not the problem of only one community (Khan 1978: 1510-12).

When Muslims assume a minority position the 'other' (Hindus) automatically becomes the 'majority'. By taking a label of minority for themselves, Muslims created political space for Hindus to assume a majority position when in fact they were not a 'majority' in the real sense of the term. If we go back to the first three decades of the post-Independence period, we find that Indian society was seen as a conglomeration of castes, sects, tribes, and religious and linguistic communities. Hindutva forces were weak. They began their grand projects of construction of a Hindu majority in the mid-1980s by questioning the 'nationalist' credentials of a minority named Muslims. Muslims are expected to surrender to the Hindu majoritarianism, which aims to accommodate all castes and communities. Muslims would also be accommodated with the explicit understanding that they would be treated as second-class citizens.

The idea of a minority gave rise to the idea of a community, whereby all Muslims, irrespective of divisions based on social or economic hierarchy, were brought onto one platform and consequently became susceptible to calls given by the political and religious leaders of the 'community'. Thus the category of 'minority' gave on the one hand a false sense of community to the majority of Muslims, who were socially and economically disadvantaged, and on the other produced a tacit and willing consent to the designs of dominant sections within the community. Sociological studies of Muslims in the Hindi heartland have brought to the fore the unequal position of Ashraf (noble or upper-class) and Ajlaf (common) Muslims. Ashrafs have a fourfold division among themselves: Sayyids, Shaikhs, Mughals, and Pathans. Ajlafs are mostly descended from families of converts from the lower castes (Ahmad 1996: 268-78). The Ajlafs include craftsmen like weavers, butchers, carpenters, oilmen, barbers, washermen, and leatherworkers. It is true that rigid caste distinctions are not found among Muslims, but it is also a fact that the Islamic tenet of equality among members of the fraternity is observed only at times of prayer in the masjid and during the pilgrimage at Mecca. It is futile to treat an entire religious community *per se* as a viable and valid category. Muslims, like Hindus, are divided not only into caste-like strata but also into classes and professions. 'This class distinction between the prince and the pauper, the landlord and the landless, the elite and the mass is rampant among Muslims. . . .' (Khan 1978: 1513). In order to nullify the League's attempt to create 'Muslim Identity' in the garb of Islam, Nehru started the 'Muslim mass contact' campaign in March 1937. The point he was making at that time was that Muslims were not a collective fraternity but a segment of an impoverished population and that the fate of the Muslim masses was not tied to their fellow Muslims *per se*, but to fellow artisans, peasants, and workers who were found in other communities as well. Nehru wanted to convince the Muslim masses in UP that the interests of Muslim peasants or labourers were not different from those of their Hindu counterparts. He believed that if this idea took root the 'myth of communalism would disappear along with the pseudo-religious mentality' (Hasan 1997: 48-9). The dominant sections among Muslims had emphasized the differences between Hindus and Muslims because they wanted to guard their special privileges during the British period, while the religious practices and even language of the Muslim masses did not differ significantly from those of the Hindu masses.

Muslim leaders belonging to the educated middle class or aristocracy were against representative government. Syed Ahmed Khan, for instance, pointed out that the Western system of representation would reduce Muslims to a 'permanent minority'. Muhammad Ali criticized the Western system as resting on 'lung power' and the 'counting of heads' (Brass 1975: 171-9). It was basically this middle class that migrated to Pakistan after Partition; the rural population, consisting of poor artisans and shopkeepers, preferred to stay back in India (Noorani 2003: 139-41). The political orientation of the Muslim masses differed from that of their leaders even after Independence. The National Emergency of 1975 was supported by all Muslim political organizations of the country, but the community at large was not happy with it. The Muslim leaders were practically unaware of the upsurge among the masses on account of excesses committed against Muslims by Indira Gandhi's government in Delhi and elsewhere. Moin Shakir has argued that there has been a persistent gap between the perception of the Muslim leaders and that of the voters (Shakir 1990: 100). A study of attitudes carried out at a district level in UP in the 1998 general elections vindicates this observation. The study points out that many villagers see no reason why the Muslim community should be isolated from others by a separate personal law, whereas Muslim leaders view personal law based on Shariat as one of the bases of identity (Dyke 1999: 122).

The difference between the upper classes and the masses is seen also in their voting behaviour. The 1993 MP election study concludes that upper-class Muslims may vote differently than lower-class ones. The relatively backward Muslim may support a party with a radical programme (Sanjaykumar 1996: 138-41). It was observed during the Lok Sabha elections of 1999 in UP that the more educated or rich Muslims 'feel a greater kinship with the Congress', while those belonging to the lower classes go with the SP (SG, SR 1999: 3421). Naushad Alvi found that the upper class generally gravitated towards the Congress in this election when the majority of working-class Muslims, like the weavers in eastern UP, favoured Mulayam Singh Yadav (Bhushan 1999: 29).

What Muslims have secured by playing the minority card is a question worth exploring at this point. They went to Congress to seek protection for their religious identity, their personal law, and Aligarh Muslim University. These were demands in which the interests of other communities were not directly involved, and no reallocation of resources was called for. However, when the interests of the Hindi-speaking elite were directly involved, the demand for the recognition of Urdu was put aside by all governments, both in

UP and at the centre. The Congress government failed to protect the Babri Masjid, another symbol of Muslim identity. The most agonizing record, however, is about the life and property of Muslims, which the law-and-order machinery in India has not been able to protect.

From the first riot after Independence in Jabalpur in 1961 to this date, Muslims have had a very bad deal as far as protection from Hindus is concerned. The Congress party has been blamed for its direct or indirect role in initiating the riots and also for not taking timely action to control the violence. Muslims have been demanding their due share in bureaucracy, education, and politics. The Congress, on whom the community relied, has given only decorative and nominal representation to Muslims. The party co-opted a few aspiring upper-class Muslim leaders in its hold-all system and demanded in return support of the Muslim 'vote-bank'. By submitting to Congress, Muslims became part of the establishment, so much so that the Jamiyat-ul-Ulama was branded as the 'sarkari party' (Puri 1993: 2142).

By extending support to Nehru, Muslims accorded sufficient space to his pluralistic politics of domination. However, Nehru could not break the alliance of higher castes led by Brahmans who were following a pro-Hindi, pro-Hindu line. He forgot what he had said during his Muslim mass-contact campaign of 1937, and co-opted upper class Muslims in his pluralistic structure. He also conveniently ignored his comment on Muslims' pseudo-religious mentality and tacitly consented to the growing control of orthodoxy over the Muslim masses. Nehru, with all his charisma and ideological rhetoric, could not touch the Muslim personal law or give recognition to Urdu as a second official language.

By siding with Indira Gandhi, Muslims became part of her populist strategy and lost whatever autonomy they had had. Muslims figured as pawns in her politics and when their support was not required, as happened after 1980, she discarded them. The Congress protected Muslims from the reformist agenda and from modernist elements, but not from violent attacks on their material existence in India. Congress also encouraged Muslim leadership to harp upon minority identity all the time. The interests of Nehru-Indira Congress and those of the Muslim dominant classes, it seems, coincided whenever it came to use and misuse of the minority card, and this exercise indirectly helped the Hindutva project of constructing a Hindu majority from the 1980s onward.

MAJORITARIANISM

One way of getting rid of this curse of minorityism would have been to join the project of Bahujanism, in which the term 'Bahujan' refers to all backward castes and communities. This project was conceived by Rammanohar Lohia, a socialist leader from UP, in the late 1950s. He said that women, Harijans, shudras, depressed Muslims and Christians, and adivasis constitute more than 85 per cent of India's population, but in four decisive fields, namely politics, the army, trade, and high government jobs, they were less than 10 per cent. Therefore, the Socialist Party should strive to give at least 60 per cent of key posts in public life to these backward sections (Lohia 1964: 121-42). Lohia sincerely believed that only through this exercise could the inequalities and backwardness be eradicated. He made it a crucial part of his socialist programme, which also included eradication of English and opposition to Congress.

Two things probably deterred Muslims from joining hands with Lohia: his pro-Hindi stance, which was a part of his plan to eradicate English, and his opposition to Congress. But it is essential to make a distinction between the Jana Sangh's (BJP's pre-1977 name) position on the Hindi language and that of Lohia. The Jana Sangh looked from a communal point of view and believed in a Hindi-Hindu equation, while Lohia took an egalitarian position. He thought that English was the language of the ruling class and Hindi that of the masses. Muslims who had stood behind Congress could not accept Lohia's anti-Congress stand. But the most important reason why Muslims did not join the Bahujans was the elitist character of the Muslim political class, which made them reject Lohia's egalitarianism. The 'depressed Muslims' probably had no agency to take decisions independently. In fact, a group of backward-class Muslims had shown the courage to stand up against the upper class long before, in the 1920s in Bihar, when Momins (handloom weavers), who form around 20 per cent of the Muslims of Bihar, refused to support the Muslim League. They backed the Congress party, which had started by that time projecting the symbol of the spinning wheel and had also promised to encourage indigenous handicrafts (Brass 1975: 247-57).

The Momins of Bihar and eastern UP had organized themselves into an all-India Momin conference in that decade (Khan 1997: 65-6). In the first few years after Independence, A. Q. Ansari had floated the Bihar State Backward Muslim Federation, which later on turned inactive. These attempts on the part of poor Muslim groups should be seen as the beginning of the politics of disadvantaged Muslims in UP and Bihar. However, it seems that these efforts could not last long; they were not the inspiration for the Bahujanism of later decades, which visualized a coalition of Hindu as well as Muslim backward classes against the ruling classes. The socialism of Hasrat Mohani and his colleagues, which had acquired a following among the Muslim workforce in Kanpur in the early 1920s, was restricted to the Muslim poor and became known as 'Islamic Socialism' (Gooptu 2001: 280).

It is a fact that there were no takers for Lohia's movement, even among Hindus, when it was proposed in the late 1950s. However, the general elections in 1967 was a time when Lohia's thesis of power to the backward classes was tested and vindicated to a certain degree in the Hindi-speaking belt. It must be noted that the defeat of the Congress in this region was due to a combination of factors and the rise of the backward classes was only one of them. Muslims, who by that time were disillusioned with the Congress, supported the opposition up to a point, but their support cannot be considered as a part of Lohia's backward-class politics. In 1977 again the backward castes rose to a powerful position: Muslims had backed the opposition. However, as we have seen in an earlier section, the Emergency excesses caused a distancing between Muslims and Congress, and that was the reason why they supported the opposition.

The 1989 elections were the third occasion when the backward castes came to prominence in the Hindi-speaking belt; again Muslims, for their own reasons, supported the Janata Dal, an instrument of backward-caste politics. And again it was also not a part of the Bahujan project. Muslims kept vacillating between the Congress party and the opposition (led by the backward-caste leaders) between 1967 and 1989 and never made a decisive choice to become a part of the Bahujan project. They therefore lost the chance to shake off the burden of minorityism, which they have been carrying since Partition.

A. G. Noorani has edited documents on how Muslims responded to post-Partition conditions. In his selection we come across extracts from the presidential address given by Badruddin Tyabji at the All India Muslim Political Convention in New Delhi on 19 December 1970. In his address Tyabji highlights the need to cooperate with organizations engaged in advancing the rights of backward classes and underprivileged people (Noorani 2003: 152). Here he does not make a reference to elite and backward classes within the Muslim community, but considers Muslims as constituting one backward community that might cooperate with others. Imtiaz Ahmad's sociological study of Muslims brings out the segmented nature of the community (Ahmad 1966: 268-78). In 1974 he proposed that each distinct stratum within the Muslim community should create a solidarity of social and economic interests with corresponding segments in other religious communities and should solve common problems in collaboration with the others (Ahmad 1974: 26). Here was a possibility of the borders of community gradually getting dissolved, and cross-community and class-like political formations based on common interests getting evolved. Since Ahmad insisted on a collaboration between each distinct stratum with a corresponding segment in the other religious community, it may be that his proposal did not visualize the two broad categories—Ashraf and Ajlaf, or advanced and backward Muslims—that are implied in the Bahujanism project. Ahmad had earlier argued that the two-fold division tends to produce a distorted picture of stratification in the Muslim community (Ahmad 1967: 890).

Lohia's thesis of uniting the backward classes to seek political power and due representation in crucial sectors was pushed further in the late 1980s—under the leadership of V. P. Singh, a high-caste leader from UP who became Prime Minister of the Janata Dal-led government in 1989, and Mulayam Singh Yadav, who became Chief Minister of UP in the same year. The V. P. Singh government accepted the recommendations of the Mandal Commission to reserve 27 per cent of government jobs for the other backward castes (OBCs). The Commission had included backward Muslim communities among the OBCs. Mulayam Singh Yadav, committed to

Lohia's bahujanism, considered the Mandal report the 'cornerstone of Lohiaite politics' (Hasan 1998: 150), which latter was not only an instrument of empowerment for the OBC but also a defence against the onslaught of Hindutva. He stopped the marches of Hindutva followers towards the Babri Masjid in 1990. He formulated and also to some extent implemented pro-Muslim programmes during his Chief Ministership. No wonder he soon emerged as the protector of Muslims (van Dyke 1999: 111). He challenged the secular credentials of the Congress and saw a similarity between the Congress and the BJP, both being urban-based and pro-capitalist parties (SG, SR 1999: 3419). Mulayam Singh believes that God is one. Ram and Allah are God's two names. Mulayam Singh appeals to people to stay away from violence, since it has no place in democracy. He claims that he is following in the footsteps of Mahatma Gandhi and Lohia (Yadav 1993: 2-7). Gandhi is seen as a symbol of Hindu-Muslim unity and Lohia as the symbol of empowerment of backward classes and castes. Mulayam Singh severed his ties with the Janata Dal and formed the Samajwadi Party (SP) in 1992. He and his party successfully established the M–Y combination (M = Muslim, Y = Yadav) in UP politics. Muslims looked to the SP with hope and supported it consistently from the 1993 Assembly elections to the 1999 Lok Sabha and 2000 Assembly elections. Voting behaviour studies conducted by the Centre for the Study of Developing Societies during the 1996 Lok Sabha elections reveal that one of the important reasons for the better performance of the National Front and the Left Front was the Muslim vote these fronts secured (48 per cent) (Yadav 1996: 48). In the 1998 elections, the United Front fared well again, due to the Muslim vote (30 per cent). It is crucial to note that in both elections, these Fronts got a higher proportion of the Muslim vote due to the impact of the SP (Yadav et al. 1998: 49).

The Bahujan Samaj Party (BSP), formed in 1984, is an offshoot of the Backward and Minorities Employees Federation (1978) and the Dalit Shoshit Samaj Sangharsha Samiti (1982). Kanshiram, its founder and ideologue, divides Indian society into the Alpjan (minority), composed of the three upper classes, and the Bahujan, consisting of backward castes, Dalits, Tribes, Muslims, Christians, and Sikhs, or all those not included in the Alpjan. Muslims are treated as a single category and the BSP has so far not made a distinction between upper-class and poor Muslims (Chandra 1999a: 68). While the Congress promises to protect the minority identity of Muslims, the BSP offers them political power. Kanshiram believes that humiliation is the real problem of Dalits and minorities, and that the only solution is political power. He holds that capturing power should be the uppermost priority and that other things will follow (Chandra 1999b: 50-1). His party allotted Muslims around 16 per cent tickets in 1996 and also in the 1998 Lok Sabha elections. Muslims have extended their support to the BSP since the early 1990s. However, the party entered into an alliance with the BJP in 1995 and 2000 to form a government in order to keep the SP out of power. Consequently the BSP's share in the Muslim vote has remained restricted to 4 or 5 per cent (Jaffrelot 2003: 401).

In Bihar, the JD and Laloo Prasad Yadav's RJD, formed in 1997, have emerged as the parties claiming the Muslim vote from 1989 onwards. Sanjaykumar's study of Bihar's electoral politics in recent years shows that the M–Y combination also holds good in Bihar and that the RJD has retained power in the state, basically due to the overwhelming backing of Yadavs and Muslims (Sanjaykumar 2000: 29).

Bahujanism reached its height in 1993, when the SP–BSP alliance defeated the BJP in UP, the heart of *Aryavarta*. This victory was seen as a sign of how caste populism of the SP–BSP alliance could counteract the onslaught of Hindutva (Vora 2003: 271-98). The 1993 Assembly elections in UP were held against the background of the demolition of the Babri Masjid in December 1992. A novel equation of Muslims (16 per cent), OBC (37 per cent), and Dalits (22 per cent) had emerged on the political scene of UP. This equation gave a hope that if these backward sections, who account for 75 per cent of the population of UP, came together, they would be able to stop the tide of Hindutva. However, these expectations did not last long, because the SP and BSP parted ways, and Muslim, OBC, and Dalit votes were split.

The Shift to OBC Parties

The shift of Muslim voters from Congress to SP, BSP or RJD since the mid-1990s has been interpreted by Javeed Alam as a shift away from 'concerns of security fostered by the Congress to those of equality and dignity'. He observes that the Muslim masses find that the OBCs and Dalits are 'adjacent' to them. It is a case, he says, of 'alignment of interests of a secular nature, a social coalition of oppressed forces' (Alam 1999: 760). A social coalition of oppressed forces is what Lohia had in mind when he proposed his majoritarianism based on the criterion of backwardness irrespective of religious distinctions. This radical potential, however, was not recognized by the majority of Muslims or by their middle-class representatives earlier; it is being recognized when the project has, to a large extent, exhausted that potential (Sikand 2004: 109-19). The following observations will substantiate this argument.

In the first instance, we should take note that Bahujanism, which is a project of constructing a majority of all the downtrodden, cannot succeed if there is internal dissension. After the 1993 experiment, the BSP and SP have never joined hands. Second, the BSP twice entered into an alliance with the BJP, which was until recently branded an Alpjan party. If Hindutva and a Bahujan party come together to capture power, that will be the end of the project of Lohia. Muslim leaders were also drawn into this opportunistic exercise of the BSP. They not only supported the BSP–BJP alliance, but also shared power. Third, it has been observed that during election campaigns Mulayam Singh Yadav treats Muslims as one category and does not bring out the internal divisions in that community (Chandra 1999b: 76-7). The SP does not differ much in this from the Congress. Fourth, it is necessary to take into account the fact that the BJP also mobilised the backward castes through its social engineering strategy and gave them a share in power—both within the party and within the government—thereby blurring the boundaries between an upper-caste party and a backward-caste party. Fifth, Muslims do support the SP, BSP, and RJD, but still consider Congress as a dependable friend, even though, as seen in earlier sections, upper-class Muslims vote Congress, while lower class Muslims prefer SP or BSP. Last, it is essential to know whether Muslims stand behind the SP or BSP in UP and the RJD in Bihar out of conviction or out of sheer expediency. Is the Muslim–SP equation similar to the Muslim–Congress equation of an earlier era? It is clear that Muslim leaders advise their followers to vote for Mulayam Singh, not because he is one of the torch-bearers of Bahujanism, but because he is a protector of their community. It is apparent that since the early 1990s Muslims have been keeping all options open. Voting behaviour studies conducted from 1989 until the 2000 elections have shown that the Muslim vote gets divided into many parties, and that Muslim preferences are determined by political conditions that prevail at the time of a particular election.

From the foregoing discussion, a fact that glaringly comes to the surface is that Muslims have lost the historic opportunity to become part of a project of constructing a majority of all backward castes and communities. They could not become equal partners in organizing the backward-class politics in the Hindi-speaking belt. A political elite belonging to backward communities among Muslims did not take the initiative in establishing linkages with leaders of the backward castes. As noted earlier, radical outfits of a backward or socialist nature initiated by Muslim leaders largely remained restricted to Muslims. Muslim backward-class leaders could not envisage a grand scenario of majority construction cutting across religious barriers. Instead of deciding confidently to work out a social coalition of the backward and the downtrodden, Muslims have vacillated between the Congress and SP or between the SP and BSP. The backward Muslim masses have not been able to uncover the motives of the political class who claimed to represent the *millat* (community) as a whole. They should have realized that the leaders exploit the appeal to Islam and community solidarity as a shield for their political designs (Hasan 1997: 51). Unless they 'deconstruct the language of minorityism', poor Muslims, whose life experience and cultural expressions are not different from those of the lower Hindu castes and Dalits, will not be able to take the initiative in building a people's movement and will not develop the expansive and inclusive tendencies required for carrying with them their counterparts from other religious communities.

By accepting the status of a permanent minority, Muslims directly helped the Hindutva forces to engineer a Hindu majority, something that until the 1990s had been a myth. Babasaheb Ambedkar never approved this tendency of self-perpetuation among minorities. While addressing the Constituent Assembly in November 1948, he said that the constitutional safeguards are not sufficient to avert this tendency. These safeguards will have to be matched by appropriate political action in the form of a party system (Noorani 2003: 9). Ambedkar found Lohia's idea of an alliance among all deprived sections attractive, and had thought of bringing his party and that of Lohia closer to each other to work out a new equation. However, he died before any of this could materialize (Vora 1995: 11-16).

PARTICIPATION IN MASS-STRUGGLES

A second course of action that Muslims could have taken would have been wholehearted participation in the social and political struggles of the masses in the country. There was a time when Muslims from the Hindi heartland participated in the nationalist movement and also in socialist and communist organizations. The Muslim middle class used to take a leading part in peasant and student agitations. However, in recent decades it either has withdrawn from such activities or is involved only in organizations catering to the needs of its own community. The Muslim middle class is not a small segment but its politics is restricted to seeking positions on Waqf Boards, Hajj committees, Urdu academies, personal law boards, or minority commissions. The political elite, which comes from this class, strives for election tickets from one of the mainstream parties, hoping somehow to get into government. In the last decade or so, they have turned to even the BJP for such favours and have stuck to power positions even after the Sangh Parivar demolished a masjid and massacred thousands of their brethren. Muslim political and religious leaders have not in recent decades gone beyond electoral politics. Their idea of democracy is limited to vote-bank politics, in return for which they receive some rewards from the mainstream parties. They play voting games on behalf of some party and are happy when that party gets elected. In short, they have assumed the role of political agents, not political leaders. They send petitions to the government or delegations to the President or Prime Minister; they organize conventions or occasionally hold rallies; they take part in electoral activities; and they hold debates in the legislature. The focal point of all these activities is grievances and demands of the community. The Muslim political class has shown little serious concern for what is happening to Indian democracy or to the masses in general. If one goes through the charters of demands submitted to the governments and ruling parties since Independence, one finds only occasional and token references to conditions of, say, the scheduled castes or the other poor. Most of the grievances that figure in Muslim leaders' speeches in conventions are about their own community and they are mostly related to religious matters and identity issues rather than material conditions.

Recently, especially after the demolition of the Babri Masjid, Muslims have begun talking in terms of reservation of seats for Muslims in legislative bodies, government administration, and educational institutions. If the Muslim backward classes had participated in the Bahujan project since its inception they would have formed an equal contingent in the struggle and would have got the benefits not because they are Muslims but because they are deprived. Even without participating on an equal footing in the backward-caste struggle for reservations, many Muslims have been considered eligible for benefits by the Mandal commission. It is a gift to them from the backward castes' struggle for social justice, a gift from a project that had its origins in Lohia's ideas of the late 1950s.

Today, when this project is almost a spent force, the only viable alternative for Muslims in the Hindi belt is to take part in the democratic struggles of marginalized sections, in people's movements, in women's and environmental movements, and also in peasant and workers' movements. Muslims' continuous and committed involvement in these social and political movements will put an end to their humiliation and dissolve their question of minority identity. Since participation in mass struggles is the best way to get a political education, the Muslim masses will come out more mature and confident to join the project of defending democracy from the aggression of the Hindutva forces.

The Hindutva forces are not only targeting Muslims. They are also targeting the very foundation of Indian democracy. Therefore, becoming involved in a mass struggle to save democratic rights and institutions is the best way to defeat Hindutva politics. In the wake of the demolition of the Babri Masjid, Muslims of the Hindi belt have not become mobilised in a democratic fashion. Secularists and liberals or modernists received a patient hearing after the demolition. A suggestion to revive a composite culture was made. A need to enlarge the community's socio-economic and educational resources through promotion of ameliorative activity was emphasized (Hasan 1997: 322-7). In 1994 and 1999, a demand for reservation of seats for the community in legislative bodies was forcefully put forward. Parties—secular parties—were appealed to field common Muslim candidates from at least 100 constituencies in the Lok Sabha elections (Noorani 2003: 281-2). Nowhere does one find an appeal to the community to get itself involved in the larger and broader struggles for rights and livelihood that are being undertaken by the masses in general. These struggles, carried out on the basis of principles of satyagraha, are what is ultimately going to save democracy in India—not the sectarian or parochial politics of minorities. Minority politics has become an ineffective tool to tackle the challenges before Indian democracy, especially after the coming of the Hindutva wave in the early 1990s. Muslims seem to have two options: either to become second-class citizens by succumbing to Hindutva's homogenization strategy, or to participate in the larger non-violent democratic struggles of the weaker sections, become part of the majority, and throw away the shackles of minorityism.

It is the failure to understand the true character of Hindutva that has weakened Muslim politics in the sacred region. Hindutva took a definite and decided turn after 1980, with a neo-fascist twist. The opposite of neo-fascism is democracy, not secularism. Secular rhetoric was all right in the days of conventional communal politics of Hindus. But since the rise of the neo-fascist politics of Hindutva it has turned into an ineffective and inadequate tool (Vora 2002: 10-15). Muslims of the cow-belt are still continuing their conventional minority politics, in which they seek protection and redressal of grievances, ignoring the fundamental transformation that has occurred in the political ethos of India and especially in their region. The usual politics of conventions, petitions, grievances, demands, and delegations is increasingly becoming insufficient to face the new challenges posed by forces that not only believe in violence but also glorify it. And this is applicable to the Hindutva brigade as well as to Islamic fundamentalist tendencies that have grown up in this very period in the region. Sectarian politics based on minorityism is not going to help Muslims in facing this challenge. Minorityism in fact is one of the reasons why fundamentalist organizations have found strength in recent decades among Muslims. It is true that West Asian fundamentalists have exported their creed to India and that Pakistan is encouraging and supporting activities of Indian fundamentalists, but it is also true that, had Muslims thought of giving up on minorityism earlier, had they joined the majoritarianism of the backward classes and the democratic struggles of the masses, they could have reversed these tendencies.

REFERENCES

Ahmad, Imtiaz. 1966. 'The Ashraf-Ajlaf Dichotomy in Muslim Social Structure in India', *Indian Economic and Social History Review* 3 (3): 268-78.

———. 1967. 'The Ashraf and Ajlaf Categories in Indo-Muslim Society', *Economic and Political Weekly* 2, No. 19 (May 13): 887-91.

———. 1974. 'An Essential Prerequisite', *Seminar*, No. 174 (February): 24-7.

Alam, Javeed. 1999. 'Is Caste Appeal Casteism? Oppressed Castes in Politics', *Economic and Political Weekly* 34, No. 13 (27 March): 757-61.

Basu, Amrita. 1996. 'Mass Movement or Elite Conspiracy? The Puzzle of Hindu Nationalism', in Ludden, ed., 1996: 55-80.

Bhushan, Ranjit. 1999. 'Real Politick Casino', *Outlook*, 18 October, pp. 28-30.

Brass, Paul. 1975. *Language, Religion and Politics in North India*. New Delhi: Vikas Publishing House.

Burman, J. J. Roy. 1996. 'Hindu-Muslim Syncretism in India', *Economic and Political Weekly* 31, No. 20 (18 May): 1211-15.

Chandra, Kanchan. 1999a. 'Mobilising the Excluded', *Seminar*, No. 480 (August): 47-51.

———. 1999b. 'Post-Congress Politics in Uttar Pradesh: The Ethnification of the Party System and its Consequences', in Roy and Wallace, eds., 1999: 55-104.

Chatterji, Nandalal. 1957. *Glories of Uttar Pradesh*. Lucknow: Publications Bureau, Uttar Pradesh.

Dasgupta, Swapan. 1990. 'Confrontation in UP: Logic of Mulayam Singh's Offensive', *The Times of India*, 24 September.

Davis, Richard M. 1996. 'The Iconography of Rama's Chariot', in Ludden, ed., 1996: 28-54.

Eck, Diana L. 1998. 'The Imagined Landscape: Patterns in the Construction of Hindu Sacred Geography', *Contributions to Indian Sociology* 32, No. 2 (July-December): 165-88.

Engineer, Asghar Ali. 1998. 'Re-emergence of Communalism in Post-Independence India', in Ram, ed., 1998: 58-76.

Ghosh, Partha S. 1999. *BJP and the Evolution of Hindu Nationalism: From Periphery to Centre*. New Delhi: Manohar.

Gooptu, Nandini. 2001. *The Politics of the Urban Poor in Early 20th Century India*. Cambridge: Cambridge University Press.

Graf, Violette. 1992. 'The Muslim Vote', in Mitra and Chiriyankandath, eds., 1992, pp. 213-40.

Gupta, Charu. 2001. 'The Icon of Mother in Late Colonial North India: "Bharat Mata", "Matri Bhasha" and "Gau Mata" ' *Economic and Political Weekly* 36, No. 45 (10 November): 4291-9.

Hasan, Mushirul. 1997. *Legacy of a Divided Nation: India's Muslims Since Independence*. New Delhi: Oxford University Press.

Hasan, Zoya. 1989. 'Minority Identity, Muslim Women Bill Campaign and the Political Process', *Economic and Political Weekly* 24, No. 1 (7 January): 44-50.

———. 1996. 'Communal Mobilisation and Changing Majority in U.P.', in Ludden, ed., 1996: 28-54.

———. 1998. *Quest for Power: Oppositional Movements and Post-Congress Politics in Uttar Pradesh*. New Delhi: Oxford University Press.

———, ed. 2002. *Parties and Party Politics in India*. New Delhi: Oxford University Press.

Heath, Oliver. 2002. 'Anatomy of BJP's Rise to Power: Social, Regional and Political Expansion in the 1990s', in Hasan, ed., 2002: 232-56.

Jaffrelot, Christopher. 2003. *India's Silent Revolution: The Rise of the Low Castes in North Indian Politics*. New Delhi: Permanent Black.

Jones, Kenneth W. 1994. *Socio-Religious Reform Movements in British India*. New Delhi: Foundation Books.

Kang, Bhavdeep and Saba Naqvi Bhaumik. 2003. 'The Milky Way', *Outlook*, 10 March, pp. 30-8.

Khalidi, Omar. 1993. 'Muslims in Indian Political Process: Group Goals and Alternative Strategies', *Economic and Political Weekly* 28, Nos. 1 and 2: 43-54.

———. 1995. *Indian Muslims Since Independence*. New Delhi: Vikas Publishing House.

Khan, Maulana Wahiduddin. 1997. *Indian Muslims: A Need for a Positive Outlook*. New Delhi: Al-Risala Books.

Khan, Rasheeduddin. 1974. 'Perspectives and Prospects', *Seminar*, No. 174 (February): 13-19.

———. 1978. 'Minority Segments in Indian Polity: Muslim Situation and Plight of Urdu', *Economic and Political Weekly* 13, No. 35 (2 September): 1509-15.

Larson, Gerald James. 1997. *India's Agony over Religion*. New Delhi: Oxford University Press.

Lohia, Rammanohar. 1964. *The Caste System*. Hyderabad: Navhind.

Ludden, David, ed. 1996. *Making India Hindu*. New Delhi: Oxford University Press.

Mitra, S. K. and J. Chiriyankandath, eds. 1992. *Electoral Politics in India: A Changing Landscape*. New Delhi: Segment Books.

Noorani, A. G. 2003. *The Muslims of India: A Documentary Record*. New Delhi: Oxford University Press.

Pai, Sudha. 2002. 'Politics of Language: Decline of Urdu in Uttar Pradesh', *Economic and Political Weekly* 37, No. 27 (6 July): 2705-8.

Pandey, Gyanendra. 1990. *The Construction of Communalism in Colonial North India*. New Delhi: Oxford University Press.

Pinch, William R. 1996. 'Soldier Monks and Militant Sadhus', in Ludden, ed., 1996: 140-61.

Puri, Balraj. 1978. 'Autonomy and Participation: Dimensions of Indian Muslim Identity', *Economic and Political Weekly* 13, No. 40 (7 October): 1706-12.

———. 1993. 'Indian Muslims Since Partition', *Economic and Political Weekly* 28, No. 40 (2 October): 2141-9.

Ram, P. R., ed. 1998. *Secular Challenge and Communal Politics: A Reader*. Mumbai: Vikas Adhyayana Kendra.

Robinson, Francis. 1995. *Separatism Among Indian Muslims*. New Delhi: Vikas Publishing House.

Roy, Ramashray and Richard Sisson, eds. 1990. *Diversity and Dominance in Indian Politics*, Vol. 2. New Delhi: Sage.

Roy, Ramashray and Paul Wallace, eds. 1999. *Indian Politics and the 1998 Election: Regionalism, Hindutva and State Politics*. New Delhi: Sage.

Rudolph, Lloyd and Susanne Hoeber Rudolph. 1987. *In Pursuit of Laxmi: The Political Economy of the Indian State*. Chicago: The University of Chicago Press.

Sanjaykumar. 1996. 'Muslims in Electoral Politics', *Economic and Political Weekly* 21, Nos. 2 and 3 (13-20 January): 138-41.

———. 2000. 'The Return of the RJD', *Frontline*, 31 March, pp. 27-30.

Sarkar, Sumit. 1986. *Modern India: 1885-1947*. Madras: Macmillan India.

SG, SR. 1999. 'Uttar Pradesh: Samajwadi Party Holds Ground', *Economic and Political Weekly* 34, No. 49 (4 December): 3419-21.

Shakir, Moin. 1990. 'Congress and the Minority Vote', in Roy and Sisson, eds., 1990: 97-108.

Sikand, Yoginder. 2004. *Muslims in India Since 1947: Islamic Perspectives on Inter-faith Relations*. London: Routledge Curzon.

Talib, Rasheed. 1979. 'A Creative Option', *Seminar*, No. 240 (August): 18-21.

Trivedi, Harish. 1995. 'A View From Pardes', *Seminar*, No. 432 (August): 48-50.

Troll, C. W. 2003. *Muslim Shrines in India*. New Delhi: Oxford University Press.

van Dyke, Virginia. 1999. 'The 1998 General Elections: The Janus-Faced

Policies of the BJP and Religious Mobilisation at the District Level in Uttar Pradesh', in Roy and Wallace, eds., 1999, pp. 105-28.

Varma, Rajani Kant, ed. 1993. *Mulayam Singh Yadav Ke Sat Sawal* (Hindi). Lucknow: Himalaya Features.

Vora, Rajendra. 1995. 'Bahujanwad Va Samajwad' (Marathi). *Samaj Vidnyan Samvad*, No. 7 (June): 11-16.

———. 2002. 'Middle Class, Democracy and Secularism: Lessons From Gujarat', Seminar, VAK and YUVA, Mumbai, 12-14 July (unpublished).

———. 2003. 'Decline of Caste Majoritarianism in Indian Politics', in Vora and Palshikar, eds., 2003, pp. 271-98.

Vora, Rajendra and Suhas Palshikar, eds., 2003. *Indian Democracy: Meanings and Practices*. New Delhi: Sage.

Wright, Gillian. 1995. 'The Decline of Congress: The Rise of Mulayam', *Seminar*, No. 432 (August): 19-23.

Wright, Theodore P., Jr. 1977. 'Muslims and the 1977 Indian Elections: A Watershed?' *Asian Survey* 17, No. 12 (December): 1207-20.

Yadav, Yogendra. 1996. 'Exit Poll: Who Voted Whom', *India Today*, 31 May, pp. 47-50.

———, Alistair Macmillan and Kanchan Chandra. 1998. 'Post-Poll: Who Voted For Whom?' *India Today*, 16 March, pp. 49-52.

Zakaria, Rafiq. 1995. *The Widening Divide: An Insight into Hindu-Muslim Relations*. New Delhi: Viking.

14

Regional Politics, City Conflicts and Communal Riots: Ahmedabad 1985-1986[1]

Sujata Patel

In a recent contribution, Ashutosh Varshney states that Ahmedabad and Baroda, together with Surat, have seen the worst communal frenzy in India, with the last phase being as recent as February-March 2002. From 1969 onwards and then in 1985-6, Ahmedabad witnessed violent communal confrontations, as did Baroda and Surat, while Godhra has had 'low intensity' communal conflict since Independence (Varshney 2002: 104-6).

This paper argues that the communal conflicts in these cities need to be evaluated against the backdrop of the regional politics of that period. It contends that inequalities (of class, caste, and religion, for example) pervading the city, and the conflicts surrounding these inequalities, were mobilized in the political confrontations that took place between, on the one hand, the upper-caste economic and social elite and, on the other, the lower-caste political leadership. In the context of the economic and political crisis affecting Gujarat, the two sides were unable to frame a common agenda for a new political bloc. This paper argues that the confrontations between the two segments of the elite relate to the incorporation of lower-caste regional interests within the existing urban upper-caste political bloc. The inability of the economic and social elite to accommodate these groups within their bloc led to a major conflict between it and the political leaders. The riots of 1985-6 became the theatre through which the two groups demonstrated their relative political strength. This political conflict was played out in and through the communal riots that held the city ransom for more than five months.

The focus in this paper is on the politics of the state in these years. I examine (a) the nature of Gujarat's politics prior to the 1985-6 riots;

(b) the upward mobility of sections among the regional groups and the Congress and the political elite's attempt to accommodate the expectations of these mobile groups; (c) the incorporation of these aspirations through the policy of extension of reservation for backward classes and through the formation of a political bloc called KHAM (Kshatriya, Harijan, Adivasi and Muslim); (d) the alienation of the economic and social elite groups from these measures and their mobilization against the Congress party through the anti-reservation movement, later supported by the opposition parties; (e) the belated attempt by the Congress and the political elite to appease the upper-caste elite by attempting to form a Hindu bloc, thereby isolating the Muslim community through acts of omission; (f) the later acts of commission of the state government and the political elite, fuelling communal conflict into a major confrontation between Hindus and Muslims; (g) the ways in which class, caste, and religious conflicts of the city were mobilized in this confrontation; and (h) the ultimate resolution of these conflicts, which arrived when the Chief Minister resigned, reinforcing the point that the issue remained political.

The communal riots of 1985-6 represent a fascist response by the elite, now divided between the mainly upper-caste economic and social elites and the mainly lower-caste political leaders, represented in the Congress party. At the heart of the conflict was the dispute as to which group should form and lead the new political bloc and what would be its ideology. After 1985 a Hindu bloc with the upper-caste elite at its helm was formed and then consolidated. Additionally the later years saw the institutionalization of communal conflict as a way to represent and solve the contradictions emerging as the upper castes formed a Hindu bloc in order to establish their own hegemonic domination.[2] Low-intensity communal conflict pervaded the cities of Gujarat for the next fifteen years, culminating in February-March 2002 with the worst communal confrontations recorded in the history of India since Partition. I would argue that the analysis of the processes that led to the 1985-6 confrontations helps us understand the later events and processes, including the 2002 conflicts.[3]

The Political Crisis of the 1970s and 1980s

Political sociologists (Khilnani 1997, Corbridge and Harriss 2000) have argued that the post-Nehruvian years heralded an economic and political crisis in India fuelled by contradictions emerging from the Nehruvian 'developmental state' and the breakdown of the system of 'one party dominance'. Also, post Nehru, the introduction of new technologies in agriculture led in many regions of the country to the growth of a new rich peasant class (the kulaks), who invested their profits in small industries and services as they moved to new towns that emerged in the country. This development paved the way for the shaping of a new alliance between the urban-based industrial and business groups, the new agrarian elite, and the bureaucracy. Politically, this change was reflected in the growth of regionalism, as a mobile agrarian bourgeoisie encouraged the growth of regional parties. It is in this context that Indira Gandhi took over the leadership of the country.

Indira Gandhi's regime attempted to resolve this political and economic crisis. On the one hand, she dismantled the Congress organization and substituted it with personality-based politics and loyalty to the Nehru-Gandhi 'family'. This brought to an end a system of patronage and accommodation used as strategies and tactics for conflict resolution by the 'Congress system'. On the other hand, she used the election process to go directly to the 'people'; an attempt was made to mobilize the lower sections of society (the restless backward castes on the margins of the processes of democracy) through a politics of economic populism. The Indira Gandhi years saw new policies being implemented: bank nationalization, the abolition of privy purses, and programmes for the poor in agriculture, all bound together in the programme of *Garibi Hatao*. It is in this period that democracy came to be equated with winning elections rather than creating opportunities for all to enter the political process.

The decade of the 1970s was characterized by contradictory trends, with uneven mobilization from below. Mobile groups of kulaks based in urban India came to a compromise with the Indira Gandhi regime as they jostled for power with the old elites. Many twists and turns took place in the political realm as the opposition confronted the Indira Gandhi regime before and after the Emergency. In search of a common agenda to build an alliance between contradictory interests, primordial identities found a space; the 1970s was a decade when caste, ethnicity, and religious sentiments found their political space, and identity movements mobilized urban and agrarian conflicts.

In her second avatar as Prime Minister, beginning in 1980, Indira Gandhi abandoned her earlier strategy of mobilizing the lower sections of society through economic populism. Instead she experimented with two other political formulae to consolidate power and defeat fragmented interests in place in the various states. The first was to incorporate religious extremists into mainstream politics in order to retain power. This experiment, attempted first in the Punjab but also in Assam and in Kashmir, brought the politics of religion onto centre stage. Over time this led to the crystallization of a Hindu bloc. The second formula was to build a bloc of the deprived by mobilizing these groups through a policy of reservations. This was first attempted in the late 1970s in Gujarat, where the bloc called KHAM was formed with a one-point agenda: an extension of reservations for backward castes.[4]

In the immediate aftermath of Indira Gandhi's death in 1984, Rajiv Gandhi, the next Prime Minister and the leader of the Congress party, approved the continuation of the latter strategy, mobilizing the lower sections to gain power in Gujarat and to defeat a conglomeration of interests bound together by a *savarna* (upper caste) ideology (Patel 1996). To gain control in Delhi, the Congress party used the other strategy, that of mobilizing Hindus against Sikhs. Both these strategies turned out to be a success, as the Congress won the election at the centre and state levels. The victory of the Congress in Gujarat was resounding and displaced for the first time the rule of the upper castes.

However, the upper castes did not accept this defeat. They immediately mobilized against the KHAM model by sponsoring an anti-reservation agitation. Initially students, and later members of the state apparatus and civil society—the bureaucracy and the police, the press and the judiciary—were mobilized. The Congress attempted to deflect this move, so soon after their victory, by allowing a localized communal conflict to escalate. They also attempted to 'appease' the upper castes through an attempt to build a Hindu bloc. This attempt proved unsuccessful, as the upper castes had by then consolidated themselves against the Congress in and through the anti-reservation movement. The Hindu-Muslim conflict that the Congress allowed to take place was exacerbated into full-scale communal conflict, with the Congress and the opposition parties competing with each other to consolidate behind the Hindu bloc, thereby making the Muslims the victims of their politics.

This action-reaction sequence continued for more than five months. It not only affected Ahmedabad but engulfed other cities as well, along with towns based in rural areas of Gujarat. In this first attempt, the opposition achieved success and the Congress was left teetering on the brink of collapse. Congress had displaced the KHAM bloc to encourage the formation of the Hindu bloc, neither of which was in a successful hegemonic position. They had also created a situation wherein the upper castes migrated to the opposition. The politics of the next two decades was that of upper castes trying to form the Hindu bloc by weaning away the kshatriyas, adivasis and harijans. As a result, the Congress lost power as well as its organizational strength among these deprived communities.

My argument in this paper is that the city of Ahmedabad, and the riots that took place immediately after the election of March 1985, became the theatre for competing regional groups to experiment with two ideological strategies to build hegemonic blocs. During the course of this paper I will show how various economic and political issues of the city came to be mobilized by these two groups in support of their political agendas. The riots stopped nearly five months later when the two groups ran out of steam; this competition left the city deeply divided on communal lines. This was the first in a series of 'historical moments', the latest being February-March 2002, when the city's politics came to be submerged in that of the region.

The conflicts in the city stretched from 18 March 1985 to 31 July 1985. Over the course of five months, the total number of deaths recorded was 178 (78 Hindus and 100 Muslims). Through police firings and stabbings 1,039 people received injuries. The cost of loss and damage to public property was Rs. 24.75 lakh, and that to private property was Rs. 855.02 lakh, of which 88 per cent belonged to Hindus and 12 per cent to Muslims. In these five months, 1,130 tenements and slums were destroyed. Of these, 600 belonged to scheduled castes and 530 to the Muslim poor. 273 persons were arrested under the National Security Act and 93 under PASA. 3,306 preventive arrests were made and 2,078 persons, 45 per cent of whom were Muslim, were booked on substantial charges (Patel 1987).

Caste, Reservation and the Formation of a New Bloc

In contemporary India, political power, ritual purity and social hierarchy have intermingled in a pattern which has been able to co-opt the colonial democratic institutions to work at the behest of the economically powerful interests who are high on the scale of ritual purity. The modern variant of the caste system as it reflects itself in the political process combines effectively the characteristics of jati and varna to aid and continue to maintain the economic interests of the upper classes over the deprived groups in the society. Solidarity of caste interests mediates to articulate class interests. The consolidation of upper-caste interests in politics took place during the national movement. In Gujarat, this meant that the Congress leaders were mainly drawn from the upper castes, the brahmans, the baniyas and the Patidars.

A hundred years ago, the Patidars were not considered an upper caste. The upper castes in Gujarat were the Brahmans, Banias and Rajputs. Below them were the peasant Kanbis; and ritually lower than them, the Kolis and castes of similar standing. Then came the artisan castes, and, at the bottom, those castes whom we term the scheduled castes (SC) today. In addition, there were tribes and other non-Hindu communities, chief among them the Muslims.

Over the last hundred years, with the integration of Gujarat with the world economy, there has been an upward mobility of the upper levels of the peasantry, the Kanbis, at the expense of the Kolis, accompanied by their rise in the ritual scale through the process of Sanskritization. The mobility of the Kanbis has been a feature of the last hundred years and has been an effect of the differential integration of various regions of Gujarat within the world economy. Initially, it was the Kanbis of central Gujarat who rose in economic and social stratum with the grant of land rights in their favour. By the 1930s, their political pressure made possible a change of their caste name from Kanbi to the status-group name Patidar (landholder). In the post-Independence period Patidar-Kanbis of north Gujarat and Saurashtra obtained rights through the Land Reform Legislation. Their rise and consolidation throughout Gujarat has occurred at the expense of the lower peasantry, the Kolis, who have been pushed to become small cultivators or agricultural labourers. This structural conflict has had important consequences for political alliances in Gujarat.[5]

By the end of the twentieth century, the Patidars of central Gujarat, the Baniyas, and the Brahmans had consolidated their position in the political arena through the Congress party and now controlled state power as well as its ideological apparatus. The representatives of these castes dominated the educational institutions, the judiciary, and the administration, while a few Baniya and Patidar families jointly controlled the economic resources of the state. The upper-caste domination of the state was complete.[6]

The social, political and economic domination of the upper castes received its first jolt soon after Independence with the formation in 1948 of the Gujarat Kshatriya Sabha. This Sabha pooled the resources of the Kolis with those of the Rajputs in a bloc which first aimed to improve its economic chances through a process of Sanskritization and participation in political dynamics. Its formation made an immediate impact on the upper-caste-led Congress in Gujarat, which did yield some seats to the Sabha. An effort was made by the Patidars to recruit the upper-caste Rajputs into an alliance, keeping a distance from the Kolis, their traditional foes. However, since its formation, this particular combination of caste groups has affected in a significant way the politics of the state mainly because of its demographic weight and the mobilization of poor peasantry.

It is difficult to estimate the population of Gujarat on the basis of caste. Most political scientists have used the 1931 census figures, which roughly indicate that in the post-Independence period the upper-caste Gujarati population is about 25 per cent (Baniyas 3 per cent, Brahmans 4 per cent, Rajputs 5 per cent, Patidars 12 per cent, and others 1 per cent). The Kolis and other similar castes (38 per-cent), with the artisan castes (6 per cent), total 44 per cent of the population. The remaining are the scheduled castes (7 per cent), the scheduled tribes (14 per cent), and the Muslims (9 per cent) and other non-Hindu communities (1 per cent). It is immediately perceivable that a coalition of Kolis and similar castes with the backward castes and the Rajputs would be formidable. Together, they constitute more than half of the population of the state (Patel 1987; Sheth and Menon 1986).

In its initial years, because of the social background of its leadership (generally upper-caste Rajputs) and its aspiration for Sanskritization, this bloc did not form itself into a coalition that was intimidating for the upper-caste-led Congress party. As a result, the lower-caste Kolis would prefer the varna term 'kshatriya' rather than jati names like Patanvadias or Talpadas. Because of a lack of consciousness of social and ideological distance from the upper castes, the Sabha had only one motive, political power. Initially, the Congress could accommodate this goal through its Rajput leaders. Later, when these ambitions became difficult to fulfil within the Congress, members of the Sabha forged an alliance with the rich Patidars to form the Swatantra Party. In the 1960s, this bloc could not realize much of its ambitions, until it came to an understanding with Mrs. Gandhi in 1969 over the issue of reservations. This alliance led to the consolidation of its identity, over the decade, as the bloc of the oppressed.

The second jolt to this specific upper-caste hegemony arrived in the form of the growth of aspirations of the middle peasantry of north Gujarat and Saurashtra, beneficiaries of the Land Reform and Land Tenancy Acts. Though based in agriculture, they were soon transforming themselves into urban traders and businessmen,[7] with an interest in using education as a means of social and cultural mobility. Profits made in agriculture were invested in small industry and retail trade. Over the years, there has been a growth of educational institutions in mofussil towns. This group demanded a share in the access to existing political opportunities available to upper castes, at the same time as the Kshatriya bloc was also demanding political power and access to political opportunities in the state. The upper-caste Congress party in Gujarat, after its formation in 1960, was able to mediate these demands with political acumen, but, over time, the options and choices were becoming limited. This is reflected in the fact that there was political instability in Gujarat, with no ministry able to last its full term until 1980 (P. Patel 2003: 127).

The 1970s found a different situation. The Congress had lost power in 1967 in a number of states in the country; later the Congress split into two: Congress (Organization) and Congress (Indira). The upper castes supported the Congress (O). Mrs. Gandhi wooed the Kshatriyas with the promise of reservations for the backward castes. Although the Congress (I) received a majority, its ministry was soon dismissed after the Nav Nirman (New Creation) Movement.

However, the movement inaugurated a polarization of class and political interests. A scheduled caste mobilization began under the aegis of a nascent Dalit Panther movement, while the Congress (I), with the support of the Gandhian constructive leaders of south Gujarat and Saurashtra, also attempted mobilization of the tribal people in addition to Harijans. The post-Emergency elections brought the upper-caste dominated Janata Party back to power for a brief period, but the 1980 election changed this pattern totally, with the Congress (I) consciously working to build a coalition of Kshatriyas (K), Harijans (H), Adivasis (A), and Muslims (M) to defeat the upper castes in the polls. Madhavsingh Solanki, a lower-caste Kshatriya, became Chief Minister. Fifteen out of twenty-two ministers of the Solanki government were from the KHAM coalition, while the Janata ministry had only seven out of twenty-three ministers. The 1980 ministry of Madhavsingh Solanki represented a new threshold in caste and political dynamics of Gujarat state. The seeds of violence lay in the fact that there was a disjunction between those who controlled economic resources and those who had political power (Patel 1987).

Given this background, it is not difficult to understand why the issue of confrontation between the two groups was not access to economic resources but access to educational opportunities and government jobs. On the one hand the upper castes of north Gujarat and Saurashtra, slowly becoming urbanized, had developed into a formidable lobby demanding educational avenues and government jobs. Unfortunately, existing opportunities were not keeping pace with demand. There was an increase of literacy in Gujarat by 13 per cent between 1961 and 1981. High schools had increased by 96 per cent and colleges by 165 per cent, with an increase of college population by more than three times its 1961 mark, from 50 to 180 thousand. Government jobs had increased by four times from 1,06,009 in 1960 to 4,43,952 in 1980. Yet the demand and supply were not keeping pace with each other (Shah 1986: 33-4).

It is at this point in time, in the early 1970s, that the reservation quota for SC and ST people was first implemented in Class I and II government jobs (it had already been implemented for Class III and IV jobs).[8] The roster system that ensured promotion and job reservations to these castes was also introduced then. In 1978, the backward castes (BC, or OBC) were given a reservation, thereby providing them with opportunities for utilizing higher education for social mobility. The stage was thus set for confrontation. It arrived as soon as the lower-caste dominated Solanki government took power. In 1981, an anti-reservation agitation erupted in the state on the issue of reservation of medical seats; the agitation led to caste clashes and even to the division of the textile workers on caste lines. It was preceded by caste tensions, and the conflict continued for almost five months.

The Chief Minister arrived at a political settlement with the upper castes on this issue and, in the subsequent months, behaved in what can be termed a circumspect way to appease the upper castes. He followed a policy of industrial development and did not in any way disturb the entrenched upper-caste interests in society; moreover, he surrounded himself with upper-caste colleagues. All the important portfolios were in the hands of the upper castes. Probodh Rawal (a Brahman) was the Home and Education Minister, and Sanat Mehta (a Bania) was the minister of finance, planning and labour. In spite of its political base, this government was in no way a revolutionary or even a pro-poor government (Patel 1986).

Each caste had its politicians represented in the government, but no effort was made to create a class bloc with the goal of seizing economic power. Party politics was not based on the articulation of a revolutionary ideology but on pragmatic considerations, family, kin, and caste. What happened was a substitution of political privileges from a coterie around the upper-caste ministry to the coterie around the lower-caste Chief Minister, who was surrounded by members of upper castes. In fact, the dangers of such a coalition were discernible easily and immediately. There were factions in the party based on regions, castes, and personalities, each pulling the party and ministry in different directions. An attempt was also made to introduce these alliances, and thus factions, among government employees and within the administration, including the police as also the State Reserve Police, the judiciary and government-aided educational institutions—the private ones being controlled by the upper castes.

It was an uneasy five years for the Congress ministry, with rampant dissidence and uncertain prospects (see Yagnik 1983). In order to gain complete power for himself and his agenda, Solanki announced, just before the state elections of March 1985, an 18 per cent increase in the reservation quota for backward castes; this increase led to a total reservation quota of 49 per cent for Gujarat State. It is no surprise to note that Solanki thus pulled off a major victory. His party secured 82 per cent of the seats in the legislature. This time, all the important portfolios were given to KHAM politicians. The divide between the two groups of elite was clear (Patel 1986).

The upper castes once again reacted to Solanki's reservation policy. The agitation started in mid-February with demonstrations, marches, and intermittent violence. It was an attempt to question the power of KHAM by using the reservation issue once again. The upper castes' and opposition political parties' response and reaction was structured by the complete political domination of lower castes in the legislature. Upper-caste political interests had no voice in the legislature.

Rioting began on 18 March 1985 and Ahmedabad erupted with violence. The army was called in at midnight of the same day, and a semblance of peace was restored within a few days. Hardly had the city quieted down and the army withdrawn, when riots again shook the city with ferocious intensity in the third week of April. If in March the rioting was restricted to certain areas of the walled city, in April it spread to the eastern suburbs, where the working classes live, and the western suburbs, where predominantly the rich of the city live. The army was recalled and continued to patrol the city, but the intensity of violence did not decrease. In fact, violence spread northwards, to Mehsana in north Gujarat. It also affected Baroda and, with less intensity, Surat, as also the rural areas of Kheda and Mehsana districts. Only after the resignation of Madhav Singh Solanki, the Chief Minister who four months earlier had led the Congress (I) to its most magnificent victory, did the violence taper off. August 1985 was Ahmedabad's first month of quiet and peace (Patel 1985; 1985a).

It is the argument of this paper that a campaign was orchestrated to create chaos in order to make the government buy political peace. The educational institutions, a significant portion of the judiciary, and, of course, the entire press, which was used very effectively, was in the hands of the upper castes. A political bargain could thus be negotiated.

If that was the intention, it need not have succeeded, if not for the failure of the state apparatus, and for the Congress (I) factionalism itself. If the violence continued over such a long period, it did so because it brought out the weaknesses of the populist regime of Solanki, of the divided and communalized police, of the caste-ridden government employees, and of the factionalized party apparatus, with its links to smugglers and illicit liquor dons and with little-to-no mass cadre base among the poor and deprived groups. Thus, when chaos was being perpetuated, narrow particularistic issues emerged and guided people's responses. The police went on strike when a colleague was lynched, further intensifying the breakdown of law-and-order machinery and making possible the perpetuation of violence.

The city became a theatre for the play of conflicts between scheduled castes and Muslims and between backward castes and Muslims, as also upper castes and scheduled castes and Hindus and Muslims. Simultaneously various sectional interests were mobilized. The SC and BC government employees took out rallies to ensure that their minimum privileges, guaranteed through reservations, would not slip away. If the violence of 1985 was an attempt by the upper castes to reach a political understanding with a government in which they had no representatives, the continuation of the violence and the destabilization it brought were a result of the inherent weakness of the bloc being formed by the Congress (I) and its government in Gujarat. In addition, the competing groups were able to mobilize local conflicts. Below I explore some of these.

Stagnation, Inequalities and Urban Policy in Ahmedabad

In this section I am going to look closely at the way the city's economy, its morphology, and its politics came to be mobilized by the two competing regional groups seeking to establish hegemony in the state. Specifically, I am going to explore the gradual decline of the economic strength of Ahmedabad city, the impact of urban policies, the growth of the spatial division of caste and community settlements in the context of the scarcity of land, and the growth of illegal and criminal interests linked to the police and the politicians, leading ultimately to the 'ghettoization' of Muslims.

The Decline of the Textile Industry

A study by Mehta attests to the decline in manufacturing occurring in the city. Meera Mehta (1984), using census data together with the Factories Inspectorate report, states, 'in terms of earning opportunities for workers in Ahmedabad, there has probably been a decline over the last two decades' (Mehta 1984: 92-127).

Mehta's work looks first at the population tables to understand and examine the growth of the population of the city, and later examines the changing character of the workforce in the city to show the decline of the manufacturing sector. A decadal growth table shows that there was a decline in population growth by nearly 4.23 per cent between 1951 and 1961, a very marginal increase of 0.52 per cent in 1961-71, and again a decline of 4.46 per cent between 1971 and 1981. After accepting limitations of data regarding the registrations of births and deaths, Mehta shows that the net migrations as a proportion of total population and in their contribution to total population are both declining. Thus the increase in population is more as a result of natural increase than because of migration. The reason may be the decline of economic opportunities of the city.

Mehta's examination of the change in the male workforce from the census data of 1961 and 1971 shows a general decline in the secondary sector and simultaneous growth in the tertiary sector. The growth of the tertiary sector was mainly in the areas of trade, commerce, and transport. The census data show a striking decline in the proportionate share of workers in the manufacturing process. On the other hand, in the service sector, the share of domestic service had increased. In addition, there had been an increase in professionals, especially teachers and government employees, as also the proportion of clerical and worker staff.

Mehta thus draws a very interesting profile of the changes in the city, despite the limited nature of her sources. On the one hand, jobs needing education had increased. So had domestic services requiring little to no education, and services like trade and transport, wherein not skill but initial investment is needed. There is an overall decline in the manufacturing sector, especially in the textile industry. The Annual Survey of Industry data for 1960-9 are quoted to show that, while capital and output rose, the workforce declined by 13.9 per cent. On the other hand, there was an increase in the manufacturing sector in the small-scale industrial estates, especially in the engineering and chemical industries. Most of these, if not all, are not governed by the Factories Act and have little to no unionization; therefore in most cases minimum wages are most probably not being implemented.

Qualitative evidence of this trend is available in another study (Patel 1985b; 1986) which analyses the casualization of the work-force in Ahmedabad. As noted above, Ahmedabad was (and is) a textile city, with nearly 80 per cent of its workers producing cloth. It had 60 mills, with over one and a half lakh textile workers. The textile workers were organized through a trade union movement and had obtained through years of bargaining a minimum average daily wage of Rs. 30. This study on the casualization of the workforce indicates that nearly 10 per cent of workers in the city's textile mills earned an average of Rs. 8 a day, instead of the Rs. 30 available to permanent employees. It also mentions that the casual workers were mainly drawn from scheduled castes and were women and children.

Other sources indicate that 17 out of 60 mills in Ahmedabad closed down in 1985, displacing nearly 40,000 employees who had to find alternate sources of employment. This displacement affected nearly 1.20 lakh of the 27-lakh population of the city (S. Patel 1985). A survey conducted by the Gandhi Labour Institute[9] of the 5000-odd displaced employees who were to be given aid and alternative employment by the government showed that there was a general decline in the workers' daily wages. If this was true for the privileged among the 40,000 displaced, can it be less true of the others, who were prey to market forces? The workers of Ahmedabad city were facing problems of survival when the riots occurred, and this factor certainly would have helped in exploding emotions and pent-up frustrations (B. B. Patel 1985).

The Walled City and the Ghettoization of Muslims

The initial conflicts started in the walled city. It is important to study the morphology of the walled city to understand why these conflicts found expression there. Walled cities have distinct and peculiar histories. Scholars have indicated that within walled cities, individuals develop distinct identities that combine notions of community, space and territory. Here space, identity and community intermix to divide the walled areas of the city into different groups separated from and related to each other via space. The walled city plays a distinct role in perpetuating cleavages between communities.

The growth of the walled city in Ahmedabad was associated with its establishment by King Ahmad Shah, from whom the city draws its name. Castes who migrated to the city lived within *pols*, living spaces belonging to a specific caste or community (Gillion 1968), which regulated its social and economic life. Each *pol* also had its own *panch*, which would adjudicate social and economic conflicts between members of the *pol*, who not only belonged to the same jati but also often had the same economic activity. The *pol* was a manifestation of a highly developed formation wherein space, society, religion, culture and economic activity interlinked and combined with each other to reproduce the *pol* community.

The forces of modernization did not destroy these linkages when new processes developed; the *pol* remained the centre of the life of its inhabitants. Economic activities diversified over time, but caste and space continued to remain intertwined. When modern institutional politics was introduced into this society, it became an element of *pol* life and integrated itself into this structure. Political mobilization was now carried out in and through *pols*. A *pol* defined a world in all its manifestations and thus controlled interactions with others outside the *pol*.

The process of spatial mobility did not break up the *pol* community but reinforced it. Members of the same *pol* set up various cooperative societies in new parts of the city. Thus economic mobility created a substratum, a class among the caste, which established its spatial settlement in a different area through housing colonies and yet maintained social, cultural and religious ties with the original *pol*. The entire western sector of Ahmedabad city, called the garden city area, is organized in this fashion. Class and caste in Ahmedabad are coterminous with space. Some families among the lower castes also experienced mobility but could not find space for themselves in the western suburbs, now an exclusive privilege for the upper classes who were also upper castes. They got relocated in the eastern areas of the city where there was a sizeable working-class population.

On the other hand, the growth of a modern professional class or of the petty bourgeoisie among the Muslims has not led to a significant change in their spatial location. The Muslims found it difficult to get land in areas of the western sector where the upper-caste Hindus lived.[10] Also, the continuous series of tensions and riots tended to reinforce a ghetto mentality. After the British took over the city, riots have been endemic. They occurred in 1942 and 1946, and a blood bath followed in 1948. Tensions continued in the 1950s, to explode into a major attack in 1969. Tensions have never dissipated after that, and, as mentioned before, have got localized in the areas of Kalupur and Dariapur, which are also the base of the bootlegging activities and big 'barons'. As a result the natural expansion of the Muslim population and its resettlement has been limited and mainly concentrated in the walled city areas, except for small areas in the eastern and western suburbs.

Because the natural expansion of the Muslim community has become restricted to one spatial area, this area has become a feeding ground for the community's ghettoization. In addition a growing proportion of the community has become involved with the expanding illegal activities relating to immigration and smuggling as also bootlegging. Soon the Muslim community came to be associated with criminal activities in this area. The spatial concentration of the community in one area, the walled city, has led the majority community to exaggerate the Muslim community's partial economic mobility as extending to the entire group. Most Hindus tended to believe that the Muslims were mobile groups and extremely rich, and that they had wealth to buy more and more property. For instance, it was alleged that one third of Bhanderi Pol, a Hindu *pol*, had now been taken over by the Muslims. The pressure of this campaign was such that the Chaudhary ministry (1985-9) (P. Patel 2003: 127) took immediate steps to ban property transfers in order to assuage Hindu feelings.

The proponents of this ideology do not compare proportionate mobility between Muslims and Hindus in the entire city. While the richer families among the Muslims stayed on in the *pol*, those of the Hindus had migrated out. The latter's place was taken by recent migrants into the city, mainly from a Hindu background, who were affiliated to castes which had lived in these *pols*. This group felt threatened by the Muslims, who they presumed were rich. The tensions between these two communities were exaggerated on account of the deterioration of municipal services to the *pols*. In rich Muslim pockets, these services were maintained and new ones provided through private initiatives and through networks established by the wealthy families with municipal officials. On the other hand, in poor Hindu *pols* such services remained ill equipped, fuelling further stereotypes of 'appeasement' of Muslims by the government. The location of wealthy businessmen in this area also involved in illegal activities such as liquor retailing made these stereotypes assume moral stances (e.g., all Muslims were involved in amoral or immoral activities). Ultimately such stereotypes inflated communal conflict and fed into the making of Hindutva ideology.

Land, Space and its Conflicts

Suburbization and the creation of garden colonies had not eliminated completely earlier villages settlements in the western sector of the city. Upper-caste housing colonies grew around them. Additionally, some new village-like settlements were established when, in the late 1940s and early 1950s, the government gave land rights to lower castes. The existence of both kinds of settlement was not welcomed by the upper castes who settled later in this region. In the course of the riots there was an effort to displace these groups by setting fire to these settlements. Both of these settlements, one in Vadaj and the other in Paldi, housed Dalits. In both areas there were caste clashes and in both areas the militancy of the Dalits led to the withdrawal if not total defeat of the upper castes.

As mentioned earlier, it was in the western parts of the city that the upper castes resettled and reconstructed their chauvinist social worlds. This process got its first jolt with the promulgation of the Urban Land Ceiling Act in 1976. This Act simultaneously froze land and released it, under special circumstances, for housing lower economic groups. Not much land within the municipal boundaries was left for housing the lower castes in the western sector of the city. But wherever they did have land, the price of the built-up area had appreciated considerably. The Act, executed at a time when the quantity of land available in the western sector was low, made possible a steep rise in the prices of the built-up area. The western sector became an exclusive area for the upper-middle and upper classes among the upper castes.

As a result, the rising middle classes among the lower castes turned their eyes eastwards, to a part of the city that had been populated almost exclusively until then by the working classes: the scheduled castes, the backward castes, and the migrant Muslim population. Higher- and middle-income houses were constructed in these areas, either through public agencies or through private developers. Pockets of middle-class, upper-caste presence developed.[11] The eastern areas of the city also became important for upper-caste, middle- and lower-middle-class settlements. The riots were a handy means to displace poor Muslim and scheduled-caste settlements. Evidence suggests that most of the clashes that took place in the eastern sector of the city were of this kind.

The Gangs, the Police and the Politicians

The Miyabhoy Commission (1983) recognized that the prohibition policy was instrumental in organizing a number of 'anti-social elements who have made it a business to manufacture, collect and transport and distribute illicit liquor in the districts of Gujarat'. These 'baron bootleggers' supplied foreign and country liquor and also drugs. Country liquor was supplied from the local distilleries, and foreign liquor through imports from wet states. The Commission's report adds that there was no other trade in this part of the state 'which could not yield the high percentage of profits which the bootleggers made'. The report also states that this wealth gave these people a status which enabled them 'to pass off as respectable citizens'. They thus do social work and 'spend considerable amounts of money by way of charities, maintenance of widows and orphans, grants of scholarships, liberal contributions in religious and social festivals and establish temples mosques and schools'.

According to the report, the data showed that the bootleggers formed 'a very important part in the political life of the state and especially on occasion of the elections', where, because of their social work activities, they had 'an influence among the voters of the area'. Election candidates, the report continues, and political parties compete with each other for their favours. These baron bootleggers were anti-social elements insofar as they were 'capable of striking terror' if any effort is made to question their power. The report also states that not only the police department but several other departments of the government, especially those that deal with black marketeers and other economic offenders, had links with these bootleggers. There was hardly any police station free from the taint of corruption. 'The result is that an honest police officer is a misfit and even suffers from ostracism from his dishonest colleagues. Moreover, in context to the influence, which the baron bootleggers have in the higher echelons of social and political life, an honest police officer is easily removed or dealt with.'

It has been difficult to trace the history of the growth of gangs in Gujarat, as prohibition was a policy of the Government of Bombay State even before its formal division into two. The Commission states (and this is collaborated by interviews with citizens and one liquor baron) that the trade of bootlegging had grown phenomenally in the decades since the 1960s. The then Additional Commissioner of Police in an interview also stated that in Ahmedabad, the bigger bootleggers had diverted their activities to drug smuggling and silver smuggling.[12] Additionally it has been suggested that the returns are extremely high. For a big baron, a daily turnover of Rs.15 lakh and a monthly profit of Rs. 45 lakh was suggested (1986 price levels). While it is difficult to judge the truth of these figures, it is still possible to make an analysis of the nature of the lumpen culture bootlegging can breed, in a context of the declining real wages of a large mass of the population, the nexus with police and politicians, and the powerful influence it can demonstrate in the city.

Trade union leaders and crime branch news reporters attested to the fact that almost every locality has its liquor den. Some localities have four to five such dens. These are places where males, young and old, meet. Rooms for gambling are set aside and a lot of brew is imbibed. A Communist Party of India (Marxist) trade union leader bitterly complained that these *addas* had replaced street-corner discussion-meetings.

The illicit liquor barons usually retained a number of helpers to conduct their business, some of whom act as protectors. A network of solicitors, retailers, and insiders gets built into the trade. Two groups, it seemed, were intrinsically connected in the network: *panwallas*, who act as retail outlets, and auto-rickshaw drivers, who in addition to being part-time employees were also couriers. Wages were exceedingly high. Thus it was no wonder that the youth, and especially the dropouts from schools, gravitated to this form of employment, which had its risks and excitements and was also ultimately a form of protest against the society.

A scrutiny of the list of antisocial elements submitted to the government indicates that members of this group also did other part-time activity or business or service, like keeping a tea stall or being a bus driver. Around them a group of people 'hung around' and could be identified through them or by the specific places where they met. Their addresses were also the same.[13] Over time these youths became the protectors of this locality. It was not surprising to find the names of children of policemen in these lists. After all, they too faced the same economic and social discrimination as others.[14] Small time crime thus flourished independent of the marketing of illicit liquor. This world had generated its own conflicts over territory, influence, power and control. One of these conflicts was expressed during the riots and left nearly 200 families destitute.

CONCLUSION

In this paper I have discussed the way city-based conflicts were mobilized by the two sections of the elites—those that represented economic interests and controlled the social and cultural life on the one hand, and those who represented politics on the other—as they attempted to evolve a new hegemonic bloc that incorporated regional groups in Gujarat. I have argued that these conflicts emerged as a consequence of an economic and political crisis—growing inequalities and a non-accommodation of political aspirations of the mobile regional groups, which until then had not found a political space or a political voice in society or in the regime.

I am also arguing that the 1985-6 riots were critical for another reason. Until 1985, the Congress party was promoting the KHAM model in Gujarat in its attempt to build a bloc of the deprived. Critical to this formation was the arithmetic regarding caste mobilization and electoral politics, including the small size of the upper castes in Gujarat, unlike some other states in India. However, what the Congress party had not anticipated was the mobilization of the upper castes against the KHAM bloc and their takeover of the second Congress experiment in north India, that of forming a religion-based political bloc for Gujarat. The Congress handed over to the rightist parties in Gujarat, and to the rest of the country, the formula of hegemonizing the lower sections in society through a Hindu bloc. Later the Bharatiya Janata Party reframed this as Hindutva.

Commentators have noted that soon after the 1985-6 riots the BJP and its various front organizations, such as the Vishwa Hindu Parishad, successfully campaigned in the tribal belt of south Gujarat (Lobo 2002), where they started an anti-Christian campaign, while in north Gujarat, Saurashtra and Kutch and in the cities they initiated an anti-Muslim campaign. These campaigns encouraged and exaggerated community divisions between religions and fomented religious conflicts between communities. Communal riots were an immediate outcome. These communal conflicts in turn further communalized the relationships among castes, classes, and religious communities in Gujarat. This was not the situation in 1985-6, as I have argued above. I have contended that the conflicts in Ahmedabad of class, caste and religion were a consequence of the contradictions emerging due to unequal access to jobs and housing and due to the limitations of the public policies practised by the government. The Hindutva agenda coalesced these conflicts into religious conflicts.[15]

The Hindutva campaign realized its political dividend when the BJP increased its vote share to 26.7 per cent and won 67 seats in the State legislature elections of 1990 (Patel 2003). By then the Hindutva bloc had consolidated itself and the BJP was able to mobilize the population of Gujarat to send the largest number of bricks for the *shilanyasa* during the 1992 campaign against the Babri Masjid. In the elections of 1995 the BJP won with a two-thirds majority, suggesting that by then the BJP had ensured that the Hindutva bloc would prevail over remnants of the other bloc and that all conflicts among the elites would be resolved through a communalization of conflict. The 2002 pogrom against the Muslims can be traced to the confrontations among the elites in 1985-6.

NOTES

1. Funds for carrying out the research on which this paper is based were made available by the Centre for Social Studies in Surat. Thanks to Mahesh Upadhyaya, who helped me to collect data.
2. In a recent paper, Priyavadan Patel (2003) suggests that communal confrontations have become a common occurrence during factional fights within the BJP.
3. An earlier version of this argument is available in Patel (1985, 1985a).
4. The Congress party promised recognition of some Muslim communities as backward-class.

5. The following analysis draws heavily upon, and follows, those that have been made by Pathak, Parekh and Desai 1966; Shah 1975; Wood 1984; Sheth and Menon 1986; and P. Patel 2003.
6. For statistics on upper-caste domination in government jobs and in education, see Shah 1986.
7. By 1981, Gujarat had 31 per cent of its population living in towns and cities. The all-India average for 1981 was 23.7 per cent.
8. Until 1969, the State government had not implemented the constitutional provisions providing reservation to SCs and STs in government jobs. In 1969 it approved reservations of 7 per cent and 14 per cent for Class III and IV and 5 per cent and 10 per cent for Class I and Class II jobs for SC and ST respectively. Only in December 1971 were these provisions also extended to Class I and II jobs. Shah 1986: 16-17.
9. B. B. Patel 1985.
10. A Muslim resident of a posh upper-caste housing society told me that his family was initially not allowed to become a member of this housing society. Only the intervention of a prominent litterateur of the city, whom the family knew, made it possible for them to own a residence in this society. Most Muslims would not even try and make this effort, knowing the Hindu upper-caste attitudes on this issue.
11. Even the land in the eastern area was frozen. Thus the *modus operandi* was to get a no-objection certificate to built flats for lower-income groups, the definition of which is people living in built-up areas. Once the clearance was given, either two flats became one or duplexes were built. In this way a lower-income flat becomes an upper-middle-class accommodation.
12. In an interview, the then DG, Gujarat, Julius Ribero, also talked about this nexus. He saw links between the gang warfare in Bombay and its extension to Ahmedabad. Others in the police department at Ahmedabad attested to the fact that they have evidence of drug smuggling from Pakistan to Saurashtra via *dhows* and the transport of drugs via Ahmedabad to Bombay. The murder of the noted smuggler Alam Zeb in Surat in December 1985 seemed to confirm the suspicions about this linkage for many. *Indian Express*, 10-1-1986.
13. For instance, one person is known as Kitlleewala (obviously someone operating a small tea shop), and another as Dadu Bus Driverwala of 137 Bus Last Stop. (The first names have been replaced from the originals.)
14. It is interesting to note that, whether at Jamalpur, in Bapunagar, or at Jamalpur Chali, attacks on the Muslims seem to have come from the police quarters. It is imperative to examine in detail how much of lumpenization is part and parcel of the nature of the Indian police force.
15. This paper takes a different view on the analysis of communalism and communal riots than that taken by Varshney (2002). First, I would argue that it is necessary to maintain a distinction between communal tensions

and ethnic tensions, and between communalism and ethnicity, because communalism and the formation of Hindutva ideology are rooted in the politics of majoritarianism and minorityism inherited from the colonial period, while ethnicity in India has very specific connotations. Second, I have tried to study at a separate analytical level the tensions and conflicts in Ahmedabad, and to evaluate how these have coalesced with the conflicts among the elites in Gujarat. I would argue that this analytical distinction is extremely important in order to assess the nature of communal conflicts in contemporary India. Last, civil society institutions do not have a separate and distinct life from institutions of the state; they are integrated with it organically. To isolate them analytically from the processes of market and politics and to assert that socialities are constructed outside of politics is both a theoretical and a methodological error.

REFERENCES

Corbridge, S. and J. Harriss. 2000. *Reinventing India: Liberalisation, Hindu Nationalism and Popular Democracy*. New Delhi: Oxford University Press.

Gillion, K. 1968. *Ahmedabad: A Study in Urban History*. Ahmedabad: New Order Book Depot.

Khilnani, S. 1997. *The Idea of India*. New Delhi: Penguin Books.

Lobo, L. 2002. 'Adivasis, *Hindutwa* and Post Godhra Riots in Gujarat', *Economic and Political Weekly* 37 (48): 4844-9.

Mehta, Meera 1984. 'The Informal Sector in Ahmedabad'. Ph.D. Thesis, Department of Economics, Gujarat University, Ahmedabad.

Pathak, D. N., M. G. Parekh and K. D. Desai. 1966. *Three General Elections in Gujarat: Development of a Decade, 1952-1962*. Ahmedabad: Gujarat University.

Patel, B. B. 1985. *Workers of Closed Textile Mills: Patterns and Problems of their Absorption in a Metropolitan Labour Market*. Ahmedabad: Gandhi Labour Institute.

Patel, P. 2003. 'Gujarat: *Hindutwa* mobilization and Electoral Dominance of the BJP', *Journal of Indian School of Political Economy* 15 (1 & 2): 123-42.

Patel, S. 1985. 'Gujarat: Debacle of Populist Politics', *Economic and Political Weekly* 20 (16): 681-2.

———. 1985a. 'Gujarat: Collapse of Government', *Economic and Political Weekly* 20 (17): 749-50.

———. 1985b. 'Ahmedabad: Nationalisation, TLA and the Textile Workers', *Economic and Political Weekly* 20 (49): 2154-5.

———. 1986. 'Contract Workers in Ahmedabad Textile Industry', Self

Employed Women's Association (SEWA) Report, December 1984 (mimeo) and *Economic and Political Weekly* 21 (41): 853-64.

——. 1987. 'The Ahmedabad Riots, 1985' (mimeo).

Shah, G. 1975. *Caste Association and Political Process in Gujarat: A Study of Gujarat Kshatriya Sabha*. Bombay: Popular Prakashan.

——. 1986. 'Middle Class Politics: A Case of Anti-Reservation Agitation in Gujarat'. Paper presented in the International Seminar on Gujarat Society, 17-20 December, Centre for Social Studies, Surat.

Sheth, P. and R. Menon. 1986. *Caste and Communal Time Bomb*. Ahmedabad: Golwala Publications.

Varshney, A. 2002. *Ethnic Conflict and Civic Life: Hindus and Muslims in India*. New Delhi: Oxford University Press.

Wood, J. 1984. 'Congress Restored? The "Kham" Strategy and Congress (I) Recruitment in Gujarat', in *State Politics in Contemporary India: Crisis or Continuity*, edited by John R. Wood. Boulder: West View Press.

Yagnik, Achyut. 1983. 'Paradoxes of Populism', *Economic and Political Weekly* 18 (35): 1505-8.

Contributors

PRACHI DESHPANDE is Assistant Professor of South Asian History at Rutgers University, Newark. She received her Ph.D. in 2002 from Tufts University. She is currently working on a book manuscript entitled 'Historiography, Modernity and Identity in Maharashtra'.

ANNE FELDHAUS is Foundation Professor of Religious Studies at Arizona State University. She has written or edited more than ten books and twenty articles on the religious history and geography of Maharashtra. With S. G. Tulpule, she edited *A Dictionary of Old Marathi* (Mumbai: Popular Prakashan, 1999/New York: Oxford University Press, 2000). Her latest book is *Connected Places: Region, Pilgrimage, and Geographical Imagination in India* (New York: Palgrave Macmillan, 2003).

JOHN RICHARDSON FREEMAN is a research scholar at the Center for South Asian Studies, University of Michigan. His recent publications include 'Rubies and Coral: The Lapidary Crafting of Language in Kerala', *Journal of Asian Studies* 57 (1998): 38-65 and 'Genre and Society: The Literary Culture of Premodern Kerala', in *Literary Cultures in History: Reconstructions from South Asia*, edited by Sheldon Pollock (New Delhi: Oxford University Press, 2003).

IRINA GLUSHKOVA is Leading Research Fellow in the Center for Indian Studies, Institute of Oriental Studies of the Russian Academy of Sciences. Her writings on regions in India include *Indian Pilgrimage: the Metaphor of Motion and the Motion of Metaphor* (Moscow: Nauchniy Mir, 2000), 'The Mental Program of the Marathis', in *India: the Country and its Regions*, edited by Yugenia Vanina (Moscow: Editorial URSS, 2000), and 'Gods Here and Now: Mythology as an Instrument of Construction of North Indian Identity', in *Vostok-Oriens*, 2004, Nos. 1-2.

DANIEL JASPER is currently Visiting Assistant Professor of Sociology at Moravian College. His work explores the relationship between collective memory and identity formation in Maharashtra.

SURINDER JODHKA teaches sociology at the Centre for the Study of Social Systems, School of Social Sciences, Jawaharlal Nehru University, New Delhi. Previously he has taught at the University of Hyderabad and at Panjab University. He has published two books, including the edited volume *Community and Identities: Contemporary Discourses on Culture and Politics in India* (New Delhi: Sage, 2001). His current research and writing deal with the contemporary Punjab.

JIM MASSELOS is Honorary Reader in History at the University of Sydney. He specializes in South Asian history. Apart from numerous articles, he is the author of *Towards Nationalism* (Bombay: Popular Prakashan, 1974), and *Indian Nationalism* (various editions since 1971 with 5th edition forthcoming). He has co-authored *Beato's Delhi, 1858-1997* (New Delhi: Ravi Dayal Publisher, 2000) and *Dancing to the Flute: Music and Dance in Indian Art* (Sydney: The Art Gallery of New South Wales, 1997). He has also edited *India: Creating a Modern Nation* (New Delhi: Sterling Publishers, 1990), *Struggling and Ruling: The Indian National Congress: 1885-1985* (New Delhi: Sterling Publishers, 1987) and *Translatings: Images from India's Half Century* (*South Asia: Journal of South Asian Studies* XXI, No. 1, 1998) and has co-edited *Bombay and Mumbai: A City in Transition* (New Delhi: Oxford University Press, 2003).

BISHNU N. MOHAPATRA was educated in Orissa, Delhi and Oxford. Since 1994 he has held an academic position at the Centre for Political Studies, Jawaharlal Nehru University, New Delhi. Currently he is working as a Program Officer for Local-Global Governance at the New Delhi office of the Ford Foundation. Apart from his scholarly interest in Orissa's cultural and social history, his current research revolves around themes of democracy, minority rights, and ideas and practices of social change in India.

SANJAY PALSHIKAR is Reader at the University of Hyderabad, where he teaches social and political theory. He has published numerous papers in this area. Currently he is working on political thought in nineteenth-century western India. He has been a visiting fellow at the Dept. of Philosophy, Liverpool University, UK, and in the Dept. of Government at the Uppsala University, Sweden.

SUHAS PALSHIKAR is Professor in the Department of Politics and Public Administration at the University of Pune. He has published numerous articles and essays on the theme of Indian politics. He has co-edited as guest editor the special issue (on politics in Indian States) of the *Journal of the Indian School of Political Economy* (Jan.-June 2003). He is also co-editor of *Indian Democracy: Meanings and Practices* (New Delhi: Sage, 2004). Since 1995 he has been associated with the Lokniti Programme of the Center for the Study of Developing Societies, Delhi. He has completed a major University Grants Commission research project on the politics of marginalized groups (2000), and is currently working on a study of Pune city titled 'From City to Metropolis'.

SUJATA PATEL is Professor of Sociology at the University of Pune. She is the author of *The Making of Industrial Relations: Ahmedabad Textile Industry 1918-1939* (Oxford, 1987) and the co-editor of three volumes on Bombay titled *Bombay: Metaphor of Modern India*; *Bombay: Mosaic of Modern Culture* (both Oxford, 1995); and *Bombay and Mumbai: The City in Transition* (Oxford, 2003), and of *Thinking Social Science in India* (New Delhi, 2002). In addition she has written articles in international and national journals on the themes of affirmative action, communalism, ethnicity, and gender. She is the Vice-President of the International Sociological Association, a member of the editorial board of *Current Sociology*, the corresponding editor for the *International Journal of Urban and Regional Research*, and a member of the Governing Board of the Global Development Network.

LEELA PRASAD is Assistant Professor in the Department of Religion at Duke University. She received her Ph.D. in Folklore and Folklife from the University of Pennsylvania in 1998. She has guest-curated and written the catalog for the first-ever exhibition on Indian American life and is the co-editor of *Gender and Story in South India* (Albany: State University of New York Press, in press).

Currently she is working on two monographs: *The Folklore Project* (Philadelphia: University of Pennsylvania Press, forthcoming), which considers invisible but pervasive linkages between folklore collection in late nineteenth and early twentieth century India and contemporary anthropological discourse about South Asia; and a book, based on her research in Sringeri, which takes an ethnographic approach to ethical enquiry.

SUMATHI RAMASWAMY is Associate Professor of History at the University of Michigan, Ann Arbor. She is currently on assignment with the Ford Foundation, New Delhi, as Program Officer for Education, Arts and Culture. She is the author of *Passions of the Tongue: Language Devotion in Tamil India, 1891-1970* (Berkeley: University of California Press, 1997) and has recently edited a volume entitled *Beyond Appearances? Visual Practices and Ideologies in Modern India* (New Delhi: Sage, 2003). A recent monograph of hers expanding on the themes of the essay published here is entitled *The Lost Land of Lemuria: Fabulous Geographies, Catastrophic Histories* (Berkeley: University of California Press, 2004). She is currently working on a new project on the social life of maps and the formation of cartographic culture in modern India.

RAJENDRA VORA is Lokmanya Tilak Professor of Politics and Public Administration at the University of Pune. He is the co-editor of *Indian Democracy: Meanings and Practices* (New Delhi: Sage, 2004); *Home, Family, and Kinship in Maharashtra* (New Delhi: Oxford University Press, 1999); and *State and Society in India* (New Delhi: Chanakya, 1990). He has also published a large number of articles on the political process and political thought in India. He is the coordinator of the UGC's Special Assistance Programme with Indian politics and Indian political thought as the thrust area at the Department of Politics and Public Administration of the University of Pune.